THE HISTORY OF THE 35th DIVISION IN THE GREAT WAR

THE HISTORY OF THE 35TH DIVISION

IN THE GREAT WAR

BY

LIEUTENANT-COLONEL H. M. DAVSON
C.M.G., D.S.O., R.A. (Retired).

LONDON:
SIFTON PRAED & CO., LTD.
THE MAP HOUSE, 67 ST. JAMES'S STREET, S.W.1.
1926

DEDICATED TO THE MEMORY OF THE OFFICERS, NON-COMMISSIONED OFFICERS AND MEN OF THE 35TH DIVISION WHO GAVE THEIR LIVES FOR THEIR COUNTRY IN THE GREAT WAR.

"And they shall be mine, saith the Lord of hosts, in that day when I make up my jewels."

CONTENTS

CHAP.		PAGE
	INTRODUCTION	xi
I.	THE ORIGIN OF THE BANTAM DIVISION	1
II.	THE MOVE TO FRANCE	8
III.	FAUQUISSART AND NEUVE CHAPELLE	12
IV.	THE SOMME	27
V.	ARRAS	56
VI.	LIHONS AND ROSIERES	87
VII.	GRICOURT	101
VIII.	GONNELIEU AND EPEHY	118
IX.	THE KNOLL AND GILLEMONT	134
X.	SEPTEMBER, 1917	151
XI.	HOUTHULST	157
XII.	POELCAPELLE	180
XIII.	GERMAN OFFENSIVE, 1918	193
XIV.	AVELUY WOOD	219
XV.	LOCRE	238
XVI.	YPRES	249
XVII.	THE FINAL ADVANCE	257
XVIII.	SWEVEGHEM	278

CONTENTS

CHAP.		PAGE
XIX. THE CROSSING OF THE SCHELDT : THE ARMISTICE		290
APPENDIX I : HONOURS.		298
APPENDIX II : CASUALTY LISTS.		306
APPENDIX III : ORIGINAL ORDER OF BATTLE.		317
APPENDIX IV : ORDER OF BATTLE, NOVEMBER, 1916.		320
APPENDIX V : ORDER OF BATTLE, OCTOBER, 1918.		323
APPENDIX VI : CORPS ROUTINE ORDERS.		328
APPENDIX VII : BRIGADE ROUTINE ORDERS.		330
APPENDIX VIII : 4/ NORTH STAFFORD REGIMENT.		332
APPENDIX IX : VII CORPS ORDER No. 248.		335
INDEX		337

ILLUSTRATIONS

MAPS

1. Somme and Ancre
2. Flanders

PLANS

1. Part of Somme Battlefield	29
2. Defence of Waterlot Farm	32
2. The Arras Trenches	59
4. Arras : Raid of Sherwood Foresters	68
5. Vermand-Gricourt	103
6. The Bird-Cage	126
7. The Knoll	138
8. Gillemont Farm	142
9. The Knoll and Gillemont Farm	147
10. Houthulst Forest	167

PANORAMAS

1. Part of Somme Battlefield	44
2. Honnecourt Wood	119

PLATES

I. Major-General Sir R. J. Pinney, K.C.B.	facing 6
II. Major-General H. J. S. Landon, C.B.	,, 86
III. Major-General G. MacK. Franks, C.B.	,, 156

ILLUSTRATIONS

Fig.		Page
IV.	Major-General A. H. Marindin, C.B., D.S.O.	facing 256
V.	(a) Brig.-General H. O'Donnell, C.M.G.	,, 100
	(b) Brig.-General W. C. Staveley, C.B.	,, 100
	(c) Brig.-General J. W. Sandilands, C.B., C.M.G., D.S.O.	,, 100
	(d) Brig.-General J. H. W. Pollard, C.B., C.M.G., D.S.O.	,, 100
VI.	(a) Brig.-General W. R. N. Madocks, C.B., C.M.G., D.S.O.	,, 192
	(b) Brig.-General A. J. Turner, C.B., C.M.G., D.S.O.	,, 192
	(c) 2nd Lieut. H. F. Parsons, V.C.	,, 192
	(d) Lieut.-Colonel W. H. Anderson, V.C.	,, 192

VIEWS

1. View from the Knoll . . . . . ,, 140
2. View from Wood House, Pilckem, looking over the Valley of the Steenbeek . . . . . ,, 158
3. Aveluy Wood . . . . ,, 220

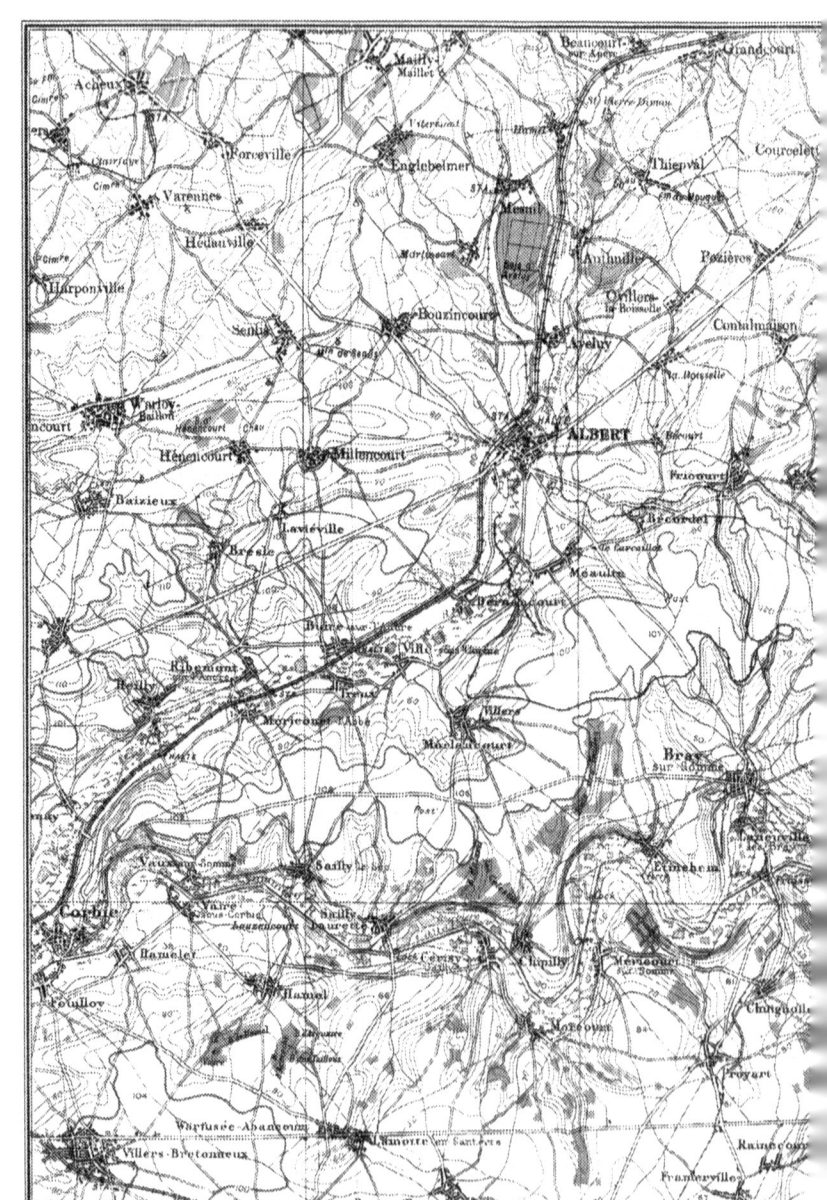

SOMME AND ANCRE

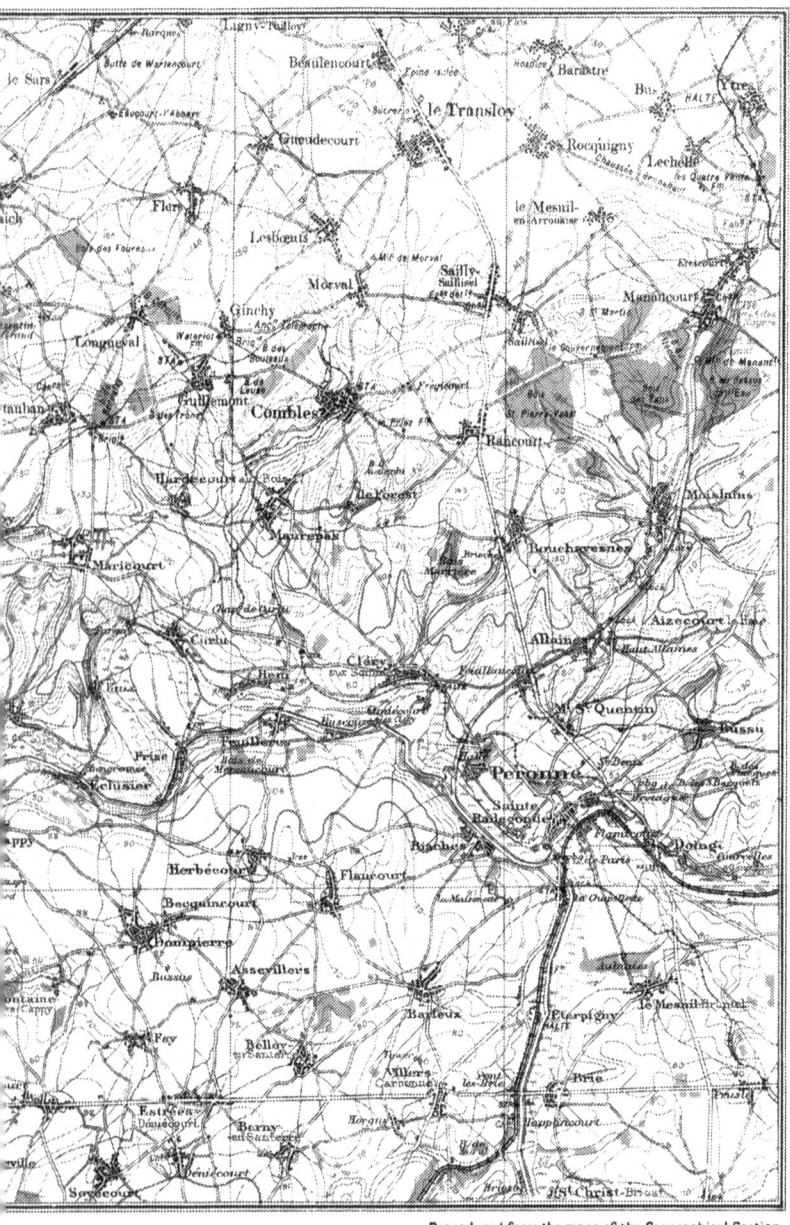

Reproduced from the maps of the Geographical Section General Staff, by permission of H.M. Stationery Office

Scale of Miles

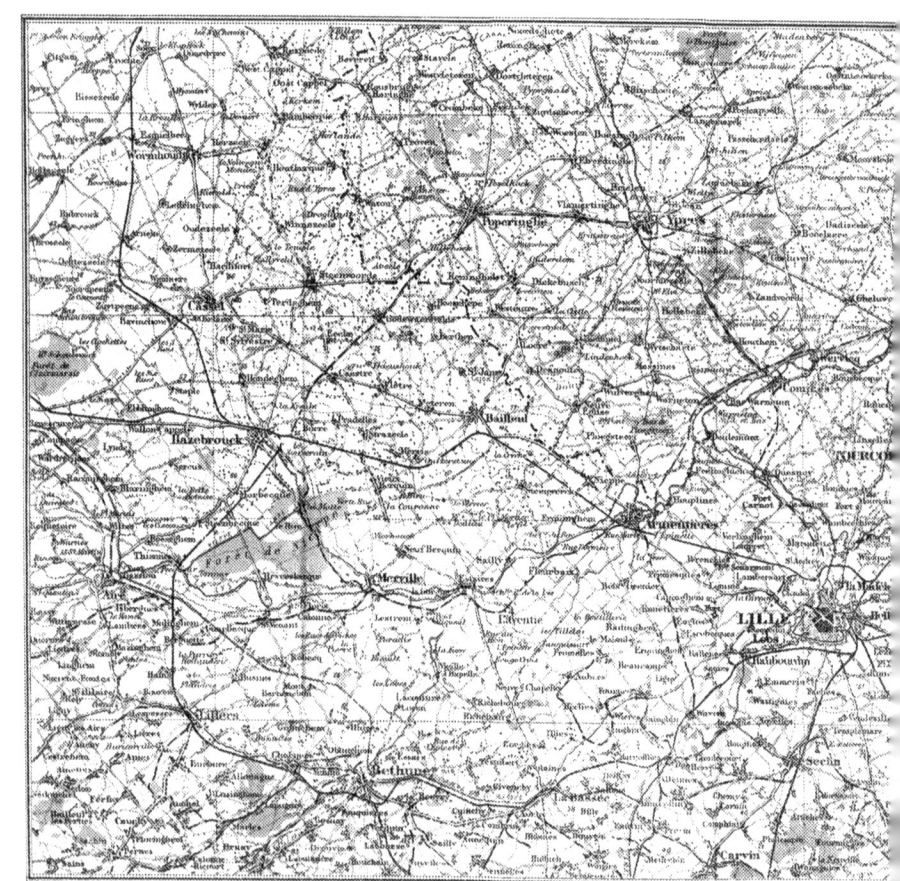

FLANDERS

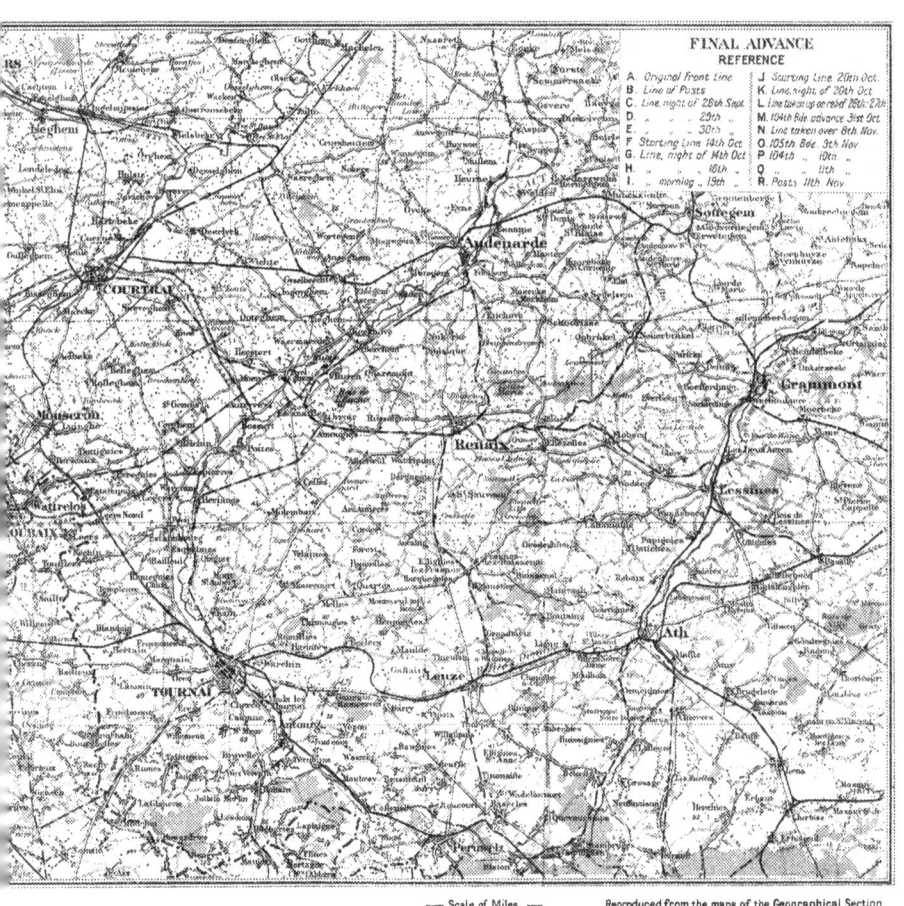

INTRODUCTION

IN publishing the History of the 35th Division, I have used the nomenclature for units as adopted in the Official History of the War except as regards the Field Artillery Brigades. For them I have retained the titles which were familiar to the members of the division. For example, the term 15/Cheshire means the 15th battalion, Cheshire Regiment, and A/157 Battery refers to A Battery, 157th Brigade, R.F.A.

The casualty lists have been taken from the War Diaries, and may not agree with the official rolls. In some cases casualties were given in round numbers, and their subsequent correction is not recorded ; in others the killed and wounded are not separated. I have endeavoured to put this right by cross-checking with divisional and brigade records, but I cannot lay claim to any accuracy.

The thanks of the division are mainly due to Mr. W. H. Riddell, who has spent a year in searching through the various records in the Historical Section of the Imperial General Staff, and in tabulating the results in such a form as greatly to lessen the labour of writing.

Mr. Riddell joined my brigade on the Somme in July 1916, and, except for those periods when he acted as Staff Captain, R.A., he was my orderly officer from that time until after the Armistice. Without his help, living so far from London as I do, I should not have been able to undertake the task.

I should also like to acknowledge the unfailing courtesy and helpfulness of the officers and officials of the Historical Section, who spared no pains in looking up any document which was considered necessary for the production of the work.

My thanks are due to Major-General Sir Reginald Pinney, K.C.B., Major-General A. H. Marindin, C.B., D.S.O., Brigadier-General W. C. Staveley, C.B., Lieut.-Colonel Harrison Johnston, D.S.O., the Town Clerk of Glasgow, the Incorporated Newcastle and Gateshead Chambers of Commerce, and to others, too numerous to mention by name, who have so kindly assisted by placing at my disposal public and private records and in supplying data of a more personal character than is found in official documents.

The prints from the ordnance maps are reproduced by kind permission of the Controller of H.M. Stationery Office.

I am conscious that there must be many shortcomings in the work and for such I trust that my brother officers may forgive me, but I have tried to make it as complete as possible in the space at my disposal, and I can only hope that the reading of it will give them as much pleasure as the writing has given to me.

H. M. DAVSON, *Lieut.-Colonel.*

HERDMANSTON,
    PENCAITLAND,
        EAST LOTHIAN,
            May, 1926.

CHAPTER I

THE ORIGIN OF THE BANTAM DIVISION

THE advisability, or otherwise, of accepting men who were below the recognized standard of physique, for enlistment in the Army, has been a matter of argument for many years. Those who were in favour of it supported their arguments with individual instances which ranged from Lord Roberts to racehorses and had no hesitation in reasoning from the particular to the general in order to support their contention. The controversy, however, received little sympathy from the authorities, even after the declaration of war in 1914, when the question of the supply of reinforcements in the field was likely to become acute, and when it was recognized that there was in Great Britain a large number of men, who, although otherwise physically fit to take their places in the ranks, were debarred by shortness of stature from fulfilling their desire.

The incident which led to a change in the official outlook has been recorded as follows :—

"A fine, sturdy little man walked into Birkenhead Recruiting Office towards the end of September, 1914. He was very angry when rejected, because he was an inch too short. He had tried four or five other recruiting offices, but always with the same result. Mr. Alfred Mansfield talked to the man and came to the conclusion that we were losing some of the best manhood of our race. Splendid little men, who were keen and anxious to do their bit, were being rejected daily. He (Mr. Mansfield) went to Mr. Alfred Bigland, M.P., who was chairman of the Birkenhead Recruiting Committee, and asked him if something could not be done to get these men into the Army. Mr. Bigland promptly took the matter up with the War Office next day. He asked permission to form a ' Bantam Battalion ' at Birkenhead—and got it."[1]

---

[1] The official answer was that the battalion might be formed if a second could be raised to supply wastage. Afterwards the formation of a division was allowed. It was said that Lord Kitchener had seen the men and was impressed by the possibilities of tapping a new source of recruits.

HISTORY OF THE 35TH DIVISION

" Three days after recruiting opened, we had over 2,000 men attested and had to form a second battalion at once. The men came from England, Scotland, Ireland, and Wales—many Lancashire, Yorkshire, Welsh, and Scottish miners being amongst them."[1]

So began the formation of the " Bantam Division."

The areas of recruitment were extended beyond the boundaries of Cheshire until they included Lancashire, Yorkshire, and the South of Scotland. Many miners from Fife, The Lothians, and Lanarkshire journeyed to Birkenhead to enlist previous to the time when bantam battalions were recruited nearer to their own homes.

The battalions which constituted the division were raised at the following centres :—

104th Brigade. 17/Lancashire Fusiliers at Oldham ; 18/Lancashire Fusiliers at Garswood ; 20/Lancashire Fusiliers at Salford ; 23/Manchester at Blackpool. The 104th Brigade had originally been the 112th Brigade, but in March, 1915, the battalions composing it were sent to join divisions which were nearly ready for service. Brigade Headquarters was moved to Chester and the brigade reconstituted upon a bantam basis. The only one of the original battalions allocated to it was the 17/Lancashire Fusiliers, which for a short time had been removed from the brigade, and was now restored to it. The Commander was Brigadier-General G. M. Mackenzie.

105th Brigade. 15/Cheshire at Birkenhead ; 16/Cheshire at Birkenhead ; 14/Gloucester was raised by the Mayor of Bristol ; 15/Sherwood Foresters at Nottingham. It was allotted the number 105 on May 1st, 1915. The Commander was Brigadier-General J. G. Hunter, C.B.

106th Brigade. 17/Royal Scots were raised in Edinburgh at the instance of Sir Joseph Dobbie, who was chairman of a committee presided over by Lord Rosebery and the Lord Provost of Edinburgh ; 17/West Yorkshire at Leeds ; 19/Durham at Hartlepool under the Durham Parliamentary Recruiting Committee, of which the Earl of Durham was president.[2] Special permission to recruit

---

[1] " Extracts from an Officer's Diary," by Lieut.-Col. Harrison Johnston, D.S.O., 15th (Service) Battalion Cheshire Regiment.

[2] Other members of the committee responsible for the battalion were Messrs. C. R. Barratt, A. B. Horsley, J. Corrie, F. W. Slater, and T. W. Dawson.

"bantams" was given by the War Office in January. The original commanding officer was Lieut.-Colonel W. Thomlinson, V.D. The 18th Highland Light Infantry was raised at Glasgow. As early as November, 1914, the Lord Provost (Sir Thos. Dunlop, G.B.E.) had been asked by the Rotary Club to form a battalion of men below the normal height and had put himself in communication with Lord Kitchener on the subject. It was not, however, until March, 1915, that final sanction was given. The corporation of the city agreed to raise and equip the battalion, and the Rotary Club gave every assistance in registering volunteers for service. It was originally intended to equip the battalion with the kilt, but difficulties were experienced which would have delayed progress so the proposal was withdrawn. Colonel John Shaunessy was originally appointed Commanding Officer. The minimum height for infantry was 5 feet 3 inches. For the Bantams, recruits were required to be not less than 5 feet nor more than 5 feet 3 inches in height with a chest measurement of 34 inches.

The Brigade Commander was Brigadier-General H. O'Donnell.

The Artillery, Engineers, Pioneers, and Signallers were not "Bantams," but were raised in the ordinary process of formation of the new armies.

The Artillery units were raised as follows :—The 157th Brigade by the Lord Provost of Aberdeen (Sir James Taggart) and Lieut.-Colonel G. Milne, an officer of local influence, and who had previously commanded a Highland Territorial Artillery Brigade, was placed in command.

The 158th Brigade was raised in Lancashire partly at Burnley, and partly at Accrington, at the request of the War Office by the two town councils concerned, in February, 1915. Captain Harwood, the mayor of Accrington, undertook the task of superintending clothing, equipment, and pay. In June, 1915, it moved to camp at Weeton, near Blackpool. Colonel T. P. Ritzema was the first commanding officer.

The 159th Brigade was initiated about the middle of January, 1916, by the Lord Provost and Corporation of Glasgow. The Corporation agreed " to raise and equip a Brigade of 4 batteries of Field Artillery, with Ammunition-Column, and Reserve, 943 officers and men. Enlistment began in March, and before May the brigade was at full strength.¹ It was assembled at Ayr and when complete moved to camp at Doonfoot, three miles away. Lieut-.Colonel W. Lamont, V.D., of the 3rd Lowland Brigade, R.F.A., was in command.

The 163rd Brigade of Howitzers was raised by the Mayor and Corporation of West Ham in the County of London.

The Royal Engineers (203rd, 204th, and 205th companies), normally recruited, and commanded respectively by Captain Pye and Majors Marshall and Murdock, joined the division in August. The C.R.E. was Lieut.-Colonel H. W. Rushton.

The Divisional Signal Company, under Major N. L. Pearson, arrived from Reading about the same time.

On June 16th there joined the Pioneer Battalion, 19/Northumberland Fusiliers (Lieut.-Colonel F. W. Daniell), the Machine Gun Sections and the Trench Mortar Batteries.

The 19/Northumberland Fusiliers was raised by the Council of the Newcastle and Gateshead Incorporated Chambers of Commerce. Authority was received from the War Office on November 16th, 1914, and the strength was complete on December 1st. Major R. Temperley, T.D., was the first commanding officer. He was chairman of the Military Committee and with Mr. George Renwick carried out the raising and organizing of the Newcastle battalions.

Major-General R. J. Pinney, who had been commanding the 23rd Brigade, 8th Division in France, was appointed to the command, and took up his duties on July 4th at Masham, Yorkshire. In August, Brigadier-General W. C. Staveley, who had been commanding the 30th Brigade R.F.A. in France, assumed command of the artillery.

The Division was first concentrated at this place, the camp being at Roomer Common. Whilst there the services on one Sunday were taken by the Archbishop of York and the Bishop of Ripon, who gave blessing to the troops on their impending departure overseas.

Towards the end of August, the Division was moved to Salisbury Plain, the Infantry to Tidworth and the Artillery to Bulford for gun practice. This was carried out under difficulties, as the full complement of horses was not received until December. When

¹ The equipment of this brigade and also of the 18/H.L.I. and other units raised by the city was completely carried out. In the early stages of the training officers and men lived in a state of comfort which they were not to experience again for many a long day.

HISTORY OF THE 35TH DIVISION

reported ready for service the division was put under orders for Mesopotamia, but this order was afterwards cancelled and eventually France was the destination.

Those who had knowledge of the division when first formed, unite in describing the original drafts as a fine body of men, whose shortness of stature was compensated for by breadth of chest and physical condition, and, if the supply of such could have been continued, the arguments of those in favour of the employment of small men would have been proved. As it happened it was found no more possible to support a bantam division consisting of well-developed men below the average height of the nation, than it was to fill up the ranks of the Household Cavalry with men above it. The result, in the former case, was that the type of recruit deteriorated. Many who joined were immature, and, with the laudable intention of serving their country, had, when enlisting, become somewhat hazy about the actual date of their birth. Others, conscripted later, were weaklings who would never be fit for the strain of active service and who were passed to the division as the supply of men of the original bantam standard had failed. These men had not the fortitude to endure fatigue and hardship, and although possibly a long period of training might have given them the mechanical discipline which would have, to some extent, counterbalanced the failing, this was denied them. The complaints of battalion commanders became frequent, and the efforts of the divisional commander to have the weaklings removed were only partially successful. Whilst in training at Masham, a certain number was withdrawn, but the recruiting authorities refused to have them discharged, and instead, sent them to the depots and kept them there. The result was that, but half-trained and as yet unsubordinated to habits of automatic obedience, they rejoined at a critical period of the war and took their places in a series of battles which tested the courage and endurance of the most highly trained soldiers of three nations.

The result was not only disastrous to these men themselves, but harmful to those who fought alongside them. The Bantams lasted until losses in battle had decimated their ranks ; the Bantam Division continued to exist some six months longer, until it was recognized that there was not a sufficient number of bantams in Britain to supply so large a unit. And so, in the spring of 1917, the 35th

(Bantam) Division passed away, and the 35th Division took its place.

It was a period of regret, for great expectation had been entertained of the success of the enterprise. The ultimate result was not the fault of the officers and men of the original battalions, who all went into battle with high hopes and desire for action, and, as one of their officers once remarked, " They were little men but had big hearts." But war is no respecter of hopes or theories, and it was to war, and war alone, that the arbitrament of their case was entrusted. The project failed, but the failure was not due to the men who gave their lives in the earlier battles, or to their comrades who survived and who took an honourable part in the succeeding years of warfare.

Major-General. Sir REGINALD JOHN PINNEY, K.C.B.
Commanding the Division January 1916 to September 1916.

CHAPTER II

THE MOVE TO FRANCE

THE first unit of the division to leave for the front was the 17/Lancashire Fusiliers, which left Salisbury Plain on January 28th, 1916. Between that date and the end of the month, all the other units followed it. The Divisional Headquarters closed down at Cholderton House, Salisbury, on the 29th, and opened at the Château de Nieppe,[1] 6½ miles east of St. Omer, on the 31st. With the exception of the 23/Manchester, 15/Sherwood Foresters, and the 18/Highland Light Infantry, the route of which was by Folkestone and Boulogne, all units crossed the channel *via* Southampton and Havre, and were concentrated in the district between St. Omer and Aire from Clety, 7½ miles S.S.W. of St. Omer, to Wallon Capelle, 10 miles along the Hazebrouck road. The concentration was completed by February 5th, and a course of training was begun. The division was allotted to the XI Corps (Lieut.-General Sir R. Haking), which already contained the Guards, 19th and 38th (Welsh) Divisions. Certain officers and N.C.O.'s from artillery and infantry units, were sent up to the Guards Division for instruction in the line. On the 4th occurred the first change of personnel, when Lieut.-Colonel Hope Johnston took over command of the 157th Brigade, R.F.A., from Colonel Milne.

On February 9th all units made a move towards the line. Divisional Headquarters to Lambres, C.R.A. to Witternesse, 104th Brigade to Wardrecques, 105th to Molinghem, and 106th from Wardrecques to Boeseghem. The units were in billets close around these places. During their marches to Wardrecques and Thiennes respectively, the 17/Lancashire Fusiliers and the 19/Durham Light Infantry were inspected by the Commander-in-Chief and by Prince Arthur of Connaught, and, on the 11th, the whole division

---

[1] It moved next day to the Distillery near the Abbaye de Woestine, one-and-a-quarter miles away.

was inspected by Lord Kitchener and the G.O.C. XI Corps. It rained all day, but the parade was successful, and Lord Kitchener expressed his satisfaction at the turn-out and appearance of the " Bantams." Thereafter the division continued its training. The weather was very bad—alternately snow and rain—but this did not damp the ardour of the troops. On the night of 17/18th the division became G.H.Q. reserve and was under orders to move at nine hours' notice, but the only movement made was a further one nearer the front to the area south-east of the Forêt de Nieppe, round Merville. During this move, Lieut.-Colonel Lamont, 159th Brigade, R.F.A., returned to England, and his place was taken by Lieut.-Colonel W. G. Bedford. Divisional Headquarters moved from Lambres to Lestrem, C.R.A. to St. Venant, 104th Brigade to Callone-sur-la-Lys, 105th Brigade to Locon, three miles north of Bethune, where it came under orders of the 38th Division for tactical requirements. The 106th Brigade was at Les Lauriers near Merville, and sent up the 17/Royal Scots and 17/West Yorkshire to Vielle Chapelle and La Gorgue, to be attached to the 19th Division for training in the front line, the 17/ and 18/Lancashire Fusiliers and the 23/Manchester had already moved up into the trenches of the 38th Division for a similar purpose.[1] About the same time the 157th Brigade, R.F.A., sent up 10 guns and wagons complete, and 2 officers and 30 men per battery for instruction under the 2nd Indian R.H.A. Brigade. The 158th Brigade R.F.A. sent 8 officers and 120 men to the La Bassée Canal; and the 163rd Brigade R.F.A. 4 officers and 116 men to Luisnes to the 120th Brigade R.F.A.

The first casualty, to the division occurred on February 20th, when 1 man of the 17/West Yorkshire, attached to the 19th Division, was killed in the trenches in the Neuve Chapelle sector. Next day the 17/Lancashire Fusiliers (attached to 113th Brigade) had 5 men wounded. Captain Hulson, of the 18/Lancashire Fusiliers (attached to the 115th Brigade) was slightly wounded also. Next day the 17/West Yorkshire suffered again, when Lieutenant Layman was severely wounded and died a few hours later, and, on the following day another man was killed.[2]

[1] In the orders for these moves there is a recurring paragraph :—" Two sandbags per man for filling and placing on the fire-step will be provided. . . . Parapets are not to be lowered."
[2] Unit not stated.

There would appear to have been a considerable skirmish on this battalion front at this time, although details are lacking. A note from Brigadier-General Price Davies has been preserved, and runs as follows :—" Please convey to your battalion (17/Lancashire Fusiliers) my appreciation of the spirit they showed in the recent encounter with the enemy. The readiness of the listening patrol allowing the enemy to approach and then dealing with them is also an excellent sign."

For the next ten days trench training was proceeded with. Companies and battalions relieved one another in the front line until all had had experience. All accounts describe the weather as very trying, snow and rain alternating with cold winds, and once or twice a note is made of the bad boots provided and the insufficiency of gas helmets. An unfortunate accident occurred to Captain R. C. Doidge, the brigade bombing officer of the 104th Brigade, who was killed by an accidental bomb explosion and Lieutenant Durandeau and 3 other ranks of the 23/Manchester were wounded at the same time.

CHAPTER III

FAUQUISSART AND NEUVE CHAPELLE

THE time had now come when the division was to take its place in the line as a complete unit. The portion of the British line which it was to hold at various points for the next four months, was that between Laventie on the north to Festubert, west of La Bassée. Like most of the Flanders Plain, it is low-lying and damp—in fact it is one of the wettest parts of Flanders. The whole country is intersected with wet ditches, and in the winter the water is so near the surface that it is impossible to dig down to gain cover which therefore had to be obtained by means of parapets.

The British line in the northern sections appeared to be dominated by the Aubers Ridge, from which the allies had been forced to withdraw in October, 1914, and, at first sight, it seemed that all movement behind the British front line must be apparent to the enemy. This, however, was not altogether the case, for owing to the nature of the country, intersected as it was by hedges with numerous trees, observation from the ground was not easy. Also, the neighbourhood of Aubers itself was 2,500 yards distant from the front line at Fauquissart, and only 60 feet above it. So that the main advantage which the enemy possessed was that the terrain over which he worked was better drained than was the case with the forces opposed to him.

On March 7th the 35th Division took over a portion of the trenches from the 19th Division, the 104th Brigade relieving the 58th Brigade in the sector Quinque Rue to Plum Street, east of Festubert, and the 106th Brigade relieved the 57th Brigade and temporarily came under orders of the 19th Division.[1]

The 105th Brigade, which had been in reserve, and had sent parties into the line later than the other two brigades, was still under instruction in the trenches of the 38th Division. The last battalions

---

[1] The 17/Royal Scots were in the sector, Signpost Lane–Moated Grange. The position of the 17/West Yorkshire is not stated.

HISTORY OF THE 35TH DIVISION

to leave the trenches—the 16/Cheshire and 15/Sherwood Foresters—marched back to Calonne on March 15th.[1]

The C.R.A. assumed command of Colonel Head's group of batteries which included two of the 157th Brigade R.F.A. The remainder of the 35th Division's Artillery was, during the next few days, gradually withdrawn from its instructional units and rejoined the division.

On the 13th, at 6.30 a.m., the enemy fired a mine under the trenches at Duck's Bill, a small salient in the front line about 500 yards N.E. of Neuve Chapelle, which was then occupied by the 18/Highland L.I., and in doing so must have outflanked our counter-mine. The casualties amounted to one officer wounded and about 30 killed and 30 wounded of other ranks.[2] The other men in the trench stood firm, which conduct was appreciated by the Corps Commander who wrote :—" I am very pleased with the action taken by you and all ranks concerned to deal with the situation at the Duck's Bill on the morning of March 14th. . . . I am also glad to hear that there was no sign of giving way amongst the men of the 18/Highland Light Infantry, who were exposed to the full effect of the mine. This shows that although these men have only recently arrived in this country, they are to be trusted to maintain their positions even in the most difficult and dangerous circumstances."

On March 29th, 2nd Lieutenant F. St. G. Yorke was awarded the Military Cross for his conduct on this occasion.

On the same day another of the battalions reported mining under its trenches, but the mining experts were not inclined to attach great importance to this. At any rate there was no explosion while the division occupied this particular sector.[3]

---

[1] The casualties in the division whilst under instruction totalled : killed, 6 officers and 10 men ; wounded, 1 officer and 31 men. In addition, Major Lumsden, 18 H.L.I. dropped dead from heart failure on the 7th inst. whilst marching from the trenches to Riez Bailleul.

[2] The divisional, brigade, and battalion diaries all vary as to the numbers of casualties as well as to the time. It is probable that the full extent of damage was not at first known.

[3] On the 15th, Lieutenant Farrar, 17/Lancashire Fusiliers, was severely wounded and died on the 17th. Captain Christie of the same battalion was also severely wounded, and on the 13th, Lieutenant Nutall was wounded. During seven days in the line this battalion had 6 killed and 9 wounded. The 20/Lancashire Fusiliers, who relieved them, in the next nine days lost 1 officer killed, 1 wounded, 8 other ranks killed and 22 wounded. The officer killed was possibly 2nd Lieutenant Duckworth, who had been severely wounded on the 23rd inst.

Two medium Trench Mortar Batteries, Nos. 68 and 71, were now attached to the division, and were renumbered X/35 and Y/35. For the time being these remained under command of the 19th Division, and on the 15th, the 159th Brigade R.F.A., as a complete unit took over the positions of the 88th Brigade R.F.A., 19th Division. The artillery then commenced wire cutting in anticipation of a raid which was about to take place.

This raid, the first which the Division had undertaken, was carried out by the 17/Lancashire Fusiliers, who had rehearsed it when out of the line at Richebourg St. Vaast. The party consisted of 3 officers and 50 other ranks under command of Captain Cowan. The raid was timed for 9 p.m., but, owing to the activity of enemy searchlights, it did not start until 9.35 p.m. The raiding party traversed No Man's Land in three groups, crossing a deep ditch by bridges, and so through the gaps in the wire made by our artillery. It reached the German front line, but the enemy were on the alert, and, after an exchange of rifle grenades, it was forced to retire under rifle and machine-gun fire with the loss of one officer wounded, one other rank killed and 10 wounded. The raid was supported by a portion of the 35th Division Artillery (157th and 158th Brigades), but as the allowance of ammunition was only 30 rounds, it presumably could not achieve satisfactory results and this fact, no doubt, contributed greatly to the lack of success.

On the 25th the division side-slipped to the north-east. That day the 104th Brigade was relieved in the Quinque Rue—Plum Street sector by the 58th Brigade, 19th Division, and on the following day, the 105th Brigade, which had spent the night in Estaires, took over the Fauquissart front from the 23rd Brigade, 8th Division, the reserve battalions being billeted in Laventie. The 106th Brigade relieved the 25th Brigade in the Petillon Sector next day. The two reserve battalions being billeted in Croix le Cornet and Rouge de Bout. The 157th and 158th Brigades R.F.A. were gradually withdrawn from action, and, with the 159th Brigade R.F.A., took over from the 8th Divisional R.A. forming two groups, with the batteries of the 163rd Brigade divided between them. The Divisional Headquarters and the C.R.A. moved to Sailly-sur-la-Lys and the brigade in divisional reserve marched there also. The weather was execrable ! A cold wind accompanied by sleet, snow, and much

April 6, 1916

mud made the change of position very disagreeable. The relief was completed on the 28th. A 2-inch Trench Mortar Battery (Z/35) joined the division on this day. Each infantry brigade had now one Trench Mortar Battery attached.

The month of April was chiefly remarkable for a considerable increase in artillery fire both on our part and on that of the enemy. During the month, the 35th Divisional Artillery fired about 5,500 rounds, and the enemy about 1,000 less. Needless to say, this fire caused considerable damage to wire and parapets, and working parties were subsequently active on both sides, especially, apparently, on the part of the Germans. Our artillery started the month well by silencing a hostile battery south of Fromelles, and two days later C/159 Battery destroyed another situated 100 yards east of that town. In reply to the first of these, the enemy fired 300 rounds, the majority of which were received by the batteries of the 19th Division on our left. A combined operation against the Wick Salient, south-east of Le Tilleloy, seems to have had a beneficial result.[1] Rifle fire also increased considerably during the month and the snipers of the division claimed many victims. That the claim was well founded was proved later from the examination of prisoners captured on the corps front. These stated that work in the line, which at this time was considerable, had been seriously impeded by sniping and, also, by the indirect fire of machine guns at night. On the other hand, it must be noted that the enemy snipers were also active and caused a fair number of casualties in the front line.

At this time a suspicious aeroplane was observed by certain units in the line. It had the British markings, but its movements were such as to throw doubt upon its nationality. The services of an officer of the R.A.F. were requisitioned and he unhesitatingly pronounced it German. Its flights continued at intervals until April 8th, when it was heavily shot at by anti-aircraft guns of both sides and did not appear again.

On the 6th the division captured its first prisoner. This was a signaller of the 17th Bavarian Reserve Regiment, a unit which had been in this part of Flanders since 1914. This man wandered into

---

[1] The position of certain batteries appears to have been noted to the enemy by a countryman ploughing with a black and a white horse, the positions of which he changed at intervals. He was watched and subsequently discovered armed, and watching a road.

the wire in front of the 15/Sherwood Foresters, and was promptly captured. He stated that he was a deserter, but, as an enemy patrol was known to have been out shortly before, it was suspected that he had lost his way.

On the 9th, Serjeant-Major Shooter, 15/Cheshire, performed a very gallant action in the bombing school. A man under instruction dropped a bomb, having previously removed the pin. Sergeant-Major Shooter sprang to it, picked it up, and threw it clear, but was wounded in the thigh in doing so. His action probably saved the lives of two officers and several men who were standing by.

The division now received orders that it was to move position southwards to the Neuve Chapelle and Ferme du Bois sectors, and on the 13th, the artillery (157th Brigade) began changing positions. Two days later the 106th Brigade and the 204th Company R.E. were relieved in the Fauquissart sector by the 115th Brigade, 58th Division, and marched to Estaires, whence it relieved the 56th Brigade, 19th Division, in the Neuve Chapelle sector, with reserve battalions at Croix Barbée. A few days later the 105th Brigade, from divisional reserve, relieved the 58th Brigade in the Ferme du Bois sector. The 1st Australian Field Artillery relieved the 159th Brigade R.F.A., and this brigade moved to position at Ferme du Bois, south of Richebourg l'Avoué, a straggling village along the Rue du Bois. When the artillery relief was completed, and the C.R.A. had assumed command of the new sector, the guns were divided into two groups under Lieut.-Colonel Bedford and Lieut.-Colonel Fawcett, who had relieved Lieut.-Colonel Ritzema in command of the 158th Brigade R.F.A.

The following changes in command took place about this time. On the 11th, Captain A. C. Whyte, commanding B/159 Battery, died, and his place was taken by Captain G. A. Hart, adjutant of the Brigade, Major Hart held this command until after the Armistice.

On the 14th, Lieut.-Colonel J. W. Sandilands, C.M.G., D.S.O., from the 7/Cameron Highlanders, assumed command of the 104th Brigade from Brigadier-General G. M. Mackenzie, who proceeded to England. Brigadier-General Sandilands commanded from this date until March, 1919. On the same day, Lieut.-Colonel Cheales, 17/Royal Scots, was taken to hospital.

On the 15th, Lieut.-Colonel W. J. MacWhinnie, 17/Lancashire

Fusiliers, gave up command and returned to England. His place was taken by Major A. M. Mills, Indian Cavalry, who was already serving in the division.

On the 16th, Lieut.-Colonel Ranken, 7th Hussars, took over command of the 105th Brigade from Brigadier-General Hunter, C.B., who also returned to England.

On the 18th, Lieut.-Colonel D. B. Stewart assumed command of the 157th Brigade, R.F.A., vice Lieut.-Colonel Hope Johnston.[1] Major Cullen, D.A.D.O.S., also left the division.

On the 19th the 104th Brigade was relieved by the 1st Australian Division and moved in two marches to divisional reserve at Vielle Chapelle, an old village with a quaint old church ; and, on the next day, Divisional Headquarters was changed to Lestrem, and the Fauquissart–Petillon Sector was finally taken over by the Australian Division. This division, since the 8th instant, had been sending parties of men up to the units of the 35th Division for instruction in trench warfare.

The change of position had been carried out without incident, but immediately afterwards a certain liveliness commenced. The enemy began using bombs which emitted a dense cloud of smoke for about thirty minutes, but no definite reason could be observed for their employment and they were apparently only used for one day, the 20th. The line otherwise was quiet, but Major H. W. Thirlwell, 15/Sherwood Foresters, was killed. Next day, the 106th Brigade carried out a minor operation supported by trench mortars and artillery against the enemy front line south-west of Bois de Biez, and the Germans retaliated by shelling the reserve battalions out of their billets at Croix Barbée. A day or two later, The Neb, a projection in the trench line 500 yards south-east of Neuve Chapelle, was heavily shelled, and the parapet breached, and Vielle Chapelle itself was shelled and several casualties resulted, two of them being old Frenchwomen and one a French soldier on leave. It will be noticed that the enemy had some knowledge of the positions of our reserve billets. The 16/Cheshire suffered considerable casualties in the line at this time.

[1] The batteries of the 157th and 163rd Brigades, R.F.A., were at this time divided between the two groups, and their commanding officers, Colonels Stewart and Symons, had their headquarters at Le Vert Lannot, near Locon, and Paradi respectively.

On the 28th the 104th Machine Gun Company arrived from England and joined the brigade.

On May 1st a strong patrol of the 23/Manchester advanced to the enemy wire at Les Brulot and bombed a machine gun on the parapet. It accomplished its task successfully, and returned with only two men wounded, and, following on this, experiments were made in wire cutting with trench mortars brought close up to the front line. The result was very effective and the gaps were kept open by machine-gun fire.[1] Brigadier-General Ranken now gave up command of the 105th Brigade on transfer to the Umballa Cavalry Brigade. His place was temporarily filled by Lieut.-Colonel F. W. Daniell, 19/Northumberland Fusiliers, until the arrival (on May 6th) of Lieut.-Colonel A. H. Marindin, Black Watch, who had lately been G.S.O. 1 of the 17th Division. Brigadier-General Marindin commanded the 105th Brigade until March, 1918, when he succeeded to the command of the division and continued in this position until the end of the war.

Considerable artillery and trench mortar bombardments of various points on the enemy's front line now took place, and were continued as long as the division occupied the sector. Generally, small infantry raids followed, and on two occasions raids on a larger scale. To make the fire more effective, B/159 Battery put forward two enfilading sections for the Neuve Chapelle—Ferme du Bois sector, one firing south from Bacquerot, south-west of Fauquissart, and one firing north from a point 500 yards east of Rue du Bois. A bombardment of the enemy salient opposite The Neb followed, and next day a further bombardment of the wire north of Les Brulot. A small raid on the part of the 23/Manchester then took place, but it came under hostile artillery fire. The raiding party reached the enemy front line, but suffered several casualties, all of whom were, however, brought in. The retaliation was very severe, and the battalion lost 8 killed and 15 wounded, including Major Bannatyne, who died of wounds some days later.[2] A few quiet days followed, during which Captain A. B. Crawford, 17/West York-

---

[1] During the night the enemy put up a yellow board in No Man's Land announcing the fall of Kut-el-Amara, and the loss of 15,000 prisoners. Kut surrendered on April 29th. The prisoners actually numbered 9,000.

[2] For their behaviour on this occasion Sergeant Hare, Corporal O'Connor, Privates Lee and Townley were awarded the Military Medal.

shire and Captain G. S. de M. Williams were unfortunately killed in the line.

On the 14th the reorganization of the artillery was ordered. The howitzer brigade was dispersed and exchanged one battery with each of the 18 pr. brigades so that in future, all brigades were armed alike, having three 18 pr. batteries and one 4.5 in. howitzer battery. The brigade ammunition columns were absorbed into the Divisional Ammunition Column. This change was timed to take place on the night 27th/28th.[1] On this day, Lieut.-Colonel Stewart and Lieut.-Colonel Symons took over command of the two artillery groups, and a few days later, Lieut.-Colonel Bedford, 159th Brigade, R.F.A., was evacuated to hospital. The artillery fire increased as the month progressed, and infantry patrols were active, which led to certain encounters in No Man's Land from which the " Bantams " emerged with credit. As was to be expected, this continuous harassing of the enemy caused extensive retaliation and certain points of the front line and the rearward area were frequently bombarded. In addition to such places as Pope's Nose, The Neb, and S.10.b, Factory Corner at Rue du Bois received considerable attention, and, on one occasion, a German aeroplane joined in the fray and bombed the 18/Lancashire Fusiliers in their billets at Les Lobes.

On the 20th one of our aeroplanes crashed in the enemy front line and guns and trench mortars promptly turned on to it and set it on fire, and, at the same time, a sniper of the 106th Brigade killed a German staff officer who was accompanying his general and others round the line. The next few days were filled up with bombardments and minor raids, but nothing of any importance took place. Lieutenant K. D. East, of the 18/Lancashire Fusiliers, was killed at this time.

On the 28th the 106th Brigade took over the Festubert sector from the 118th Brigade, 39th Division and the left group of the 39th Divisional Artillery came under General Staveley's command. This sector was a succession of island posts, many of which had not

[1] This change was calculated to save 265 personnel, 310 animals, and 44 G.S. wagons. It, however, necessitated 100 rounds of ammunition being dumped at the 18 pr. gun positions.
On May 9th the divisional cavalry (Lancashire Hussars) were withdrawn from the division.

been connected up, and reliefs could only be done at night. The division had now all three brigades in the line. Major E. L. Maxwell, promoted from the division took command on this day of the 23/Manchester vice Lieut.-Colonel Smith, who returned to England.

On the 29th the 15/Cheshire carried out a raid against the enemy front line opposite The Neb and in front of Bois du Biez. This was preceded by an artillery demonstration supported by the 15/Sherwood Foresters opposite the front held by them. Following an intense bombardment of trench mortars and an artillery " Box " barrage, the raiding party started, but met in No Man's Land a German covering party to a working party which had been held in place by the barrage, and a bomb fight ensued. The enemy then retired and the raiders pursued, and, after crossing a deep ditch, another enemy party was encountered, which in turn was driven in. All this caused delay, and when the party had arrived at within 40 yards of the enemy front line the time limit had been reached and the artillery fire ceased. The party lay down and waited, but, as there appeared to be no object in continuing the attack, the commanders (Lieutenant Frost and Lieutenant Wolstenholme) decided to withdraw. All wounded men were safely brought in. It was unfortunate that so many of the enemy were encountered in advance of their front line, but the probable explanation was forthcoming on the following night.

At 7.20 p.m. the enemy put down a heavy bombardment on the fire and support trenches held by the 15/Sherwood Foresters, who were in process of being relieved by the 14/Gloucester. The fire was particularly heavy at the salient known as S.10.5, 1,300 yards east-north-east of Richebourg l'Avoué, where the front was practically obliterated and severe casualties caused to the garrison. Our artillery counter barrage opened at 7.26 p.m., and the heavy artillery joined in shortly afterwards. Captain R. W. Ainsworth, who commanded the right company of the battalion, in order to save casualties, ordered his men to clear to the flanks. At 8.15 the barrage lifted and was intensified to the flanks. At 8.45 the left company of the battalion under 2nd Lieutenant M. M. Harvey attempted to reoccupy the line, but was held up by the barrage. Shortly afterward the 18/Lancashire Fusiliers, the left of the 104th

May 30, 1916

HISTORY OF THE 35TH DIVISION 21

Brigade, discovered the trenches on their left to be unoccupied, and the Lewis guns of the 17/Lancashire Fusiliers, which were in the line in anticipation of an inter-battalion relief, occupied the gap, whilst a company of the 18th was brought round from the right. About 9.30 p.m. this company gained touch with the Sherwood Foresters coming down from the north and the line was restored. It was discovered that the enemy had penetrated the line and carried off the wounded who had been left when the line was evacuated. Unexploded bombs were found in the line and some shovels, which gave the idea that something more than a raid was intended, and the opinion was that the support of the attack had broken under our artillery barrage. Two companies of the 14/Gloucester were sent up in support, and they assisted the Royal Engineers and Pioneers in repairing the front trenches and relieved a portion of the 15/Sherwood Foresters in the line. This work was completed before daylight.

The trenches had been practically destroyed by shells and trench mortar bombs, and the parapet had been breached in several places. When the divisional commander visited the scene early next morning the men were still engaged in digging out remnants of dead bodies.[1]

On the following night a German patrol penetrated to the wire in front of the trench and threw bombs, one of which fell near Captain Kinred, 14/Gloucester, who promptly threw himself upon it. The bomb exploded and blew him up, but his action saved the lives of five men who were standing beside him. Captain Kinred's life was saved by a steel waistcoat which he was wearing. Although his legs were severely injured, he still continued to control his men and organize fire against a hostile attack which was now expected. Later he was removed to the dressing station.[2]

[1] Two battalions of the 38th Division were placed at General Pinney's disposal during this attack.
 Some importance was attached to this raid by the higher authorities who feared a counter offensive to delay the Somme operations. Congratulations on the result were received from Corps and Army and from the Commander-in-Chief. *Vide* Appendix.
 The following letter was received by the C.R.A. from the G.O.C., 35th Division :—
 " The infantry at the points attacked last night all stated that the prompt support and the straight shooting of the artillery saved the situation. General Pinney is quite of their opinion and congratulates all ranks on the 35th D.A. in the way they stopped the German attack." The 18 pr. guns fired 2,770 rounds and the howitzers 340.
[2] For this action Captain Kinred was awarded the M.C.

The casualties amongst the 15/Sherwood Foresters, 14/Gloucester and Machine Gun Corps amounted to 3 officers wounded and 2 missing, 13 other ranks killed, 46 wounded and 27 missing. In addition, 2nd Lieutenant R. C. Davies and 5 men of the 19/Northumberland Fusiliers, were killed whilst repairing the trenches.

The next few days were quiet, except that The Neb (then held by the 16/Cheshire) was again bombarded by the enemy and the parapet breached. No attack followed. On June 6th 2nd Lieutenant B. L. Hitchen, 17/West Yorkshire, was killed in the line. On this day Captain S. J. le P. Trench, Staffordshire Yeomanry, joined as Staff-Captain, R.A., vice Captain R. M. Rendel invalided.[1]

On the 8th a very successful raid was carried out by the 14/Gloucester against the trenches opposite the Pope's Nose at the road junction south-west of Les Brulots. It commenced at 9 p.m. with a box barrage round the point of entry and a bombardment of the whole line. The enemy replied in a few minutes, and unfortunately Colonel Roberts, commanding the battalion, was killed by the first shell that came over. Captain Toop, the adjutant, took command and started the raiding party, Major Vernon, 2nd in command, being cut off by the counter barrage. The raid was under the command of Captain H. A. Butt, and deployed in No Man's Land in three parties. When the barrage lifted, these advanced but were met by rifle and machine-gun fire. The wire, however, had been well cut and they forced their way into the trenches and all had hand-to-hand fights with the enemy, who still manned the trenches in spite of the barrage. Captain Butt, who was with his left party, was seriously wounded and was carried out of the trench by Private Bull, but was hit a second time and killed, meanwhile Sergeant Rainbird took command and bombed the dugouts.

The right party, under 2nd Lieutenant Meldrum, came upon a machine-gun in action, killed the detachment, bombed all dugouts, and carried the gun back to our lines. This was stated to be the first machine-gun captured in the XI Corps area. A second was

---

[1] A German " Booby trap " appeared in No Man's Land which consisted of a flag from a pole. When the halliards were pulled a mine exploded, and a machine-gun opened fire on the spot. It was investigated by the infantry without any injurious result.

June 12, 1916

HISTORY OF THE 35TH DIVISION 23

also captured, but was abandoned on the way back and never brought in. This gun was sent home by General Pinney in charge of Lieutenant Meldrum, and was received by the Mayor and Corporation of Bristol who placed it in the Town Hall. The centre party (2nd Lieutenant Brown) also came upon a machine-gun in action. In the scuffle which ensued, Lieutenant Brown was wounded, but Sergeant Upson took command. The party bombed its way up a communication trench and destroyed another machine-gun. It then withdrew. A clearing-up party under 2nd Lieutenant Menendez also entered the enemy line, but found that all their work had been performed by the raiding parties. Having satisfied himself that all bombers had withdrawn Lieutenant Menendez withdrew his party also. On his return this officer heard that Captain Butt was still out in No Man's Land, and he retraced his steps to fetch him. He found him in a shell hole about 80 yards from our lines and, thinking him alive but dangerously wounded, he returned and fetched a stretcher and brought in Captain Butt's body under machine-gun fire. All the parties were in the German lines for about twenty minutes, and were back in their own lines by 10 p.m.

The brigade signallers, under Sergeant Hobson, managed to lay out a line to the enemy's trench which was of great assistance, and Lieutenant R. N. Aylward of the R.E., with a corporal and two sappers, entered the enemy line with the infantry and demolished several works. They brought in one of our own wounded men on their return.

Heavy rain fell during the operation, and, in addition to this, the battalion cannot be said to have been favoured by fortune. All the greater credit is therefore due to operations being entirely successful, and congratulations were received from the G.O.C. First Army, the G.O.C. XI Corps, and the G.O.C. Division.[1]

On the 11th commenced the relief of the 35th Division by the 39th Division from the Guinchy sector, when the 117th brigade took over the trenches of the 106th, but active operations continued to the end. On the 12th a small but unsuccessful bombing raid was undertaken by the 18/Lancashire Fusiliers. The party came

---

[1] Casualties were :—killed : Lieutenant-Colonel Roberts, Captain H. A. Butt, 3 other ranks. Wounded : 2nd/Lieutenant A. Brown, 15 other ranks. Missing : 4 other ranks. The total party consisted of 3 officers and 60 other ranks.
It was on this day that Compulsory Service was instituted in Great Britain.

under shell fire. Lieutenant Vesey Strong, who commanded, was killed, and Lieutenant Stansfield was wounded in attempting to bring in his body.

Next day an enemy party attempted a raid against the 15/ Cheshire, but it was destroyed.

On the 15th Major C. M. T. Hogg, 4th Ghurka Rifles, from the 31st Division, joined the divisional headquarters as G.S.O.2, vice Major V. C. Climo, who was ordered to England.[1]

On the 16th the 104th Brigade was relieved by the 116th and 117th Brigades, and the 105th Brigade by portions of the 39th and 61st Divisions. The 106th Brigade was now at Mt. Bernanchon and Hingette moving westward. Next day the divisional headquarters moved to Busnes, the artillery headquarters to Lillers and the relief of the artillery commenced. The infantry were then concentrated in the area Fouquières-Fouquereuil—Busnes-Hinges, but most of the artillery and the trench mortar batteries remained in the line under the 39th and 61st Divisions. Five batteries under Lieutenant-Colonel Stewart, the Royal Engineers, and the 19/ Northumberland Fusiliers, were preparing for an attack of the 39th Division on Boar's Head. The attack at first was a success, but after holding the captured positions for three hours the assaulting parties were compelled to withdraw.

The following letter was received by the Corps Commander from Major-General Dawson, commanding 39th Division :—" I should like to bring to the notice of the Lieut.-General commanding XI Corps my appreciation of the valuable assistance that I received from the 35th Division in the preparation for, and carrying out of, the recent assault on the enemy trenches at the Boar's Head. The preparations made by the Royal Engineers of the 35th Division were in an advanced stage when I took over the Ferme du Bois Section, and the Batteries R.F.A. of the 35th Division which were lent to me for the occasion were a very great help."

A complimentary message from the Corps Commander accompanied this letter when forwarded to the Division.

A few days later the division became Army Reserve with orders to move at six hours' notice. On leaving the command of the XI

---

[1] Lieutenant and Adjutant Gardiner, 18/Lancashires, was awarded the M.C., and Corporal Bloor the D.C.M. on this day. Lieutenant G. B. Oliver, 157th Brigade, R.F.A., was killed on the 16th.

Corps, the following letter was received from the General Officer Commanding (dated July 2nd) :—

"On the departure of the 35th Division from the XI Corps, I should be glad if you will convey to all ranks my appreciation of the fine fighting qualities they have displayed since they have been in France. The Division has carried out four successful raids into the enemy's trenches and has developed a fine fighting spirit.

"The work done by the artillery under Brigadier-General Staveley and the engineers under Lieut.-Colonel Rushton has been exceptionally good.

"I hope in your new surroundings that you will be given the opportunity of defeating the enemy : an opportunity which I know will be welcomed by you all."

On the 23rd the 105th Brigade was inspected by the General Officer Commanding First Army (Sir Charles Munro) who expressed his appreciation of the appearance of the troops.

Between the 19th and 27th the following changes occurred : Captain R. T. Holland took over the duties of Brigade-Major R. A. vice Major P. G. Robinson appointed Staff Officer II Corps Artillery. Lieut.-Colonel C. Mayne, 20/Lancashire Fusiliers, left the battalion for special duty. Lieut.-Colonel H. M. Davson, from the 6th Division, assumed command of the 159th Brigade, R.F.A., and remained with it until it was disbanded at Ripon in April, 1919. Major Furnival (C/157 Battery) left to command the 175th Brigade, R.F.A., 34th Division, and his place was taken by Major Parsons. Captain Keith, from the ammunition column, assumed command of A/163 Battery, and, earlier in the month, Captain Goss took command of D/163 Battery. Captain Glover succeeded Captain Milward as Brigade-Major, 105th Brigade, and Captain Hamilton was appointed Staff Captain vice Captain Hall.

On the 28th the 159th and 163rd Brigades, R.F.A., marched to Monchy Breton and the headquarters 159th Brigade went to Arras for special service under the 5th Division. After a few days the prospective arrangements were cancelled, and the brigades resumed their march south.

On the 29th, the last unit of the 35th Division (C/159 Battery) was withdrawn from action and rejoined the divisional artillery.[1]

[1] The 157th Brigade was at this time at Houvelin, and the 158th at La Thieuloye.

CHAPTER IV

THE SOMME, 1916

ON the night of July 2nd/3rd the infantry brigades entrained for the Third Army Area, the 104th Brigade at Fouquereuil for Bouquemaison, and the 105th and 106th at Chocques for Bouquemaison and Frevent respectively.[1] The divisional headquarters moved to Doullens, and the artillery proceeded by march route and billeted in the neighbourhood at Grouche, Milly, and Authieule.[2] The division was now allotted to the VIII Corps (Sir A. G. Hunter-Weston). At this time the 19/Northumberland Fusiliers was attached to the 29th Division for pioneer work,[3] and Major E. L. Makins joined the headquarters staff as G.S.O. 2. The 204th, 205th, and 206th Companies R.E. were split up between the 29th, 48th, and 4th Divisions respectively, at Mailly, Sailly au Bois, and Beaussant, and on the 9th all commanding officers reconnoitred the positions to the north of Albert. The intention had been that the 35th Division should attack from this direction whilst forces which were fighting in the neighbourhood of Montauban gained ground to the north. The brigades were under orders to move into the battle area, but on the 10th these orders were cancelled and the division marched to the south. Headquarters moved to Contay.

Between the 6th and the 13th instant the infantry brigades moved as follow : 104th Brigade, Bus les Artois, Lealvillers and Harponville, Bouzencourt (by lorry) to billets in Aveluy Wood (a place which the brigade was to be well acquainted with at a later date), Morlancourt, Happy Valley [4] ; 105th Brigade, Leucheux, Beauval,

---

[1] Battalions were billeted at Bouquemaison, Neuvilette, Lucheux, Sus St. Leger, le Souich, and Ivergny.
[2] Two days later these billets were changed to Hem, Gezaincourt, and Bretel.
[3] It re-joined on the 12th inst., having worked for both VIII and X Corps.
[4] There were two Happy Valleys. The one referred to here, and to which further references occur, was situated a mile north of Bray and was an infantry rest area. The other " Happy Valley " was a shallow depression extending from the north of Maricourt to the south end of Bernafay Wood. The title was euphemistic.

Bus les Artois, Warloy-Baillon, Heilly, Bois des Celestines, Grovetown ; 106th Brigade, Bois de Warnement, Varennes Bresle, Bois des Celestines, and Bois des Tailles and thence to Billon Copse. The division now came under the orders of the XIII Corps (Lieut.-General W. N. Congreve, V.C.), the headquarters being at Morlancourt and advanced headquarters in a steep bank about one mile north-west of Bray.

The 35th Division was now in the area of the battle of the Somme, and it may not be out of place to recall to those who fought there some of the chief features of the country.[1]

The River Somme rises a few miles north-east of St. Quentin and flows into the English Channel between Boulogne and Dieppe. In its upper reaches it pursues a sinuous course which is comparable to the Forth between Aberfoyle and Stirling, or to the Tees below Darlington. It is a river which has had a marked influence on the strategy of opposing armies from the earliest times. In 1346 the English Army crossed this river at the ford of Blanquetaque above Noyelles to fight the battle of Crécy, and in the Great War, twice in two years, were definite battles fought upon its banks.

In 1916 the portion which concerned the 35th Division was that lying between Hem and Suzanne. Here the river makes a double bend, like the letter S tilted forward, and on the upper and north-western loop, lay Fargny Mill, on which, on July 1st, rested the right of that part of the allied front line which was situated north of the river. From this point the original line ran north for one-and-a-half miles and encircled the northern edge of Maricourt Wood when it turned westwards for about four miles, lying south of, and close to, Mametz and Fricourt, and then turned northwards again in the direction of La Boiselle and Thiepval.

When the 35th Division arrived in the area the British Army had advanced two miles northwards from Maricourt, and, after severe fighting, had gained possession of Trones Wood, Bernafay Wood, and Montauban. The French Army on the right had pushed forward a similar distance to the east and north-east, and the junction of the two armies was near Maltz Horn Farm, half-a-mile south of Trones Wood. Two ruined villages, Guillemont and

---

[1] It may be of interest to note that the first intimation which the divisional commander received of the Somme offensive was through a casual conversation in London in April.

Ginchy, lay on the right flank of the British advance, and farther to the south lay Falfemont Farm. This originally had been a trilateral group of buildings situated in a rectangular park of about seventeen acres which are surrounded by a spinney, but it was now reduced to a heap of ruins and some stumps of trees. All these points were strongly fortified by the enemy and were situated in the original German reserve line.

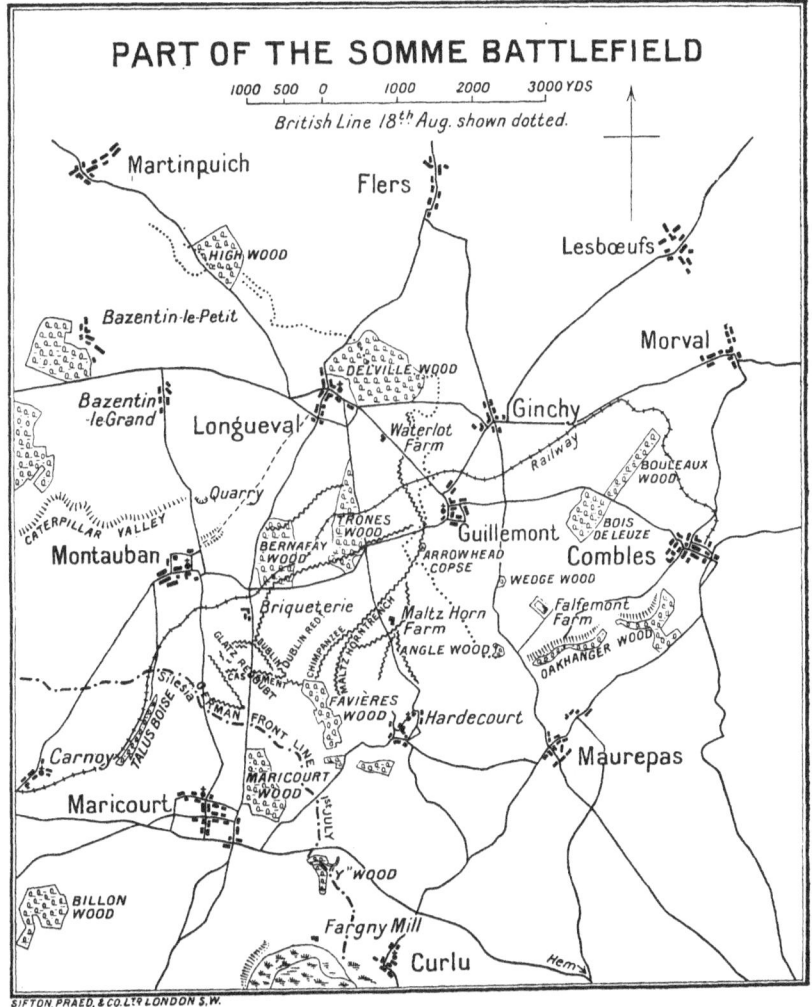

The nodal point, as far as the 35th Division was concerned, was Maricourt, which was the centre of the area from which developed all the attacks which the battalions were called upon to undertake. Through it, also, ran the main track which led to Briqueterie, a disused brickwork occupying a commanding position, and to Bernafay Wood. Twenty months later this village became a decisive factor in the battle which the division fought in this area.

The XIII Corps was due to attack, on July 14th, with final objectives, Longueval Village, Delville Wood, Bazentin le Grand. The attack was to be undertaken by the 9th and 3rd Divisions, on right and left respectively, with the 18th Division forming a defensive flank to the right. The 35th Division was in corps reserve.

The attack was successful and all objectives captured. The 105th Brigade being ordered to Billon Wood and the 106th Brigade to Talus Boisé, a long strip of wood in low ground a mile north-west of Maricourt, arrived at these places about 3.30 p.m. when the 106th Brigade was placed under orders of the 9th Division, and, a few hours later, the 105th came under orders of the 18th Division in anticipation of an attack on Guillemont and Ginchy. The units then commenced work on trenches in Bernafay Wood and Montauban Alley.

Meanwhile the Artillery had marched *via* Harponville and Warloy to the Bois des Tailles where it arrived on the 15th, but it did not go into action until the 20th, when it occupied positions amid serried ranks of guns in the Happy Valley, north of Maricourt, on the edges of Oxford Copse (north-west of Maricourt), the northern fringe of Maricourt Village and in the valley south of Trones Wood.[1] Owing to the exceptional nature of the warfare and the intensity of the hostile fire it was deemed imperative that many of the batteries of the 35th Division should take over the guns of the 30th Division *in situ*. This was regrettable as the 35th Division guns were new and in excellent order whereas the others had been subjected to severe strain and soon afterwards began to show signs of wear.

---

[1] The artillery was amalgamated with that of other divisions into four groups which were commanded by Major T. Kirkland (149th Brigade), Lieutenant-Colonel H. M. Davson (159th Brigade), Lieutenant-Colonel F. A. Dixon (151st Brigade), and Lieutenant-Colonel D. B. Stewart (157th Brigade). Each group consisted of five to seven batteries.

From now, except for a brief period, until its service in the Somme battle came to a close, the 35th Division ceased to act as a complete unit, and no definite action was carried by it as a whole, although brigades, and sometimes separate battalions, were continuously employed under other commands. The Corps' Commander was reluctant to employ the division in this manner during its first battle, but the situation then prevailing left him no option.

WATERLOT FARM AND MALTZ HORN FARM

On the night 16th/17th the 105th Brigade relieved portions of the 53rd and 54th Brigades in the line stretching from the north of Bernafay Wood to the south of Trones Wood, and the battalions came under the orders of the commanders of these two brigades. The orders were only received by telephone at 5 p.m. on the 16th, and the troops marched from Billon Farm at 8.45 p.m. and completed the relief at 5.20 a.m. next morning. The mud in the communication trenches was deep and holding, and taxed the men greatly. Heavy rain was experienced about this time. One company of the 15/Sherwood Foresters was subsequently moved during the night and relieved the 7/Buffs in the Maltz Horn Farm Trench, whilst one company of the 16/Cheshire took over Waterlot Farm between Guillemont and Longueval from troops of the 54th Brigade (18th instant). The battalions were heavily bombarded during this time, and Lieut.-Colonel Browne Clayton was unable to move the company of the 16/Cheshire ("W" Company) until 12.30 a.m. on the 18th, but having got there, the company, assisted by the Pioneer Battalion, set to work to strengthen the position. The bombardment now increased in intensity, and the enemy were observed creeping along the railway embankment from the south.

At 3.30 p.m. Lieutenant Ryalls, who commanded the post, asked for reinforcements and sent a Lewis gun team and some bombers to a brick wall 250 yards south-east of the farm (Point D on Sketch). A hand-to-hand fight took place at the wall and the enemy was thrown back. This proved to be an advanced party of a force estimated at 300 strong with two machine-guns. A Vickers gun was placed in the angle of the trench (Point C) which checked the advance. On hearing of this Colonel Browne Clayton sent a machine-gun under Lieutenant Frazer, M.G.C., to a shell hole, 300 yards

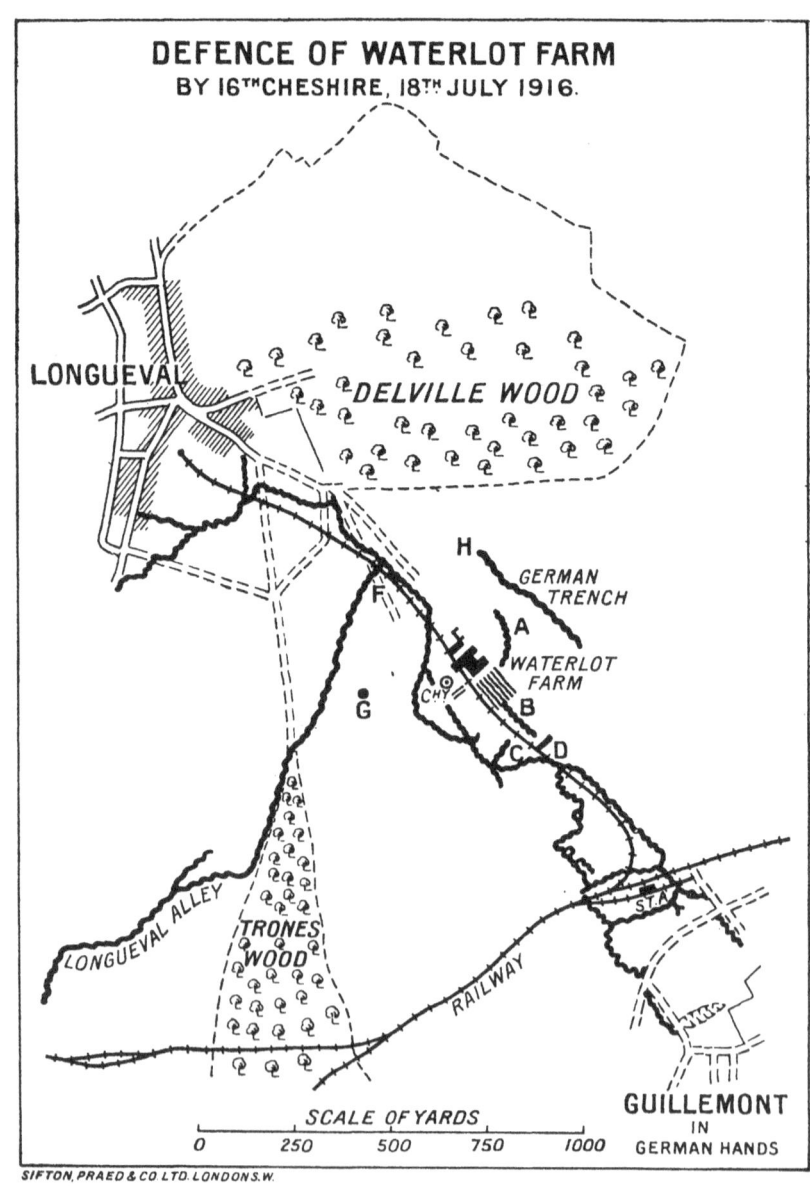

west of the farm (Point G) which effectually stopped the attack and frustrated all attempts on the part of the enemy to work round to the south. After this artillery support was obtained and the enemy was driven back from this direction.

Meanwhile, on the north-east of the farm a company of the enemy issued from the south-east corner of Delville Wood and entered the German trench (Point H) and at the same moment a force estimated at one battalion issued from the trench and advanced upon the farm in six lines.

2nd Lieutenant Schofield, who commanded two platoons in a trench in advance of the farm (Point A), which had been secretly occupied, opened fire with rapid fire and a Lewis gun at point blank range. The enemy, in close formation, could not withstand this and fled back to the starting-point in disorder. Unfortunately, in the action Lieutenant Schofield was severely wounded and died a few hours later. Sergeant Cook then assumed command of the party.

On the 19th no enemy infantry attack took place, but the area was heavily bombarded and the trench (A) quite obliterated. The remnant of the garrison with the gun, which had been buried three times, moved into the trench south-east of the farm (Point B). To cover the now exposed left flank of Lieutenant Ryall's party, a Vickers and Lewis gun were placed in a strong point (Point F), and Lieutenant Ryall was able to maintain his position.

At 8.30 p.m. on the 19th the enemy were reported to be advancing from Guillemont. The 14/Gloucester was moving up to relieve the garrison who were preparing to resist the impending attack. But the hostile advance had been observed, and at this moment a rapid artillery barrage was opened on the enemy trenches north of Guillemont and no attack developed.

The casualties had been heavy. Lieutenant A. C. Styles was killed and 2nd Lieutenants A. McLaren and R. B. Schofield died of wounds. In addition 6 other officers were wounded including the commanding officer. Of the other ranks 32 were killed, 194 wounded and 7 missing.[1]

[1] The O.C. Battalion especially mentioned Lieutenant Ryall for his conduct during the action.
This action was mentioned in Sir Douglas Haig's despatch of December 23rd, 1916.

The brigade was now again reunited under General Marindin's command after having been split up for two days.

At 6.30 p.m. on the 19th Major-General Pinney arrived from a corps' conference and went to brigade headquarters, Stanley's Hole, an evil-smelling dug-out about 400 yards south-west of Maricourt. He gave orders that the brigade should capture the enemy trenches from Maltz Horn Farm to Arrowhead Copse, about 1,000 yards of trenches, on the next day (20th). The French were also to attack.

Some difficulty was experienced in getting orders through to battalions which were well in advance of brigade headquarters and subjected to continuous shell fire.[1]

The 15/Sherwood Foresters who were in the trenches opposite were chosen to make the attack, but the undertaking was complicated by the fact that observed artillery fire on the trenches near Maltz Horn was impossible and that the front was too long to be attacked in its entirety by one battalion. It was, therefore, decided to attack at two points; one near Maltz Horn Farm and the other near Arrowhead Copse, and it was hoped that, having entered the enemy's lines, the storming parties would be able to bomb along the trench and affect a junction. The artillery could only bombard the visible part of the line and then lift and form a barrage round the south-western edge of Guillemont and down the valley to Angle Wood. It was an arrangement which left much to be desired, but time was short and satisfactory observation stations almost impossible to find.[2]

Colonel Gordon, 15/Sherwood Foresters, did not reach Stanley's Hole until 8.30 p.m., and left at 9.15 p.m. At 12.30 a.m. Major Cochran arrived with a message from him to say that the battalion was badly shaken by shelling and gas—the men had been in gas masks for four hours—and that only two companies were fit to attack. The divisional commander, therefore, ordered the 104th Brigade to supply supporting troops and two companies of the 23/Manchester reached Colonel Gordon at 3 a.m.

---

[1] The 14/Gloucester was in the northern edge of Trones Wood; the 16/Cheshire in trenches south of Bernafay Wood; the 15/Cheshire in Glatz Redoubt, 500 yards south-west of Briqueterie.

[2] Artillery commanders in July, 1916, had the greatest difficulty in giving effectual support to the infantry in front of them. The front line was always changing and never accurately defined, and a close barrage of indirect fire would have been a danger to advancing troops.

HISTORY OF THE 35TH DIVISION

The attack commenced at 5 a.m., which as it turned out, was too late, as the rising sun illumined the troops as they advanced on their objectives. The right company reached its objective but was driven out by machine-gun and rifle fire and fell back on its original trench, now occupied by a company of the 23/Manchester. The left company were even more unfortunate, as, when they topped the ridge, they came under a devastating fire and dug themselves into shell holes. The survivors dribbled back by degrees on to the line held by the 23/Manchester.

As the right of the attack near Maltz Horn Farm was at the junction with the French, who were attacking simultaneously and had made progress, it was important that headway should be made, and the two companies of 23/Manchester already in the line were ordered to advance, two other companies being sent up in support. The Field Artillery drew in the barrage close behind the enemy front line whilst the heavy guns bombarded the trench south of Arrowhead Copse—the original right objective.

The attack was launched at 10.45 a.m. The second two companies of 23/Manchester had only arrived a quarter of an hour previously and one was ordered to follow the attack and the other to hold the trench. An intense hostile bombardment lasted all this time. The assaulting waves again reached what remained of the enemy trench, but there was no cover there, and as they were swept by machine-gun fire they were compelled to return.

Word of a counter attack from the east of Guillemont was now received from the French. The troops were not in a fit state to contend with this. The 15/Sherwood Foresters had been four days in the line and had been shelled and gassed the whole time, the 23/Manchester had made a very trying forced march followed by an unsuccessful and costly assault, and the front trench was broken in many places. The officers worked hard to rally the exhausted troops and put the line in a state of defence and Colonel Gordon sent for reinforcements and also sent up the S.O.S.

Fortunately no counter attack took place and the front line was eventually completely re-occupied and linked up with the French.

The losses were heavy. The 15/Sherwood Foresters lost 10 officers killed and 9 wounded, 39 other ranks killed, 146 wounded, and 36 missing. The 23/Manchester lost 9 officers, including the commanding officer, and 162 other ranks.

The brigade was then relieved by the 104th Brigade and by the 8th Brigade, 3rd Division.

Next day General Magnan, of the French 153rd Division, wrote a letter to General Pinney in which he said that the advance of the 23/Manchester had been noted by several of his observing posts (from a flank). The advance was made as if on parade, but the position being on the forward slope of the hill gave the battalion no chance of holding it. General Pinney in his reply congratulated the French general on the success of his own enterprise. The French right flank had advanced about 2,500 yards.

An hour or two later an arrangement was made that the exhausted 35th Division should form a defensive flank, and that fresh troops (*i.e.*, 30th Division) should be used for the assault. This arrangement was afterwards modified.

•

To turn to the 106th Brigade which was employed in the neighbourhood of Bernafay Wood and Montauban, the 18/Highland L.I., being at the disposal of the 27th Brigade, and the 17/West Yorkshire supplying working parties.[1]

On the 17th the former battalion had two companies in action in the quarry north of Montauban under the 9/Scottish Rifles, and, at 6 p.m., two more companies relieved the 12/Royal Scots at Longueval. These companies became involved in the heavy fighting during the strong counter attack on Delville Wood. All ground was maintained. On this day officers of the 17/Royal Scots and 17/West Yorkshire reconnoitred Delville Wood and Ginchy when Lieut.-Colonel Cheales and two other officers were wounded.

On the 19th the 17/West Yorkshire, attached to 9/Seaforth Highlanders, 8th Brigade, 3rd Division, consolidated the captured ground at Montauban, the 18/Highland L.I. were withdrawn from Longueval and the 19/Durham L.I. occupied a line from Longueval to Delville Wood. The headquarters and reserve battalions were at Caftet Wood, south-west of Carnoy.

---

[1] On July 14th four men of the 18/H.L.I., who had been discharged from hospital at Bethune, rejoined. They had walked the whole way in five days.

HISTORY OF THE 35TH DIVISION

The 104th Brigade had alone remained under the command of the 35th Division, and, as it was ordered that the division should relieve the 18th Division after the capture of Guillemont, the officers reconnoitred the front.[1]

The battalions moved first to Maricourt and then to Talus Boisé, whence, on the 20th, the 23/Manchester relieved the 15/Sherwood Foresters at Maltz Horn Farm.

Following on the fight there the 23/Manchester was withdrawn to Talus Boisé; the 18/Lancashire Fusiliers took over the front line from Trones Wood to Maltz Horn Farm; the 17/Lancashire Fusiliers were in support at the south edge of Bernafay Wood and the 20/Lancashire Fusiliers in Dublin Trench south of Briqueterie.

At 5 p.m. on the 21st orders were received that a strong raid was to be made on the enemy trenches running from a point southeast of Arrowhead Copse to Maltz Horn Farm with a view to demolishing the wire so as to allow attacking troops to pass.[2]

As time was short the 18/Lancashire Fusiliers (holding the line) were ordered to concentrate and prepare to attack, and were relieved in the line by the 17/Lancashire Fusiliers. By the time this was done and the company commanders had received their orders, it was 9 p.m. The attack took place in two columns at 1.30 a.m. The left column was unable to reach the enemy trench. The right column reached its objective but was forced to retire. In his report upon this action the Brigade Commander was of opinion that the time allowed was too short to permit of proper organization of attack in the New Armies, but probably the continuous shell fire impeded the officers in the necessary preparations. The battalion was then withdrawn to Talus Boisé.

On the 23rd at 3.40 a.m. the 21st Brigade, 30th Division, attacked Guillemont whilst the 104th Brigade held the line behind it. The attack did not succeed, and about 9.30 a.m. the remnants of the assaulting companies fell back on the 17/Lancashire Fusiliers. This battalion naturally came in for a good deal of shell fire, but the casualties were not heavy. Lieut.-Colonel Mills and Sir H. Havelock Allan, the Second-in-Command, were wounded during this fighting. Major Crook assumed command of the battalion.

A prospective German attack on the Ginchy-Flers line put all

[1] Guillemont was not captured.
[2] Apparently this wire was not visible from any artillery observing station.

battalions on the alert. The 105th Brigade was ordered forward in support, but the attack never took shape. It was possibly delayed for some reason and an artillery concentrated barrage, which was put down north-east of Delville Wood about midday on the 24th, may have stopped the project altogether.

OPERATIONS OF THE 106TH BRIGADE, JULY 30TH AND 31ST

During this time the 106th Brigade was employed in the neighbourhood of Montauban, supplying working and carrying parties. The battalions suffered a certain number of casualties without having the excitement of taking part in any attack. Lieut.-Colonel Stoney, commanding 17/West Yorkshires, was unfortunately injured by a runaway ammunition mule and had to be evacuated, when Captain Huffam took command of the battalion.

The work, however, was important, and General Pinney expressed his appreciation as to the thorough manner in which it had been carried out.

When the attack from Ginchy-Flers was expected XIII Corps ordered that the whole of the 106th Brigade should be attached to the 3rd Division. The 17/Royal Scots and the 17/West Yorkshire were already with it, and, at 2.30 a.m. on the 24th, these two battalions took up position north of Bernafay Wood, where they had to withstand a considerable amount of fire. The 19/Durham L.I. and the 18/Highland L.I. moved to Caterpillar Valley, arriving at 5 a.m. Brigade Headquarters was in the quarry, Montauban.[1] At 2 a.m. on the 25th the 17/West Yorkshire again came under brigade orders, and the three other battalions were relieved by battalions of the Royal Fusiliers and marched back to Caftet, being much troubled by gas shelling en route. The losses in the last two days had been considerable. Battalions moved again into the reserve trenches next day. Major Foulkes, commanding 17/Royal Scots, was injured, and Captain Scougal took his place. At 8 p.m. orders were received to move at half an hour's notice in support of the 2nd Division, which had just completed the capture of Delville Wood. The brigade was to prepare for a counter attack and come under the orders of the G.O.C. 2nd

---

[1] Owing to the expectation of this German attack the orders for the attack of the 30th Division on the line Guillemont-Falfemont Farm were temporarily withdrawn. Caterpillar Valley is north of Montauban.

Division, and on the 29th became reserve of the 89th Brigade, 30th Division, during the postponed attack on Guillemont-Falfemont Farm.

The instructions were that the brigade should carry through the assault of the attacking battalions, and, in the event of finding itself leading the attack, to take and hold the final objectives.

The attack was timed for 4.45 a.m. (July 30th), and at that hour the 17/West Yorkshire left Dublin Trench and moved forward to Bernafay Trench [1] only to find that it was still occupied, and the battalion was obliged to lie down in the open behind the trench until it was vacated by the advancing troops about half an hour later. As the trenches in front were occupied it was decided that the battalion should pass by these trenches and occupy Maltz Horn Trench which was empty. This was done and the trench occupied about 7 a.m. Meanwhile the 17/Royal Scots had also passed Bernafay Trench and occupied Dawson Trench. Both battalions were now completely blocked by the congestion in front. The 19/Durham L.I. and half the 18/Highland L.I. advanced to Bernafay Trench; the remainder of the 18/Highland L.I. was sent to reinforce the 90th Brigade on the east of Trones Wood and occupied a trench between Arrowhead Copse and the railway, where they remained until they were relieved in the evening.[2]

About 9.45 a.m. the Officer Commanding 17/Royal Scots sent forward a platoon to Maltz Horn Farm to report on the situation. This platoon, led by Lieutenant J. Blair, reached the line 150 yards east of the farm, which had been taken and held by the 20/Liverpool. The platoon remained there, helping this battalion to consolidate, until relieved there at 5 a.m. on the 31st. For this action General O'Donnel specially commended Lieutenant Blair to the notice of the Divisional Commander. On the following day the brigade marched back to Sandpit Valley.[3]

---

[1] An advance of about one mile.

[2] Maltz Horn Trench extended from a point 300 yards north-west of Maltz Horn Farm to a point between Faviere Wood and Hardecourt. The northern portion is here indicated. Dawson Trench was behind it. The railway referred to was a light railway linking up various villages. It passed through Trones Wood and north of Guillemont.

[3] The following letter was received by the G.O.C. 35th Division from Maj.-General Shea, G.O.C. 30th Division : " In the name of my division I wish to thank you and yours most sincerely for all you did for us. You gave us all help you possibly could, and it is our earnest hope that some day we may be able to repay you. We much deplore your losses but will always remember the gallantry of your men."

We must now return to the 104th Brigade, which was in occupation of the area north and east of Bernafay Wood, with one battalion in the front line facing Guillemont. On the 24th, when information was received that the 30th Division would attack Guillemont, there was some doubt if the left of the brigade linked up with the 3rd Division. Two companies of the 20/Lancashire Fusiliers were accordingly sent forward, and these, advancing partly across the open, closed the gap.

The 23/Manchester and 20/Lancashire Fusiliers then held a line from Maltz Horn Farm to the north end of Trones Wood. At 9.20 p.m. the artillery F.O.O. at advanced headquarters reported heavy shelling in front of these two battalions, and a few minutes later the S.O.S. was sent up by the 23/Manchester which reported heavy shelling and considerable casualties, and the artillery put down a barrage. All communications were cut. Reinforcements were sent up from the 18/Lancashire Fusiliers but the shell fire gradually subsided and no attack developed.

The probable reason of the shelling was the move of the 20/Lancashire Fusiliers to reinforce the right of the 3rd Division, which, being under observation, was probably interpreted by the enemy as an attack. It is possible that the artillery barrage broke up an enemy attack, as troops had been reported massing behind Ginchy. The German wireless communiqué mentioned the fact that "an impending British attack from Trones Wood had been broken up on July 24th." There was no attack from Trones Wood on this date. Next day the 20/Lancashire Fusiliers were relieved by the 17/Royal Fusiliers, 5th Brigade, 2nd Division. The 18/Lancashire Fusiliers relieved the 23/Manchester, and the 16/Cheshire relieved the 17/Lancashire Fusiliers. Next day the 105th Brigade completed the relief.

The 105th Brigade, on receipt of information of the German attack from Flers, had been hurried forward to reserve trenches between Montauban and Bernafay Wood and in advance of Maricourt. In accordance with divisional orders Briqueterie was made into a strong point and garrisoned by a section of the machine-gun corps. This was promptly shelled by the enemy. The attack on Guillemont was cancelled for 48 hours.

A considerable amount of gas shelling on the part of the enemy upon the ridge of which Briqueterie stood caused some casualties and much inconvenience to troops carrying out reliefs. It seemed evident that the German command objected to the fortification of Briqueterie.

The brigade relieved the 104th Brigade on the 26th, and, on the 29th, it was relieved by the 89th and 90th Brigades except the 15/Sherwood Foresters who were relieved by the 106th Brigade in Dublin Trench. The brigade then moved back to Sandpit Valley, and thence to Bois de Tailles.

The 104th Brigade, after performing various subsidiary duties to the troops holding the line, were also withdrawn on the 31st and marched to Morlancourt. They were joined there next day by the 19/Northumberland Fusiliers, who, since the 16th, had been doing excellent work on the forward line between Trones Wood and Arrow Head Copse. On the 20th, "W" Company (Captain A. W. Muir) for a time held a trench which had been dug overnight and acted as a support to the other infantry battalions during the attack.[1]

ARTILLERY OPERATIONS

During this period the artillery was engaged in covering the attacks which were made on the enemy's positions, in wire-cutting, and in answering calls for assistance. All operations in which the infantry were engaged were covered by guns of the 35th Division, except that on July 20th when the officers were engaged in a search for observation stations which would give a good view of the front line and yet afford a reasonable chance of keeping in telephonic communication with their batteries. Besides those operations undertaken by the 35th Division, the guns were engaged in the following actions :—

The attack on the 21st Division on Guillemont (158th and 159th Brigades). On this occasion the 157th Brigade were able to break up a German counter attack from Delville Wood. The attack on Longueval and Delville Wood when all groups fired a heavy defensive barrage round Ginchy, and the further attacks of the 30th Division. Firing continued day and night and naturally induced a great deal of retaliation, but, considering that in most cases the

[1] For his work on this day Captain Muir was awarded the M.C.

cover for the detachments was very slight, the casualty list was smaller than might have been expected.

The batteries of the 157th Brigade, south of Trones Wood, were persistently shelled, and D/157 and D/159 batteries in the wood below Maricourt were so heavily bombarded on the 23rd, that, after a second dose on the same day, it was judged necessary to move the position of the latter battery. In this case the cover in the old trenches round the village was good and what might have been a heavy casualty list was partially avoided. The equipment, however, suffered. Captain S. Browne, R.A.M.C., was blown up whilst attending to the wounded. He refused to stay in hospital and returned to the brigade two days later.

On the 30th, during the fight for Guillemont, an enemy battalion advancing from Bois de Leuze to Falfemont Farm was decimated by the fire of A/159 Battery. Lieutenant Marshall, the observing officer, in a new station, discovered by Major Pinney, the Commanding Officer, in the French lines east of Maricourt, was able to bring all guns to bear on this force at once with most satisfactory results.[1] The success of this post was such that the Brigade Commander decided to move the whole brigade to that area if permission could be obtained. The French authorities, when approached, made no difficulty—in fact they gave all possible assistance—and on August 2nd all batteries moved to positions on, or behind, the ridge on the Curlu road about a mile east-south-east of the cross roads just south of Maricourt. This was one of the best artillery positions occupied during the war, and the observing station became so popular with officers wishing to view the line that, lying as they did off the main French communication trench to Maurepas, steps had to be taken to confine the number of sightseers to those whose duty made it necessary that they should study the positions.[2]

On the 31st the area about a thousand yards south of Briqueterie

---

[1] *Vide* sketch attached. Lieutenant Langtree was mortally wounded during the change to the new position.

[2] An amusing incident occurred on the previous day when Major Pinney first found this post. Disturbed at the delay in connecting up he went back to investigate and found his signallers in custody of a French guard, with the intimation that they would be shot. It appeared that they had fallen under suspicion by laying German wire—there being no other available—and voluble explanations in broad Scotch had confirmed the misgivings. They were released with mutual apologies.

August 12, 1916

was heavily bombarded for some time, and the batteries of the 158th Brigade suffered considerably. Captain F. C. Stevens, who left the telephone dug-out to assist the drivers of an ammunition wagon, which had been upset by shell fire whilst passing along the track northwards, was killed whilst doing so.[1] Two days later Captain Riley was severely wounded and died shortly afterwards.

On this night the batteries of the 157th and 163rd Brigades took up new positions 900 yards south of Montauban, forming one group under Colonel Stewart. Colonel Symonds, who had lately been commanding a group in Happy Valley (Maricourt), handed it over to Colonel Sheppard, 275th Brigade, R.F.A., and took command of his own brigade. This group now covered the 2nd Division.

On August 1st Major Harisson, C/159 Battery, made a most valuable reconnaissance which helped to solve the difficulty about observing stations, and, for the time being, afforded an accurate description of the front line. Starting out alone he spent the whole day quartering the line from the east of Trones Wood to Maltz Horn Trench, and noting positions from which the various portions of the fighting zone could be seen and the best means of securing co-operation.[2]

The first week of August was comparatively quiet, but on the 8th the battle renewed its intensity. On the 8th the 2nd and 55th Divisions attacked Guillemont in conjunction with the French, and the 158th and 159th Brigades, R.F.A., supported it. The 165th Brigade and the French advanced 260 yards, but the left of the attack was not so successful. The assault was renewed next day with small success.

On the 11th and 12th the 157th, 158th, and 163rd Brigades, R.F.A., were relieved in action and withdrew to Bois de Tailles. The 159th Brigade, R.F.A., remained in action on the Maricourt-Curlu ridge, and on the 12th supported the 165th Brigade, 55th Division, which was co-operating with the French VII and XX Corps in an attack against the southern part of Maurepas. The French were entirely successful and reached the Hardecourt-Guillemont road. Next day in the afternoon they occupied Maurepas by a

---

[1] Colonel Fawcett in reporting the event, described the action as " one of purely unselfish self-sacrifice under exceptionally heavy shelling of heavy artillery." He adds, " Captain Stevens was a very gallant, efficient, and valuable officer."

[2] For this act Major Harisson afterwards was awarded the D.S.O.

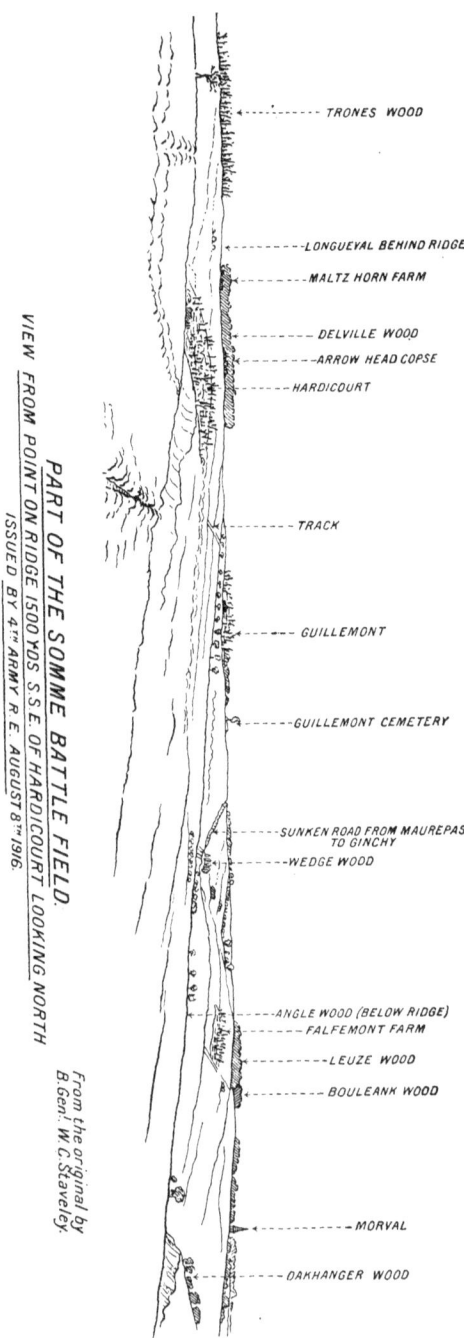

series of movements which were much appreciated by those who were privileged to witness them.

On the 15th the 159th Brigade was relieved by the 23rd Brigade, R.F.A., and withdrew to Dernancourt-sur-Ancre and subsequently to Corbie. The 158th and 163rd Brigades moved to Treux and Ville-sur-Ancre respectively.

The vivid green of the river valleys and the picturesque villages nestling amongst the trees was a welcome sight to the troops after the smoke and dust of the battlefield. Unfortunately, the valley of the Ancre was infested with flies and mosquitoes which considerably interfered with quiet rest. When the troops of the 35th Division next occupied this valley the flies and mosquitoes were there no longer. Objects less desirable filled the air.

OPERATIONS : AUGUST 9TH TO 30TH

After relief on August 1st the Divisional Headquarters and C.R.A. moved to Corbie, and the 104th Brigade, then in Happy Valley, celebrated Minden Day. After which the Brigade Head-quarters moved to Sailly-le-Sec and battalions to that place, Vaux, and Corbie. On the 5th the brigade moved by train from Mericourt-sur-Somme to Salleux and marched to rest billets in the area of Molliens Vidame, ten miles west of Amiens. The battalions, taking them in order of seniority, were billeted at Montagne le Fayel, Molliens Vidame, and Camps les Ameuris. At the same date the 105th Brigade left Grovetown by train and, having reached Salleux, marched to Molliens Vidame, Oissy, and Riencourt.

The 106th Brigade entrained at Mericourt and moved to Saisseval, Saissemont, Le Mesle, and Fourdrinny. The 19/Northumberland Fusiliers were at Reincourt.

The infantry of the division were now in the X Corps area (General Sir T. Morland, K.C.B.), and were supposed to enjoy a well-earned rest, but the work of reorganizing the new drafts (which contained many men of very poor physique), and making them fit to go into the line demanded a considerable amount of attention from the officers concerned, and left little time for rest or recreation.

It had been expected that the division would remain in this area for a week or more, but, on the 9th, orders were received to move once more into the battle area, and the transport started the same day. Next day the battalions entrained at Airaines and Hangest, detrained at Corbie and Mericourt and marched to Sailly-le-Sec (104th Brigade), Citadel (105th Brigade and Pioneer Battalion), and Morlancourt (106 Brigade). Divisional Headquarters moved from Cavillon to Corbie.

The 105th Brigade began supplying large working parties which lasted until the 19th when the two Cheshire battalions occupied the line in Chimpanzee Trench (north of Favière Wood) and Arrow Head Copse. On the 15th the 104th Brigade marched to Happy Valley, and next day the 106th Brigade moved to Sandpit Valley.

The 104th Brigade remained in Happy Valley until the 18th, when in anticipation of an attack by the XIV Corps it was moved to Talus Boisé,[1] and next day it advanced into action and took over the front held by the 24th Division.

At 12.45 a.m. on the 19th the 104th Brigade was ordered to send two companies to occupy Montauban, and this was complied with by 8 a.m. On the same night the 35th Division relieved the 3rd and part of the 24th Division in the front line in touch with the French XX Corps, the celebrated "Corps de Fer." The 104th Brigade relieved the 76th and 9th Brigades in the Maltz Horn Farm trenches, and the 105th Brigade relieved that part of the 73rd Brigade, 24th Division, south of the Trones Wood–Guillemont Road. In accordance with the above orders the 17/Lancashire Fusiliers occupied Dublin Trench in brigade reserve; the 18/ Lancashire Fusiliers, Casement Trench in rear of it; the 20/Lancashire Fusiliers took over Arrow Head Copse from the 2/Northumberland Fusiliers and the 8/East Yorkshire, and the 23/Manchester occupied the extreme right of the British Line in place of the remains of three battalions of the 76th Brigade.

The 16/Cheshire relieved the 1/North Staffordshire in the neighbourhood of Arrow Head Copse; the 14/Gloucester relieved the 2/Leicester in Lancaster and Dawson trenches; the 15/ Cheshire were in Glatz Redoubt and Silesia Trench. The 15/ Sherwood Foresters remained at Citadel.[2]

[1] The XIV Corps did attack this day in conjunction with the French XX Corps, which assaulted Maltz Horn Ravine on our right. Lieut-General Congreve was ill, and Lieut.-General the Earl of Cavan was now commanding. The XIV Corps received the XIII on the night of August 16th/17th.

[2] Lancaster Trench lay north and south about a mile east of Briqueterie. Silesia Trench was the old German front line north of Maricourt.

August 21, 1916

HISTORY OF THE 35TH DIVISION 47

The 24th and 35th Divisions, then holding the XIV Corps front, were ordered to make preparations for an attack on Guillemont. The immediate objective of the 35th Division was a double line of trenches from a strong point about ninety yards east of Arrow Head Copse to an orchard in the south-west outskirts of Guillemont, a front of about 400 yards. Any tactical point in front of this objective was to be seized at once and consolidated. The 16/Cheshire was detailed for this attack. Advanced Divisional Headquarters was established at Billon Farm (south-west of Maricourt) and the two brigade headquarters were in Chimpanzee Trench.[1] The artillery of the 3rd Division covered the divisional front.

On the 20th at 8.30 a.m. the G.O.C. 35th Division took over command of the divisional front as a preliminary to the main attack which was now postponed until the 21st. The XIV Corps ordered that the before-mentioned strong point should be captured on this day. It was arranged that heavy artillery should bombard this point and that the field artillery should form a box barrage round it when the heavy artillery ceased. Meanwhile, the trenches which were to be evacuated during the heavy bombardment should be reoccupied. Zero hour was fixed for 9 p.m., but a few minutes before this the Officer Commanding 16/Cheshire reported that the heavy artillery still continued to fire, and to fire short, and that it was impossible for him to get ready to attack, that the trenches were blown in and most of the Stokes ammunition buried. The Brigade Major, Captain Glover, was sent to the Officer Commanding 16/Cheshire to say that the attack must take place at 10 p.m. At the same time arrangements were made to relieve the 16/Cheshire by the 14/Gloucester and to carry out a raid on the strong point if the attack of the former battalion failed.

A subsequent message from the officer commanding stated that he considered the battalion demoralized, and that it would be unwise to attempt any enterprise that night.

On Captain Glover's arrival at Colonel Browne Clayton's headquarters it was arranged that a party should reconnoitre the strong point, and if it were found to be unoccupied, to seize it and consolidate it. Eight volunteers (mostly bombers) under Lieutenant

[1] North of Favière Wood.

Milne were chosen as the patrol. Colonel Browne Clayton, Captain Ryalls, and Captain Glover accompanied them to the front line, which was found to be destroyed, except for a short length of trench north of the Guillemont road where two Stokes guns were in position. Lieutenant Milne carried his patrol to the First Barrier, which was on the Guillemont Road, close to the strong point, where he remained, whilst Captain Glover returned and sent up reinforcements to consolidate it.

On the arrival of the 14/Gloucester at 4.30 a.m. a strong patro was sent out to the strong point but met wire and came under machine-gun fire so that it had to return, the leader, 2nd Lieutenant Mitchell, being wounded. The Brigade Commander attributed the failure of this enterprize to (i) the heavy artillery firing beyond the specified time and thus giving no time to organize the infantry attack ; (ii) to the heavy artillery firing short and demoralizing the men in the trenches although the casualties were not heavy ; and, (iii) to the class of new recruits being no longer " bantams " proper, but either half-grown lads or degenerates.

As regards (iii) the opinion was not confined to the General Officer Commanding the 105th Brigade. The original " Bantams " had done all that was expected of them, and, indeed, until the end of the war, the survivors manfully played their parts and earned a large share of the military awards which were from time to time gained by the members of the 35th Division. But when losses occurred, the men who were sent to take their places were, in most cases, not " Bantams " at all, as the term was originally understood, but undeveloped men, who had been previously rejected by the commanders, and who were unfitted, both morally and physically, to take their places in the fighting ranks of the British Army. This was recognized at a later date, and the unfit amongst them were withdrawn. Their retention appeared likely to endanger the *moral* of the whole division.

The short shooting of the heavy artillery as mentioned above, like other unfortunate incidents of a similar nature, must be regarded as controversial. Subsequent investigation tended to show that a considerable amount of damage was done by hostile fire. It is a fact that high angle fire from a flank has been mistaken by experienced troops for shell falling from our own artillery in rear, but, whichever theory is correct, there can be no doubt that the fire was greatly responsible for the failure of the attack.

At this time there were numerous German batteries grouped round Le Sars which lay to the north-west and only 7,000 yards from the trench held by the 16/Cheshire, and also between that village and Flers, which was situated but 4,000 yards to the north of the trench. If these German battery commanders cared to risk killing their own infantry they could have fired into the rear of the British front line facing Guillemont.

The casualties in these four days in this brigade were 28 killed, 244 wounded, and 24 missing.

Owing to this failure the 35th Division did not continue the proposed attack, but, by order, confined itself to assisting the 24th Division by a discharge of smoke, trench mortars, and machine-gun fire. This feint attack was very effective and succeeded in drawing heavy machine-gun and rifle fire from the strong point previously mentioned.

Meanwhile, the 104th Brigade had consolidated, and in some respects slightly advanced the line. That position taken over by the 23/Manchester was in very bad condition. The parapet was badly damaged and the relieved battalions, which apparently had suffered heavily, had had no opportunity of evacuating or burying their dead. The Manchesters, however, ignored these imperfections, and on the 20th were able to dig a trench in advance of the line, which they named Bantam Trench, and also to link up an isolated work with the original front line. Next night the battalion raided a German dug-out and captured a machine-gun.

During the afternoon Lieutenant Rose from Brigade Headquarters had been sent to reconnoitre the right of our line with a view to a possible advance in that direction. Having proceeded beyond the advanced post this officer entered a dug-out inhabited by a German speaking through a telephone. The German turned and addressed the officer, who, being unarmed and alone, promptly withdrew and returned to our line. Arrangements were immediately made for a raid on this spot, and, after nightfall, Lieutenant Rose, accompanied by forty men, returned to the neighbourhood, bombed all the dug-outs which were there and brought back the machine-gun and a certain amount of equipment.

As regards the 106th Brigade, as soon as it reached Sandpit Valley 500 men of the 18/Highland L.I. were sent up to dig communication trenches south of Trones Wood, and, on the 20th, the remainder of the Brigade was moved to Caftet Wood and Carnoy. Next day the 17/Royal Scots were engaged as a working party at Maltz Horn Farm, after which the battalion relieved the 16/Cheshires in Silesia Trench where it was joined by the 17/West Yorkshire. At the same time the 19/Durham L.I. relieved the 23/Manchester, and the last battalion to come into the line was the 18/Highland L.I., which, having finished its work at Trones Wood, was sent up in relief of the 15/Cheshire.

On this night, the 22nd, the 17/Lancashire Fusiliers took over the trenches at Angle Wood from the French 433rd and 127th regiments and the 18/Lancashire Fusiliers relieved their comrades of the 20th and that portion of the 23/Manchester, which had not been relieved by the 19/Durham L.I. This battalion suffered heavy casualties during the relief and subsequent repairing of trenches.

Next day the 105th Brigade made further attempts to capture the German strong point which had caused so much trouble, and strong patrols were sent forward by the 15/Sherwood Foresters and 14/Gloucester. As soon as these advanced they came under heavy machine-gun fire and, as a strong attack was in process of preparation, the raiding parties were ordered to be withdrawn. During the night the 105th Brigade was relieved partly by the 2/Leicester and partly by the 106th Brigade.

On the afternoon of the 24th the 104th Brigade was ordered to make an attack in conjunction with the French attack on Oakhanger Wood, south of the Falfemont Farm Ridge. The brigade was to advance on the left of the French and enter the enemy line running from a point south-east of the farm to the farm itself. This was to be carried out by strong patrols followed by two companies which were to establish themselves in the captured trench and hold it. This operation meant attacking the main German line with one battalion on a front of 350 yards, and, as no troops were to advance on the left of the battalion used, its left would therefore rest in the air near Falfemont Farm—still in German hands—and about 500 yards in advance of the next British battalion. A representation was made to divisional headquarters pointing out that in such circumstances the attack had little prospect of success; but the situation made it necessary that it should be proceeded with. The 17/ Lancashire Fusiliers were accordingly ordered to undertake it and the 19/Northumberland Fusiliers were ordered to dig assembly trenches.

At 9 p.m. the enemy commenced a heavy bombardment of our whole line. The Pioneers, led by the Brigade Liaison Officer, lost their way in the confusion caused by the shelling, and one party eventually found itself in rear of the German advanced lines where it engaged in a hand-to-hand fight, but eventually gained our trenches. Other details were similarly split up, as well as parties carrying ammunition and stores, so that at daylight no trench had been dug and only one company of the 17/Lancashire Fusiliers was formed up ready. General Pinney, having visited the front line, reported the situation to the Corps Commander, cancelled the attack and ordered that the 17/Lancashire Fusiliers should advance their right only in conjunction with the French and hold a line from a point south-east of Falfemont Farm to the north end of Angle Wood. At 5.45 p.m. the French advanced against Oakhanger Wood and reached their objectives, and at the same time, the 17/Lancashire Fusiliers advanced their line about 300 yards and dug themselves in.[1] They were not unduly disturbed during the night and had only about sixty casualties. The Brigade Commander visited the new line next morning and, in spite of intermittent barrages of great intensity, found the battalion firmly established on the southern slope of the Falfemont Farm ridge and feeling quite confident that they could hold on. This they did throughout the day which passed without other incident except spasmodic but heavy shelling, an abortive counter attack which was dispersed by artillery fire, and a sharp brush with enemy patrols near the farm in the evening. At night the Battalion was relieved by the 20/Lancashire Fusiliers.

Meanwhile, the 17/West Yorkshire of the 106th Brigade was covering the 19/Northumberland Fusiliers who were engaged in

[1] This was the French 1st Division, commanded by General de Fonclare. It had relieved the 153rd French Division on the 20th. On the 27th, on the division being relieved, this general wrote to General Pinney referring to the shortness of time allowed: *"L'œuf est dans la coque, et la victorie est dans la preparation."*

linking up the trenches which had been dug by the 23/Manchester. A heavy bombardment lasted through this time, which caused the battalion about seventy casualties. In the evening a counter attack of the enemy was reported and our artillery was called upon for a barrage, but if any counter attack was intended it did not materialize. During the next night the 35th Division was relieved in the line, the 104th Brigade by the 13th Brigade, 5th Division (10/Warwick and 1/West Kent), and the 106th Brigade by the 15/Warwick and 1/Devon. The 104th Brigade withdrew to Citadel and the 106th to Happy Valley. The Division was then transferred to the VI Corps, Third Army, and, on the 30th, entrained at Heilly for Candas, about five miles south-west of Doullens. The 104th and 106th Brigades were billeted in areas north-east of this place and the 105th Brigade south-west of it. The 19/Northumberland Fusiliers remained with the 5th Division until 1st September.

To return to the Artillery, the 158th and 163rd Brigades, R.F.A., which had been relieved on August 12th, went into action again on the 17th, the former near Montauban covering the zone north of Guillemont and the latter in the orchard east of Maricourt, covering the area between Wedge Wood and Oakhanger Wood. These two brigades covered the various attacks on Guillemont and also supported the French attacks on the right of our line. The 158th Brigade was withdrawn from action on August 22nd, and the 163rd on the night of the 25th/26th. It joined the 157th Brigade at Bois de Tailles, where it had been waiting in readiness, without being called upon, since the 12th. Since its relief on the 15th, the 159th Brigade had remained in billets at Corbie, and on the 29th it marched to Daours.

The period of the Battle of the Somme cannot be considered to have been either a happy or a successful time for the infantry of the division. The serious losses suffered at the commencement, whilst battalions were either engaged in digging trenches or serving under other commands, had an undesirable effect upon all ranks, and, when the opportunity finally came to act as a division and carry out attacks, which a month previously would no doubt have been crowned with success, the men who could have executed the orders were no longer there, and those who had taken their places were in many cases unfitted for the work which they were called upon to perform. A successful attack at the commencement, or a share of good luck towards the close would undoubtedly have altered the record of performances on the Somme. Evidence of individual leadership and of isolated actions of small parties all go to prove what result might have been expected under different circumstances. The time came later when such expectations were to be realized.

It must be taken into consideration, however, that when the 35th Division arrived in the Somme area, the salient at Longueval-Delville Wood was a critical position, which the XIII Corps had to hold at any cost, and it was necessary that the 106th Brigade should have been advanced to strengthen the troops holding it.

The same may be said of the use of the 105th Brigade on the right flank.

The praise which was given to the work of the division by army and corps commanders testifies to the importance of the duty and the manner in which it was carried out.

Before the division left the Somme area discussions took place as to the advisability of evacuating men of poor physique and especially those who had arrived with the later drafts. It was determined that such a course was necessary, but it was also decided by the G.H.Q. that the changes should not take place until the division had left the Fourth Army. As a matter of fact it was delayed longer than this.

It may be of interest to those who took part in these operations to learn the further history of Guillemont and the strong point south-west of it, known as S.30.b.7.1. This point formed part of the First Objective of the general attack on Ginchy-Guillemont-Falfemont Farm, originally planned for August 24th, but subsequently postponed until midday, September 3rd. The interval was occupied in making more careful preparations for the attack than had hitherto been possible.

The attack was undertaken by the 59th Bde. 20th Division (Brig.-Gen. Shute) and a " Push Pipe " mine was driven from a point on the Hardecourt–Guillemont road towards the hostile strong point. When this was exploded a trench was formed and

Flammenwerfer turned on to the objective. As a result, the strong point gave no trouble to the troops in the advance.

By 1 p.m. the 59th Brigade had captured the strong point and the greater part of Guillemont but, as the attacks on Ginchy and Falfemont Farm were both held up, the brigade had to undergo two more days of heavy fighting before relief.

The losses of this brigade during these three days were 5 officers killed, 20 wounded, 5 missing ; 117 other ranks killed, 402 wounded, 416 missing. This meant a loss to the fighting strength of 30 officers and 935 men.

As the brigade apparently made no retirement, most of the missing were presumably either blown up or buried. Falfemont Farm was captured on September 5th.

CHAPTER V

ARRAS

AT the end of August, 1916, the division was quartered in and around Doullens, with headquarters in the town, except for the artillery which was still in the Somme battle area. On September 1st units commenced their movement in the direction of Arras, preparatory to taking over the defence of that sector.

The new period covers a continuous service of three months in the trenches as regards the infantry, and almost four for the artillery. During this time all three brigades were in the line, and the period was destitute of incident that calls for any special comment. The enemy holding the front were, like the 35th Division, resting from exhaustive efforts on the Somme, and, in addition, were apparently short of artillery, or, at least, of ammunition with which to supply it. The main feature of the fighting was the great increase in numbers and efficiency of trench mortars which for some months were to take the chief part in the system of trench warfare.

On September 2nd divisional headquarters closed at Doullens and opened at Le Cauroy, about fifteen miles west of Arras. The 104th Brigade had by this time reached the area of Grand Rullecourt and moved thence by motor omnibus to Wanquetin. The 105th Brigade had come by motor omnibus from their former billeting areas and were also established at Wanquetin and Agnez-les-Duisans. The 106th Brigade moved by omnibus from Sus St. Leger to the same area. On the 3rd the brigades entered the town and took over from the 21st Division as follows :—

The 104th Brigade relieved the 2nd Brigade in " I " Sector, which extended roughly from a point south of the Cambrai road, one mile east-south-east of Arras, to the banks of the Scarpe at Blangy. The reserve battalions were in the Cemetery and the Faubourg St. Saveur. The 105th Brigade took over " J " Sector from 110th Brigade. This sector extended from the Scarpe to a point north of the Douai road and included at its nothern point the three craters Claude, Cuthbert, and Clarence. The 106th Brigade relieved the 64th Brigade in " K " Sector which extended from a maze of derelict trenches known as The Gridiron, to a point 1,000 yards north-east of Roclincourt. It was the left section of the VI Corps and Third Army front. The 104th Brigade had two battalions in the line, one in brigade reserve and one in divisional reserve. The 105th had three battalions in the line and one in brigade reserve, which was quartered in Arras. The 106th had two battalions in the line, one in brigade reserve and one in divisional reserve at Dainville. There were thus for the defence of the Arras sector, seven battalions in the line, three in brigade reserve, and two in divisional reserve.

As soon as the division had entered the line, after having raised the fire-steps to enable the " Bantams " to fire over the parapet, they set to work to revet and improve the trenches which they had taken over, and which, although in good order, did not fulfil all requirements. Owing to incessant work, and in spite of heavy trench mortar bombardments of the front line, these trenches in the Arras sector eventually became a model of what trenches should be. In a short time they were not only cleaned, revetted, and fully duck-boarded, but, by making use of the waterpower of the Scarpe, battalion headquarters, etc., were eventually lit by electric light. It must be acknowledged that the soil of Arras lent itself to good trench-making, and similar results might not have been obtained in certain other portions of the line without a prodigious amount of labour.

The divisional headquarters was at Duisans, a village situated just south of the St. Pol road and about three and a half miles west of the town. The infantry and artillery brigade headquarters were in the town, from which the front lines were easily accessible as the communication trenches radiated outwards from the suburbs. The names of those in " I " Sector all began with the letter I ; the most important being Iceland Street and Imperial Street, south of the Cambrai Road, and Ivory Street between Blangy and the railway. Those in " J " Sector were called avenues and named after the months of the year beginning with January, a short length close to the Scarpe. Several of them were unused and the most important were March, May, July, October (trench tramway), and November.[1] In "K" Sector the avenues were named after the days of the week, the two most in use being Sunday and Wednesday, the latter of which passed the dominating point known as Les Quatre Vents.

The reliefs were completed on September 4th, and all battalions were in position except the 19/Northumberland Fusiliers which arrived by lorry at Agnez-les-Duisans on the 6th.

The artillery had remained in the Somme area until the 3rd, on which day the march to Arras commenced.[2] The artillery reliefs were completed in the Arras Sector on the 10th. Prior to coming into the line the artillery had been again reorganized. On the 8th the 163rd Brigade was disbanded, and its guns and personnel divided amongst the other three brigades which now consisted of three 18-pr. batteries of six guns and one battery of four 4.5 howitzers. The brigade commanders remained as before, namely, Lieut.-Colonel Stewart (157th), Lieut.-Colonel Fawcett (158th), and Lieut.-Colonel Davson (159th).

From now onwards, except for a few slight modifications, each artillery brigade covered a definite infantry brigade. The 157th R.F.A. covered the 104th, south of the Scarpe; the 159th R.F.A. covered the 105th in "J" Sector; and the 158th covered the 106th in "K" Sector. It was an organization which greatly simplified the co-operation between artillery and infantry, and the arrangement was taken advantage of by officers of both arms. The batteries were located behind the trench lines in and around the Faubourgs of the town, except B/159 Battery which held a commanding position in the walls of Arras close to the Porte Baudimont (the St. Pol Gate) whence an uninterrupted view was obtained of the approaches to Arras from the Douai direction as far as Le Point du Jour. In addition to the divisional artillery the 124th Brigade,

---

[1] In "J" Sector the trenches were occupied by the "rolling stone" method. That is they were divided into three sectors, each portion being occupied by one battalion with a long period in and a short period out. The fourth battalion relieved each in turn. By this method the permanent battalions took great interest in the improvement of the trenches.

[2] The R.A. marches were as follows :—

4th, Daours; 5th, Villers Bocage, Pierregot, and Molliens au Bois; 6th, Le Meillard, Outre Bois, Occoches (these places were from four to six miles to the west of Doullens); 7th, Frohan le Grand, Romesnil Outrebois, Mezerolles; 8th, Ivergny, Sus St. Leger, Brevillers, Le Souich; 9th, Wanquetin, Arras, Hautville.

September 12, 1916

HISTORY OF THE 35TH DIVISION   59

R.F.A., came under 35th Division Orders and covered the whole front. The trench mortar batteries of the division arrived on the 12th

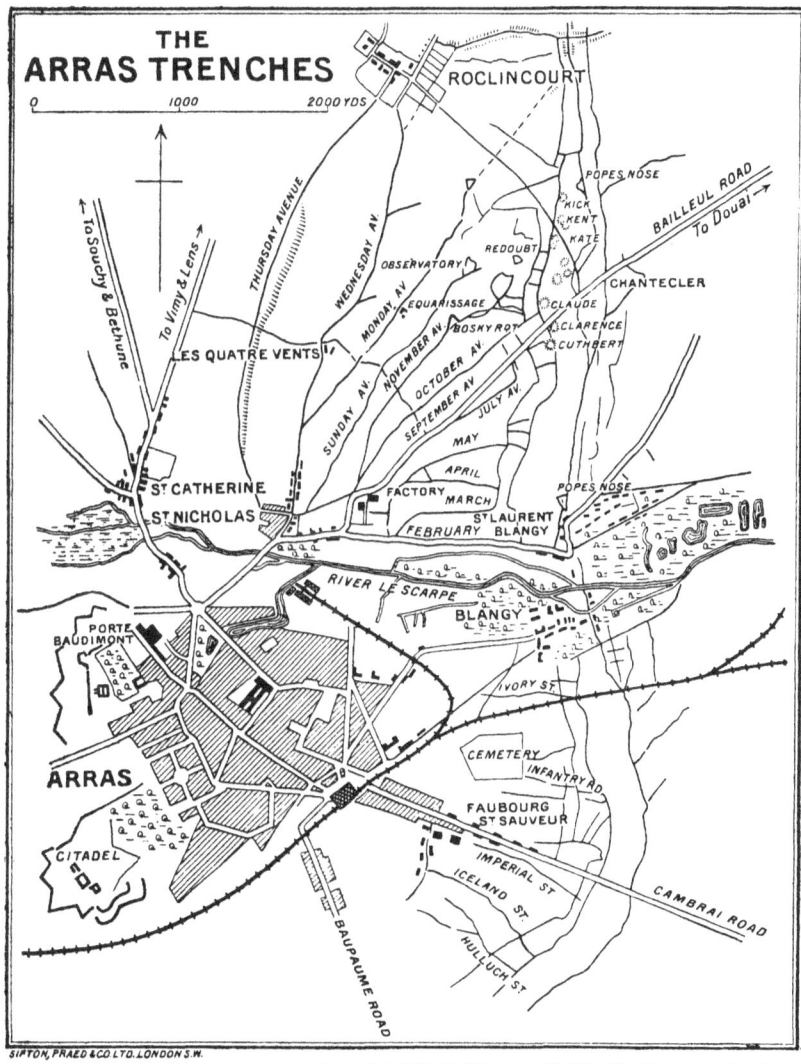

and went into action, as also did V/35 Heavy T.M. Battery, which consisted of four 9.45 heavy mortars. This latter reinforcement was much appreciated as the enemy's mortars overpowered ours, and already, on the 8th and 9th, both " I " and " J " Sectors had suffered severely from heavy bombs to which no adequate response could be made. A small, but satisfactory, reprisal was executed by the 104th Brigade when a sniper having shot a German, others of the enemy ran to his assistance and a Stokes bomb was successfully dispatched into the middle of them.

This beginning was but a foretaste of what was to come, and from now onwards the daily summaries regularly quoted damage to trenches at night and the rebuilding of the same. As our own trench mortar batteries settled down and became active the intensity of the bombardment increased. All through the period under review the enemy mortars appeared to be more numerous than ours, to be better sited for the work in hand, and many were of heavier calibre, so that, but for our superiority in field artillery, the combat might have been one-sided. The difficulty of siting and preparing proper emplacements for V/35 was also a handicap in this respect.

On the 10th at 11.40 p.m. the enemy attempted a small raid against the 106th Brigade at Kate Crater. Lewis gunners opened fire upon the party which threw a few bombs and then retired. A thirst for information was possibly the origin of the attempt. On the next day an installation of gas cylinders was begun on the left of " K " Sector, and this was completed on the 13th. Elaborate orders were issued as to its use, and it was to be discharged at the first favourable opportunity. Altogether 960 cylinders were installed, and 4,000 rounds were allotted to the artillery in support of the prospective discharge. The favourable opportunity did not come for some time, and the delay was not attractive to those who had to live in close proximity to gas cylinders exposed to the fire of artillery and trench mortar bombs.

On September 14th the 124th Brigade, R.F.A., was relieved by the 156th Brigade (Colonel Rochfoot Boyd, D.S.O.), but by VI Corps orders it was shortly withdrawn again. On this day the Commander of the VI Corps (Lieut.-General Sir A. Haldane) visited the units in the line and expressed approval of the trenches. At night the 15/Cheshire made a raid upon the enemy trenches just north of the Bailleul Road. This portion of the enemy line was known as the Three Craters Salient, owing to three small mine craters being situated in front of the German trenches. The programme was that the artillery should bombard the enemy front and support trenches, and then lift and form a box barrage round the point of entry for an hour. Diversions were created by the R.F.A. brigades covering other sectors and by trench mortars and Stokes guns.

The raid advanced in two parties which had had a previous rehearsal on a course laid out at Duisans. The artillery barrage opened at 8 p.m., and at 8.16 four large Camouflets were fired between Cuthbert and Clarence Craters, the shock of which was felt in Arras. At the same time the raiding party, following close behind the artillery barrage reached the enemy trenches where they unfortunately suffered a few casualties from short bursts. The light was still just sufficient to enable the men to see for a few yards.

The wire was cut and the trenches at the point of entry severely damaged, but the rest of the enemy front line inside the box barrage did not appear to have suffered sufficiently from our artillery fire, so that, as soon as the bombing party appeared at the point of entry, the Germans again lined their parapet and opened rapid rifle fire. Taking into consideration the heaviness of the barrage along their front it must be conceded that the enemy displayed conspicuous gallantry.[1] Three bombing parties followed by a clearing up party entered the trench and started bombing their way outwards, but, owing to the enemy being present in the trench on either side, the progress made was slow, and the opening was not widened sufficiently to enable the remainder of the raiding party and the party of New Zealand miners, which had accompanied the raid, to enter the trenches in the time allotted. On account of this the officer commanding the raiding party moved his men to a flank outside the trench and bombed the parapets from there. The recall signal was made at 9 p.m. after the party had been in the trenches forty minutes. All men returned by 9.45 p.m. except 2nd Lieutenant Jones, who was wounded, and four men who stayed to assist him, also an officer [2] and sergeant of the New Zealand Miners, who, in spite of three search parties having gone out during the night and one in charge of Captain Le Mesurier, having searched along the enemy wire, were not again heard of. 2nd Lieutenant

[1] The 159th Brigade fired 1,400 rounds in this enterprise.
[2] Name not mentioned.

Jones and party were brought in about 10.30 p.m. as well as three other wounded men.

Although the enemy casualties appeared to have been numerous the support line was not sufficiently damaged by the Field Artillery barrage, and it was able to be manned by riflemen as our parties entered the trenches. It was reported that there seemed to be great confusion among the German units, accompanied by much shouting and blowing of horns. The shouting, etc., however, appeared to have had the effect of forcing individuals back to their fighting position.

The casualties were 1 officer wounded, 1 missing, 2 other ranks killed, 27 wounded and 2 missing, one of which was known to be with the New Zealand officer.

A feature of the raid was the almost total lack of enemy artillery fire, and their trench mortar retaliation was also weak. Our artillery and trench mortars appeared to have been wholly successful in keeping down hostile machine-gun fire.

At 9.43 p.m. a large crimson flame which looked like a burst of ammonal was seen. It was thought probable that the New Zealand officer had succeeded in reaching a mine shaft, but no confirmation could be obtained, and probably it will never now be definitely known. Whilst hoping that such was the case, it must be taken into consideration that the raiding party had left the enemy trenches some forty minutes previously.

Communications throughout worked without a hitch. Constant reports of proceedings were received at Headquarters from 2nd Lieutenant F. D. Stephenson, B/159 Battery, stationed in Claude Crater, and from Major R. D. Harisson, C/159 Battery, who was in Saps, 98 and 99.

Possibly, as a result of the previous night's raid the enemy trench mortars showed considerable activity on the 15th and did a fair amount of damage. Iron Street in " I " Sector was blown in, as was the left support headquarters of the 15/Cheshire close to November Avenue. Our artillery in retaliation scored some successes. A/157 Battery obtained eleven direct hits on a snipers' post opposite their front and D/158 demolished a new German post in course of erection. Next day this battery spotted a German working party behind the line and dispersed it with loss.

On the night of the 16th a raid was attempted by the 23/Manchester for the purpose of obtaining identification. The spots chosen were the saps running parallel to and immediately north and south of the Arras-Lens railway where it crossed the German line. These had been bombarded on September 14th by field howitzers and medium trench mortars for the purpose of smashing them up and cutting the wire. The fire of the mortars was disappointing as patrols reported that the wire, although damaged, was not destroyed. The light was bad for observation, and much of the ammunition was said to be defective. It was decided, however, not to draw further attention to the proposed raid and to attempt to cross the remains of the wire by means of mats.

The raid started at 2.30 a.m. At ten minutes before zero two parties of twenty men each, led by an officer, and a covering party of ten men moved out to beyond our wire. Five minutes before zero an intense artillery barrage was put down on the enemy front line and as it lifted the parties advanced. The party north of the railway could not effect a passage through the wire which was thicker than had been anticipated, and, after bombing the sap, it withdrew. The party south of the railway, led by 2nd Lieutenant Abraham, had also considerable difficulty in crossing the wire, but they ultimately succeeded in doing so and entered the sap which was found to be deserted. The enemy from the main line now advanced and after an exchange of bombs Lieutenant Abraham withdrew his men.

The enemy retaliation was very feeble as only two men out of the fifty engaged were hit. This was attributed to the accuracy of the barrage, and it was generally considered that had the wire been properly cut the raid would have been a definite success. As it was, it must be considered to have failed in its object, as, although certain articles of equipment were brought back by the raiders, no identifications of value could be obtained from them.

The 20/Lancashire Fusiliers relieved the 23/Manchester after this operation and immediately experienced a stroke of bad luck by having 3 men killed and 6 wounded by a single rifle grenade. At the same time the 18/Lancashire Fusiliers next door to them had 2 men killed and 6 wounded by a single grenade which exploded in Iodine Sap. Next morning, however, Sergeant Tinsley revenged his regiment by shooting 5 Germans out of a working party at a range of 750 yards.

On the 18th Lieut.-Colonel E. Vaughan, Manchester Regiment, from the 2nd/7th Royal Welsh Fusiliers, assumed command of the 20/Lancashire Fusiliers.

The rest of the month was quiet, and beyond a certain amount of trench mortar activity on both sides no operations took place which are worthy of comment.

About this time the artillery commenced to calibrate their guns, that is, they tested each gun separately under expert supervision, and arranged the sighting apparatus so that all weapons might be relied upon to shoot alike at varying ranges. Previous to this the extra wear of certain pieces had conduced to a difference of range with the same setting of sights, and in pre-war days the protests of battery commanders that their guns did not shoot alike were merely looked upon as an excuse for inferior fire control. One advantage of the European War was the knowledge obtained that a gun's shooting power varied according to its length of usage.

On the 22nd the 156th Brigade, R.F.A., returned to the command of the 35th Divisional Artillery and resumed its function of covering the whole front.

On the 23rd Major-General A. J. S. Landon, C.B., assumed command of the division in exchange with Major-General Pinney who went to command the 33rd Division, and on the same day General Allenby, commanding Third Army, accompanied by Lieut.-General Haldane, inspected a portion of the line. The 104th Brigade successfully blew up a chimney in the No Man's Land of Blangy which the Germans had been using as a night observation post, and following on this, one of their snipers who saw a German carrying a heavy object fired at him. He missed the man but hit the object which exploded. It was suspected that the man was hurt.

On the following morning a German (hatless) was seen wandering about No Man's Land at "Stand To." He was shot at and disappeared. It is possible that he was one of a patrol and had been lost. At the same time the 105th Brigade successfully engaged an enemy trench mortar emplacement north of Blangy. As judged by the subsequent sounds which proceeded from the spot considerable damage must have been done.[1]

On September 27th a bombing party went out in " I " Sector and bombed a sap in the German lines about 500 yards north of the Cambrai road. The episode was entirely successful, and it is believed that all the enemy present in the sap were accounted for.

The only other records of this month are a series of trench mortar bombardments and counter bombardments and much work done to trenches both in improving what existed and rebuilding what had been blown down the night before. It became increasingly apparent, also, that the enemy's chief wish was to be left alone and a succession of heavy rains which damaged the trenches helped him in this respect.

OCTOBER, 1916

On October 1st divisional orders were issued that the medium trench batteries should come under the direct command of the R.A. group commanders, and that the Divisional Trench Mortar Officer should act as technical adviser to the C.R.A. The intention was that the trench mortar batteries should receive more assistance by being attached to artillery units than when acting independently. No doubt this result was achieved, but, seeing that most of the trench mortar positions were blown to bits nearly every night, the scheme entailed much extra labour to the R.A. brigade commander concerned. About a month later the order was rescinded.

On this day also the 20/Lancashire Fusiliers had an engagement with the enemy in No Man's Land, in which 2nd Lieutenant Bates, the leader, and two other ranks were either killed or captured. At the same time in the trenches 2nd Lieutenant Lennox was severely wounded.

A considerable amount of trench mortar activity followed, and some damage was done to our trenches, especially in " J " Sector. Following a bombardment of artillery and trench mortars on the enemy's wire opposite Kick Crater, a patrol of the 106th Brigade attempted to enter the enemy's trenches at Pope's Nose, but was

[1] This was the day (September 26th) of the capture of Thiepval and the sounds of battle were plainly audible to all sections on the Arras front, seventeen miles away.

unsuccessful. Pope's Nose was severely bombarded next day, and on the following afternoon a combined shoot was carried out against the Three Crater Salient. There was little retaliation, but in the evening the enemy sallied out and attacked one of our bombing posts. The occupants went out after them and they retired to their own line. Part of the gas cylinders were now removed from " K " to " I " Sector, and the result was that orders and counter orders for the discharge came over the telephone with painful frequency for some considerable time.[1]

The details of what took place may be of interest to those who were present in the trenches. At 7.10 a.m. on the 6th gas discharge was ordered to take place at 9.30 p.m. At 9.10 p.m. divisional headquarters were ordered to cancel this, and the counter order was received by the 104th Brigade at 9.22 p.m. It was then too late to warn all the gas emplacements, and, for a few minutes before it could be stopped, gas was discharged from about ninety cylinders in front of Blangy. The wind had veered south-south-east and most of the garrison of the front line had been withdrawn. When the men came back eight of them were slightly gassed. The 106th Brigade received the orders in time to cancel the discharge.

At 11.42 p.m. a fresh notification was received that gas would be discharged at 1 a.m. on the 7th. At 12.50 a.m., the discharge was cancelled for both " I " and " K " Sector. At 6.10 p.m. gas discharge was ordered for 8.15 p.m., but was cancelled at 7.30 p.m. The 106th Brigade, already mystified by these proceedings, was further unsettled by the enemy cutting a ten-feet gap in his own wire opposite Kings Crater, and it was assumed that this was a prelude to an attack.

At 6.45 p.m. on the 8th, the division was ordered to discharge gas at 8.45 p.m. This was done. Artillery and trench mortars co-operated and at 10.45 p.m. patrols went out from the 104th [2] and 106th [3] Brigades to investigate the result.

The enemy was on the alert and no information was obtained except that the gas was heavy in the enemy's trenches and some of our own men suffered slightly from its effect. Subsequent infor-

---

[1] This work was carried out by the 17/West Yorkshire. At the same time the 18/Highland L.I., who were in the line, had one officer and four men killed, and two men wounded by a single trench mortar bomb which fell in the trenches.

[2] 17/Lancashire Fusiliers and 23/Manchester.

[3] 19/Durham L.I., 2nd Lieutenant Smith, the leader, was mortally wounded.

OCTOBER 20, 1916

HISTORY OF THE 35TH DIVISION 67

mation from prisoners revealed the fact that twenty-five of the enemy were gassed, and that most of them died from the effects.

Following on this operation there was an activity with trench mortars and aerial torpedoes, also a certain amount of sniping in which our marksmen gained the upper hand.[1] The enemy erected a periscope opposite King's Crater which was carefully left alone as our observers, by means of it, were able to see what was going on in the German lines and to describe the appearance of officers and men. It was, however, ordered to be destroyed.

On the 17th a combined artillery and trench mortar shoot was made against the enemy trenches near Cuthbert Crater. This inflicted a considerable amount of damage on the enemy front line, but also brought upon us the usual retaliation. The 106th Brigade reported that very good practice was made on its lines by an 8-inch trench mortar.

President Poincaré visited Arras on the following day, and our artillery activity died down, but after his departure both guns and trench mortars opened with redoubled energy, and, on the 20th, the 104th Brigade (23/Manchester) made an attempt to enter the enemy's lines through a gap in the wire opposite Infantry Road. The raid was unsuccessful, and after an exchange of bombs the party retired, 2nd Lieutenant Hines, the leader, and his N.C.O. both being wounded. Two days later the 105th Brigade carried out a surprise raid near the three small craters. The raid was divided into three parties, but only the centre one was able to penetrate the wire and enter the trenches which it found unoccupied. The party extended outwards but were unable to obtain any identifications and retired on the recall signal being shown. The casualties were 8 men wounded.

The weather now became very bad and the damage done to trenches by weather and bombs was considerable. It was apparent that work on the supposed Hindenberg Line which could be seen on the high ground about four miles to the north-east was increasing in intensity and rumours were heard that the Germans shortly intended to retire. These were, however, without foundation.[2]

[1] Major G. S. C. Willis, D.S.O., assumed the duties of brigade major, 106th Brigade, on the 9th.
[2] On the 22nd three officers of the 159th Brigade, R.F.A., whilst riding to Arras from the wagon lines, were attacked by a German aeroplane. After circling round and firing at them for a few minutes it disappeared in a westerly direction. There were no casualties.

On the 25th the 15/Sherwood Foresters carried out a raid upon that portion of the enemy trenches just south of the Bailleul road, and opposite Clarence and Cuthbert Craters, where there were two saps protruding from the enemy front line. Zero hour was fixed for 8 p.m.

The artillery programme was that a barrage should be put down on trenches " B," " C," and " F," [1] from 8 to 8.20 p.m., and then to switch on to the support line [2] until 8.45 p.m. or until the raiders

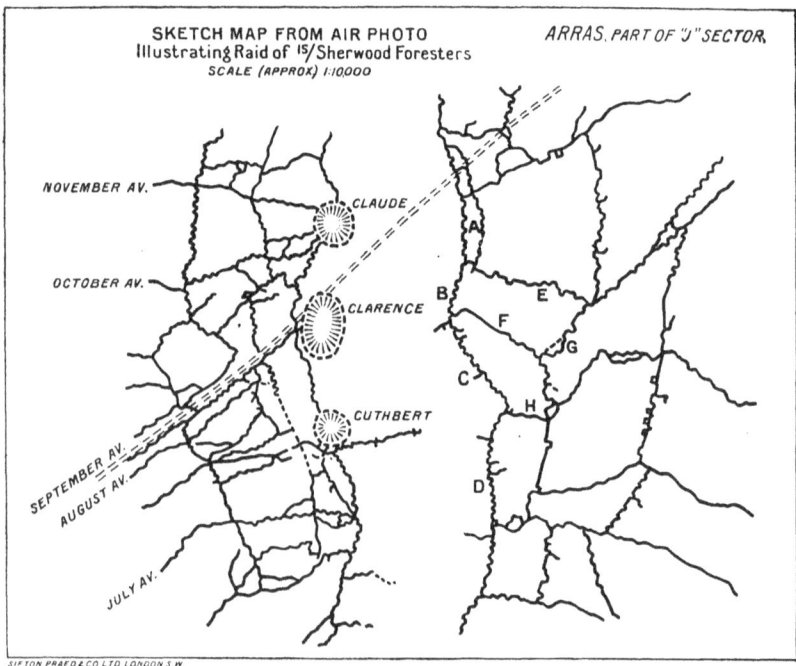

returned. Also at 8 p.m. a heavy barrage assisted by 6-inch howitzers and trench mortars was opened on trenches " A," " E," " G," " H," and " D." From 8.15 to 8.25 the artillery created a diversion by firing on Pope's Nose and co-operation was also obtained from trench mortars, Stokes guns, machine, and Lewis guns, and infantry on both flanks.

[1] See Sketch Map attached.
[2] G 12.a.85.20 to G 6.c.95.00, including Trench G.

September 25, 1916

The raid had been carefully rehearsed for several days at the Divisional School at Duisans. Sergeant-Major Wilcocks, Army Gymnastic School Staff, rendered excellent service in instructing the party.[1] The raiding party did not go up to the trenches until just before the time of the raid. It was composed as follows:—

A bombing party under 2nd Lieutenant Warburton of thirty men divided into three squads.

A clearing party under 2nd Lieutenant Dunn [2] of thirty-four men divided into three squads.

A demolition party consisting of one N.C.O. and six men of the 204th Field Company Royal Engineers.

An intelligence party of ten men.

A covering party under 2nd Lieutenants Judge and Swallow of forty-two men with bombs, rifles, and Lewis guns.

In addition, two scouts (Privates Rhodes and Hinton) who had explored the way across No Man's Land, were detailed to guide the raid by tapes from our lines to the point of entry and to keep ahead of the bombers and enclose them within the tapes.

The three bombing parties, who were all volunteers, began crawling forward from their assembly positions at 8.15, but, owing to the darkness, mist, and heavy going (it had rained for several days) their progress was very slow. Also, the centre and right parties managed to stray wide despite the tapes, and only the left party kept direction and found the point of entry with the wire completely cut. Lieutenant Warburton who was in charge of the bombing parties lost direction with the centre party. He sent the party back and attempted to find the others, but failed to do so.[3]

The right party of the clearing parties also went astray but Lieutenant Dunn eventually got them to the hostile trenches where they had a hand-to-hand fight with some Germans and put them to flight. In this engagement Lieutenant Dunn was slightly wounded in the face, and as the time limit had expired and he had no bombers with him he led his party back to our lines. The centre and left parties both got into the enemy's lines and captured a prisoner. This man, on his way back, tried to throttle one of his captors,

[1] This N.C.O. volunteered to go over with the raid but was not allowed to do so.
[2] He was in charge of the whole party.
[3] This officer was reported missing.

but was overpowered and forcibly brought back to our lines.[1] The raiders saw several dead in the trenches all being partially buried, and it is interesting to note that the men who engaged Lieutenant Dunn's party were wearing gas masks.

The Royal Engineers, when they got into the trenches, had not sufficient time to make a systematic search for the mine shaft which was supposed to be in the neighbourhood, but they found two dug-outs both occupied by the enemy and destroyed them with their inmates. The time limit then obliged the party to return to our own lines. The casualties were many. Besides Lieutenant Dunn and Lieutenant Warburton one other officer was reported missing,[2] and one officer of the 15/Sherwood Foresters and one of the 14/Gloucester were killed by the enemy retaliation. The Sherwood Foresters lost 2 other ranks killed, 18 wounded and 8 missing in the raid itself. The artillery fire was reported as excellent. The Royal Engineers stated the wire to be completely cut although it was forty feet thick in two series. The raiding parties encountered little opposition in the trenches, and although some parties remained beyond the scheduled time there was no attempt at a counter attack. The retaliation was weak, possibly as battery positions within range and heavy trench mortar emplacements were kept under fire by our heavy artillery and trench mortars. A somewhat elaborate system of artillery communications operated without hindrance.

The rest of the month passed quietly. More gas cylinders were moved from " J " Sector to " I " Sector, and some sniping and artillery activity were the only events of note. An enemy relief, the date of which had been extracted from the prisoner, was successfully dealt with in the " J " Sector.

NOVEMBER, 1916

On November 2nd the enemy commenced a heavy trench mortar bombardment on " J " and " K " Sectors, and much damage was caused to the sodden trenches in addition to several casualties.

---

[1] The captors were Privates Wharton, Jefferies, and Newton. It was reported that five prisoners were taken, but only one was brought back. Private Rhodes, the left tape man, reported seeing five Germans in a shell hole outside their wire. He threw two bombs at them and later found that four of them were killed. It is possible that these were the prisoners unaccounted for.

[2] His name is not given in any report. One wounded officer was found by a patrol in No Man's Land on the 27th instant and brought in.

In " J " Sector, February Avenue was badly damaged, and in the centre of the sector the front line and support line were in many cases completely destroyed. The whole of the trench known as 101 was wrecked as well as the obstacle line between Claude and Cuthbert Craters. Several communication trenches behind these places were rendered impassable. Further north, in "K" Sector, many trenches behind Kick Crater were quite destroyed. A combined artillery and trench mortar shoot took place in retaliation with satisfactory results, although it was reported by the 106th Brigade that our trench mortars appeared to be overpowered by the superior weight of those of the enemy.[1]

At 1.38 a.m. next morning the 17/West Yorkshire raided the enemy trenches opposite Victoria Street about 400 yards north of the Bailleul Road. The wire had been cut by hand on the previous evening, and the gap was completed by the discharge of two Bangalore torpedoes of 17 inches and 14 inches respectively, and the moment of their explosion was signalled to the artillery by rockets. The guns then opened fire. The raiding party experienced no difficulty in entering the enemy's trenches. Six Germans were killed and two dug-outs bombed. The party returned at 2.30 a.m., having suffered only one casualty, and bringing back identification of the 89th Grenadier Regiment. The party consisted of 2 officers and 32 other ranks, but the names of the leaders and details of attack are not available.

Owing to the bad weather many of the damaged parapets entirely collapsed and repairs became increasingly difficult. The men were working up to their knees in mud. The artillery and trench mortars continued the work of retaliation for the damage which had been done, but the enemy made little or no reply. Work of destruction was observed in the back areas and four explosions in one day were reported in Plouvain, about seven miles east of Arras. At 5.30 a.m., a patrol of the 15 Cheshire captured a German wearing a mask just south of Clarence Crater. He belonged to the 90th Fusilier Regiment. It was uncertain whether he was a deserter or a scout.

On the 9th a British aeroplane came down in No Man's Land just

---

[1] The 15/Cheshire had 1 officer, 2 sergeants, and 2 men buried who were dug out alive, but next day 22 men were buried, of whom 7 were killed.

south of the Cambrai Road in " I " Sector. The pilot escaped to a shell hole and at dusk crawled into the lines of the 18/Lancashire Fusiliers. He had been wounded in two places and his engine damaged in a fight with two enemy machines. The Germans, whose curiosity made them expose themselves on the parapet, were suitably dealt with by our snipers, and our trench mortars destroyed the machine. The new battalions in the enemy line were reported as more venturesome than their predecessors: they were also smarter in appearance. The two facts might be regarded as analogous.[1]

At this time the 508th Howitzer Battery (Major Potter) came under the orders of the division and was attached to the 159th Brigade, R.F.A. It was sited in the Faubourg St. Saveur, facing north, and rendered valuable assistance during the time the division remained in the Arras Sector.

A successful bombing raid in " I " Sector was followed by further orders for a gas discharge, but, owing to a change of wind it was subsequently cancelled. Although the weather had moderated the wind continued variable, and when, in a few days, this, too, became more settled, the rain gave place to fog which lasted intermittently until the end of the month. The fog and mist handicapped artillery work, but the absence of rain was a boon to battalions which were making heroic efforts to repair the trenches.

At this time a particularly heavy mortar in the German lines opposite " J " Sector was causing a considerable amount of annoyance. It was used, apparently, from two (or three) emplacements which were bomb-proof and must have been run on a trolley from one to the other.[2] As all local efforts to silence it failed, application was made for the services of a 12-inch howitzer. The Captain of the detachment accordingly took up his position in the trenches in front of Observatory Redoubt. A burst of Stokes mortar fire was replied to by this monster and disclosed its position close to the cross road at Chantecler. It fired two rounds. Then the first 12-inch shell arrived from seven miles away and burst within twenty

---

[1] On the same night one of the enemy shouted to the sentry of No. 1 Sap in K Sector, " It's cold to-night, Jock." It may have been a coincidence, but it is remarkable that on this particular night both the Scottish battalions of the 100th Brigade were in the line.

[2] It was spotted by two infantry observers (a number had been trained for this duty) by the mist which rose from the ground, and the artillery F.O.O. confirmed the observation.

yards of it. The mortar ceased fire. Seven more shells were fired from the 12-inch and a direct hit was obtained on the emplacement. The mortar henceforward ceased from troubling. Three days later this howitzer engaged a similar mortar in " I " Sector close to the Cambrai Road. The result was not so successful, but considerable damage was done to the vicinity of the emplacement. A similar weapon firing from a point 500 yards further north was effectively silenced by the divisional artillery.

Following on this the enemy's medium mortars showed renewed activity, and combined shoots on our part were arranged in retaliation. It was generally considered that the enemy received more than he gave, and reports of working parties being fired at were frequent. The 20th and 21st were foggy in the morning, but on the fog lifting heavy toll was taken of enemy working parties in " J " and " K " Sectors. On the other hand the advanced portion of February Avenue was again blown to pieces. But on the following day the two Pope's Noses (*i.e.*, in " K " and " I " Sectors) were heavily bombarded by our artillery and in both cases concrete emplacements were exposed.[1]

It now became apparent that the enemy was preparing for something of greater moment than the ordinary trench fighting. The number of trench mortars appeared to have increased, and one battalion on one occasion reported to have seen six bombs in the air at once. Aerial torpedoes also made their appearance. The hostile patrolling became more vigorous, and our patrols had several minor encounters in No Man's Land. In one of these a party of 17/Royal Scots, whilst attempting to capture a German sentry at Pope's Nose, found themselves engaged in a fierce hand-to-hand combat in which Lieutenants Willis and McKnight were wounded. Finally, definite efforts were made to cut our wire at certain points —on one occasion by hand—and one morning at dawn a German officer was discovered in an unoccupied sap in " I " Sector. He took to flight leaving behind him his revolver and rifle. As certain raids and a discharge of gas were in preparation these symptoms did not receive the same attention as they would have had had the front been more quiet. As it happened, three simultaneous hostile raids were made on the divisional front.

[1] Every sector of the British front contained a " Pope's Nose."

74 HISTORY OF THE 35TH DIVISION

EVENTS ON THE 26TH NOVEMBER

At 3 a.m. on the 25th the 15/Cheshire attempted a surprise raid on the enemy trenches just south of Chantecler. The party consisted of twenty men under Lieutenant Fitzgerald. Although the wire had been shot at continually by 2-inch trench mortars, it was reported as insufficiently cut, and the raiding party, according to orders, did not attempt further progress. There were no casualties.

Meanwhile, in front of the 104th Brigade, a gas discharge had been ordered for 11.45 p.m., but at 11.35 p.m. it was cancelled. At 12.35 a.m. the gas discharge was ordered for 2.35 a.m., and was then carried out in two flotations, one at 2.35 a.m. and one at 4.5 a.m. During the discharge our artillery fired on the enemy support lines and communications about 1,000 yards behind the front. During the day the trenches on the right of this sector and on the left of the 12th Division (which was on our right) were heavily bombarded by trench mortars and suffered considerable damage. The wire was practically blown to bits. The flank battalion of the 12th Division appears to have vacated about a dozen bays on their left, and General Sandilands sent a notification of this to the G.O.C. 35th Brigade, who forthwith arranged for their defence. At the same time orders were sent to Lieut.-Colonel Mills, 17/Lancashire Fusiliers, to take special precautions, and fresh companies were filtered in to take the place of those which had suffered during the afternoon. The damaged trenches were incapable of being held, but blocks were built at the extremities, and these were held by strong parties. The 12th Division adopted the same means of defence, but owing to incessant bombardment these could not be completed before 2 a.m. 2nd Lieutenant Powell, on duty with the right sentry group, had taken a wounded man back to the stretcher-bearers in Iceland Street, and, on his return, he found the sentries much shaken and the corporal in charge absent. When discovered, he was found to be in an unfit state for duty and was replaced. A patrol was sent out between 10 p.m. and midnight and found all quiet. Lieutenant Powell on visits between 1 and 1.30 a.m. also reported all quiet. Meanwhile, on the right of the 17/Lancashire Fusiliers all posts in the front line had been withdrawn on account of the gas discharge, only the Lewis gun at the top of Hulloch Street remaining.

Lieutenant Powell, having given orders to send out a patrol at 2 a.m., returned to the company headquarters dug-out, where he found that the officer who was due to take the first watch was uncertain of his way and he offered to guide him. The two officers started soon after 2 a.m., but, owing to the blocks, they had to go round by the support trenches in order to reach the front line. On their way they were caught by a hostile trench mortar barrage which began about 2.20 a.m., and, in the darkness and shell fire, they lost their bearings, and it was an hour later before they found their way back to the dug-out, having failed to reach the front line and being in ignorance that a raid had taken place.

The evidence concerning the raid is confusing. The intense bombardment mentioned above was continued until 3 a.m. At 2.53 a.m. C/157 Battery was requested to open barrage fire—the rest of the artillery being engaged in supporting the gas discharge. Further evidence from the men of the sentry post in 16 Street, who apparently retired in confusion up Iceland Street ; from a Lewis gun team at the bottom of 49 sap who were half buried but uninjured ; from a man who was captured in a dug-out in 19 Street and escaped ; and from the officers and men who arrived after the Germans had left, leads to the conclusion that the enemy entered at two points in the derelict area and, after destroying the sentries at the blocks, worked their way towards one another and up 19 Street as far as the Lewis gun stationed there.

As far as could be ascertained the garrison offered little opposition, except (i) the Essex Lewis gun detachment at the top of Hulluch Street which saw six or seven Germans crawling in the wire and emptied four drums of ammunition at them ; (ii) the two Lewis gunners at the bottom of 16 Street, one of whom was shot and the other knocked over before they could bring their gun into action ; (iii) the Lewis gunners in 20 Street who fired at the raiding party as they were leaving, and (iv) the Stokes gunner in an emplacement off 19 Street who continued to fire although told to surrender and eventually after firing all his ammunition, escaped with his gun.[1]

The remainder of the garrison either retired or surrendered without

[1] A tale was current at the time that a German appeared at the lip of the crater where this gun was placed and shouted " You voss my prisoner." The gunner replied " Oh, voss I ? " and fired the mortar. The bomb and German exploded together in mid-air.

offering, as far as is known, any appreciable resistance. If a fight had taken place the noise of it must have been heard, but, as a matter of fact, no one near was aware that a raid was in progress. The first news came from a man who reached the reserve platoon in the support line about 2.30 a.m. and called to Sergeant Rhodes " The Germans are in." Sergeant Rhodes hastened forward with his party only to find that the Germans had left. This also happened to a party from " Y " Company on the left, which hurried forward to try to relieve the situation.

The casualties to the battalion were 2 men killed, 7 wounded, and 24 missing.

Whilst these events were taking place in " I " Sector the 19/ Durham L.I. in " K " Sector was about to make a raid on the enemy's trenches, but before this was accomplished a somewhat similar accident befell the 106th Brigade as had occurred to their comrades of the 104th.

Three days previous to the raid the enemy had intensified his trench mortar shelling of the trenches in rear of King's Crater, but, beyond this, there was nothing to indicate a contemplated raid.

The two lines were very close together. The outer lip of King's Crater was not more than fifty yards from the enemy front line, and the wire round the crater, for some reason, was thin.

Normally, there were two sentry groups of six men in each at the northern and southern entrance to the crater, but, as the 19/ Durham L.I. was about to make a raid on the enemy trenches about 700 yards north of the crater, the garrison had been thinned to a minimum to avoid unnecessary casualties from enemy retaliation, and the two posts were now held by three men and two men respectively, whilst, at another post in Cecil Avenue, near by, were three more men on sentry and four in a dug-out close at hand.

At some time between 2 and 2.30 a.m. the enemy re-opened the trench mortar bombardment of the crater and its vicinity. At 2.15 a.m. Lieutenant Mandy, commanding the right company, accompanied by a sergeant, visited the post south of the crater. After remaining there about ten minutes, he entered the crater on his way to the north post and encountered a German raiding party, which had apparently penetrated into the crater from the northern edge. Lieutenant Mandy was shot and fell. The sergeant made his escape. He passed the southern post and shouted something, and was finally stopped at the junction of Wednesday and Bogey Avenues by the battle police. Corporal Stevenson, in charge of the southern post, went into the crater, found and brought back Lieutenant Mandy, and then collected some bombers and sent them into the crater.

The Germans, after shooting Lieutenant Mandy, went to the northern post. On seeing them the corporal in charge and a sentry ran away. Private Hunt, the other man of this sentry group stood his ground and was captured. The corporal and private ran down the front line to Cecil Avenue and shouted to the sentry group there to "run for the Germans are on you." The private afterwards returned to his post, but the corporal was stopped by the battle police at the junction of Wednesday and Bogey Avenues. The sentry group at the top of Cecil Avenue had, however, unfortunately been infected and retired from their post until they were stopped by a sentry of the 17/Royal Scots.

Shortly afterwards 2nd Lieutenant Harding and Sergeant Napier (the officer and N.C.O. of the watch) were going their rounds. Unaware of anything unusual having happened they approached the crater. They met the raiders north of Cecil Avenue, challenged them and were both shot. Sergeant Napier managed to get back to a dug-out in Cecil Avenue where there were two stretcher-bearers. The raiders searched Lieutenant Harding, proceeded a short way down the front line bombing dug-outs, and then returned to their own lines. The strength of this party was estimated as between eight and twelve men.

Lieutenant Howes, O.C. supporting platoon in Bogey Avenue, first heard of the raid by the shouts of the sergeant who had deserted Lieutenant Mandy. He ordered out his platoon and attempted to lead them across the open to the front line but only four of eight men followed him. Leaving these in a fixed position he returned and collected four more and led the eight men to the crater where he met 2nd Lieutenant Maclachlan with some bombers who reported all quiet. The line was then re-established. The casualties were Lieutenants Mandy and Harding wounded, 3 other ranks, wounded, and Private Hunt captured.

At 3 a.m. the contemplated raid, undeterred by the preceding events was launched. As soon as it was apparent that the line was clear, a torpedo was taken out by Lieutenants Welbourne and Forester and placed in position. On its discharge the party advanced. 2nd Lieutenant Johnson and four men entered the German trench and moved to the right. 2nd Lieutenant K. Smith entered and moved to the left and four other men entered behind them. The gap in the wire was excellent and the party got in without opposition, but the remainder of the raid, which consisted of two officers and forty-five men, was prevented, or at any rate, discouraged from reaching the German trench by our own shells which were reported as dropping thickly in No Man's Land and round the point of entry. A report to this effect was also received from Lieutenant Pearson, who commanded the covering party, and from Lieutenant Dillon, Royal Engineers, who was in Sap 120 A, from which place he had discharged the torpedo.

Lieutenant Johnson proceeded as far as the first traverse to the right, bombed an occupied dug-out, and then found that he had no men with him. Lieutenant Smith, moving to the left, found an entrance to a dug-out, saw a man on the steps and shot him with his revolver. Passing on he found another dug-out entrance, threw a bomb down the stairs and round the next traverse killed a sentry. Finding now he had only two men with him he returned to the point of entry to get more and there found Lieutenant Johnson on the same quest. As there were no men available they decided to withdraw. Our own shells were now falling on the German front line, but they brought back with them the body of one of their own men who was killed on the German parapet. The casualties were 2nd Lieutenant Welbourne wounded, 2 other ranks killed, and 8 wounded.

The enemy made one more raid on the night, namely, against the 105th Brigade in " J " Sector, but as far as the Germans were concerned, it was a failure. This was to a large extent due to the fact that General Marindin had ordered the line to be held in the usual manner, and no modifications were made on account of the gas discharge.

During the afternoon and evening of the 25th the trenches round Claude Crater were bombarded by trench mortars at the rate of about two a minute, and an organized retaliation by our 4.5 howitzers failed to stop it. It then became evident that a raid was to be expected, and, as about fifty yards of trench line had been practically obliterated, blocks were established at the ends of the area blown in and special sentry groups posted in the support line to overlook the part evacuated. At 2.30 a.m. on the 26th the enemy again opened fire with trench mortars on this area, and formed a barrage between the front and support lines. At the same time a mine was exploded under the southern lip of Claude Crater.

The officers commanding left and right companies of the 15/ Sherwood Foresters (Captain Bryce and Lieutenant Boot) both concluded that a raid was imminent, and sent up S.O.S. rockets. The Artillery barrage came down on the S.O.S. lines thirty seconds after the signals had gone up.

The raiders reached our trenches at the same time, somewhere near the top of July Avenue, and found one man who had been wounded in the leg during the bombardment. He refused to be taken prisoner, was stabbed and fired at with a revolver, but survived. The party then turned south and ran into the block established at the southern end of the gap. Our sentry group being outnumbered, fell back fighting to the next sentry group, where they were reinforced by a fresh party under Lieutenant Henstock. The combined parties counter-attacked and drove the enemy out of the lines. One of the enemy, who had apparently lost his way, and who seems to have been a Bavarian pioneer, refused to surrender and was shot close to the support line parapet. He died before he could impart any information and carried no identification marks. Another German, slightly wounded, was captured in front of our wire between Claude and Clarence Craters. He belonged to the 90th Fusilier regiment and stated that the raiding party consisted of thirty men but none of our own men who were engaged in the fight placed the number above a dozen.

A box which apparently contained some nature of explosive was found in a recess in the trench. It was surmized that the enemy mistook this place for a mine shaft. Patrols followed the enemy into No Man's Land and there found other explosive charges as well as rifles, bombs, belts, etc. The general opinion was that the majority of the raiding party got caught by the artillery barrage and failed to enter the trench. The action of all parties in the

80 HISTORY OF THE 35TH DIVISION

trenches was prompt and effective, and the behaviour of the men who had been subjected to a more than usually heavy bombardment for several hours earned the praise of those in authority.

So ended a busy night, and also the last fight in which the division took part as a "Bantam" division. Although the general result of the enemy raids was much to be deplored it may be said to have had one good effect. It brought forcibly to notice that which commanding officers had been reporting for some time, namely, that the major part of the recently received reinforcements could not be trusted to hold the line.

The next day was quiet on all the fronts, and on the following day (the 28th) the fog was so dense that nothing could be seen beyond twenty or thirty yards. This state of affairs was welcomed by officers of all arms. The infantry were enabled to examine and repair the broken parapets and wire whilst trench mortar officers walked about over the top of reserve trenches discovering their guns which had been buried and reconnoitring new positions for future use. Unfortunately the day was attended by some casualties. Captain Wolstenholme, 15/Cheshire, was killed whilst examining the wire from the front trench. 2nd Lieutenant G. N. Slinger, 159th Brigade, R.F.A., was killed in No Man's Land where he had gone to find out the exact lie of the trenches,[1] and 14 men of the 18/Highland L.I. were killed by snipers and bombs whilst repairing parapets and wire.

After this the usual trench mortar bombardment continued,[2] and on December 1st orders were received that the 35th Division was to be relieved by the 9th Division in the Arras Sector. The next day the 106th Brigade was relieved by the 27th Brigade and on the 3rd the 105th Brigade was relieved by the 1st South African Brigade. The relief of the 104th Brigade by the 26th Brigade followed. The artillery remained in the line, being reinforced by "J" Battery,

[1] Lieutenant Hanrick, who had accompanied Lieutenant Slinger, attempted to bring in his body, but lost his direction and took him nearer the German line. He returned, and at dusk obtained the assistance of Lieutenant FitzGerald, 15/Cheshire, who accompanied him in a search which was unsuccessful and Lieutenant FitzGerald was wounded. Much later, after the British advance, a grave was discovered in one of the German cemeteries, which was inscribed "To a Brave British Officer who was killed whilst examining our wire on November 28th, 1916."
[2] During November the Divisional Trench Mortars fired 2,927 bombs.

R.F.A. (Major R. Maitland). Some changes amongst the officers took place about this time in addition to the replacement of casualties. Lieut.-Colonel Mills, who had been wounded on the Somme, returned to duty and reassumed command of the 17/Lancashire Fusiliers. Whilst Lieut.-Colonel Crook went home to the Senior Officers Course, Major E. G. K. Goss was appointed to command the 17/Royal Scots.

On November 24th Lieut.-Colonel Browne-Clayton was appointed to the command of a brigade and Lieut.-Colonel E. T. Saint (1/Cambridgeshire) took command of the 16/Cheshire. Lieut.-Colonel P. H. Fawcett, 158th Brigade, R.F.A., was posted to command the 48th Heavy Group, R.G.A., and left the 35th Division.

THE CHANGE IN THE DIVISION

On December 5th the G.O.C. 9th Division took over command of the front from the G.O.C. 35th Division, but General Staveley remained at head-quarters commanding the artillery. The 52nd Brigade, R.F.A. reinforced the 35th Divisional Artillery and Lieut.-Colonel H. T. Belcher, commanding the brigade, took over command of the left group, R.F.A. The relief caused no alteration in the trench mortar counter-action which continued as usual.

The infantry battalions on relief moved some seven or eight miles to the west of Arras, except for those of the 106th Brigade, which had two battalions billeted in the town.[1] The time was occupied in supplying working parties for the Royal Engineers, Tunnelling Companies,[2] Army Signals, etc., and also in undergoing inspections by the higher commanders with a view to weeding out men who were unfit for duty or active service.

On December 8th the G.O.C. VI Corps and the G.O.C. 35th Division, again reported the low physical and moral standard of some of the infantry, and all battalions were inspected by the A.D.M.S. Then followed several days of inspections by various officers when the men underwent a searching examination as to

[1] The 18/Highland L.I. made a 15 mile march to Maisnil St. Pol, and spent the time in rest and training.

[2] These were engaged in improving the communications through the catacombs with a view to the future offensive. There was a series of deep underground passages at the eastern side of Arras which had been in existence for a great number of years.

their physical fitness. Between the 8th and 21st of December 2,784 men were reported as unfit for infantry work in the line.[1] Unfortunately, and possibly unavoidably, many men, whom regimental officers would have been only too willing to keep in their commands, were rejected for some physical disability which so far had not affected them in any way. These men were naturally very disappointed and received sympathy from all who had served with the "Bantams." They were duly sent to the base, and reinforcements were received from disbanded yeomanry regiments and from men in training at the cavalry depôt. These were men of good physique who took an honourable part in the future achievements of the division, but although the word "Bantam" was no longer to be used and the divisional signs had been changed to the well-known one of the seven fives on a circle, it required for some time great watchfulness on the part of commanding officers to guard against previously rejected men being again received as reinforcements. When the alterations had been carried out the Army Commander inspected all battalions and expressed satisfaction at the change, but naturally, when so many men had come from another arm of the service, a certain amount of training was necessary before they were able to take their full share of infantry duties.

As far as the infantry was concerned, working parties, inspections, and training, occupied the battalions until the end of the month.

Captain G. de C. Glover was transferred to the Portuguese Corps and his place as Brigade Major, 105th Brigade, was taken by Captain G. R. P. Roupell, V.C., from Army Headquarters.

ARTILLERY OPERATIONS, JANUARY 13TH TO FEBRUARY 4TH

Meanwhile, the artillery, which had remained in the line, was occupied in operations which had previously become familiar to the infantry of the 35th Division. A slight difference occurred in that the enemy began to use lachrymatory shell, and this became more frequent as the days passed. On the 14th the infantry sent up an S.O.S. signal in "J" Sector, and over 1,000 rounds were

[1] There is a discrepancy in the numbers here, but some reports no doubt include men who would have been evacuated in any case. Other battalion diaries do not give concrete figures.

fired before it could be stopped. It was afterwards learned that it was intended as a test. Next day the 210th Siege Battery, R.F.A., engaged several heavy trench mortar emplacements with conspicuous success.[1] The 51st Brigade, R.F.A., now relieved the 52nd Brigade R.F.A. and Lieut.-Colonel Cape assumed command of the left group instead of Lieut.-Colonel Belcher. On the 20th, the left group co-operated in a raid on the enemy's trenches by the 3rd Canadian Division, about 1,500 yards north-north-east of Roclincourt. This raid, which started at 3.15 p.m., was a complete success. The three companies engaged reached their objectives and returned to their own trenches within an hour and a half having captured 42 prisoners with a loss of only 2 killed and a few wounded. A secondary raid which attacked at a point about 500 yards to the south-east one and a half hours later failed owing to heavy hostile shelling.

On the 26th the relief of the 35th Divisional Artillery commenced, and next evening, whilst the relief was in progress, a heavy bombardment of gas shell was put down round the Porte de Baudimont. The enemy must have had knowledge of this relief, and also that this was the exit by which the troops would leave the town. It was calculated that from 10 p.m. on the 27th to 3.30 a.m. on the 28th between 2,000 and 3,000 gas shell fell in the north-west area of Arras. The greatest sufferers were B/159 Battery, which, as already stated, was situated in this part of the town, and also the battery which relieved it, but all troops and civilians in the vicinity were affected by the bombardment. Next day the C.R.A., 9th Division (Brig.-General Tudor) took over command of the Arras Sector. The 157th Brigade R.F.A. remained in action until January 7th.[2] The 159th Brigade withdrew to Rebreuve until January 8th

[1] After this the enemy began to use puffs of smoke whenever their trench mortars were firing to disguise the actual situation of the emplacements.

[2] Previous to the artillery quitting Arras on Christmas Day an interesting competition took place between J Battery, R.H.A., and the 508th Howitzer Battery, R.F.A. A certain portion of the enemy line required punishment and the two battery commanders concerned were of opinion that they each could fire a heavier bombardment (measured by weight of shell) into it than the other in a given time, which time was half a minute. In consideration of the heavier shell to be handled Major Maitland allowed Major Potter to have his guns loaded (each battery fired four guns). The 508th Battery fired 18 rounds at 35 lbs. each, viz., 630 lbs. J Battery fired 41 rounds at 13 lbs each, viz., 533 lbs. But for Major Maitland's magnanimity the result might have been different, but, considering that the shooting was accurate, the test was meritorious.

when certain batteries returned to the Arras front in relief of the 158th Brigade, R.F.A., which was now disbanded and divided amongst other artillery units. The R.F.A. of the 35th Division henceforward consisted of two brigades (the 157th and 159th : Lieut.-Colonels Stewart and Davson) each consisting of three 18 pr. batteries of six guns and one 4.5 howitzer battery, also of six guns. On the 14th the headquarters of the 159th Brigade moved back to Arras as well as some batteries of the 157th Brigade. The C.R.A., 35th Division, took over command of " I " Sector with Lieut.-Colonel Stewart as group commander. Four batteries of the 35th Division remained in action here until February 5th, when they were relieved by the 12th Divisional Artillery and marched to billets at Estrée Wamin and Berlancourt.[1] The only item of importance during this final tour of duty in Arras was the support of a raid by the 8/Black Watch and 10/Argyle and Sutherland Highlanders, which was highly successful and penetrated into the enemy support line. The rest of the time was spent in trench routine.

During this time the infantry were in reserve billets situated from eight to fifteen miles west of Arras. The 104th Brigade at Manin, the 105th at Lattre St. Quentin, and the 106th at Foufflin Ricometz.

The time was spent in evacuating discharged " Bantams," in supplying working parties in Arras, and in training the new drafts. For this latter purpose a depôt battalion was formed with Lieut.-Colonel Dent, 19/Durham L.I., in command. The instructional staff was formed from officers and men drawn from each infantry battalion. The staff formed a cadre of one company per brigade ; each company had four platoons—one from each battalion.

The object of the Depôt Battalion was (i) to instruct all reinforcing drafts, whether trained or untrained, and to pass all through a course of musketry, and (ii) to enable training to continue whilst the division was in the line by the periodical withdrawal of one platoon per battalion and so give officers and men a rest from the trenches.

This depot battalion was first located at Averdoignt with accom-

[1] It may be noted that D/157 Battery remained continuously in action from September 10th, 1916, to February 4th, 1917.

modation for 1,200 men. The first draft arrived on January 4th and by the 5th the 1,200 men had been obtained. A week later its strength had risen to 1,350. It was disbanded on March 14th having, during its short period of existence, carried out a considerable amount of useful work.

Soon after Christmas frost set in, and it became more severe as the month advanced. Heavy snow fell at intervals which made life in general unpleasant for all concerned, especially for those who had to dig in unyielding ground. This weather lasted until well into February and the thaw, when it did come, was worse than the frost.

Plate 1

Major-General H. J. S. LANDON, C.B., C.M.G.
Commanding the Division September 1916 to July 1917.

CHAPTER VI

LIHONS AND ROSIERES

ON February 5th Divisional Headquarters moved from the Roellecourt area to Boquemaison, and, next day, to Vignacourt, about twelve miles south-west of Doullens. The 104th Brigade proceeded by march route to the neighbourhood of Naours, the 105th to Fleselles, and the 106th to Vignacourt. The artillery were at Hem and Occoches. Training was continued at these places. The division now passed under control of the IV Corps, and, on February 12th, a visit was paid by its commander. On the following day orders were received from Headquarters, Fourth Army, that men cast at the Second Commanding Officers' Inspection should not be evacuated, and these were temporarily retained with the units.[1]

The next three days were spent in reconnaissance of the new line which was to be taken over from the French 154th Division in the Caix Sector. Thaw had now set in, and there was slight rain which made walking difficult. On the 17th, the 104th Brigade entrained at Fleselles for Marcelcave, and thence by road to what was known as " A " staging area, around Wiencourt-l'Equipée. The 105th followed next day and billeted at Wiencourt and Demuin. On the 20th the 106th Brigade arrived at Marcelcave and billeted there. The artillery followed by march route, and, on the 20th, went into action alongside the French batteries—the 157th Brigade east of Rosières, and the 159th Brigade in and around Meharicourt. The 104th Brigade relieved the 413th and part of the 414th, regiments in the Lihons sector having three battalions in the line.[2] The 105th Brigade took over the right subsection from the 413th and 416th regiments.[3] The front extended from a point on the north between

---

[1] Up to this time 1,872 rejected men had been evacuated to the base and labour battalions. Excepting the 15/Sherwood Foresters, of which the numbers are not available.

[2] 18/L.F. on right ; 23/Manchester, centre ; 20/L.F., left.

[3] 14/Gloucester on right ; 15/Sherwood Foresters, centre ; 15/Cheshire, left.

Bois Triangulaire and Chaulnes to a point 1,500 yards south of Chilly. Each brigade held approximately 2,000 yards of front. The infantry found the trenches in very bad condition. The rapid thaw had caused a great portion of the parapets to fall in, and the débris in the bottom of the trenches had become glutinous mud, which in some cases was as much as three feet deep. The reliefs, therefore, became extremely difficult, and after that was concluded the supply of rations and ammunition taxed the endurance of the men to such an extent that they were frequently heard to remark that they would prefer a heavy bombardment. On the other hand, the relief was much simplified by the care which had been bestowed on details by the French authorities, and the utmost sympathy existed between the two armies.[1] This was especially the case with the artillery, which was unable to register owing to the mist, and so the French batteries remained in their positions and covered the line until it should be safe. Officers and men extended their hospitality to the relieving troops.

During the relief some slight discharges of gas were made by the enemy, and, at 7.45 p.m. on the 23rd, a heavy bombardment was put down on the front of the 105th Brigade. The German infantry must have been surprised at the retaliation as, although the French batteries were due to quit their positions within an hour, they opened their barrage fire along with the British batteries, which were now registered, and a deluge of fire was poured in upon the German lines. In the early morning the French batteries withdrew amidst many expressions of cordiality on both sides.[2]

The next few days were marked by bombardments and counter bombardments, and, on two occasions, front line sentries reported enemy parties advancing on our lines. These were dispersed by artillery fire. A hostile attempt to cut wire in front of the 105th Brigade was rendered ineffective by means of Lewis gun fire.

With a view to holding the front with two battalions per brigade, the 105th Brigade extended its line to include about 200 yards of trench of the Lihons sector, and the brigade boundary was now

---

[1] One battalion diary reports " The handing over by the French regiment was excellent. All documents, air photos, etc., were in perfect order."

[2] Divisional and C.R.A. Headquarters were at Caix, and Brigade Headquarters at Rosières. The 106th Brigade was in divisional reserve. The Headquarters of the 159th Brigade R.F.A., had at first been established at Meharicourt. It was withdrawn to Rosières on the 25th.

fixed at the communication trench known as the Boyau Brisbane. When this movement was completed the 106th Brigade relieved the 104th in the Lihons sector. A hostile bombardment followed this relief, and, at dawn on the 27th, an enemy raid was made against the front of the 14/Gloucester at a point known as the Triangle Sap, south of Chilly. Two of our sentries were shot by revolver fire, one was killed and the other wounded. Two other men were taken prisoners. A Lewis gun team saw the enemy leaving the trench and opened fire. One of the enemy was hit as also was one of the prisoners, who then managed to escape and return to our lines.

The repulse of even a small raid was not easy, as the depth of mud in the trenches made rapid movement impossible. In addition, No Man's Land, according to reports of patrols, was a mass of waterlogged shell holes. At this time our men began to suffer from "Trench Feet" and many had to be evacuated in consequence.[1]

The condition of No Man's Land did not deter the enemy from attempting raids. Two days after the one mentioned above, an officer's patrol in the Lihons sector discovered that the enemy had cut some of our wire east of Bois Brownig, just south of the railway, and had laid a tape to this point. The patrol returned and prepared to receive the enemy but the enterprise appears to have been abandoned. Others, however, were to follow. At 6.45 p.m. on March 2nd, a heavy bombardment of trench mortars and guns of all calibres descended on the front and support lines of the 16/Cheshire, forming a barrage round the sap about 1,000 yards north-east of Chilly and extending to about 400 yards on either side of it. At the same time the batteries in the vicinity were shelled with 150 m.m. guns and with gas. The batteries opened fire. but immediately afterwards all communications were cut, and it was not until 7.30 p.m. that any information of the raid was received at battalion headquarters.[2] It then transpired that hand-to-hand fighting had

---

[1] A medical officer in Rosières weighed the clothes of one of the stretcher-cases brought to him. They were clogged with mud and water and turned the scale at 90 lb.

[2] Lieutenant Baxter, accompanied by his servant, went forward during the bombardment to obtain information. He met two Germans and fired at them but was wounded by a bomb, and his servant was knocked senseless by a blow from a spade.

taken place, that 1 of the enemy had been killed, and 1 or 2 wounded, and that the remainder had been driven back. The Cheshire losses were 2 officers wounded, 2 other ranks killed, 10 wounded and 1 missing.

At 5.30 a.m. on the 3rd, the bombardment re-opened in a similar manner except that, on this occasion, the central point was known as Lunette II and involved the left subsection of the 16/Cheshire and the right platoon of the 19/Durham L.I. A hostile raiding party of between forty and fifty strong entered our trenches by a sap at the end of the Lunette and proceeded to bomb north and south along the front line. On the south the attack was stopped by a sentry post just north of the Boyau de Rennes, whilst the northern limit was between Boyaux Tomasali and Brisbane. Heavy artillery engaged the support lines and batteries. Our Lewis guns were in action throughout the raid until the enemy withdrew under cover of smoke bombs, leaving behind a large quantity of bombs (including 184 stick bombs), rifles and equipment, as well as three dead men and one badly wounded, also a hymn book marked 175 I.R.[1] Twenty-one men of the 16/Cheshire were missing, but a portion of these was probably buried during the bombardment. A Vickers gun of the Durham L.I. was captured. Judging from the violence of the bombardment and the rigour with which the attack was pushed home, something more than a casual raid was evidently intended. Whether it was from a desire for further intelligence, or as a cover for the impending retreat, could not be ascertained, but, whichever it was, due credit must be given to the enemy for the determination with which the men fought their way along about 200 yards of trenches where movement was not easy at any time.

Orders were now received that the men previously considered as unsuitable for infantry should be sent to the base. This involved a draft of 800 men. At the same time 500 men, in addition, were classified as untrained and sent to the Depôt Battalion.[2] On the 6th the 104th Brigade came into the line in the Chilly Sector in

[1] Subsequent reports from patrols, etc., led to the conclusion that the enemy losses were considerable. The wounded prisoner subsequently died. He was a Pole, but was wearing a Russian cap badge. There were no other identity marks.
[2] This, with casualties from wounds and trench feet, reduced the fighting strength of the battalions. On the 12th the 15/Cheshire reported their trench strength as only 400 rifles.

place of the 105th Brigade. Snow fell at this time which altered conditions for the worse.

The artillery now carried out the experiment of using a roving gun at night which could be fired on definite targets without drawing fire on the battery positions, which were well known to the enemy. The first trial was made by A/159 Battery, but the result was not successful, and, after a few days, the attempt was not persisted in. Both brigades, however, succeeded in pushing a gun forward to very short range, and these pieces were made use of for wire cutting. It was found that the effect of shrapnel on the German loose concertina wire, even at short range, was not commensurate with the amount of ammunition expended.

The enemy still continued tentative raids, which, however, were not pushed home, and in view of subsequent events, must be regarded as being more in the nature of defensive than offensive warfare. On the 5th a small party advancing against the Chilly sector was dispersed by rifle fire. Next day, after a bombardment of La Demi Lune (a semi-circular spinney in our front trench, south-west of Chaulnes), an attempt was made on one of our bombing posts in Bois Triangulaire, but was repulsed. On the following evening, however, after a heavy bombardment, a more determined attempt was made by a party about sixty strong. This time about twenty of the enemy succeeded in forcing their way into what was known as Bombrag Sap, north of La Demi Lune, and captured 5 prisoners from the 17/West Yorkshire. In addition, 1 man was killed and 1 wounded. The gap was filled by the 17/Royal Scots.[1] Vigorous patrolling on the part of the 104th Brigade possibly prevented similar enterprises on the Chilly front. 2nd Lieutenant C. R. Chaffey, 23/Manchester, was killed in a patrol action on this day.

On the 9th the division side-slipped to the right. The left battalion of the 106th Brigade (the 18/Highland L.I.) was relieved by the 7/Worcestershire, 61st Division, and the 104th Brigade handed over its left battalion front to the 106th Brigade, and in turn took over a battalion front from the 97th Brigade, 32nd Division. The bad condition of the trenches seriously interfered

[1] The German wireless claimed 18 prisoners, but this was not the case. On this day one of the enemy is reported to have shouted in English " Don't worry, we are throwing up the sponge in a fortnight."

92 HISTORY OF THE 35TH DIVISION

with this change of positions and temporary adjustments became necessary. Rain on the next day did not improve the situation, but the reliefs were completed by the infantry, and the zones of artillery altered accordingly. The batteries were able to alter their zones of fire without moving position, except A/159 Battery, which quitted Méharicourt for a point on the Vrély-Méharicourt road.

THE GERMAN RETREAT

Evidence of an impending enemy retirement now became more apparent. Fires were observed behind the German lines, and the counter battery fire diminished. It was plain, however, that the line was still held, as patrols were fired upon and shelling of the trenches by field guns continued as before. Reports of gas shelling became more frequent, and the position of B/159 Battery was heavily shelled by 150 mm. during the whole day of the 13th and suffered considerable damage.

On the 15th the 105th Brigade relieved the 106th in the Lihons Sector, and, at the same time, orders were issued for operations in support of an attack which the French were to deliver in the south. This attack took place on the 17th, and an intense bombardment was opened on the enemy's trenches at 7 a.m., also a smoke demonstration from the front line. There was no reply of any kind from the German lines, and early in the afternoon the infantry occupied the enemy trenches. The 17/West Yorkshire [1] were in possession at 2.30 p.m. The artillery limbered up and followed. The artillery brigades were now attached to the infantry brigades.

By 8 p.m. the 17/West Yorkshire, attached to 104th Brigade, had pushed patrols as far as Fransart where it was in touch with the 32nd Division, and the 17/Lancashire Fusiliers had reached Punchy without encountering any hostile party. This indicated an advance on the whole front of about two miles. Brigade head-quarters was established in Chilly. Owing to the road between Chilly and Hallu not having been completely destroyed, the batteries of the 159th Brigade R.F.A. were able to keep close touch with the infantry and took up positions around Hallu.

[1] This battalion received the congratulations of the G.O.C. for being the first to enter the German lines. Special mention was made of the work done by Lieutenant H. F. O. Jenkins and 2nd Lieutenants A. D. Rose and White.

HISTORY OF THE 35TH DIVISION

Meanwhile on the left the 105th Brigade, at 5 p.m., had advanced along its whole front, and in ten minutes had occupied the German front line. By 8 p.m. the patrols of the 15/Cheshire and 14/Gloucesters had pushed forward nearly two miles in advance of this. Brigade headquarters, having established an advance section, remained at Rosières. As the road from Lihons to Chaulnes was practically obliterated, the 157th Brigade R.F.A. had the greatest difficulty in getting the guns across No Man's Land. The batteries spent the night in the neighbourhood of Bois Brownig whilst the Royal Engineers assisted the gunners in the preparation of roads across the trench systems in the neighbourhood of Chaulnes railway station. Subsequently, orders were received that the brigade should use the Chilly-Hallu road. The brigade advanced by this line on the 19th.

So began the German Retreat of 1917.

At 4 a.m. on the 18th orders were received from IV Corps (Lieut.-General Sir C. L. Woolcombe, K.C.B.) that the division should advance to the line Hattencourt-Punchy-Puzeaux-Bois de Hambourg, with the 104th and 105th Brigades in the line and the 106th in reserve. From this line patrols were pushed out to the line Curchy-Barsaucourt, about two miles forward. Division Headquarters moved forward to Rosières, the 104th Brigade and the 159th Brigade R.F.A. to Chilly, the 105th Brigade to Hallu, the 106th Brigade to Le Mans, and the 157th Brigade R.F.A. to the railway south of Lihons.

The 17/West Yorkshire were now at Hattencourt; the 18/Lancashire Fusiliers in the Trench d'Ingan, a German work northwest of Curchy; and the 20/Lancashire Fusiliers in Curchy itself. The line was continued northwards as far as Bersaucourt by the 16/Cheshire and 15/Sherwood Foresters, who occupied the old German reserve line known as the Trench du Vieux Boche. The cavalry corps reported that the enemy had retired across the Somme, blowing up the bridges. He had, also, laid waste the whole countryside. Every tree had been felled and every house demolished; large craters were found at all cross roads and the wells were reported to have been poisoned. In addition, certain " booby traps " were left behind for the purpose of deceiving the innocent and causing loss of life. Fortunately, these efforts were unsuccessful.

At 10.15 p.m., much to everybody's disappointment, orders were received that the infantry of the division would not advance further, but would detail parties to work on the roads and railways. This order was the outcome of the converging nature of the pursuit with the result that the 35th Division was pinched between the 61st and 32nd. Accordingly, the advance was stopped and the battalions distributed as follows :—17/Lancashire Fusiliers and 23/Manchesters at Fouquescourt and Parvillers for road making ; 15/Cheshire and 14/Gloucester at Lihons mending roads for the 61st Division ; the 15/Sherwood Foresters marched to Vermandovillers and commenced salvage work, but the whole of the 105th Brigade was immediately afterwards ordered to repair the Rosières-Nesle railway and certain billets were altered accordingly. The 106th Brigade marched to Hallu and Rosières (18/Highland L.I.) and commenced work on railway and roads. The 17/Royal Scots being moved from Rouvroy for this purpose.

The 157th and 159th Brigades R.F.A. were attached to the 61st and 32nd Divisions respectively.

During the period under review the following changes in commands and appointments had taken place. In December, 1916, Lieut.-Colonel C. B. J. Riccard had assumed command of the 17/Royal Scots vice Major Goss. On January 26th Major C. B. Darley and Captain R. B. Lascelles were attached to the division for horse management duties, and, on the same date, Captain K. J. Nicholson, R.F.A., left the division on appointment as staff captain R.A., 14th Division. On January 30th Major C. H. F. Metcalfe, G.S.O.3, became brigade major 104th Brigade vice Captain B. C. Montgomery who was appointed G.S.O. 2, 33rd Division. Major Metcalfe's place on the divisional staff was taken by Lieutenant R. F. Lawrenson. On this date Lieutenants Waller and Pulford were appointed to command V/35 and Y/35 Trench Mortar Batteries.

During March, Major E. S. G. Willis, D.S.O., Brigade Major, 106th Brigade, was ordered to India. Lieut.-Colonel Dent returned from the depôt battalion and was appointed to the command of the 16/Cheshire in place of Lieut.-Colonel Saint, who went to command the newly formed Divisional School at Boves. Major Greenwell became Officer Commanding the 19/Durham L.I. Captain Trench, who had been sick in England since January 6th, returned to duty as staff captain, R.A., vice Captain A. M. Burke.

FROM ROSIERES TO THE HINDENBURG LINE

Artillery Operations

Whilst the battalions were thus stopped in the pursuit, the two artillery brigades continued to advance with the divisions to which they had been attached, General Staveley and his staff being placed under orders of the IV Corps for reconnaissance.

The artillery advance was to some extent influenced by the wintry weather which affected the condition of the horses, and also by the destruction of the roads which obliged teams to work across country. Fortunately the nature of the country was very open and no great difficulty was experienced as regards this. The question of supply, however, became acute, so that towards the end of the month it was decided to retire the wagon lines to Rosières. The ammunition supply became more arduous, but no great amount was required before the end of the month when road conditions improved.

On March 19th, the 157th Brigade, having advanced by Chilly, Hallu, and Curchy to Potte, occupied a position of observation to defend the line of the Somme where it remained until March 28th, on which date it moved forward to Tertry, and the batteries took up positions covering the advance to Soyécourt.

The 159th Brigade, on the 19th, pushed forward from the neighbourhood of Hallu and Punchy *via* Fonchette, Mesmil le Petit, and Mesnil St. Nicaise to the west bank of the river d'Ingou opposite Rouy le Petit, a distance of about nine miles.

Next day the batteries marched to Voyennes on the Somme, the headquarters was ordered to Langvoisin in order to be in touch with the 96th Brigade. On the 21st, however, the headquarters rejoined the brigade at Voyennes, which, being the most advanced artillery, was attached to the 14th Infantry Brigade.

At 11.30 a.m. on this day, by order of Brigadier-General J. A. Tyler, the C.R.A. 32nd Division, a mounted patrol of " C " Battery under Major R. D. Harisson was taken out in order to obtain contact with the enemy in the neighbourhood of St. Quentin, and to bring in a German "alive or dead." Major Harisson took with him Lieutenant Burt, Battery-Sergeant-Major Taylor, and six rifles, and was accompanied by Major Lumsden, G.S.O. 2, 32nd Division.

The patrol moved to Germaine and then to Savy at which place it was noticed that the enemy was holding the line Bois d'Holnon-l'Epine de Dallon (south-west of St. Quentin). Passing by Savy Station, it surprised an infantry outpost in a crater on the road 300 yards east of the village. This outpost ran back to a trench and two men were seen to drop to our fire. On observing this, Major Harisson remounted, and calling upon Lieutenant Burt, the sergeant-major, and four rifles, galloped forward and captured one of these who proved to be only slightly hurt. The other was picked up by his comrades and carried off. An attempt to cut off this party failed as the enemy manned the parapet of the trench and opened rifle and machine-gun fire at 400 yards range. The patrol retired to the crater which was then held by three rifles in order to cover the withdrawal of the horses and prisoner into Savy. The prisoner, Hermann Schmidt, Feldwebel of the 115th Hesse Infantry Reserve, was handed over to the 32nd Division Headquarters at Nesle at 8 p.m. There were no casualties to the patrol. Lieutenant Burt, however, was unfortunately accidentally wounded next day, and had to be evacuated.[1]

On the following day forward positions were reconnoitred and one section of " C " Battery under Captain White was attached to a small force of mounted men (King Edward's Horse) and cyclists operating against Savy Wood. As the roads had been destroyed movement of guns was difficult, but about 2 p.m. the section was engaged with enemy infantry near Bois d'Holnon, who left their trenches in order to capture some of the force who had been wounded. These were driven back and the guns then turned on to a battery east of Savy Wood and forced it to retire. The reconnoitring force then withdrew.[2]

On this day, owing to a rearrangement of the forward line, " A," " B " and " D " Batteries were ordered to retire to Rouy. " C " Battery and Brigade Headquarters remained in Voyennes until the 28th, when the whole brigade advanced to positions which had

---

[1] For his behaviour on this day, B.S.M Taylor was awarded the D.C.M.
[2] Major Harisson himself accompanied this force.

been previously chosen in the vicinity of Lanchy. The headquarters moved to Quivières. On the 30th the brigade advanced to Roupy except one battery which was in action near Beauvois covering another infantry brigade. Headquarters were at Fluquières.

On the 30th, the 157th Brigade left Tertry and advanced to Caulaincourt, the batteries being in action to the west of the village, except one which was close to Poeuilly, and on the following morning two were pushed forward to positions between Caulaincourt and Vermand.

On April 2nd the brigade covered the attack of the 61st Division on the enemy position astride Bihecourt and the Omignon River. For this purpose " B " and " C " Batteries had been advanced to within a thousand yards of Vermand. The attack was completely successful, and they followed up the advance to positions east of Vermand from which place, next day, they were successful in breaking up a German counter attack on Maissemy. On the 5th the other two batteries of the brigade were moved to the north of St. Quentin Wood in support of the projected attacks of the 183rd Brigade on the high ground south of Berthaucourt, and of the 184th on the Pontru Ridge north of Maissemy. On the 6th Fresnoy-le-Peitt was captured but it was lost in the evening. The batteries moved forward, and on the 8th the village was captured and held. Early next morning the Pontru Ridge was also taken possession of.

There followed bombardments of the Gricourt-Pontruet line, the batteries moving on as opportunity offered, and, on the 14th, General Stavely assumed command of the group, the 306th Brigade on the right, 157th in centre, and 307th on left. The infantry of the 35th Division had begun taking over from the 61st Division two days previously and the 157th Brigade R.F.A. henceforward co-operated with its own infantry.

The 159th Brigade, however, remained in the neighbourhood of Savy under the 32nd and later the 61st Division until May 8th, and supported the attacks which ended in the capture of Savy Wood and Cepy Farm, as well as the French attacks on the southwestern outskirts of St. Quentin.

Savy Wood was an irregular thicket, shaped like the badly cut tail of a horse, which lay north and south on the western slope of a hill about 450 feet high, situated two miles west of St. Quentin. To gain possession of this hill, which commanded the town, it was necessary first of all to capture the wood as well as the villages of Selency and Francilley-Selency to the north of it. The French had already made good the low ground along the St. Quentin canal to the south and were awaiting the time when these high lands should be captured in order to improve their artillery positions.

The attack of the 32nd Division on Savy Wood was planned for April 1st, and the batteries of the 159th Brigade had been placed west of Roupy in support of it. Owing, however, to an alteration in the plan of attack, it was not considered that efficient support could be given from the positions which the batteries occupied to the west of the village, and so, in the morning, they were moved forward to positions to the north-east of Roupy which brought some of them to within 5,000 yards of the Hindenburg Line. At 2.30 p.m. the brigade supported the attack of the 96th Brigade on Savy Wood, which was entirely successful, and by evening the whole of Savy Wood and Savy Wood South was in our hands as well as some 80 prisoners. Originally, the 159th Brigade R.F.A. was to share the barrage with another brigade on the left, but circumstances necessitated the 159th undertaking part of the task allotted to this brigade as well as their own share. This was successfully accomplished. The ammunition expenditure amounted to 5,300 rounds.[1]

In the early morning of the next day the infantry advanced from Savy Wood and captured Francilley-Selency, when the 159th Brigade supplied the greater portion of the barrage. The enemy abandoned a six-gun battery of 77 mm. in Francilley. In the afternoon the batteries moved to positions between Savy Village and Holnon Wood, and next day " C " Battery sent up teams to

[1] Extract from Report of 32nd Division operations April 1st and 2nd : " The movements of the Field Artillery on April 1st are worthy of note. Batteries moved in daylight over the open to positions south of Savy, and came into action under fire as in open warfare. When the movements over the open were ordered to be carried out on the morning of April 1st, there seemed at first to be some doubt as to whether such operations were possible. The Artillery, however, carried out their orders with the utmost energy and ability and the fact that six batteries were moved up within a few hours to support the attack of the 96th Infantry Brigade on the Bois de Savy is a useful reminder that the artillery must now be prepared to go into action over the open as in open warfare, and that the tendency to think that such movements can only be carried out under cover of darkness is incorrect."

April 2, 1917

remove the captured guns, but, owing to heavy shelling, the attempt had to be postponed until nightfall. During the night the guns were removed by a battery of the 32nd Division and on the following evening A/159 brought away the wagons.[1]

[1] One of these guns was presented to the 159th Brigade and handed over by it to the City of Glasgow.

Brig.-General J. A. Tyler, C.R.A., 32nd Division, wrote as follows to Brig.-General Staveley :—" I want to tell you how very well your 159th Brigade has done during the recent operations. Colonel Davson has given me every possible assistance and support and carried out all orders with praiseworthy promptitude. Major Harisson, with a small party, did a very fine performance on March 21st, and brought back a prisoner."

Plate V

BRIGADIER-GENERAL H. O'DONNELL, C.M.G.
Commanding 106th Brigade June 1915 to
May 1917.

BRIGADIER-GENERAL W. C. STAVELEY, C.B.
Commanding Royal Artillery July 1915 to
October 1917.

BRIGADIER-GENERAL J. W. SANDILANDS, C.B.,
C.M.G., D.S.O.
Commanding 104th Brigade April 1916 to March 1919.

BRIGADIER-GENERAL J. H. W. POLLARD, C.B.,
C.M.G., D.S.O.
Commanding 106th Brigade May 1917 to March 1919.

CHAPTER VII

GRICOURT

WE must now turn to the infantry which, as previously mentioned, had on March 20th been allotted tasks to repair the communications across the abandoned area. The first billeting area was roughly on a line Parvillers-Fouquescourt-Lihons, but as the work progressed more advanced billets were chosen until about ten days later, the majority of the battalions had reached the Somme.

The work on road and railway, uncongenial as it was to most of those engaged upon it, was well and expeditiously carried out, and praise was given for the spirit and energy displayed. Those units engaged on the railway kept well ahead of the French platelayers and were even able to afford them some assistance. The weather during this time was most inclement. The trenches in the Rosières-Lihons sector had suffered from thaw and rain, but as soon as the German lines were crossed, snow fell, and, from this date until the April 20th, there was a continuous repetition of frost, snow, sleet, and rain, which would have been unwelcome even to those who could house themselves in comfort, and who did not require to spend their lives in the open air. Owing to the wholesale destruction of the countryside, very few villages afforded any shelter at all for the advancing troops until they had leisure to provide some for themselves.[1]

By the beginning of April all battalions were at work in the forward area across the Somme,[2] and, on the 9th, orders were received to relieve the 61st Division in the left sector of the corps front. In accordance with this order the 104th Brigade took over the line from Fresnoy-le-Petit to the River Omignon, whilst the

---
[1] On the night of the 10th the wind blew down the buildings where the horses of the H.Q., 20th L.F., were sheltered and all were killed.
[2] Battalions were quartered roughly as follows : 104th Brigade, Germaine, Vaux, Beauvois ; 105th Brigade, Canizy, Voyennes, Offoy, Hambleux ; 106th Brigade, Ennemain, Flez, Athies.

106th Brigade continued the line from the river to a point south-east of Les Verguier. The 17/Lancashire Fusiliers relieved the 25/Warwickshire at Fresnoy-le-Petit ; the 23/Manchester, the 8/Warwickshire at Maissemy ; the 18/Highland L.I., the 5/Buckinghamshire at Soyécourt ; and the 19/Durham L.I., the 4/Royal Berkshire at the Tumulus, north-east of Bihecourt, Brigade Headquarters was at Villevecque and Bihecourt respectively. The Divisional Headquarters moved to Beauvois, and, on April 12th, General Landon took over command of the line. The 105th Brigade then relieved the 184th Brigade in divisional reserve and headquarters was established at Cauvigny Farm, north of Tertry. During the following night the boundary between the brigades was shifted, the 106th Brigade extending its right to include what was known as Hill 120, half a mile south of Berthaucourt. This portion was held by the 17/Royal Scots, and forward posts were established as opportunity offered. The enemy guns were active and casualties were reported by all battalions in the line.

The 32nd Division was due to attack Fayet and The Twin Copses north of it on the 14th, and the original plan had been for the 104th Brigade to attack Gricourt on the following day. This plan was changed, and it was decided not to attack Gricourt itself but to squeeze it out by a converging movement of the two brigades.

The variation from the scheme which followed might be quoted as an example of a pre-existing tactical principle that the initiative for the assault must come from the firing line. For, although instructions as to the various moves followed the usual course, the actual impulse to go forward was communicated from the front and anticipated the wishes of those who were directing affairs in rear.

At dawn on the 14th the 97th Brigade, 32nd Division, assaulted and captured Fayet, and advantage was taken of this by the 17/Lancashire Fusiliers to push patrols towards Gricourt, which had been shelled by the 157th Brigade, R.F.A., in support of the 32nd Division attack. At 6 a.m. a strong point was raided, but strenuous opposition was met with, and it was not until 2.30 p.m. that, after a flanking movement, assisted by a hurricane bombardment of 2 Stokes mortars, the strong point surrendered with 45 prisoners.

APRIL 14, 1917

HISTORY OF THE 35TH DIVISION 103

The attack on Fayet having been pushed home, the enemy was seen to be evacuating Gricourt, and the 17/Lancashire Fusiliers

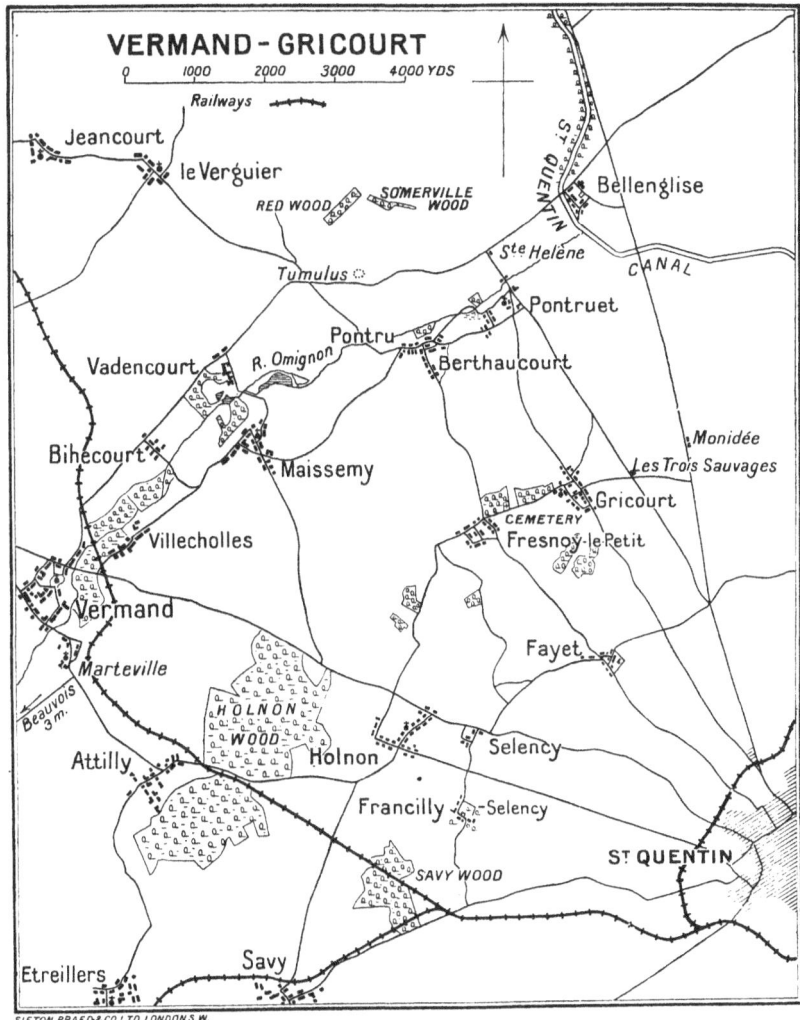

advanced and captured the cemetery. In face of some opposition they then cleared the village and, by 5.30 p.m., had established themselves upon the eastern edge. A further batch of 53 prisoners belonging to the 451st I.R. (234th Division) was captured in the village as well as 4 Granatenwerfer. The casualties were 1 officer wounded, 13 other ranks killed, and 34 wounded.

The battalion also succeeded in shooting down a hostile aeroplane with Lewis gun fire—an incident so unusual as to be remarkable.

Half a mile to the east of Gricourt on the summit of a ridge and on a bye road between Pontruet and St. Quentin stood a farm known as Les Trois Sauvages. It was decided to take advantage of the confusion of the enemy, by pushing the 18/Lancashire Fusiliers through the 17/Lancashire Fusiliers to occupy this position. Accordingly, at 4.15 a.m., an artillery bombardment was commenced upon the trenches round the farm, and under its fire two companies of the 18/Lancashire Fusiliers under Captain G. A. Duncan, which had formed up in the road east of Gricourt, advanced to the attack. The farm was found to be occupied by about twenty of the enemy, who were either killed or captured, and the advance continued. The intention had been that the companies should dig in on the ridge about 200 yards in advance of the farm, and one company did so, but the other continued in pursuit of the enemy beyond the Le Catelet-St. Quentin road, where they stormed a trench and engaged in a hand-to-hand conflict with the enemy, killing and wounding about a 100 and capturing 21 prisoners. Unfortunately, they then came under machine-gun fire from both flanks and suffered some loss. The company was accordingly ordered to withdraw, and this movement was carried out by alternate sections under cover of the Lewis guns of " Z " Company, which had now consolidated its position.

At 6 a.m. " X " Company was ordered up in support, and, having captured two machine-guns east of Gricourt, it established itself to the north of Les Trois Sauvages. A combined artillery and machine-gun barrage eventually silenced the enemy machine-guns, but as the position gained was commanded by the ridges to the east and south-east, it was deemed advisable to withdraw the three companies at dusk, and they dug themselves in to the east of Gricourt and left the farm unoccupied.

The casualties were 3 officers wounded, 1 officer missing, 30 other ranks killed, 50 other ranks wounded, 16 missing.

Meanwhile to the north the 20/Lancashire Fusiliers were

engaged in an assault upon some trenches on the Pontruet Ridge with ultimate objective the sunken track before mentioned, which led from Pontruet past Les Trois Sauvages. The assault was quite successful, and the battalion established itself on the position gained and linked up with the 18/Lancashire Fusiliers on its right. On the left the 106th Brigade established posts to cover the left flank, and penetrated north of Pontruet. Some casualties were inflicted, and a Lewis gun team of the 17/Royal Scots, which was covering the left flank of the 20/Lancashire Fusiliers, was completely destroyed.

At 2.30 a.m. next morning, two raiding parties of the 20/Lancashire Fusiliers, each consisting of 2 officers and 30 men, went out to a new trench which the enemy had dug, extending for about 800 yards south-east of Pontruet. The trench was empty and incomplete. A second visit at night was without result, although the party waited for an hour in expectation of the enemy appearing. In the early morning, also, a strong party of the 23/Manchester entered Pontruet which was found to be deserted. Meanwhile, on the left, a force of the 17/West Yorkshire, advancing to investigate an enemy trench near Ste. Hélène, north of Pontruet, encountered a hostile force which retired to a crater at the cross roads in front of it. The crater was rushed and the enemy fled. At night a raiding party passed through this company and advanced to the trench under an artillery barrage of the 307th Brigade R.F.A. The wire was found to be very strong, and the enemy opened machine-gun fire which checked a portion of the force. Two platoons, however cut gaps in the wire by hand, entered the trench, and drove out the garrison. Owing to the barrage, which had not yet ceased, pursuit of these was not possible, but artillery and rifle fire between them accounted for a good many of the German garrison.

On the night of the 16th/17th, in pouring rain, the 105th Brigade relieved the 104th Brigade from Gricourt to Maissemy, having the 14/Gloucestershire on the right and the 15/Cheshire on the left.[1] The 104th Brigade marched back to Trefcon, Villecholles, and Tertry. During its tour in the line it had suffered about 400

[1] On this day the following telegram was received from Corps :—" General Rawlinson wires as follows :—Please convey to 32nd and 35th Divisions my best congratulations on the phenomenal success of their operations. . . . I offer my best thanks."

casualties. The position of C/157 Battery was also rendered untenable, and the battery commander, to avoid further casualties, moved forward under the shelter of the hill north of Berthaucourt. From the 14th to the 16th of the month the 157th Brigade R.F.A. fired 7,700 rounds of ammunition.

On the 20th the 105th Brigade took over what was known as the Twin Copses, south of Gricourt from the 96th Brigade, and on the 21st a patrol of the 16/Cheshire reconnoitred the sunken road between Pontruet and Les Trois Sauvages, at a point a 1,000 yards south of the former place and found it strongly held.

On the following morning two platoons raided a strong point on the road. The enemy was on the alert and hand-to-hand fighting took place in which several of the enemy were hurt. Having taken 1 prisoner (452 I.R.) the party withdrew with a loss of 2 officers wounded, 3 other ranks killed, and 1 missing. Next night " W " Company of the battalion attacked this same road, but found it unoccupied. Posts were then established along it. On the night 23rd/24th a company of the same battalion rushed the enemy position on the sunken road farther north. This was found to be unoccupied and was consolidated and held. At the same time the 15/Sherwood Foresters established a post at the cross roads 500 yards north of Les Trois Sauvages.

At this time the 104th Brigade relieved the 106th in the northern sector. The 23/Manchester immediately established posts at Lone Tree on the high ground a mile north of Pontru, whilst on their left the 59th Division occupied some woods farther north. At 2.30 a.m. on the 24th, the 17/Lancashire Fusiliers raided Pontruet under an artillery barrage, but found that the enemy had evacuated the village.

The 23/Manchester, however, after a brush with the enemy at the crater west of Ste. Hélène, obtained identification of the 156th I.R., and, on the following night at the same place, identification was obtained of the 452nd I.R. (234th Division).[1] A demonstration against the enemy trench at Ste. Hélène, after an initial success, proved abortive owing to uncut wire. As this movement, however,

---

[1] This division had only been recently raised and contained a large proportion of young soldiers. After meeting them in a series of conflicts the soldiers of the 35th Division nicknamed them "The Rabbits." They were somewhat lacking in warcraft.

was only undertaken to draw attention from an operation of the 59th Division, the party withdrew without trying to force an entry. The 17/Lancashire Fusiliers twice reconnoitred the bridge over the River Omignon at Pontruet, and reported it as fit for traffic. Some of the bridges in this neighbourhood had been left undisturbed by the enemy, which points to the fact that he meant to hold the line in advance of them.

On the 28th the 18/Lancashire Fusiliers established posts in the village, and a few days later the river crossings north of Berthaucourt were also guarded.

Meanwhile on the right of the sector the 105th Brigade were making progress. An officer's patrol of the 15/Cheshire under 2nd Lieutenant Mowle had a successful encounter with a hostile patrol and brought in a prisoner. Following on this, an attempt was made to cut out an enemy post beside a copse some 1,400 yards in advance of our line. The post was bombed but, on strong hostile reinforcements arriving. the patrol withdrew under bursts of rapid fire which took effect upon the enemy. On this day one of the observers of this battalion named Private Johnson, spotted a hostile battery and informed the artillery. The battery, which was in action to the east of Bellenglise, was located by Major Keith ("A" Battery, 157th Brigade) from his observation post on the Pontruet-Gricourt road. He calculated the range and called for the assistance of " D " Battery (howitzers). The result was that direct hits on three guns were obtained, a large quantity of ammunition exploded, and the detachments were scattered. The battery was put out of action.[1] This episode revenged the treatment which had been meted out to " B " Battery of this brigade some days previously, when it had been heavily shelled with 150 mm. for forty-eight hours and had been forced to move its position.

In consequence of the raid of the 15/Cheshire, the 16th were ordered to attack the two copses situated about 600 yards west of the St. Quentin-Le Catelet road.

Three companies under Captain Playfer assembled in the sunken road close to the old windmill about 1,200 yards north of Gricourt, of which two were to assault, and one to be held in reserve. The assaulting companies moved forward at 1 a.m. on the 29th, under

[1] The corps' commander sent his congratulations to all concerned.

an artillery creeping barrage, which was transformed into a standing barrage along the Le Catelet road. The attack carried the northern copse, which was the principal objective, killed some of the enemy and captured 6 prisoners, and then, forming up 50 yards north-east of the copse, sent forward patrols. The enemy opened artillery fire behind the assaulting troops, but ceased when our barrage finished at 2.15 a.m. The attacking force then withdrew unmolested. The casualties were 1 officer wounded (Lieutenant Wood), 3 other ranks killed, 24 wounded, and 2 missing.

On the 30th the 105th Brigade was relieved by the 106th. Whilst the 16/Cheshire was engaged in this enterprise the 20/Lancashire Fusiliers sent out a patrol from Lone Tree to reconnoitre a copse beyond that which the 59th Division had previously assaulted. This copse, which afterwards became known as Somerville Wood, was of straggling growth, about half a mile long, and was situated one and a half miles north of Berthaucourt, the same distance west of Bellenglise. The patrol entered into a hornet's nest, and was fired at at close range by strong enemy forces. The leader (Lieutenant Gibbons) was hit, as was also the N.C.O., after firing a few rounds. One man rushed the enemy and was killed, the two remaining escaped. Another patrol, later, brought in the N.C.O and the dead man, but no trace could be found of the officer. Strong patrols went out on the next night, and these drove off the enemy with casualties. After this the patrols withdrew.

The month of May opened quietly, and such activity as took place was mostly confined to artillery fire. Except for a party working in the copses near Pontruet, patrols reported the country clear of the enemy as far as the Le Catelet road. To the joy of everybody the weather suddenly changed, and the first week of May was decidedly hot. The whole aspect of the countryside was altered, as hedgerows and trees burst into leaf. Holnon Wood, St. Quentin Wood, and the whole valley of the Omignon from Villeque to Maissemy all at once became green, and the troops awoke to the fact that they were fighting in a really beautiful country. It is not in the natural order of things to admire scenery when one is living in squalid quarters in frost and snow, but when both weather and reserve billets improved so did the general outlook on life.[1]

[1] It is interesting to note that fruit trees felled in the orchards blossomed on the ground, and some were reported to have borne fruit later.

On the 3rd a patrol of the 17/West Yorkshire advanced to investigate a trench to the east of Les Trois Sauvages, but, in doing so, was fired at from the farm itself, which the day before had been empty. The patrol, therefore, attacked the farm from the west and came upon concertina wire. This was passed, and the farm captured with 1 prisoner, a Pole, 452nd regiment. Posts were then established north and south of the farm, which was shelled by the enemy, and as an infantry attack followed the consolidating parties were compelled to withdraw. Patrols attempted to re-occupy the farm, but were held up by hostile fire.

At 2.30 a.m. on the 5th, a force consisting of 6 officers and 189 other ranks of the 23/Manchester, captured Somerville Copse. The main party (5 officers and 159 other ranks) advanced from the west under cover of a heavy artillery barrage in which the R.A. of the 59th Division and the 89th Heavy Artillery Group co-operated. At the same time a demonstration with Lewis guns and grenades was opened by the remainder of the party against another portion of the copse. This party completely misled the enemy, so that the main party entered the copse from the north-west with but little opposition. Dug-outs and shelters were bombed and destroyed, and 4 prisoners were captured.[1] The 17/Lancashire Fusiliers then established posts in the wood and the 23/Manchester withdrew. The Fusiliers captured 2 more prisoners. Three were from the 156th I.R. and 3 from the 22nd I.R. Sixty dead Germans were found in the wood. During the morning the German artillery heavily shelled Maissemy, and, in the afternoon, Vermand and the Vermand-Poeuilly road were shelled by a high velocity naval gun without any appreciable result.

At 10 p.m. the enemy attacked the posts of the 17/Lancashire Fusiliers in the copse, and after hand-to-hand fighting drove them back, but at midnight a strong counter attack regained all that had been lost and captured another prisoner. In addition, 9 of the enemy were killed and a considerable number is known to have been wounded. Our own casualties were slight.[2]

Whilst the above events were taking place on the north of the sector a somewhat larger attack was in progress on the south. " Y "

---

[1] The wood was subsequently named after the officer who led this raid.

[2] For gallantry on this occasion Lieutenant R. S. Heape was awarded the Military Cross and Lance-Sergeants Stringer and Williamson the Military Medal.

and "Z" Companies of the 19/Durham L.I., under Captain W. J. Oliver here made an attack on Les Trois Sauvages, and the new German line beyond it. This new line ran in a curve from a little north of the farm to a point on the Le Catelet road to the east of it. "W" Company, under Captain J. W. Waller, was detailed to establish posts north and south of the farm during the operation.

The day had been very hot, but a severe thunderstorm descended in the evening, and the operation was carried out in pouring rain. The attack advanced under an artillery barrage and met with no opposition until it arrived at a point about 300 yards south of the farm. Then it came under heavy rifle fire, and, as the barrage was still on the farm, the advance was delayed. At this moment a German artillery barrage of heavy guns and trench mortars descended on the second and third waves of the attack, and some of our own shells were reported as falling short. As the barrage lifted on to the new German line, Captain Noakes, commanding "Y" Company, gave the order to attack, sending word to Captain Oliver and to 2nd Lieutenant Blenkinsop, commanding "Z" Company, that he had done so. Captain Oliver never received this message, and Lieutenant Blenkinsop, who apparently did, was killed immediately afterwards. The men reached the wire round the farm, and finding it uncut, lay down under fire whilst a message was dispatched by Lieutenant Gray to inform Captain Oliver of the situation. This officer was severely wounded, and the message was not delivered.

By this time part of "Z" Company had reached the wire in front of the new line, the remainder had conformed to "Y" Company's movement and swung to their left. Captain Oliver, deeming the situation critical, moved up with the reserve through the hostile barrages. He was met by Sergeant Staff, himself seriously wounded who reported that of the two officers of "Z" Company, one was killed and the other wounded, and that the men lying close to the wire of the German trench would not retire without an officer's instructions. Captain Oliver placed his reserves and Lewis guns to cover the right flank and sent orders to withdraw. He then went across to Captain Noakes and informed him of his decision. The withdrawal was carried out with great steadiness, and all wounded that could be found were brought in. Sergeant Carver was specially mentioned for going forward on three occasions and bringing wounded men in on his back as he crawled through the barrage. Lieut.-Colonel Greenwell reported that he considered Captain Oliver thoroughly justified in ordering the withdrawal when he did.

Meanwhile, " W " Company had succeeded in establishing the posts. Two were formed a few hundred yards north of the farm and a third to the south of it. These were held after the companies retired. 2nd Lieutenant Haddon and Corporal Dibb were specially mentioned for good work in creating these posts. The casualties were 3 officers and 58 other ranks' killed and wounded.[1] Two days later one of these posts was attacked by a hostile patrol which was driven off. A second attack made by 40 or 50 men obliged the post to withdraw, but when fresh troops were sent to restore the situation, it was found that the enemy had retired. This event happened just as the 19/Durham L.I. were being relieved by the 15/Sherwood Foresters. It was the latter who finally re-established the post.

At the same time the 16/Cheshire relieved the 17/Royal Scots in the Fresnoy Section, and the G.O.C. 105th Brigade assumed command of the right sector and also a portion of the 104th Brigade, the front of which now extended from the River Omignon to a point 150 yards north-west of the Vermand-Bellenglise road.

On the night of the 9th the 15/Sherwood Foresters made another attack on Les Trois Sauvages. This place had been kept under artillery fire since the last attack, and on the morning of this day it was shelled and practically demolished. It was then kept under intermittent fire by the divisional artillery.

At 9.45 p.m. two platoons of the Sherwood Foresters advanced to the cross roads, 500 yards north-west of the farm. Here one party stopped and consolidated a position, a second advanced some 400 yards eastwards to act as a covering party; a third swung to its right and attacked the farm itself, but was met by rifle and machine-gun fire and stopped by wire. Several attempts were made to rush the farm, but these were unsuccessful, and about midnight, having exhausted its ammunition and grenades, the party withdrew under cover of that which was consolidating the cross

[1] 2nd Lieutenant G. F. Golightly died of wounds.

roads. The covering force had been subjected to heavy fire and had been forced to withdraw a short time previously. The only result of the raid was that posts were established north, south, and west of the farm, and also that the enemy losses were evidently severe.

Our losses were 4 killed, 13 wounded, and 2 missing. Both these latter were hit, and one was believed to have been killed.

The enemy was evidently in strength and was reinforced after the attack commenced. He even made an ineffectual attempt to outflank the right of the attack as it was withdrawing. It had been previously reported that the Germans appeared to attach importance to its position, and the fact that they reoccupied the farm after the heavy artillery bombardment and reinforced it at the first sign of attack is confirmation of this opinion. Apparently, it was to be held, or at least denied to us, regardless of casualties.

On the 10th the Corps Commander visited General Marindin and gave instructions that although the farm might be raided it was not to be captured and held. Its possession would, no doubt, have formed a rather dangerous salient, whilst some dead ground in front would have made a further advance necessary. Apparently the importance of the position was not considered sufficient to compensate for the loss of life involved by its retention.

On May 7th and 8th the 159th Brigade R.F.A. was relieved in the Fayet-Savy Wood neighbourhood by the 306th Brigade, which had been withdrawn from the 35th Division Artillery on the 2nd instant for this purpose. The 159th Brigade then moved to Marteville.

After the capture of Savy Wood the batteries took up more advanced positions, and headquarters moved to a hen house in Etreillers, where it remained until the brigade was relieved. On April 13th " B " and " C " Batteries, then in the north-east corner of Savy Wood, supported the left flank of the French attack on the outskirts of St. Quentin. The attack failed, but was renewed in the evening when the positions were carried.[1]

Throughout the 14th the brigade was employed in supporting the 97th and 14th Brigades in their attacks on Fayet, Cepy Farm,

---

[1] The greater part of the ground gained was voluntarily relinquished later.

and the German line of trench east of the Gricourt-St. Quentin road. All these attacks were successful, and " A " Battery then occupied a position on the eastern fringe of Francilly-Selency, and " C " Battery was in a sunken road between that village and Savy Wood. These positions could not be maintained. Between now and the end of the month the enemy consistently shelled all the battery positions on the front. As the batteries were nearly all in the open without cover a considerable amount of damage was done to the equipment, and three guns were entirely destroyed. Considering the number and weight of shells fired at the units the casualties to personnel were remarkably few, but a number of officers and men was put out of action, including Major Harisson, who was struck on the head by a splinter whilst standing in his battery position south of Francilley. This battery and " A " Battery in Francilley were so severely dealt with that changes of position became a necessity if the guns were to maintain their freedom of action, and alternative positions were taken up until such time as they were able to occupy properly prepared ones in Savy Wood.

On April 21st the 61st Division relieved the 32nd Division and the brigade remained in action under its command. On May 7th the batteries were relieved [1] in the line and withdrew to Douchy and then to Marteville, and on the 10th it relieved the 307th Brigade north of Vadencourt with headquarters in the grounds of the Château, and the next night supported an attack of the 20/Lancashire Fusiliers who successfully raided Fisher Crater, as the crater west of Ste. Helène on the Vadencourt-Bellenglise road had been named.[2] The raid, under 2nd Lieutenants Irvine and Kennedy, was a complete success. The party divided into two as it approached the crater and was challenged and fired on by about fifteen or twenty rifles. Orders were given to rush the crater and this was done. The enemy fled. Several casualties were inflicted and, it was thought that the artillery barrage accounted for some more.[3]

On the 13th, A/159 Battery R.F.A., which had remained in Savy Wood with the 61st Division, rejoined the 35th Division and went

---

[1] " B " Battery had had to be withdrawn two days previously in order to refit. " A " Battery remained at Savy until the May 11th/12th.
[2] After the officer who commanded the 23/Manchester in this raid of April 25th.
[3] For his action Lieutenant Irvine was awarded the Military Cross.

into action north of Gricourt under the 157th Brigade. At the same time " Q " and " U " Batteries R.H.A. joined the division and took up positions north of Vadencourt under the 159th Brigade R.F.A.

It had been reported by the infantry that the enemy was in the habit of evacuating Les Trois Sauvages at dawn. In accordance with this report an officer of the 157th Brigade R.F.A. was stationed in an advanced post at the cross roads north-east of Gricourt in telephonic communication with the battery. At dawn on the 13th the enemy was seen to leave the farm, and the battery opened rapid fire. Machine-guns of the 14/Gloucester co-operated by indirect fire, and some forty or fifty casualties were inflicted on the enemy.

At this time Lieut.-Colonel Gordon, who had been in command of the 15/Sherwood Foresters since they arrived in France, broke down in health and was invalided to England. His place was taken by Major Crellin of the same battalion. Lieut.-Colonel Newell, 15/Cheshire, who had been wounded on the Somme, returned to duty and resumed command of the battalion. Lieut.-Colonel Cochran became second in command. Brigadier-General O'Donnel vacated command of the 106th Brigade, and was succeeded by Brigadier-General J. H. W. Pollard, C.M.G.

On the night of the 14/15th the Canadian Cavalry Brigade, ommanded by Brigadier-General Seely, D.S.O., relieved the 104th Brigade in the sector north of the River Omignon, and the battalions withdrew to the Poeuilly-Villevecque area. The 17/Royal Scots marched to Villecholles in support of the 105th Brigade.

At midnight on the 15th/16th the 15/Sherwood Foresters made yet another raid on Les Trois Sauvages. " X " and " Y " Companies formed the assaulting party, and two platoons of each formed up at the previously mentioned cross roads north-west of the farm, and moved off in a south-easterly direction with a view to entering the farm from the east. The other platoons remained at the cross roads as a support. The advance was covered by a barrage of artillery, Stokes mortars, and machine-guns. Unsuspected wire was encountered about fifty yards east of the farm buildings and found to be impassable. Three attempts were made to cut gaps and force an entry but without success, and, as the rifle fire increased in intensity, the force withdrew. Two further attempts were made to reach the buildings from a point farther west, but these also failed. The attack was then abandoned. The casualties amounted to 1 officer wounded (2nd Lieutenant J. B. Farmer), 2 other ranks killed, 23 wounded, and 15 missing.

The 15/Sherwood Foresters had been relieved on the 13th by the 14/Gloucester, and at the time of the above attack the latter battalion was holding the line, including the advanced posts and suffered some casualties during the raid. At dawn on the 16th Private Blick, of the Gloucesters, noticed several wounded men of the Sherwoods still lying out between our advanced posts and Les Trois Sauvages. He crawled out to them and, although he was noticed and shot at, tried to bring one wounded man in. He was hit through his steel helmet by a bullet and, for the time being, had to abandon the attempt. At noon he went out again but found that the man was dead. He went on to the others and succeeded in bringing in one of them. The rescued man survived.

Following on this the 6-inch howitzers bombarded Les Trois Sauvages on the 18th. The shooting was good, and it was reported from the outposts that from the sounds heard it was believed that casualties had been inflicted. The enemy retaliated to some extent but the only damage done was to B/157 Battery, which was stationed north-east of Vadencourt Château, and, for the second time within a brief space, was overpowered by a deluge of shell. A hundred rounds of 150 mm. shell were fired at this battery in the afternoon. Fortunately the battery was not firing at the time, and the detachments were able to clear the position before much damage was done. The final result, from the enemy's point of view, was quite disproportionate to the amount of ammunition expended. One gun was buried, another destroyed. Six men of a gun detachment were buried, but were all dug out alive, and beyond that the casualties amounted to 2 men wounded. The battery changed position and was in action again next morning.[1] Two days later D/157 Battery suffered the same experience. It was shelled intermittently from 10.30 a.m. to 11 p.m. Result: 1 gun destroyed, 1 officer (2nd Lieutenant Woodrow), and 5 N.C.O.'s wounded.

[1] On this day Major R. Worthington, second-in-command of the 16/Cheshire, was killed whilst visiting the posts in Pontruet. His place was filled by Captain H. Hodson, 15/Cheshire.

On the 19th the command of the section north of the River Omignon was handed over to the 5th Cavalry Division. The C.R.A. 35th Division and the officer commanding 159th Brigade relegated their commands of the left section to the C.R.A. 5th Cavalry Division, and the officer commanding 16th Brigade, Royal Horse Artillery. The 106th Brigade marched to Peronne.

The time had now come when the divisional sector was to be handed over to the French. Preparations for this move had been in hand for some days, and on the 19th the 105th Brigade was relieved by the 87th French Division.

This relief was delaye das owing to the lightness of the night the 16/Cheshire delayed occupying one of their advanced posts until 10 p.m. When the party arrived the post was found to be occupied by the enemy. Some fighting ensued. The post was duly handed over to the French about 12.30 a.m.

Next day the G.O.C. IV Corps handed over to the G.O.C. French XI Corps, and the 35th Division Headquarters moved to Peronne and came under orders of the XV Corps (Lieut.-General Sir J. Du Cane). The artillery (less 159th Brigade *en route* for Doingt) came under tactical command of the French 87th Division until the 21st, when, on the 157th Brigade handing over to the French, the headquarters moved to Peronne. The 104th Brigade also marched there.

CHAPTER VIII

GONNELIEU AND EPEHY

THE situation on May 22nd was as follows. Divisional Headquarters were at Peronne, as was the 104th Brigade. The 105th Brigade was in rest in the Tertry-Trefcon neighbourhood ; the 106th on the march, the 19/Durham L.I. and the 17/Royal Scots to Templeux la Fosse, and the 17/West Yorkshire and 18/Highland L.I. about five miles farther north at Sorel le Grand. The 157th Brigade R.F.A. was at Marteville and the 159th at Doingt.

The division was now to hold a portion of the line which afterwards became so well known on account of the Cambrai battles of November. It was about eight miles to the north of the sector recently held, and about fifteen miles due east of the area in which the division had been engaged in July of the previous year.

On the 23rd the 106th Brigade took over the right brigade sector of the 40th Division from the 120th and 121st Brigades. This extended to about 3,000 yards of front in advance of Villars-Guislain. The 104th Brigade took up the camps and billets vacated by the 106th and the 105th marched to Peronne. On the 25th the 17/ Lancashire Fusiliers relieved the 13/East Surrey, south of Gonnelieu and linked up with the 106th Brigade in the depression known as Twenty-Two Ravine. The 104th Brigade for a short time had only one battalion in the front line ; the 18/Lancashire Fusiliers were in support in Gauche Wood ; the other battalions in reserve at Sorel. The 105th Brigade was stationed at Templeux le Fosse and Aizecourt le Bas.

The country in which the division was now operating was similar to that which it had just left except that it was less wooded. Wide stretches of open grassland interspersed with woods, the remains of important villages, and valleys, which varied in depth from 50 to 300 feet, formed the chief features. About a mile in advance of

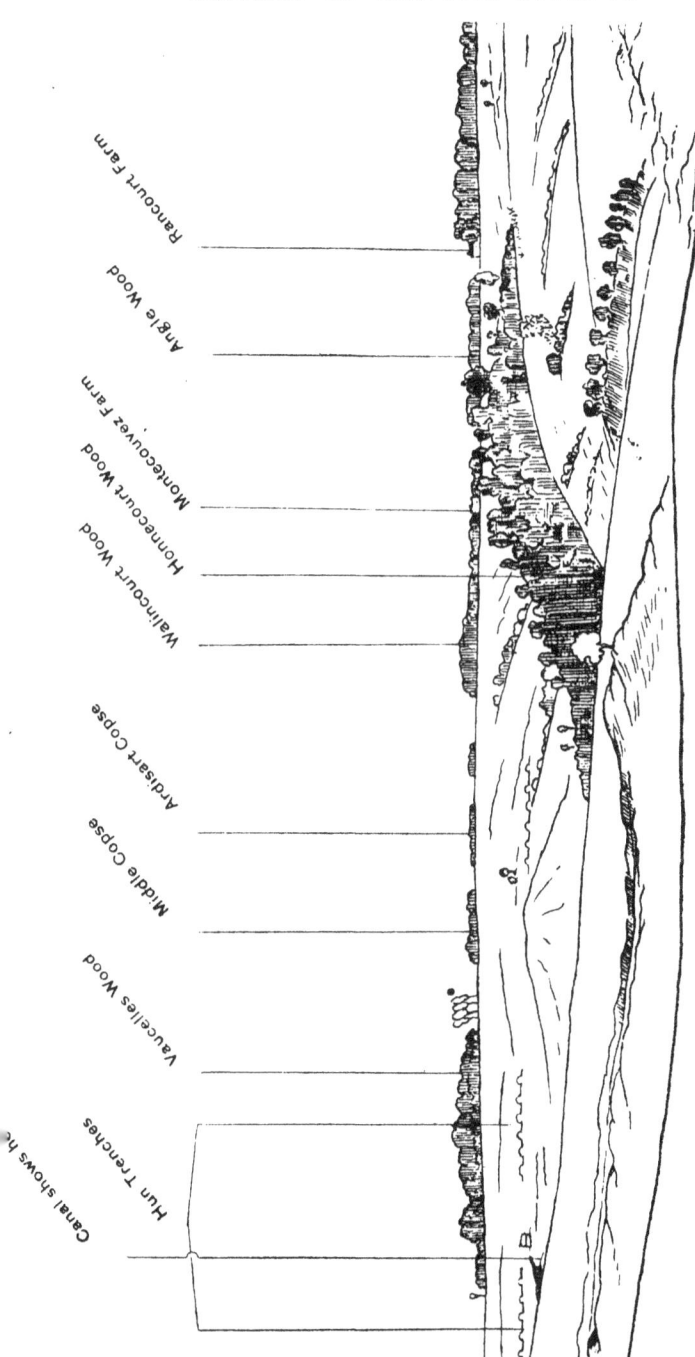

HONNECOURT WOOD: taken from a point 1200 yards South-east of Villers-Guislain.
From a sketch by Brig.-Gen. W. C. Staveley.

the front line, but hidden from view by the features of the ground, lay the Canal de L'Escaut (St. Quentin Canal) which connects the upper reaches of the Somme at St. Quentin with those of the Scheldt at Cambrai.

Behind the centre of the position held by the division lay the village of Villers-Guislain, situated on a prominent feature of the landscape and half-a-mile in rear of it lay Gauche Wood, which extended to about thirty-five acres and afforded useful cover for guns and reserves. On the enemy side of the line opposite Villers-Guislain on the slope towards the canal at Honnecourt lay Honnecourt Wood, a name which will appear later in the narrative.

About two miles behind the front line, running practically north and south was the Cambrai-Peronne railway line. This line was steeply embanked and these banks were made use of. Chapel Crossing, south-west of Gauche Wood, was much used by all units. At Epéhy the line to Bapaume and Arras branched off to the west, and in its banks were situated sundry brigade headquarters. The front line was not continuous, and, in some places at first merely consisted of a series of detached posts which in other fronts would have been impossible. The enemy, however, was not aggressive, and officers of higher commands were able to ride most of the way up to the front line and then walk over the open to the trenches. The weather was fine and the exercise was appreciated.

The division was now the right division of the XV Corps front. The others, in order from right to left, were the 40th, 59th and 42nd. Divisional Headquarters were in huts in Gurlu Wood, close to Aizecourt le Bas.

On the night of the 25th/26th the 159th Brigade relieved the 178th Brigade and occupied positions in and around Villers-Guislain and Gauche Wood. The 157th Brigade R.F.A. remained in the St. Quentin area until the 26th and then marched north. On the 30th it relieved the right group of artillery covering the 59th Division. As soon as the positions were occupied, " A " Battery was heavily shelled and two guns were put out of action.

Although the front was quiet when the division took over there was a certain amount of activity amongst patrols. On the 27th, a small party of the enemy rushed a post held by the 17/West Yorkshire in the sunken road between Villers-Guislain and Honnecourt. This took place in daylight. The sentry was wounded and captured ; the other three men in the post were also wounded. The hostile party got safely away. Next morning Sergeant Watson of the same battalion crawled out to a hostile post about 500 yards north-east of this one, shot the sentry and one other man, and then returned to our lines. No action worthy of note took place during the remainder of the month. The enemy fired a moderate amount of shells. Gas was used on one occasion against the front of the 17/Lancashire Fusiliers, and Villers-Guislain was once or twice bombarded. On one of these occasions Captain E. G. Hadow, M.C., 17/West Yorkshire, was killed. About 1,000 rounds were fired by our artillery during the last five days of the month, which included a bombardment of Honnecourt Wood and Village.

On the 31st the 18/Lancashire Fusiliers took over the left company front of the 106th Brigade. The brigade boundary was now at a point in the sunken road midway between Gonnelieu and Honnecourt.

During the month of June no operation of importance was undertaken by our troops or by the enemy. Numerous patrol encounters took place, but the Germans showed no desire to prolong the meeting. During the first half of the month hostile fire was mainly directed on villages and batteries, and our trenches were neglected ; but in the second part this procedure was reversed. The enemy also adopted means to cover his battery positions by flash reducers, dummy flashes, smoke puffs, and by several batteries firing simultaneously. The 105 mm. was the gun most used, but the counter battery work was uncertain, inaccurate, and did little damage. In all, about 5,000 rounds were fired, of which 1,600 were against battery positions.

Work on the Hindenburg line continued, but, except for the wire which was kept in good repair, not much work was done on any trenches west of the canal.

On our part, continuous work was carried out on what was known as the " Brown Line," which had claimed the attention of all reserve battalions in the Gricourt sector, and, in addition, at this time a " Green Line " was also traced which gave employment to those who were not actually fighting.

On the night May 31st/June 1st the 18/Lancashire Fusiliers

advanced the line to the sunken road in front and consolidated it. The Royal Engineers put out protective wire. The Gonnelieu-Honnecourt sunken road was reconnoitred to within 50 yards of the village without molestation, and at the same time a hostile trench in front of Gonnelieu was found to be unoccupied. It became evident that the enemy trenches in front of Honnecourt were not occupied by day. On the other hand he did attack one of our patrols which was covering a local relief and inflicted some casualties. According to the statement of a wounded prisoner belonging to the 123rd Grenadier Regiment, 27/Wurtemburger Division, the order of battle from north to south was the 123rd Grenadier, the 120th Infantry Reserve, and the 124th Infantry Reserve.

On the 2nd the 35th Division came under command of the III Corps (Lieut.-General Sir W. P. Pulteney) on the withdrawal of the XV Corps from the line, and, on the same day the 105th Brigade relieved the 106th in the right sector, with 16/Cheshire on the right and 14/Gloucester on the left. The former battalion, patrolling out towards Honnecourt, found a crater in the road occupied by the enemy, but an attempt to eject him failed, and a similar fate overtook the 14/Gloucester on the left. The enemy showed a slight increase of activity in the front line, and his artillery fire definitely increased. Villers-Guislain about this time was continually shelled.

On the 3rd the 106th Brigade Trench Mortar Battery had been lent to the 2nd Cavalry Division on our right to assist in a raid carried out by the Scots Greys on the night of the 9th/10th. The raid was successful, and the Stokes batteries received great praise for the way in which they assisted.

On the 10th the 106th Brigade relieved the 104th in the Gauche Wood sector, and on the night of the 10th/11th a patrol of the 17/West Yorkshire had an encounter with a hostile patrol north of Honnecourt Wood. After a sharp flight the enemy was routed and took to flight. Our casualties amounted to 1 officer and 3 men wounded.

The next few days passed quietly with minor patrol incidents. Some of our patrols advanced as much as 700 yards in front of the line without opposition. The enemy artillery was active, but no great damage was done. Our own artillery was also active and

JUNE 17, 1917

obtained some successes. The bridge over the canal at Honnecourt was destroyed as was also an enemy observation post on our left which was engaged by C/157 Battery.[1] Banteux and Bantouzelle were subjected to a bombardment and, as it was found that opportunities of dealing with the enemy on the west of the canal were rare, the batteries of the 159th Brigade were gradually pushed forward closer up to the front line so as to give a more extended range. D/159 Battery fortified itself amongst the débris in Villers-Guislain, and other guns were also advanced beyond the normal. It was reported that a gunner of B/157 Battery was shot in the back by a sniper when digging gun pits.

On the 15th the 15/Cheshire successfully "jumped" an advanced trench north of Honnecourt Wood in order to gain better observation. The 15/Sherwood Foresters supplied patrols to protect the digging parties, and one of these had an encounter with a hostile patrol which was driven off. Eventually a trench 800 yards long and 4½ feet deep was dug. It was wired during the night by the Royal Engineers. There was no interference with the work during the night, but a hostile patrol approached at dawn. It was fired at and bolted, leaving one wounded prisoner, belonging to the 124th Regiment, in our hands. The Sherwood Foresters then occupied the trench.

On the 17th the 159th Brigade R.F.A. supplied a creeping barrage for strong patrols of the 16/Cheshire under Lieutenants Wood and Hasler, which attempted to enter Honnecourt Wood from the north-west and south-east. The enemy strenuously opposed this, and the attempt was not persisted in.[2]

The 105th Brigade was then relieved by the 104th and withdrew to Heudecourt, Aizecourt, and Templeux. At this time the 16/Cheshire received a congratulatory message from the French with reference to the relief in the Fresnoy Sector when the battalion had remained in the line and re-established the lost posts before handing over.

[1] A curious incident happened in this brigade on the following day, when a gunner walked in front of one of the guns when it was firing and was killed. The accident is probably unique.

[2] On the same night, two and a quarter miles to the north, the 157th Brigade supported a raid of the 2/4 Lincolnshire to the east of Trescaut. A strong patrol was met on the way over and a fight ensued in which two prisoners were taken. The hostile patrol retired to the trench which was bombarded. In retaliation the enemy fired 150 rounds on the two batteries in Gouzeaucourt Wood. No damage was done except to the wood.

On the 22nd the enemy raided the Cavalry Division on the right. The raid was repulsed, but 2nd Lieutenant C. W. Blackwell, R.F.A., of the Heavy Trench Mortar Battery, which had again been lent to the Cavalry, was killed.

Next night the 106th Brigade, in conjunction with the 40th Division, dug a new trench from 50 to 100 yards in advance of the present line south-east of Gonnelieu. The enemy did not interfere, which was surprising, as during the day his artillery had been active, especially on Villers-Guislain, Gauche Wood, and portions of the front line situated north of Honnecourt Wood, and this was continued on the next day. On this day the 18/Lancashire Fusiliers suffered several casualties.

A raid by the cavalry in which our artillery and right battalion co-operated took place on the 24th, and next night the 105th Brigade relieved the 106th in the northern sector.

For some days it had been noticed that Fawcus Avenue, a communication trench connecting Targelle Ravine with a farm in the front line opposite Les Tranchées, was in receipt of a larger quantity of hostile shells than other places in the neighbourhood. A renewed bombardment on the 29th prompted General Sandilands to send a warning to commanding officers in the line that a raid was to be expected. The anticipated raid took place at 6 a.m. on the following morning, when a hostile party of 20 or 30 men entered the head of Fawcus Avenue, then held by the 23/Manchester. They were at once ejected, leaving behind one wounded man, a sergeant, who had only joined the battalion the night before. Lewis guns from both flanks opened on the enemy and caused some loss, but owing to a thick mist it was impossible to estimate the casualties.

Meanwhile various points had been registered by the enemy on the front held by the 15/Cheshire and 14/Gloucester, and from the events of the last 24 hours, General Marindin concluded that a further raid was to be expected and precautions were taken accordingly.

The night of June 30th/July 1st was a busy one. It was also noisy and confused. The 104th Brigade, after careful reconnaissance, had planned an attack on Honnecourt Wood, and this was delivered at 1.30 a.m. under a barrage of the 159th Brigade R.F.A., as well as Stokes mortars and machine-guns.[1] The night was dark

---

[1] The medium mortars had been lent to the cavalry.

JULY 2, 1917

and rainy, but the raiding party of 100 men, under Lieutenants Hobson, Wolfe, and Topham, reached the northern edge of the Wood. The darkness then obstructed the raid and enabled several of the enemy to escape. One German, however, was captured, and one or two more killed, and the barrage was reported to have accounted for several others. Some valuable information was extracted from the prisoner.

No sooner had the artillery started the barrage on Honnecourt Wood than the S.O.S. signal was sent up on the left of the 105th Brigade at the point known as Newton Post, and one battery was switched on to this line. A heavy hostile barrage was placed on the three posts, Turner Quarry, Crook Quarry and Newton Post, which, after a quarter of an hour, was lifted on to the old front line. The situation then became more clear and the garrison, the 14/ Gloucester, was able to see a party of Germans in the act of negotiating the wire, and a fight with rifles, Lewis guns, and bombs took place. The enemy withdrew, leaving behind 3 dead and 1 slightly wounded officer, who were all brought in. They belonged to the 123rd Regiment. Meanwhile another party had made an attempt to break through to the north of Newton Post. Sergeant Board and Private Balderson left the trench and attacked them with the bayonet. They wounded and captured one man. The remainder fled.[1] The bombardment slackened at 3.30 a.m., but did not cease until an hour later. The casualties were 2 killed and 8 wounded. For this action the battalion received the congratulations of the G.O.C. III Corps and the G.O.C. 35th Division.

On the night of the 2nd the infantry battalions were relieved in the line by units of the 40th Division, and marched to reserve billets at Aizecourt, Villers Faucon, and Longavesnes. Next day the 159th Brigade R.F.A. was relieved by the 40th Divisional artillery and moved directly into action under the 3rd Cavalry Division about one and a half miles farther south.[2] The 157th Brigade remained in action under the 40th Division until the 5th, when it moved to wagon lines near Roisel.

[1] This sergeant was one of the original "Bantams."
[2] Just before the relief "C" Battery was heavily bombarded in Gauche Wood, and suffered some damage.

126 HISTORY OF THE 35TH DIVISION

THE EPEHY SECTOR

The division was now to side-slip to the south and relieve the cavalry corps which was in the Epéhy sector.

The new line to be taken over was composed of a series of detached posts which extended from a short distance south of Hargicourt on the south to Targelle Ravine in the north. These posts were situated on the high ground west of the canal, except at two points, Gillemont Farm and The Knoll, features rising to a height of about 400 feet and 35 to 40 feet above our nearest posts. The area around

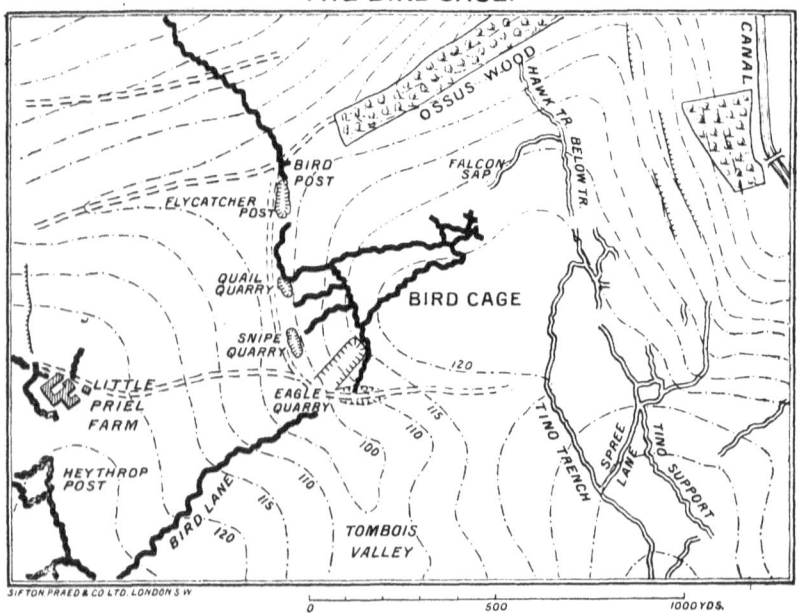

THE BIRD CAGE.

Gillemont Farm was held by both armies, but The Knoll was in the hands of the enemy. It commanded a good view of our positions to the south and also, to a lesser extent, to the north. Our nearest posts, Fleeceall and Ego (so named by the cavalry after the undying characters of Surtees) were on low ground about 750 yards from it. About a mile to the north-west, and in front of Vendhuille, was The Birdcage, a network of trenches on the reverse slope

JULY 6, 1917
HISTORY OF THE 35TH DIVISION 127

of a hillock. This post had originated in the process of sapping up to obtain view from the crest, which had not achieved success. The duty of holding it was not highly esteemed by commanders or by units. Valleys sloped down to the canal at intervals along the front, the chief of these being Macquincourt Valley, Ossus Wood and Canal Wood. The former was behind the German line, the others were practically No Man's Land. In the centre of the line, on a hillock immediately west of The Birdcage, stood Little Priel Farm, and two miles to the west of it were the conterminous villages of Peizières and Epéhy. A further two miles to the south-west lay Villers-Faucon, where was divisional headquarters.

On the west bank of the canal and almost invisible from the British lines lay the large village of Vendhuille.[1] About a mile to the south-east of Vendhuille the canal entered a tunnel and continued so until Bellenglise, well past the right flank of the division. The enemy made full use of this tunnel for the purposes of protection. Other places on the German side of the canal, visible from the high ground were Putney, Guizancourt Farm, Beaurevoir, Bellevue Farm, Le Catelet, Gouy, and Brancourt Church Spire. Some of these places were about seven miles distant from the front line, but those who fought in these parts will remember them standing out clearly in the evening sunlight.

Such is a rough description of the country in which the 35th Division was to spend the next three months. The distance from Cat Post on the right to opposite Honnecourt on the left was about 8,000 yards.

On July 6th the 106th Brigade relieved the 4th Cavalry Brigade (Brigadier-General Pitman) in the right sector which extended as far north as Tombois Farm, and, next day, the 105th Brigade relieved the 3rd Cavalry Brigade (Brigadier-General Bell-Smythe) in the northern sector. Both brigades immediately commenced to link up the posts and put out belts of wire. On this day Major-General G. Mac K. Franks, C.B., assumed command of the division in place of Major-General Landon, and a few days later Lieut.-Colonel Stewart, 157th Brigade, R.F.A., left the division on appointment as C.R.A., 66th Division.

[1] It was at this village that the 4th Division crossed the canal after the battle of Le Cateau.

During the succeeding days the Ossus Posts, four separate posts in front of the 105th Brigade, were gradually linked up, and patrols went forward in search of the enemy. The Germans on this front did not appear to be more combative than in the sector recently vacated, and several posts which were expected to be held were, when visited by patrols, found to be unoccupied. After a few days more enterprise was shown, and, at midnight on the 12th/13th a raid was attempted on Gillemont Farm. This was repulsed, but an hour later a determined attempt was made to cut out an advanced post west of The Knoll. The party of the 18/Highland L.I. which held it, fell back fighting to the main post bringing the wounded with them. The enemy then withdrew and the advanced post was reoccupied. One German, who belong to the 49th Reserve Regiment, was captured.

At the same time in the other sector a raid was made upon the Birdcage, which was then held by the 15/Sherwood Foresters. A heavy artillery bombardment was opened, which was lifted onto the quarry and sunken road in rear. A party of the enemy was then seen in front of the wire to the right. It was dispersed by rifle fire and got caught by our artillery defensive barrage. The hostile artillery ceased about 1.30 a.m. A patrol of the 16/Cheshire under Captain Burnett, which had gone out earlier in the night, was cut off by the barrage and formed itself into a flank guard until all was over, when it returned to our lines.

The casualties in these two raids amounted to 92, a considerable number of which was suffered by the 19/Northumberland Fusiliers, which was assisting in remaking the trenches. 2nd Lieutenant Gledsdale of the 15/Cheshire, who was to have led a raid on this night, was found to be missing. His body was discovered by a patrol next day.

The day was productive of artillery activity on both sides. B/157 Battery was heavily shelled by 210 mm., but little damage was done. Our artillery bombarded the enemy's trenches and shelled Bony with gas, and wire-cutting began on The Knoll. Beyond this the day was quiet. A deserter of the 49th R.I.R. was taken by the 20/Lancashire Fusiliers. He announced that storm troops were about to attack the Birdcage.[1] Next day a man of the 2nd

---

[1] This was confirmed by a second deserter, an Alsatian, captured on the 22nd.

R.I.R., one of a party which made an attempt on the east communication trench of The Birdcage, was brought in.

On the 15th the 104th Brigade relieved the 105th Brigade in left sector.[1] Following a bombardment of hostile trenches to catch a relief the day was devoted by the enemy to heavy fire on the south end of Epéhy, on Malassise Farm, 1,000 yards south-east of it, which was unoccupied, and on C/159 Battery's position in Tetard Wood, 500 yards east of Epéhy. This latter bombardment lasted from 9 a.m. to 8 p.m. There were a few minor casualties and two guns were damaged.

On the 19th the enemy registered various points in the right sector and at 11.30 p.m. he began a systematic bombardment of Gillemont Farm and Rifleman Post (almost on the extreme right of the line). At 2.30 a.m. (20th inst.) both these positions were raided. The 17/Royal Scots in Gillemont Farm had no difficulty in disposing of the raid at that point, but the attack on the 19/ Durham L.I. in Rifleman Post was carried through with greater determination. The Germans succeeded in making their way through the damaged wire and reached the forward post, but could make no further advance. On their retirement they left behind two dead, 1 Bangalore torpedo, 6 rifles, and about 30 bombs. The identifications were of the 29th Regiment and the 34th Pioneers.

During these few days the enemy continued bombardment of battery positions. C/157 Battery and A/159 Battery were both steadily shelled for some hours, but the fire was erratic and little damage was done. The former battery lost its cook-house and cooks, which was the cause of a certain amount of inconvenience. " D " Battery, 210th Brigade, which had been attached to the 159th Brigade since the 12th instant, and was located in Ronssoy Wood, also received 300 rounds on the 25th.

On the 23rd/24th the 105th Brigade relieved the 10th Brigade in the right sector.

On the 25th two parties of Germans, consisting of 10 men each, crawled up in the long grass towards Fleeceall Post and attempted to rush the advanced post to the south-east of it. They managed

[1] Brigade Headquarters of the left brigade was in the western of the two railway embankments, east of Epéhy. The 159th Brigade Headquarters was in the eastern embankment. The right brigade Headquarters was in the chateau garden at St. Emilie. The 157th Brigade Headquarters was close to it.

K

to get close to the post and threw about a dozen bombs into it, but the garrison, which consisted of Corporal Rose and 8 men only, opened rapid fire and drove the raiders off.

OPERATIONS IN THE NORTHERN SECTOR

For some days the units of the 104th Brigade had reported that a raid appeared to be imminent, and, in the early hours of the 26th, that expectation was realized, although not in the spot where it had been foreseen. At 4.30 a.m. the enemy's artillery opened a barrage on Little Priel Farm, and at 6 a.m. the fire was distributed along the front line from The Birdcage to Turner Quarry, as well as on the battery positions of " B " and " C " 159th Brigade, and on Epéhy itself. All units stood to arms, and the artillery opened fire on the S.O.S. lines. At 6.10 a.m. the raid took place against the right of the 40th Division at the junction of the front line and Fawcus Avenue, and part of our barrage was shifted northwards to deal with it. The 17/Lancashire Fusiliers, who were on the left and close to the point of entry, opened with rifle and machine-gun fire. The enemy, however, succeeded in entering the trenches and captured a few prisoners from the 13/Yorkshire. On his return, however, he was caught by the artillery barrage and by the rifle fire of the 17/Lancashire Fusiliers and suffered many casualties, so that, in the confusion, some of the prisoners were able to escape back to their own lines. One company of the 104th Brigade sent very prompt and accurate information to B/159 Battery as to the whereabouts of the retreating enemy, and the commanding officer, Major Hart, was able to deal successfully with the situation. The incident afforded a striking illustration of the value of close cooperation and good communications.

Our casualties in the line were heavy. The 17/ and 18/Lancashire Fusiliers between them lost 3 officers wounded, 9 other ranks killed, and 58 wounded.

At 2.45 a.m. on the 29th the 23/Manchester made a successful raid on Hawke Trench, an enemy advanced line north of Ossus Wood. This was preceded by an intense artillery bombardment and machine-gun barrage of five minutes duration, after which the guns formed a protective barrage round the point of entry.

The raiding party, under Captain Gibbon, was divided into four groups, of which the two centre ones, under Lieutenants Burkett and Mason, were the principal elements, the others being largely for protective purposes. These groups started from points in front of our line about 400 yards from the enemy's position, and both parties reached it without opposition. Lieutenant Burkett's party was delayed by the wire and suffered a few casualties before breaking through. Those composing Lieutenant Mason's party had no such difficulty. At the point of entry they found a machine-gun with the crew of 4 men lying dead beside it. Turning northwards up the trench they counted 30 dead Germans of the 124th Regiment, and at a point about 150 yards on they secured a second machine-gun. Then, having bombed a dug-out, they returned to our lines, bringing both machine-guns with them. The casualties were slight. No prisoners were captured nor were any of the enemy seen alive. If any survived the barrage they apparently fled.

At midnight on the following night (29th/30th) a force of 3 officers and 60 men of the 20/Lancashire Fusiliers, under Lieutenant F. J. Butler, raided Tino Trench, which was situated 500 yards in advance of The Birdcage and lay north to south covering Vendhuille.

The raid was supported by a creeping barrage, an intense bombardment of the enemy front line, and a standing barrage of the enemy support line. A small diversion was carried out on Hawke Trench and Ossus Wood.

At zero the whole party moved out in two groups close under the barrage. Each party carried a torpedo to destroy the wire, but the right party rushed the wire and crossed it with the assistance of mats whilst the torpedo was being placed. The party actually entered the trench before the barrage lifted and was able to make bombing attacks on four shelters, two of which contained six men each who were engaged in firing over the parapet. These were all killed except two who were captured. One of these unfortunately offered a vigorous resistance and had to be summarily got rid of. The other was sent to our lines. More of the enemy were overpowered in a large shelter at the point where the Vendhuille Road crossed the trench.

Meanwhile the torpedo group of the left party came upon a German listening post of two men and captured them. One broke away and was shot, the other was safely removed. The torpedo was exploded and the men passed the gap and entered the trench. A large dug-out, under construction, was next encountered. It was inhabited by eight men who showed fight when told to surrender and were killed. The trench was then searched and the garrison suitably dealt with. This party claims to have disposed of twenty of the enemy.

The communications between the infantry and artillery worked excellently. Lieutenant H. B. Barclay, " D " Battery, 210th Brigade, from a forward position, sent back full reports of the progress of the attack.

Meanwhile the diversion mentioned above had been carried out by the 17/Lancashire Fusiliers on Hawke Trench. It was covered by a light artillery barrage to which the enemy replied with an intense bombardment of trench mortars. The party, which consisted of 2 officers and 25 men, reached the trench and bombed the enemy at close range. Several casualties were inflicted.

The above-mentioned prisoners belonged to the 8th Jager Regiment. They had only been in the trench two hours when the raid commenced. Our casualties were slight.

Since the beginning of April, in addition to those previously mentioned, the following changes in command had taken place :—

On April 13th, Lieut.-Colonel R. D. Cheales was invalided home and his place in command of the 17/Royal Scots was taken by Major S. Huffan, 19/Durham L.I., and later by Lieut.-Colonel P. S. Hall. On June 5th Lieut.-Colonel R. E. M. Heathcote assumed command of the battalion, Lieut.-Colonel Hall being transferred to the 17/West Yorkshire.

On July 20th Major Metcalf relinquished the appointment of Brigade Major, 104th Brigade. His place was taken by Captain F. K. Simmons, M.V.O., Highland L.I.

On July 26th Bt.-Colonel L. M. Wilson, D.S.O., assumed command of the 157th Brigade R.F.A., vice Lieut.-Colonel Stewart, D.S.O., who had been appointed C.R.A., 66th Division.

CHAPTER IX

THE KNOLL AND GILLEMONT

PREVIOUS mention has been made of the commanding positions held by the enemy at The Knoll and Gillemont Farm, and, about the middle of July, it was decided to raid the enemy's trenches at the latter point with a view to damaging his defences and delaying any intention on his part to gain complete possession of the spur.

On July 24th approval was received for reinforcements of heavy artillery, and for the amount of ammunition required to carry out this operation.

As there seemed to be a probability of a considerable concentration of heavy and field artillery on the Corps' front, and in order to take full advantage of it, proposals were submitted for more extensive operations which were to combine the capture of The Knoll with the raid on the Gillemont Trenches, and to include a subsequent raid on the trenches between Ossus and Canal Woods. On the 29th provisional sanction was granted for this procedure, and an estimate of guns and ammunition required for all operations was submitted.

In addition to the artillery one infantry brigade was asked for to hold a portion of the line and to enable those troops which were to carry out the attacks to be pulled out for training.

Approval of all these requests was received on August 5th and the Dismounted Brigade of the 4th Cavalry Division took over the whole of the left sector on the following day.

The original date fixed had been August 15th, but, owing to the heavy artillery being delayed, it was postponed until the 19th. At the same time the scheme of attack on Gillemont was enlarged and it was decided to capture and hold the enemy front line opposite the farm.

The 105th Brigade was detailed for The Knoll attack, and, on the night of August 1st/2nd it was relieved by the 106th Brigade, which took over the whole front including that portion of the line held by the 104th Brigade south of the Ossus Wood-Malassise Farm Road. The 104th Brigade took over the right battalion front of the 121st Brigade, and thus extended its boundary to a point 500 yards north-east of Honnecourt Wood. The 18/Highland L.I. did not go into the line. It had been detailed for the attack on Gillemont, and, since July 24th, had been engaged in practising the attack on a course laid out in replica by the Pioneers at Gurlu Wood.

The 105th Brigade withdrew to Aizecourt le Bas where a full-sized course of The Knoll trenches was laid out, and on this the two battalions destined for the attack ; the 15/Cheshire and 15/Sherwood Foresters, practised continuously from the 6th until the date of attack. All details as to the supply of ammunition, stores, and trenching materials were carefully worked out, and arrangements were made for rapid fortification of the position with the assistance of collapsible canvas crates, and for these, together with rations, water, etc., to be brought forward by carrying parties on the first sign that the position was occupied.

On the night 4th/5th, the 16/Cheshire and 14/Gloucester relieved the 17/Lancashire Fusiliers and the 23/Manchester, the two battalions which had been detailed for the raids on the Ossus Posts, in the right subsector of the Epéhy front, and two nights later the remainder of the 104th Brigade, as well as these two battalions, was relieved by the 4th Dismounted Cavalry Brigade.

At 3.15 a.m. on the 6th, under cover of a thick mist, the enemy made a raid on the front and both flanks of the trenches at Gillemont Farm. There was no preliminary bombardment and the trenches were entered on all sides. The 17/Royal Scots, who were holding the position, fell back from the forward posts, many individuals having to fight their way back through the encircling enemy. About a hundred yards back the companies reformed and advanced again. The Germans withdrew and the trenches were re-occupied. The casualties were 1 killed, 15 wounded, and 2 missing. The strength of the enemy was calculated at 150 men, and several casualties were known to have been inflicted on him.

From now onwards preparations for the various attacks were hurried forward.

The enemy artillery was very active and much movement was

seen behind his lines. The wire on The Knoll was strengthened, and it was suspected that he had received some indication of the projected attack. Our own artillery chiefly devoted itself to harassing fire behind the German front line.

Reinforcements of artillery arrived consisting of " Q " and " U ' Batteries, R.H.A., and the 296th Brigade, R.F.A.[1] On the 14th the enemy fired 850 rounds on the position of A/296 Battery in Ronnsoy Wood. The only damage done was one gun slightly injured and 30 rounds of ammunition destroyed. Most of the ammunition was saved by the gallantry of officers and men in extinguishing the burning camouflage under fire. It had seemed at one time as if the damage was likely to be considerable.

A day or two later, the 21st, 27th, and 44th Heavy Artillery Groups arrived and proceeded to register, and also A/178 and C/181 Batteries, lent by the 40th Division. The Heavy Artillery consisted of 8 9·2-in. Howitzers, 10 8-in. Howitzers, 35 6-in. Howitzers and 13 60-prs., organized in three groups under Brigadier-General A. E. J. Perkins, G.O.C. III Corps, H.A.

The principal work in preparing the ground for the attack was the provision of brigade and battalion battle headquarters, and of accommodation for the increased number of troops in the forward area ; the making of forming up trenches for the attack on The Knoll ; buried cable routes, and emplacements, and dug-outs for trench mortars. Battle headquarters for one brigade and three battalions were made by extending existing mined company headquarters, and splinter proof shelters for 300 men were made in a sunken road at Lempire. Mined dug-outs were prepared for trench mortar batteries of all calibres, and a forming-up trench for the right battalion of The Knoll attack was cut 400 yards in advance of the line of posts with a communication trench to Ego Post.

Between 3,000 and 4,000 yards of cable trench, six feet deep, was dug, connecting up company headquarters, Gillemont and battalion battle headquarters at Fleeceall and Ego to a central telephone dug-out in rear of Sart Farm, whence cables were laid above ground.

---

[1] The artillery was grouped as follows :—
   Right Group : Colonel L. M. Wilson, 157th Brigade and 295th Brigade.
   Centre Group : Lieut.-Colonel B. H. Shaw-Stewart, " Q " and " U," R.H.A., C/159, A/178, A/296, D/210.
   Left Group : Lieut.-Colonel H. M. Davson, A, B and D/159, B and D/296, C/181.

The artillery preparation was carried out on August 17th and 18th. Previous to this, 500 rounds per gun of 13-pr. and 18-pr. and 300 rounds per 4.5-in. Howitzer were dumped at the gun positions and extra telephone lines were laid under the superintendence of the Divisional Artillery Signal Officer. The approximate amount of twisted cable laid was 120 miles.

On the 17th the heavy artillery carried out counter-battery work with 6-in. howitzers. In order to give the enemy no indication of the concentration of heavy guns, the 8-in. and 9.2-in. howitzers did not commence firing until the following day. The field batteries concentrated on hostile observation posts, lighter defences, and wire along a front of about 3,000 yards. The weather was favourable for aeroplane reconnaissance and satisfactory results were obtained.

The artillery officers, as well as those of other arms interested in the attack, had attended the rehearsals and studied the method of advance, and on August 15th the Army and Corps' Commanders were present and expressed themselves as well pleased with all that they had seen.

On the 10th the 16/Cheshire had moved up into the line and relieved the 17/West Yorkshire on the front of assault. From now onwards this battalion was engaged in preparing jumping-off places, in putting out dummy wire and generally making preparations for the attack. On the next day the 19/Durham L.I. was relieved in the line by the III Corps Cyclist Company, except for one company which was left as a reserve.

AUGUST 19TH. THE KNOLL

On the 16th Brigadier-General Marindin moved his headquarters up to the northern end of Lempire where it was accommodated in cellars and dug-outs, and, on the next day, the two assaulting battalions moved to camps near St. Emilie. The 14/Gloucester was in readiness in Lempire and St. Emilie, and the 16/Cheshire, as already stated, in the line. On the night of the 18th the attacking battalions marched to their assault positions. Routes had been carefully laid out so that there should be no mistake in the advance. The battalions left camp at 10 p.m. and reached their advanced dumps about 1.10 a.m., where stores were issued to companies as they filed past. All companies were in their battle positions 40 minutes before zero and at 15 minutes before they left the trenches and alined themselves on tapes previously laid out. This position was taken up with but two casualties (15/Sherwood) owing to a burst of fire on Fleeceall Post.

The artillery bombardment commenced at 4 a.m. on the 19th. The 13- and 18-prs. barraged the front line and lifted in steps of 100 yards as the infantry advanced. Low-burst shrapnel was used and the density of the barrage was 17 yards per gun. The

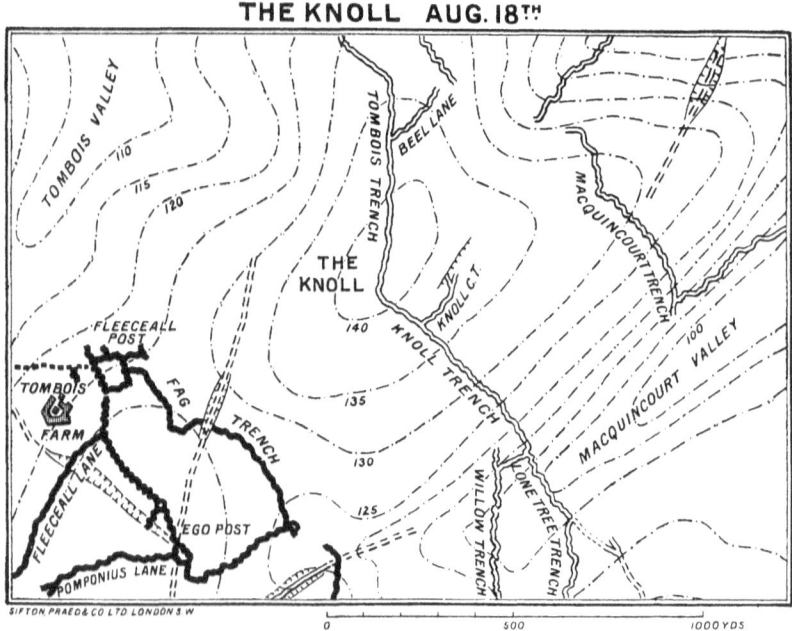

4·5-in. howitzers formed flank barrages, and fired on trenches behind the front line and on trench junctions. The 2-in. trench mortars formed a right flank barrage at Gillemont Farm; one 9·45-in. trench mortar blocked a trench junction in the same area and another (from Tombois Farm, 2,000 yards away) fired on the cross roads at Vendhuille.[1]

From zero onwards the heavy artillery neutralized hostile bat-

[1] The latter only fired five rounds and was then put out of action by a direct hit. The former fired twenty rounds under heavy hostile shrapnel fire. Z/35 Medium Trench Mortar Battery had both emplacements destroyed by direct hits.

teries, also trench mortars, machine-guns, and dug-outs. The 60-prs. searched the lines of approach.

At 4 a.m. the infantry advanced. The 15/Cheshire was on the right, the 15/Sherwood Foresters on the left. Wire had been cut for 500 yards on each side of The Knoll. Air observation reported it as generally destroyed and this was confirmed by the assaulting troops. The battalions assaulted on a two-company front, each in two waves of two lines, and advanced directly under the barrage. They reached the enemy trenches on The Knoll just as the barrage lifted and passed over the position leaving the support companies to "mop-up" and consolidate. The 16/Cheshire held the original line and supplied carrying parties. Entrances to the old German line were blocked, carrying parties followed with crates and the work of consolidation commenced. The whole assault had only occupied fifteen minutes. A small counter-attack from the direction of Lone Tree was scattered by Lewis gun fire. The assaulting companies, which had formed covering parties during consolidation, were gradually withdrawn, and, with the wounded and prisoners, were back in their own lines by 5.40 a.m.

The spirit of the troops had been excellent. All attempts at resistance on the part of the enemy had been blotted out, and, as a further example, it may be mentioned that at daylight, after the assaulting companies had been withdrawn, two men of the consolidating company of the 15/Cheshire, Lance-Corporal Morgan and Private Winstanley, marked 10 Germans standing near a dug-out in front of our new line and immediately rushed them. They killed 3, wounded and captured 2 more, and the remaining 5 fled. Three 77-m.m. trench mortars were found in the dug-out and triumphantly brought in.

Meanwhile the 15/Sherwood had worked some distance down Tino Trench and established a block. The party reported the trench as unoccupied for another 300 yards. As a matter of fact, it was reported by artillery F.O.O.'s in the neighbourhood of Grafton Post as obliterated and empty as far as the road leading from Little Priel Farm to Vendhuille, and it is much to be regretted that troops were not available to occupy and consolidate this as its possession would have had an effect on the operations which followed. Communication by visual and buzzer was quickly established, and, in a remarkably short time, a telephone wire was run out by Lieutenant Almack, " Q " Battery, R.H.A., who was acting as artillery F.O.O. This line was of great value to all concerned, and for some time was the only telephone communication with the front line.

The casualties to our troops were not heavy. The 15/Sherwood Foresters lost 27 killed, 51 wounded and 5 missing. The 15/Cheshire lost Captain G. E. Shultz, the leader of one of the assaulting companies, who died of wounds. 2nd Lieutenant T. Grace was killed as well as 23 other ranks. 2nd Lieutenant C. F. Tissington, commanding the reserve company, and 96 other ranks were wounded. There were also 7 other ranks missing. The 16/Cheshire had 14 wounded, including Captain Bacon and 2nd Lieutenants Johnston and Miller, and the 14/Gloucester, 1 killed and 4 wounded.

The enemy suffered severely. Seventeen prisoners, including 1 officer, were captured, and the assaulting troops reported a large number of dead upon The Knoll in addition to those killed in hand-to-hand fighting during the attack. Three 4-in. and two light trench mortars were brought in in addition to a considerable amount of equipment.

Work was now commenced on a new trench on the forward cres which was completed on the following night. The Pioneers constructed a communication trench back to the sunken road, and a second was dug later. These were named Crellin and Cochran Avenues, after the two battalion commanders, and connected The Knoll with Fleeceall and Ego Posts. All these new trenches were fully wired.

The first organized counter-attack (on a small scale) took place at 6 a.m., but the work of consolidation, covered by an artillery smoke screen, went on for an hour later. The Knoll was heavily shelled at intervals throughout the day, and several counter-attacks were attempted but driven off. Work was continued without intermission ; new trenches were made and wire put up. The enemy assembled once or twice on the 20th but no attack materialized. On the 21st, however, at 3.15 a.m., a determined assault was made, covered by flammenwerfer. The 14/Gloucester were holding The Knoll at the time, and for a short period, in face of the flammenwerfer fire, gave ground on the right. This ground was immediately recovered and the enemy retired, leaving behind dead which were

VIEW FROM THE KNOLL, LOOKING NORTH.   From Sketch made August 27th, 1917.

identified as belonging to a new battalion. The fact that the artillery barrage had been thinned on account of the raids to the north increased the difficulty of the defence.

A conspicuous act of gallantry is recorded on the part of 2nd Lieutenant Hardy Falconer Parsons, of this battalion, who was in charge of the southern bombing post. The bombers holding the post were forced back by the blasts of the flammenwerfer " but 2nd Lieutenant Parsons remained at his post, and single-handed, although severely scorched and burnt by liquid fire, he continued to hold up the enemy with bombs until severely wounded. This very gallant act of self-sacrifice and devotion to duty undoubtedly delayed the enemy long enough to allow of the organization of a bombing party which succeeded in driving back the enemy before they could enter any portion of the trenches. The gallant officer succumbed to his wounds."[1]

GILLEMONT FARM

The object of the attack of the 18/Highland L.I. was a semi-circular trench which was situated to the east of the farm and ended about 250 yards north and south of it. Two companies were detailed for the assault under Captains Bryan and Barrie, the whole force being commanded by Captain W. A. Murray.

The companies were in position west and south of the farm at 2 a.m., and, unfortunately between that hour and zero, the left company was subjected to a severe trench mortar bombardment, and a number of casualties was caused. The casualties were replaced, and the companies advanced at the appointed hour. The hostile trenches were found strongly garrisoned and hand-to-hand fighting took place. The enemy was driven out, and the work of consolidation commenced. The casualties in the actual assault were not many. Most of them occurred before the attack was launched. The total was 4 officers wounded, 22 other ranks killed, 86 wounded, and 4 missing. Two machine-guns and 13 unwounded prisoners were captured.

[1] His Majesty the King wrote, October 24th, 1917 :—" It is a matter of sincere regret to me that the death of Temporary 2nd Lieutenant Hardy Falconer Parsons deprives me of the pride of personally conferring upon him the Victoria Cross, the greatest of all awards for Valour and Devotion to Duty." This award was granted posthumously. 2nd Lieutenant Parsons was a student in the Medical School of the University of Bristol, and eldest son of the Rev. J. Ash Parsons of Bristol.

The enemy took his defeat very quietly, and it was not until 4.20 a.m. next morning that, under cover of an intense bombardment and ground mist, he made a determined counter attack. This

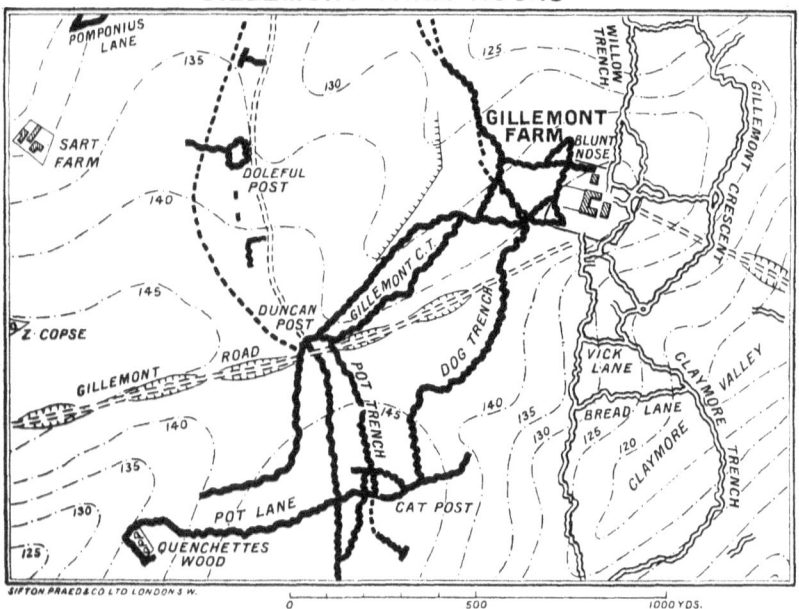

GILLEMONT FARM AUG. 18TH

attack developed along the whole front of the captured position. The artillery defensive barrage descended at once and caught the second hostile wave as it advanced, completely demoralizing the assault and inflicting severe casualties. The leading troops were destroyed by rifle fire, Lewis gun fire, and bombs.

The old German line was fortified and communication trenches cut by the Pioneers through to the forward slope. The whole captured trench—600 yards—was wired by the Royal Engineers and 100 infantry during the night.

THE RAIDS ON OSSUS

On the 19th/20th the 104th Brigade relieved the Secunderabad Dismounted Cavalry Brigade in the right section of the Epéhy front, and at 4.25 a.m. on the 21st a raid was carried out against the enemy trenches between Ossus and Canal Woods. This was entrusted to the 17/Lancashire Fusiliers and to the 23/Manchester.[1] In spite of a considerable amount of intermittent shelling during the night the forming up of the raiding parties was carried out without a hitch.

Unfortunately, at 4 a.m. an S.O.S. went up from The Knoll. The subsequent barrage drew retaliation from the enemy, and the 23/Manchester suffered severe casualties whilst the parties were waiting to start off.

In order to give no indication of the coming raid, it had been decided that no preliminary wire cutting should take place, but that the raiders should trust to the artillery barrage to enable them to cross the wire, which was reported to be thin. It was, however, found to be much thicker than had been anticipated, and this caused such delay that the barrage had been lifted off the trenches before it had been cut.

As a result the enemy was able to man the parapet and to open fire and throw bombs. In spite of this, the raiding parties forced their way into the trenches where a sharp fight ensued. The hostile resistance was overcome and the parties proceeded to their second objective, but time was not sufficient to allow of their completing it. Several dug-outs were bombed and considerable casualties inflicted on the enemy. Ten prisoners belonging to the 10th Bavarian Division were brought in. The casualties amounted to 7 officers wounded,[2] 7 other ranks killed, and 95 wounded; many very slightly.

In this battle the men of the Lancashire Fusiliers went into action with red and white roses in their steel hats as their predecessors had done 156 years before. The difference being that their former enemy was now their ally and the descendants of their former allies were fighting against them.[3]

Farther to the north, at 11 p.m., a company composed of 75 officers and men of the 20/Lancashire Fusiliers under Captain Cressy raided the enemy trenches west of Les Tranchées.

As a result of the morning's experience, it was decided to cut the

[1] " W " and " X " Companies of the 17/L.F. and 14 officers and 259 other ranks of the 23/Manchester.
[2] Including Lieutenants G. MacKenzie, M.C., W. B. K. Glass, and J. R. Hamilton. The 10th Bavarian Division was new to this front.
[3] The 17/L.F. celebrated Minden Day on August 8th. The other two battalions observed it some days later.

wire here, and, during the afternoon, 100 rounds from 6-in. howitzers were fired into it with observation from the air. The raiders, however, found the wire not properly cut and very strong, but a gap was blown in it by a Bangalore torpedo, through which some of the party passed whilst others crossed with the aid of mats. During the delay the enemy opened a trench mortar bombardment on his own wire, which caused some casualties.

The trenches, when entered, were found to be deserted and no identification was obtained. The casualties were 2nd Lieutenant Campbell and 20 other ranks wounded.

The day of the 22nd was comparatively quiet, and no infantry attacks took place. The hostile artillery was active, and on two occasions our guns were called upon for counter-preparation barrage in front of The Knoll and Gillemont. The northern end of Lempire was heavily shelled, and General Marindin was forced to move his brigade headquarters. Nearly all the battery positions were subjected to bombardment, as also was Ronnsoy Wood. The artillery was now reorganized into two groups, nearly all the reinforcing batteries withdrew from action, and the S.O.S. lines were modified.

The 104th Brigade relieved the III Corps Cyclist Battalion and the Sialkot Cavalry Brigade in The Birdcage and Honnecourt subsections, and so, except for the temporary addition of three field batteries, the 35th Division remained *in statu quo ante bellum*.[1]

THE LOSS OF GILLEMONT AND THE KNOLL

In addition to the above mentioned withdrawal of guns, certain batteries had been lent to the 34th Division for an impending

[1] The ammunition expenditure for the period August 19th to 23rd was as follows :

CORPS H.A. (approx.)		35TH D.A.	
Guns	Rounds	Guns	Rounds
6 in. how.	16,500	13 prs.	6,958 (12 guns)
8 in. ,,	3,400	18 prs.	47,473 (58 guns)
9·2 in. ,,	1,800	4·5 in. how.	14,466 (24 guns)
60 prs.	1,200	9·45 in. T.M.	104 (2 guns)
		2 in. T.M.	652 (8 guns)

From noon August 18th to noon August 19th the rounds *per gun* were :

Guns	Rounds	Weight		
13 pr.	406	2 tons	7 cwt.	14 lbs.
18 pr.	504	4 ,,	1 ,,	0 ,,
4·5 in. how.	389	6 ,,	5 ,,	4 ,,

The machine-guns of the division during the period 19th to 23rd fired 1,161,750 rounds.

attack on Malakoff and Cologne Farms which lay respectively northeast and east of Hargicourt on the right of the front held by the 35th Division. A Chinese attack was carried out on these objectives at 5.30 a.m. on the 25th.

During the previous night the 18/Highland L.I. had relieved the 19/Durham L.I. in the Gillemont Farm trenches, and, at 4 a.m., the enemy began shelling the rear of the farm, and this fire increased until 4.15 a.m., when an intense bombardment of guns and trench mortars was opened on the defences. The fire was accurate. Heavy losses were incurred by the garrison, and the Lewis guns were put out of action.

Our counter barrage, unfortunately, was weak and slow in opening. The batteries of the left group were engaged in replying to an S.O.S. call from The Knoll, and from the right group 14 guns were laid on the 34th divisional front, and it was some minutes before these were able to switch back on to their barrage lines. Profiting by this, the enemy attacked up their old communication trenches leading to the farm, and also from right and left along their old front line towards the bombing blocks.

The right flank held and beat off the attack. The left flank suffered severely. All 3 officers were disabled, and, out of 70 men, only 20 survived. The enemy was thus enabled to effect an entry. He bombed along the front line trench for about 200 yards until held up by one of the posts. The garrison of this offered stubborn resistance, but was outflanked and compelled to retire, thus obliging that on the right flank to do likewise. After a short retirement a block was formed, and, on reinforcements arriving from Doleful Post, a counter attack was made under command of Captain Jackson. The men rushed over the open but were caught in the hostile barrage, Captain Jackson being killed and another officer wounded. A further attempt to advance up the trenches having failed, the garrison fortified the position in which they found themselves, which was in rear of our original front line. The casualties amounted to about 160, including 7 officers, so that the battalion had become somewhat disorganized, and all the Stokes mortars and machine-guns were either lost or damaged.

Under these circumstances it was deemed inadvisable to make any further effort at the moment, and it was arranged that the

19/Durham L.I. should attack in the evening. Meanwhile, two batteries of heavy howitzers were placed at the disposal of the G.O.C. 35th Division, with which to carry out a deliberate bombardment of the enemy positions throughout the day.

This attack was delivered at 7.30 p.m. The battalion had advanced from Lempire across the open to Duncan Lane and from assembly positions in advance of it. Under a close artillery barrage, three weak companies advanced to the assault. The enemy in front was kept down by the barrage, but rifle fire from a flank caused some casualties. A party of Jägers offered stubborn resistance at a salient in the old front line known as the "Blunt Nose," but this was overcome and 6 of the enemy were killed. The old front line was re-established, and 3 Stokes mortars and a Lewis gun recaptured, as well as a German machine-gun. The Germans made two counter attacks from Willow Trench and one from the south-east, but all were repulsed.

In this fighting Captain G. R. Forster and 2nd Lieutenant G. W. Berry were killed, as well as 10 other ranks. Thirty-eight men were wounded. The battalion then relieved the 18/Highland L.I. in the line.

On the 26th the 34th Division captured the Cologne Farm Ridge which helped to ease the situation on the divisional front. To assist this a barrage was put down in front of The Knoll and at the same time the Stokes mortars from there bombarded a German bombing post about 80 yards south of Dolan Post.[1] Under cover of this, Sergeant Wilkinson, 16/Cheshire, led out a party and rushed the post. Six dead Germans were found. A dug-out was bombed and the post destroyed. In spite of having been bombed as it advanced, the party returned without casualties.

A portion of the 296th Brigade, R.F.A., which still remained in action under the 35th Division, was now withdrawn, and the divisional artillery alone covered the front.

Except for some bombardments of Gillemont, where the enemy evidently feared a counter attack, the next three days passed quietly. The 27th and 28th were very wet and windy. The 106th

---

[1] The two posts on the right and left flanks of The Knoll were named Dolan and Smisson respectively, after the two chaplains attached to the 15/Cheshire and 15/Sherwood Foresters. They had accompanied their respective units in the attack.

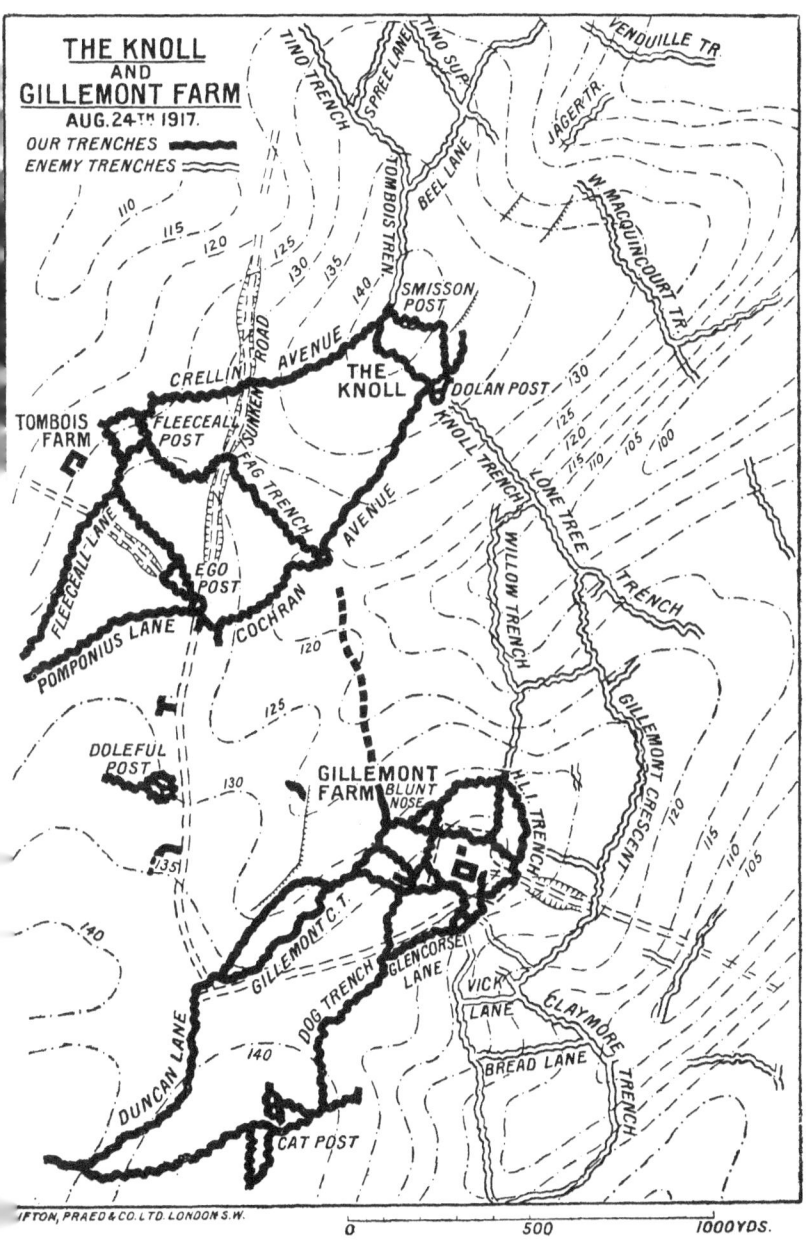

Brigade relieved the 105th in The Knoll subsection, and the 17/West Yorkshire occupied The Knoll itself.

On August 30th The Knoll was shelled all day as also were all the battery positions, and at 4.30 a.m. next morning an intense fire was opened on The Knoll, Gillemont, and Cologne Farm. The S.O.S. signal was sent up from all three places almost simultaneously. The available guns for reply to the 35th Division call were 26 18-prs. and 12 4·5-in. howitzers; the remaining 10 18-prs. were detached under the 34th Division. There was also one 9·2-in. howitzer battery and 1 6-in. howitzer battery. It will be seen that the answering barrage of our guns was not very dense.

The hostile bombardment of The Knoll was particularly violent. Trench mortars were used against the position itself whilst the artillery fired on the approaches, supporting points, and batteries.

What actually happened is somewhat obscure as there was a mist on the ground and the enemy attacked through a smoke barrage. Also all communications were cut at once, and information as to the progress of events could not be obtained. The enemy appears to have made his main attack from the north, having apparently used Tombois Trench as a jumping-off place, but a subsidiary attack was made on Dolan Post. No further information was received for some time except from the 19/Durham L.I., holding Gillemont, who reported that no attack was taking place and this permitted of more guns being switched on to The Knoll.

The enemy, however, gained a footing on The Knoll and overcame the two companies of the 17/West Yorkshire which were holding the position. The survivors withdrew and formed blocks in Crellin Avenue just west of the sunken road and in Cochran Avenue just east of Fag Trench.

At 7.55 a.m. the situation became sufficiently clear to admit of our guns opening fire on Tombois Trench and subsequently on The Knoll itself. Meanwhile, General Pollard had ordered forward all available troops, and, at 9 a.m., the barrage on The Knoll was intensified, and a third company of the 17/West Yorkshire, which had been moved up from Sart Lane, advanced along Cochran Avenue in an endeavour to re-take the lost position. This company got within 80 yards of the top of the hill but was unable to advance further. It then withdrew to the blocks. By order of the

Divisional Commander no further attacks were to be launched for the time being.

The casualties to the battalion amounted to 2 officers killed, 6 wounded, and 5 missing. Of other ranks, 7 were killed, 56 wounded, and 53 missing. The artillery F.O.O., 2nd Lieutenant P. R. Forster, was also killed on the position. The casualties amongst the other battalions were slight.

Although the recapture of The Knoll and Gillemont Farm was a disappointment, it is not to be assumed that the victory which had been gained by the troops of the 35th Division was thereby rendered negative.

In the first place it brought together a large concentration of hostile troops. Previous to the attack, the enemy had held the line from Gillemont Farm to The Knoll with one battalion belonging to the centre regiment of the 195th Division. During the fighting the following identifications were obtained, namely, 6th, 8th, and 24th Jäger Regiments, 16th Bavarian Regiment, 20th Bavarian Pioneers, and 5th Battery, F.A. Regiment. In addition, if only for 10 days, a complete view was obtained of German positions along the canal and sketches of these were preserved. Finally, the losses inflicted on the enemy were severe, and must have greatly exceeded our own, which approximately amounted to 60 officers and 1,200 men killed, wounded, and missing.

CHAPTER X

SEPTEMBER, 1917

THE opening days of September were noticeable for some heavy shelling on the part of the enemy. In addition to such places as Little Priel Farm, Lempire and certain battery positions, a good deal of fire was directed on Ronnsoy Village and the quarry 1,000 yards to the south of it.

The 105th Brigade relieved the 106th in the right subsector, but, as the brigade advanced headquarters was being persistently shelled, the Divisional Commander gave instructions that the former headquarters in St. Emilie should be used.

At midnight on the 2nd/3rd, a violent bombardment opened on Gillemont and Cat Post, and the S.O.S. signal went up from the former place. Artillery and machine-guns opened fire until word was received from the 14/Gloucester that the signal had been sent up by the enemy, and that no infantry attack was being delivered.

A good deal of movement was observed behind the enemy's lines and he dug a new trench north of Canal Wood. After a few days the movement subsided, and the hostile fire became normal.

On the 9th the 34th Division made a further attack upon the enemy trenches, and the 35th Divisional Artillery co-operated. The attack was successful and the positions retained.[1] Advantage was taken of this by the 16/Cheshire, when a party under 2nd Lieutenant Barber tried to rush the enemy bombing block at Gillemont Farm. The wire was found to be too strong, the enemy too alert, and in the subsequent trench-mortar bombardment several casualties were incurred. Lieutenant Barber was himself hurt in trying to bring in some of the wounded.

[1] On the 10th a heavy concentration of guns and storm troops forced this division to relinquish most of the ground lately gained. This day, the 9th, was the occasion of the somewhat well-known story of the captured German watchdog. He was standing savagely beside a wounded man, and an officer was about to shoot him. The dog slunk behind him and followed him about all day. He eventually became a regimental mascot, but would allow no stranger to approach his new master.

Next day the forward part of The Birdcage, which had been demolished and wired up for some days, was finally evacuated and the main line was withdrawn some 250 yards west of the point of the work. By this means the defence was strengthened and the necessity obviated of holding an advanced salient which gave no advantage of view or field of fire.

At midnight four days later the enemy heavily bombarded The Birdcage. As an attack appeared imminent the S.O.S. signal was sent up, but, as far as could be ascertained at the time, no attack developed. Some casualties were caused to the 17/West Yorkshire, who were holding the position. During the next two nights two German bombs and two boxes of explosives were discovered in our wire at the north-east corner, from which it appeared evident that some form of attack was intended.

On the 6th the 106th Brigade had relieved the 104th in the northern sector, and on the 11th the 104th took over the Lempire front from the 105th.

On the 16th at 9 p.m. the 17/Royal Scots raided the enemy trenches in the valley immediately south of Canal Wood.

The raid was made by 3 officers and 36 other ranks under an artillery barrage. No difficulty was experienced in crossing the German wire, and three parties entered the centre of the trench and bombed right and left. Inhabited dug-outs were bombed and several of the enemy were killed in the trench. The raiders then returned bringing with them 2 prisoners belonging to the 16th Bavarian Regiment. 2nd Lieutenant Struth was killed and 4 other ranks wounded. Unfortunately, Major R. D. Harisson, R.F.A., who was acting as artillery liaison officer in Pigeon Quarry, also lost his life. He had gone forward with Lieutenant-Colonel Heathcote and Captain Rycroft, the brigade major, to speed the raiding party, and was mortally wounded by a machine-gun bullet. He died twenty minutes later.

At this time the 18/Highland L.I. received drafts of four officers and 230 other ranks from the Glasgow Yeomanry and the official designation of the battalion was altered to the 18th (Glasgow Yeomanry) Battalion, Highland L.I.

On the 18th the 106th Brigade was relieved in the right sector by the 105th.

September 24, 1917

The next few days were chiefly noticeable for artillery activity. The enemy persistently shelled Ego and Fleeceall Posts, Eagle Quarry, Little Priel Farm, and Villers Guislain, but without any appreciable result. As Little Priel Farm was never occupied, except by an occasional artillery observing officer, ammunition fired at it was wasted. On our side, the 4·5-in. howitzers carried out a destructive shoot with aeroplane observation on a heavy trench mortar situated close to Franque Wood, south of Honnecourt, and a roving gun of A/159 Battery was pushed forward and fired a large number of rounds into Richmond Quarry, which was situated just behind the Hindenburg Line, about a mile north-east of the canal at Putney.

On the 24th the 104th Brigade carried out two raids on the hostile trenches south of The Knoll.

From 3 to 6 p.m. howitzers cut the wire at two points, one just south of Dolan Post and another at the trench junction in Willow Trench due east of Doleful Post. At 10.45 p.m. under a heavy artillery and trench mortar barrage, in which 4 6-in. howitzers co-operated and which extended from The Knoll to Gillemont, the raiding parties advanced. Lieutenant A. Wallis and 46 other ranks of the 17/Lancashire Fusiliers assaulted Willow Trench, and 3 officers and 56 men of the 18/Lancashire Fusiliers attacked Knoll Trench. It was found that the wire had been repaired and it had to be re-cut with Bangalore Torpedoes. In Willow Trench no enemy was found, but identification of the 184th Regiment was obtained from a greatcoat. In Knoll Trench the enemy was encountered and overcome; several dug-outs were bombed and destroyed, and the party returned with 4 prisoners of the 440th Reserve Regiment. It was reported that several of the enemy had been buried during the bombardment. Lieutenant Wallis was wounded, also a few men.

In answer to this the enemy gun fire increased again. The Ossus Posts were this time chosen and destructive shoots with aeroplane observation were carried out against B/159 and C/159 Batteries. Four hundred rounds were fired with the result that two empty gun pits in front of the position of C/159 were destroyed.

Our artillery and trench mortars bombarded Honnecourt Wood with high explosives and Thermite as a diversion for operations of the 40th Division on our left. A patrol afterwards reconnoitred the wood, but was held up by wire.

The 106th Brigade then relieved the 104th in the right sector, and, in the early morning of the 27th, the enemy bombarded a point of the trenches held by the 18/Highland L.I. on the north side of Gillemont. The garrison, a Lewis gun detachment, moved to an alternative position, but two of the men got separated and had an encounter with five Germans who entered the trench. One man, although wounded, fought his way through, but the other was apparently captured.

On the 29th, a patrol of the 14/Gloucester consisting of two officers and 25 other ranks attempted a raid on Crawford Crater opposite Les Tranchés. It started in a mist at 1 a.m., but, on getting to the wire, the mist cleared and fire was opened. The men cut the wire but were unable to enter the crater and withdrew with a loss of one officer and 4 other ranks wounded.

On the night of September 30th/October 1st, the 166th Brigade relieved the 105th in the left sector. The 105th then withdrew to Aizecourt. On the 2nd/3rd October the 106th Brigade was relieved by the 165th, and on that day the command of the line passed to the 55th Division.

On September 16th the following letter was received from Army Headquarters, dated the 13th :—

"The Army Commander has the greatest pleasure in communicating the following message received from the Commander-in-Chief, and wishes to add his sincere congratulations to those who have prepared and carried out these successful operations.

"' The Commander-in-Chief congratulates you and your troops on the repeated successes gained in your local operations which show excellent spirit and skill. These successes help appreciably in the general plan.'

"(Signed) LOUIS VAUGHAN, M.G.G.S.,
"Third Army."

Meanwhile the following alterations had taken place in the personnel of the division.

On August 9th Lieutenant C. W. Farrish, who had previously

been Presbyterian chaplain to the artillery, rejoined the division as a combatant officer, and was posted to the 157th Brigade, R.F.A.

On September 3rd Colonel C. R. Newman, G.S.O.I., was, much to everybody's regret, transferred to the 61st Division. This change was rendered necessary owing to the fact that both the commander and the G.S.O.I. belonged to the Royal Artillery. Colonel Newman was succeeded by Lieut.-Colonel H. W. B. Thorp, King's Own Yorkshire L.I.

A few days later, Lieut.-Colonel H. Farmar succeeded Lieut.-Colonel Hare as A.Q.M.G. of the division, and at the same time, Lieut.-Colonel Rushton, commanding Royal Engineers, was appointed C.R.E. of a corps, and his place was taken by Lieut.-Colonel Skipwith.

Plate III

MAJOR-GENERAL G. MACK. FRANKS, C.B.
Commanding Division July 1917 to March 1918.

CHAPTER XI

HOUTHULST

IN the beginning of October the infantry brigades moved to the area west of Arras. The 104th Brigade to Manin, the 105th to Warlus, and the 106th to Agnez les Duisans. The 19/Northumberland Fusiliers and the Royal Engineers, after having withdrawn to Bapaume, rejoined the division in the Arras area on October 6th. The artillery brigades were relieved in the line on the 3rd/4th/5th, and marched to Buire, east of Peronne.

Whilst in these areas battalions and batteries refitted, and the former went through a course of training in the conditions prevailing in the battle area of the Passchendaele Ridge, to which the division was now due to proceed. This training was continued until the 12th, and on the following day the 104th Brigade entrained at Aubigny for Esquelbecq and marched from there to Eringhem and Zeggers Cappel. The 105th Brigade entrained at Arras for Cassel and Bavinchove, and marched to Arneke and Ledringhem; and the 106th Brigade at Arras and Aubigny for Cassel *en route* for Rubrouck and Zeggers Cappel.

The 157th and 159th Brigades, R.F.A., entrained at Chapelette and Peronne for Proven and Esquelbecq respectively. The 159th Brigade marched from there to White Hope Corner near Elverdinghe, and the 157th to a camp south of Boesinghe. On the 12th, divisional headquarters had moved to Lederzeele, and on the 17th it arrived at Elverdinghe Chateau.

Meanwhile, the infantry brigades had proceeded by train to the Proven Area,[1] and, on October 16th, the 104th Brigade relieved the 3rd Guards Brigade in the left division front of the XIV Corps. The front extended from the Ypres-Staden Railway to a point 250 yards south-east of the Faidherbe Cross Roads.[2]

The division was now to take part in what afterwards became

---

[1] Proven is four miles north-west of Poperinghe, on the Dunkerque road.
[2] Vide sketch map p. 167.

known as the Third Battle of Ypres, and it was fought under conditions of bad weather and a heavy concentration of hostile fire which tried the spirit and endurance of the troops engaged in it to the very utmost. August had been very wet, and that, and heavy shells had turned the battlefield into a sea of mud, thickly pitted with water-logged shell holes. The one and only advantage obtained from this was that a fair proportion of the heavy shells which were fired upon the area either failed to burst at all or else burst so deep in the ground as to have but a local effect. With a firmer surface the casualties would have been even more severe than they were. Probably the enemy also benefited on this account, but, as, judging from air photographs, the ground behind his lines was not so churned up, it is possible that the effect of our shells was greater.

From a point four miles south of the city, at the northern end of the Wytschaete-Messines Ridge, the high ground ran roughly northeast for ten miles to Passchendaele,[1] and then northwards for a further two miles to Westroosbeke after which it sank into the Flanders Plain. A less elevated spur on this chain left the old British front line in the neighbourhood of Hooge, and continued north-west for about four miles until just beyond Pilckem and the Ypres-Staden Railway. The south-eastern portion of this had been in British hands since 1914, but the north-western portion, known to those who had held The Salient as the Pilckem Ridge, had passed out of the allied possession in April, 1915, and the front had been retired to the line from Wieltje to the canal at Boesinghe.

Four miles to the north of Pilckem lay the wooded area known as Houthulst Forest, a domain of irregular shape, extending to about 1,500 acres and composed of enclosures of deciduous trees in various stages of growth and divided by roads, rides, ditches, and fences, into rectangular portions from ten to twenty acres in extent. For the most part these enclosures were covered with thick undergrowth, and movement off the rides was difficult. The infantry of the division were destined to become well acquainted with this.

With a view to keeping pressure off the French in the southern portion of the war front, and also in the hope of denying to the enemy the use of the Belgian coast, it was decided to capture the

---

[1] This is pronounced Paskendaal in Flemish. To the British troops it was, and always will remain, Pashendale.

VIEW FROM WOOD HOUSE, PILCKEM, LOOKING OVER THE VALLEY OF THE STEENBEEK.

high ground referred to. The Battle of Messines, in June, had resulted in the capture of the Wyteschaete-Messines Ridge, which was strongly fortified and commanded a view over the British front south of Ypres, except such portions of it as were covered by Kemmel Hill and Sherpenberg.

On July 31st the main operation started, and resulted in the capture of the Pilckem Ridge and the gradual progression of the allied front to a line in advance of Passchendale, Poelcapelle and Bixschoote.

As already stated the 104th Brigade had taken over the line from near Faidherbe Cross Roads to the railway. The headquarters was at Fouche Farm on the rising ground south of the Steenbeek, and on the 16th the 105th Brigade relieved the 2nd Guards Division in the support area north-east of Elverdinghe with headquarters at Benson's Farm, west of Woesten. The 106th Brigade was in reserve in the Woesten area. On the left of the divisional front was the French 2nd Division, and on the right the 34th Division. Approach to the front line from the canal was obtained by means of two duckboard tracks known as Clarges Street and Hunter Street, which maintained a devious course between large shell holes filled with water. To step off these usually meant immersion, or at best, an extra coating of wet mud, and this accident was by no means rare, as it is not attractive to anyone to maintain a vertical position on a narrow board when shells fall close, particularly at night. These tracks crossed two marshy streams named the Steenbeek and the Broembeek, on which were many of the battery positions. They were persistently shelled with high explosive, and gas, especially at the points where the tracks crossed them. These bottoms were full of gas three nights out of four, and it will therefore be deduced that the management of reliefs and supplies to the front line was a matter of some difficulty. Assistance was obtained from the light railway which ran along the Staden railway line nearly as far as Langemarcke Station, and supplied the dumps of trench stores, bombs, and ammunition for heavy guns, but ordinary supplies were carried forward on the two tracks referred to except that the artillery pack horses carrying ammunition made a detour by a road slightly to the west which was kept in repair for the purpose.

On the 18th the 106th Brigade relieved the 104th in the line, and the latter retired to rest billets near De Wippe Cabaret, southwest of Woesten. At the same time the 105th Brigade Headquarters moved to Zommerbloom Cabaret, north of Elverdinghe.[1] The artillery covering the front as taken over by the C.R.A. 35th Division, was the 74th and 75th Brigades (Guards Artillery), 157th and 159th Brigades (35th Division). The group was commanded by Brigadier-General F. A. Wilson, Guards D.A. Under General Staveley's orders were also five brigades of artillery forming the right group of the corps' front under command of Brigadier-General Stevenson, G.O.C. 29th H.A.

In order to provide a strong left flank for the main advance it was arranged that the XIV Corps in conjunction with the French should advance northwards into Houthulst Forest. It was decided that the first attack of the 35th Division should be made by the 104th and 105th Brigades, and that the 106th Brigade, which was numerically weak,[2] should be kept in hand for a further advance. Accordingly, on the 20th, the 104th Brigade took up the line from Aden House to 5 Chemins with headquarters in Martin's Mill on the Langemarck-Wijdendrift road. The 105th Brigade continued from this point to the strong point north of Louvois Farm. The headquarters were in Wood 15. Fourche Farm, a mere shell reinforced with concrete, had been bombarded with 150 mm. (5·9-in.) shell throughout the day of the 19th, and with 8-in. during the morning of the 20th. After that, General Pollard felt obliged to move his headquarters to Saules Farm about half a mile in rear. This "pill box" was inadequate for a brigade headquarters, and so the blockhouses in Wood 15 were utilized.

The battalions, reading from right to left, were now 23/Manchester, 17/Lancashire Fusiliers, 16/Cheshire, and 14/Gloucester in touch with the 1st French Division.[3] The 157th Brigade, R.F.A., moved three batteries to the Wijdendrift Road, about half a mile west of Martin's Mill with headquarters at Lapin Farm. The 159th

---

[1] Just before the 17/Lancashire Fusiliers quitted the line the battalion headquarters at Vee Bend was visited by the Prince of Wales, then Staff Captain to the B.G.G.S. XIV Corps. The duckboard track ended at this point—beyond that the direction to the front line was only indicated by tapes laid over the mud.

[2] The strength of the 17/West Yorkshire was under 450 rifles.

[3] The 18/Lancashire Fusiliers were in close support, and during the attack came up between the 17/L.F. and the 23/Manchester. The 20/L.F. were in reserve on the line Vee Bend-Pascal Farm, and the 17/Royal Scots behind them on the line Koekuit-Namur Crossing.

Brigade, R.F.A., were in the valley of the Steenbeek with headquarters in an old German concreted battery position near Saules Farm. The whole of the artillery carried out a heavy bombardment throughout the day of the 21st to which the enemy replied. During the night the 105th Brigade captured a prisoner belonging to the 103rd R.I.R. (58th Division) which indicated that the enemy line had been strengthened.

Although for a few days prior to the attack the weather had been fine, a change occurred at the time when everyone desired the best of climatic conditions. The night 21st/22nd was bitterly cold. Rain commenced to fall about midnight and continued at intervals throughout the next day. The troops waiting in wet shell holes suffered severely, but their ardour was not damped although their clothing was. Hopes of having fairly dry ground for manœuvre were quickly dissipated and, in addition, the mechanism of the rifles suffered from rain and mud, and in many cases Stokes guns could not be brought forward.

OCTOBER 22ND : ATTACK OF THE 104TH BRIGADE

At 2 a.m. on the 22nd the battalions formed up on tapes in advance of the original line. This was done in order to escape the hostile shelling which covered the front line at dawn. The objective was the line from Six Roads to the junction of Conter Drive and the Colombo House road which was about 500 yards longer than the line then held and necessitated a diverging attack. The attack was launched at 5.35 a.m. under an artillery creeping barrage at the rate of 100 yards per 8 minutes. The 23/Manchester had been unable to gain touch with the 101st Brigade, 34th Division, on the right and this unfortunate accident had a serious influence on the succeeding operations.[1] The battalion, nevertheless, pushed on and reached the first objective in an advance of about half a mile. From this point the resistance became more stubborn, and the battalion was exposed to heavy machine-gun fire on the flanks from

[1] The reason of this was that the 101st Brigade was unable to take up a forward starting point owing to heavy hostile fire, and afterwards the barrage of its own artillery was reported as being so close in that the assaulting companies had to withdraw slightly until the barrage moved forward. Touch was never properly obtained although the left company reached, and for a short time held, the ultimate objective.

M

sets of huts which appear, to have been overlooked in the advance. All the officers and a large proportion of the N.C.O.'s were either killed or wounded, and the men were unable to make further progress. The survivors of the leading waves, in all about 50 men under command of a company-sergeant-major, were gradually withdrawn to the original line.[1] The losses were :—officers, 8 killed, 5 wounded, 1 missing; other ranks, 20 killed, 115 wounded, 55 missing. The 20/Lancashire Fusiliers were then ordered up in support. The 17/Royal Scots were in support behind them on the line Koekuit-Namur Crossing.

On the left flank the 17/Lancashire Fusiliers (Lieut.-Colonel Crook) advanced with resolution close under the barrage along the Colombo House-Marechal Farm Road in touch with the 16/Cheshire on their left. The left company (Captain Heape) passed Colombo House before 6 a.m., and at 6.45 messages were received from three company commanders simultaneously that the troops were on their final objective. All the company commanders were wounded in this attack. Unfortunately, a company of the 18/Lancashire Fusiliers, to whom fell the duty of filling the gap which would be left between the two battalions as they advanced, lost direction and moved too far to the left and had to be brought across, which caused delay. It then, however, went forward and entered the forest, being subjected to heavy machine-gun fire from the right flank, which was in the air. The Company Commander, Captain M. R. Wood, was killed here. 2nd Lieutenant Torrance, who had previously behaved with great gallantry, was wounded, and he and those with him were not seen again. The company was compelled to withdraw to the edge of the wood. " Y " Company had meanwhile kept touch with the 17/Lancashire Fusiliers and reached its objective on Conter Drive.[2] As the right flank was now exposed, at 8.35 a.m., General Sandilands sent up two more companies of the 20/Lancashire Fusiliers[3] to cover this, and at 10 a.m. these companies took up a line from a point 100 yards in advance of

---

[1] It is to be noted that the 16/Royal Scots, 34th Division, reported having given fire support to some of the 23/Manchester who were attacking a pill box near Six Roads. Reports from the battalion make no claim of having reached this point. The Royal Scots were forced to withdraw and no further information is available.

[2] A road through the forest passing Marechal Farm and continuing to Vijfwegen.

[3] Major Heelis was in command of the battalion. Lieut.-Colonel Vaughan had remained at De Wippe Cabaret.

October 22, 1917

Angle Point to one 200 yards in front of Aden House. Touch was then gained with the right of the 17/Lancashire Fusiliers, but no touch was obtained with the 34th Division except that a patrol found five wounded men. At midday the line held ran from Marechal Farm for a short distance along Conter Drive, then back to some huts about 500 yards north-east of Angle Point and so to Aden House. Except for the extreme left portion, this line was held until the brigade was relieved on the night 23rd/24th.

The 17/, 18/ and 20/Lancashire Fusiliers all used Egypt House as a battalion headquarters. The wounded were brought there also. It consisted merely of a group of small pill boxes. The accommodation was quite inadequate, and, being in a conspicuous position, it was heavily shelled by the enemy. But there was no alternative.

ATTACK OF THE 105TH BRIGADE

The 105th Brigade had occupied the line with the eventual support companies of the assaulting battalions, and the companies for the attack were in shell holes in rear.

On the night 21st/22nd these companies moved forward into assembly positions. The 15/Sherwood Foresters were in support on the line Strong Point, north of Louvois Farm–Obtuse Bend. The 15/Cheshire was in reserve in the neighbourhood of Wijdendrift. Right battalion headquarters (Lieut.-Colonel Dent) was in a pill box on the road 350 yards west of 5 Chemins, and the left battalion (Lieut.-Colonel Foord) at Louvois Farm.

The troops started close under the barrage, but, owing to the state of the ground, found some difficulty in keeping up with it. The right of the 16/Cheshire in touch with the battalion on the right gained ground rapidly and reached the final objective at Marechal Farm. The centre and left, however, were held up by fire from block-houses in the wood about 500 yards north-west of Colombo House. Colonel Dent went forward himself and superintended the capture of these points, but another check was sustained a short distance farther on. A line was consolidated there, linking up with " Z " Company (Captain Millington) which was consolidating Marechal Farm, and with the 14/Gloucester on the left. Meanwhile, a company of the 15/Sherwood Foresters occupied Colombo House.

On the left the 14/Gloucester had pushed forward in spite of opposition and occupied its first objective including Panama House at 6.15 a.m. Several casualties had occurred including Captain Baker, commanding the right company, who was severely wounded at the commencement of the advance. 2nd Lieutenant Draper had his knee-cap smashed at the same time, but he managed to struggle forward until the final objective was reached.

The left company was checked by a farm on the extreme left of the final objective but this was rushed by Captain Russel and a small party. A pill box in front of the right also gave some trouble, but by 7.45 a.m. the whole battalion was on the final objective and support lines were being consolidated. Touch had been lost with the right battalion, but Captain Russel, who was now in charge of the front line, managed to obtain contact and then called for assistance from Captain Harvey, 15/Sherwood Foresters, who led forward a platoon of his company to close the gap.

The very thorough reconnaissances which had been made by the officers of this battalion prior to the attack no doubt contributed greatly to the success of the operation.

Close touch had been kept with the French by means of a platoon detailed for the purpose by the brigade commander. The liaison between the two armies worked perfectly, and during the morning the French 201st Regiment had overcome all opposition and were in line with the 105th Brigade.[1]

As soon as he was aware of the check in the centre, General Marindin ordered up two companies of the reserve battalions to Louvois Farm–Obtuse Bend, and the remaining two companies to Wijdendrift. This battalion was not used at the time as, owing to future commitments, the divisional commander issued orders that the ground gained was to be held but local attacks were not to be attempted. The 17/West Yorkshire was lent to the brigade as reserve and moved to Koekuit.

THE COUNTER ATTACKS

From 2 p.m. to 4.30 p.m. the front remained comparatively quiet, but, at the latter hour, the enemy launched a determined

[1] As a result of this liaison General Marindin was appointed Officier of the Legion of Honour and Colonel Mangin, the French Commander, received the C.M.G. Several other officers of both armies received minor decorations. *Vide* Appendix.

OCTOBER 22, 1917

HISTORY OF THE 35TH DIVISION   165

counter attack against the left of the 16/Cheshire, and broke through the line. The remnants of the three companies of the 16/Cheshire and one company of the 15/Sherwood Foresters, which had come up in support, finding themselves isolated and partly surrounded, fell back from the forest for about 100 yards and there offered further resistance. They were eventually compelled to withdraw to the original line. This exposed the left of " Z " Company holding Marechal Farm, and the flank was thrown back to link up with the other companies on the road in rear. The right of the company still held a line in advance of the farm. Unfortunately, the officer commanding the left company of the 17/Lancashire Fusiliers, which had been firing into the flank of the enemy's advance, was misled by the refusal of the left of " Z " Company, 16/Cheshire. Being unaware that part of the company still remained in front of the farm and considering that the withdrawal placed his men in a dangerous salient, he also, about 6 p.m., decided to withdraw to the support line in order to conform to the movement. The remainder of " Z " Company were now quite isolated and Captain Millington ordered its withdrawal to Colombo House. The 18/Lancashire Fusiliers continued the line on the right as far as the neighbourhood of the huts.

The only battalion left on the original objective was the 14/Gloucester. The counter attack here was caught by the artillery barrage and was not pushed home, so that the troops had no difficulty in holding the ground gained. The right flank, however, was slightly refused in order to link up with the 16/Cheshire, and a platoon of the 15/Sherwood Foresters was placed in the gap.

Whilst these events were happening on the left the enemy were reported massing in the wood in front of the 17/ and 18/Lancashire Fusiliers. Artillery fire was called for and the area bombarded. Nevertheless, the enemy advanced to the attack, but was repulsed with heavy loss.

Communication at this time became extremely difficult. Heavy hostile barrages were put down behind our lines. and the neighbourhood of the various battalion headquarters was systematically shelled. Units, also, had become mixed up, and the men of the assaulting battalions were at length showing signs of exhaustion. The weather grew worse, and movement over the country became increasingly difficult. Fortunately, successful efforts to carry forward tea and rum to a great extent alleviated the sufferings of the troops. No further action took place on the 22nd, and the line was reorganized. The 23/Manchester was withdrawn, and its place filled by the 20/Lancashire Fusiliers. The 17/Royal Scots were moved up to Koekuit and placed under orders of the 104th Brigade. Both the assaulting battalions of the 105th Brigade were relieved, and the line was held with the 15/Cheshire, the 15/Sherwood Foresters being mostly in support.

OCTOBER 23RD AND 24TH

As General Sandilands considered that the huts situated 1,000 yards north of Aden House had been overlooked in the advance, and that the heavy losses of the 23/Manchester were partly attributable to this fact, he gave orders that the 20/Lancashire Fusiliers should raid them. This raid was carried out at 2 a.m. by a party under 2nd Lieutenant Harris. It surprised and captured a hostile machine-gun post, but when advancing against the huts the S.O.S. signal was sent up by the enemy, and an artillery barrage opened as well as machine-gun fire. Lieutenant Harris and another officer both fell, and considerable casualties were inflicted on the rank and file. As it was found impossible to occupy the huts the party withdrew.

At 5.30 a.m. the enemy again attacked the left flank of the 105th Brigade at its junction with the French. The line at this point was now held by the 15/Cheshire and one company of the 15/Sherwood Foresters [1] and the troops immediately opened rapid fire. The artillery defensive barrage descended at once, and the enemy was caught between that and the rifle fire and suffered severely. About twenty of the enemy gave themselves up, and it was considered that more were preparing to do so, but were shot by their own men from behind. Considerable numbers of the enemy were seen in shell holes, but it was impossible to get at these. The field batteries were then asked to cover the area with shrapnel, which was done. Forty dead Germans were counted in front of

[1] This company (X) had already been in action under the 14/Gloucester and was left holding its position when the 15/Cheshire took over the line. The other three companies of the 15/Sherwood Foresters were in support.

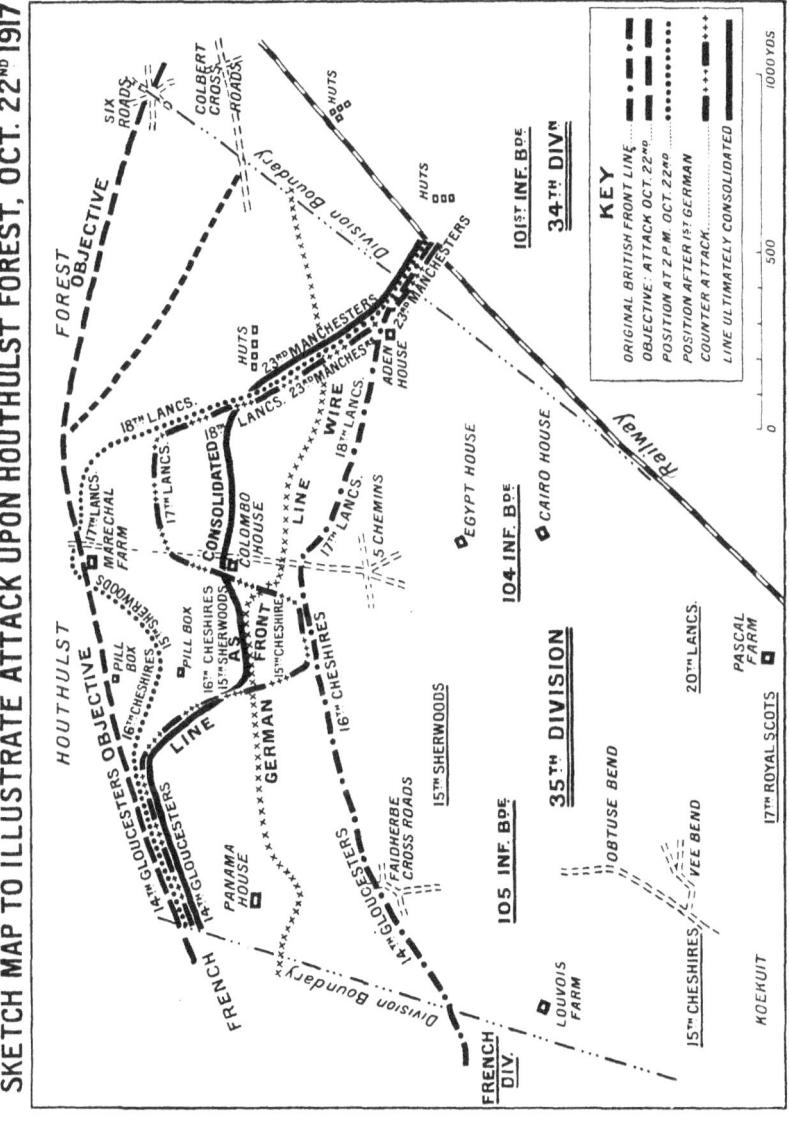

the position. The rest of the day passed without incident, and at night, in accordance with divisional orders, the 15/Cheshire advanced from the old front line at the base of the re-entrant and consolidated a position from just north of Colombo House for some 500 yards westward along the Panama House road. This meant an advance of 200 yards to the original first objective at this point.

During the night 23rd/24th the 106th Brigade relieved the 105th Brigade, less the 15/Cheshire, which remained in the line. This battalion was relieved on the following evening. The 17/Royal Scots remained at the disposal of the 104th Brigade.

On the evening of the 23rd the artillery groups were reorganized. General Staveley remained in command of the left group of the Corps Artillery which was now constituted as follows :—Right Group : (Lieut.-Colonel Davson, with headquarters at Wood House, Pilckem) 157th and 159th Brigades and certain batteries situated on the Broembeek ; Left Group : (Lieut.-Colonel Bethell, Guards D.A.) 74th and 75th Brigades. During the 22nd and 23rd the divisional artillery and attached brigades had fired 66,521 rounds of ammunition.

At 5.15 p.m. on the 24th the enemy made yet another counter attack on the left of the line. The battalion mostly concerned was the 19/Durham L.I., but the 15/Cheshire, which was in process of being relieved by the 18/Highland L.I., was also involved. The hostile bombardment was very heavy, and when signalled by red lights the barrage moved forward. It was calculated that the enemy force consisted of between three and four hundred men. The attack failed completely. Some sixty or seventy dead were counted in front of the position of the 19/Durham L.I., and a few prisoners were captured.

The day of the 24th was occupied by bombardments on the part of our artillery in preparation for the next attack. Seven thousand rounds were fired in area shoots along the front of the position, and extending back for a thousand yards. The hostile shelling to some extent died down.

During the night the 50th Division relieved the 34th Division, and the 7/Northumberland Fusiliers, 149th Brigade, relieved the 20/Lancashire Fusiliers and part of the 17/Royal Scots. The right boundary of the 35th Division was fixed at the road junction about

HISTORY OF THE 35TH DIVISION 169

600 yards north of Aden House. The 18/Highland L.I. extended their right of this point relieving the remainder of the 17/Royal Scots who went into brigade reserve. The 19/Durham L.I. held the left of the line. The 104th and 105th Brigades were in rest west of the canal. Divisional Headquarters, which had been at Zommerbloom Cabaret since the 23rd, withdrew to " J " Camp near St. Sixte.

In order to rest the troops just relieved from the battle front, the 51st Brigade, 17th Division, was placed at the disposal of the G.O.C. 35th Division, from the 26th to the 30th of October, and during the nights 26th/27th and 27th/28th two of its battalions relieved the 19/Durham L.I. and the 18/Highland L.I. in the line. The 106th Brigade withdrew to the Proven Area.

On the 26th, also, the 50th Division attacked on the right and the French on the left. The 35th Divisional Artillery fired in support of both operations. The left battalion of the 50th Division reached its objective, but, as the centre and right were held up, it had to be withdrawn at dusk. The French gained all objectives and succeeded in holding them. The enemy barrage caused a considerable number of casualties to the 106th Brigade.[1]

On the night 29th/30th, the 105th Brigade relieved the 51st Brigade in the front line, the 15/Sherwood Foresters being on the right and the 14/Gloucester on the left. Patrols pushed out through mud and water for 200 yards, but gained no contact with the enemy.

On the 30th the 35th Division passed from the XIV to the XIX Corps on the former being withdrawn.

The attack described above, the first attack on a large scale which the division had undertaken since its reorganization, earned the praise of the commanders of the Fifth Army and XIV Corps. This was all the more creditable seeing that the time for preparation was short and that the troops were unused to the shell hole line of trenches and bad communications.

The fact that the attack was not a complete success may be attributed to various reasons. Firstly, the loss of touch with the 34th Division which left the right flank isolated and so allowed

[1] The artillery supported further attacks by the French on the 27th and the XVIII Corps on the 29th. Some successes were obtained in both cases.

parties of the enemy to escape and eventually to bring fire to bear upon the flanks and rear. Secondly, certain strong points, notably the huts north of Aden House, were overlooked and caused considerable trouble and loss.

After the positions had been won, circumstances which could not have been foreseen by officers in framing the battle orders caused considerable annoyance to the troops. Low flying hostile aeroplanes harassed the men in the front line. On one occasion, when contact aeroplane was flying over our line calling for flares, an enemy plane followed some 800 yards behind dropping white lights wherever our ground flares were lighted. This brought down a hostile barrage. An 18-pr. gun of the 159th Brigade, R.F.A., was moved up towards Koekuit to try and prevent such action, but it is doubtful if the experiment achieved any great success.

The trees in the forest beyond the advanced line were made use of by German snipers, and, although a shrapnel barrage succeeded in reducing the number, they continued to be a source of irritation until the division was relieved. Also, the roadway known as Potte Drief, parallel to and about 200 yards north of Conter Drive, was camouflaged and the enemy was making use of it without being seen.

Although the pace of the barrage had been carefully calculated by all concerned as that most likely to suit the situation, it was found by some units, which had to struggle through woodland amongst thick undergrowth and fallen trees, to be too fast, and by other, which advanced over open country, to be too slow. In the former case, men either lost the barrage altogether, or, having kept up with it, arrived in such a state of exhaustion as seriously to interfere with their fighting efficiency.

Between October 18th and 25th 85 prisoners were captured by the division belonging to three different German divisions and the enemy losses were known to have been very severe.

The losses of the 35th Division between the 18th and 29th amounted to 368 killed, 1,734 wounded, and 462 missing. In addition, the brigades of artillery of other divisions which were attached to the 35th D.A. for the battle, lost 27 killed, 165 wounded, and 2 missing.

In spite of the above-mentioned trials, the **execrable weather** which prevailed, and the difficulty of getting up hot food and stores, the moral of the troops was of a high standard throughout the operations.

NOVEMBER, 1917

POELCAPELLE

In the beginning of November some further regrouping of the artillery took place. Towards the end of October, Brigadier-General Staveley had fallen a victim to influenza and was evacuated to hospital. His place in command of the Left Artillery of the Corps had, in the first place, been filled by Brigadier-General Wilson, and, on November 2nd, Brigadier-General W. Evans, D.S.O., 18th Division, assumed command. The 157th and 159th Brigades, R.F.A., still remained in the same positions and they, with the 150th Brigade, continued to form the right group (Lieut.-Colonel Davson). The left group, now commanded by Lieut.-Colonel Vickery, consisted of the 74th and 75th Brigades, R.F.A. These two brigades were replaced by the 108th Brigade, R.F.A., on the 2nd/3rd. At this time Brigadier-General W. Madocks, C.M.G., D.S.O., arrived to command the 35th Divisional Artillery in place of Brigadier-General Staveley.

During the first three days of November the enemy heavily bombarded all the batteries on the Broembeek, the Steenbeek, and Wijdendrift Road with gas and heavy shell. Gas shelling continued practically all night and the high explosive bombardment began at dawn. At midnight, 3rd/4th, an intense bombardment was opened on the front line on our right, to which the batteries replied. A hostile infantry attack followed but failed. The 19/Durham L.I., which was in support in the neighbourhood of Koekuit and Wijdendrift also suffered severely from these bombardments, and during these days in the line lost 13 officers and 125 men, most of whom were gassed.[1]

The 106th Brigade had relieved the 105th Brigade in the front line on the night 1st/2nd, and on the 3rd and 4th the 106th Brigade

---

[1] These included the commanding officer, Major Huffan, the adjutant, and all the company commanders. Lieut.-Colonel Greenwell had been gassed on October 20th and was still unwell. Major V. E. Gooderson, 18/H.L.I. took command on the 8th instant.

was relieved by the 53rd Brigade, 18th Division. The brigades entrained for the Proven Area except the 17/West Yorkshire, which was now formed into one company under Lieutenant Richard, and which marched there. The 104th, from the Boesinghe camps, and the 105th, from the De Wippe area, also moved to the area of Proven. On the 8th the 104th Brigade moved about five miles westward to Heerzele, at which place a certain intimacy developed between it and the 1st French Corps at Bambecque, about a couple of miles away. On this day, also, the 16/Cheshire returned to the Elverdinghe area for work on tramways under the C.E. II Corps. The 203rd Field Company, R.E., and the 19/Northumberland Fusiliers had remained in the forward area. The infantry brigades remained in these training areas until November 14th.

Meanwhile the artillery remained in the line and was chiefly occupied in counter preparation bombardments and barrages in support of minor attacks of other divisions.

On the 5th, the batteries of the 157th Brigade on the Wijdendrift Road were heavily shelled by 150 mm. for three hours, and next afternoon D/159 Battery suffered such a severe bombardment that for some hours the battery ceased to exist. Every gun was buried, and four of them were destroyed. The two remaining were dug up next morning and moved to a position half a mile down the Steenbeek close to Wijdendrift Bridge. New guns were supplied from the base with praiseworthy promptitude.[1] On this day the right group, Left Artillery, was broken up and the two brigades of the 35th Division became " D " Group, Left Artillery ; the whole artillery being commanded by Brigadier-General Evans.[2] During the next two days the brigades fired creeping barrages in support of successful operations carried out by British and Canadian troops north and west of Passchendaele, and, on the 10th, Brigadier-General Madocks took command of the Left Artillery from Brigadier-General Evans.

On the 11th, rain descended in torrents and the Steenbeek rose in flood. All the battery positions were inundated, and B/159 was marooned in midstream. Fortunately, in order to gain a better

---

[1] The new position was flooded out, and the battery had to move a week later.

[2] On this date a congratulatory message was received from the G.O.C. stating that the conduct of the personnel of the 157th and 159th Brigades throughout the recent operations had brought credit on the division and on themselves.

platform, the guns had been sited on spots which were slightly elevated and they, therefore, remained capable of being fired, but detachments had to carry ammunition waist deep through the water as the shells dumped beside the guns were useless. Firing was necessary as the German artillery was active, especially on the new positions captured the previous day. The water subsided almost as quickly as it had risen, and, with considerable labour, gun positions were shifted so that set barrages could be fired in support of further enterprises on the right which took place on the 14th. On the 15th the enemy attacked along the front, but was repulsed.

On the 14th the infantry of the division were transferred from the XIX to the II Corps, and on this day the 106th Brigade (less 17/West Yorkshire) moved by train to Siege Camp, half a mile south of Elverdinghe. Next day it marched to Kempton Park, a collection of Nissen Huts at a road junction midway between Wieltje and Pilckem, to relief the 174th Brigade, 58th Division, and, on the 16th, the 17/Royal Scots took over the front line in the left subsection of the Poelcapelle Sector, which extended from that village (on the north) to the Lekkerboterbeek.

On the previous day the 4/North Staffordshire (Lieut.-Colonel W. Appleyard) joined the brigade in place of the 17/West Yorkshire which marched into the XIX Corps area and passed out of the 35th Division. The 4/North Staffordshire took up a position in support partly on the Canal Bank, east of Brielen, and partly at Kempton Park.[1]

Meanwhile the 105th Brigade was concentrated at Brake Camp, north-west of Vlamertinghe, and relieved the 173rd Brigade in divisional reserve.[2] The 104th Brigade was moved to Siege Camp on the 17th.

The 35th Division was now situated between the 1st Division (on the right) and the 17th Division, XIX Corps, on the left, and remained in this position throughout the remainder of the month. General Franks took over command of the line at 10 a.m. on the 17th, and on this day the 106th Brigade extended its flank southwards as far as the Paddebeek, the 18/Highland L.I. relieving the

---

[1] *Vide* Appendix.
[2] The 16/Cheshire and part of the 15/Sherwood Foresters had been detached on duties connected with works.

2/Welch of the 1st Brigade. Divisional Headquarters were on the canal bank near Essex Farm, east of Brielen.

The artillery brigades remained in their original positions and did not now cover the 35th Division.[1] So far the front had been fairly quiet, but, on the 19th, hostilities became more active. On this day hostile patrols attacked the front posts of the 19/Durham L.I. which on the previous day had relieved the 17/Royal Scots in the left sector.

About 5.15 a.m. a strong patrol approached a pill box on the right front of Tracas Farm, which was the head-quarters of the left half of " X " Company (2nd Lieutenant R. Smith). Private Pinkney, the sentry, challenged and fired. He killed one man, and on a brisk fire being opened, the remainder withdrew. The German officer in charge then led his men round to the rear of the pill box, and, on again being challenged, replied in English that it was " all right." It was now light enough for the sentry to notice the officer's soft cap so he shot him and called upon the platoon for fire. At this the hostile patrol again withdrew, but later it appears to have made another attack. This time its losses were 12 killed and 6 prisoners.

At 7 a.m. another attempt was made on Meunier House, 500 yards to the north, by a force estimated at 30 men. This effort was dispersed by Lewis and machine-gun fire.

At 3.35 p.m. a small party of Germans approached Helles House on the left of the line. Corporal Coyle killed one, and the others scattered, lost their bearings, and eventually surrendered to other posts. Corporal Coyle and some men pursued some of them and brought in a wounded prisoner. The identifications were 7 of the 466th I.R., 1 of the 44th M.G. Company, and 1 of the 468th M.G. Company.

The conditions of mud and water in this sector were not in any way superior to those which had been so noticeable on the fringe of Houthulst Forest, and the means of communication were equally bad. Heavy rain fell on the following day, and the state of affairs did not appear to favour an attack. Nevertheless, no doubt in

---

[1] On November 24th, General Sir H. Plumer and the staff of the Second Army proceeded to Italy. General Sir H. Rawlinson assumed command in his place. On December 20th the designation was changed to Fourth Army.

consequence of the loss of three patrols, a further attempt was made on the part of the enemy.

On the night 20th/21st the 104th Brigade relieved the 106th with the 18/Lancashire Fusiliers and the 23/Manchester in the front line. At 6.15 p.m. on the 21st Lieutenant Short of the former battalion, who was on patrol, observed about 250 Germans advancing on Tracas Farm, and sent information to 2nd Lieutenant Parry who made immediate preparations to repel the impending attack. The S.O.S. signal was sent up at 7.10 and again at 7.20, but it was not answered for half an hour.[1] The Very Lights revealed the enemy advancing in several waves and the fire was withheld until these were within close range. Then rapid fire from machine-guns, Lewis guns and rifles threw the enemy into utter confusion. The attacking troops withdrew in disorder having suffered heavy casualties. Fifteen dead were counted close to our posts and one wounded man was brought in who subsequently died also. The identifications were the same as before, namely, the 466 I.R. General Franks sent a telegram of congratulations on what he considered a very creditable performance, especially by the junior officers.

The 18/Lancashire Fusiliers suffered no casualties as the hostile barrage fell behind their lines. The next few days were wet, misty, and comparatively quiet. The only peculiar incident being that Kempton Park was shelled by a high velocity gun. One shell struck the brigade office hut and another buried itself, without exploding, beneath the hut where some officers of the 18/Lancashire Fusiliers, now reserve battalion, were asleep. No damage was done to personnel.

On the night 24/25th the 105th Brigade relieved the 104th. Unfortunately, the 15/Cheshire, whilst relieving the right battalion, was caught in a hostile barrage and suffered 22 casualties. The posts in front of Meunier House were pushed forward about 80 yards in order to cover some dead ground. Two days later patrols of the 15/Sherwood Foresters, who had relieved the 16/Cheshire in the left sector, captured 2 prisoners, one a machine-gunner of the 204th Division, and another an infantryman of the 414 I.R.

---

[1] There is no record of the artillery which was covering this front at the time and, therefore, no explanation of this delay is available.

The brigade was relieved by the 106th Brigade on November 28th.

DECEMBER, 1917

The month of December was quiet. On the first two days the machine-guns of the 35th Division co-operated in an attack of the 32nd Division on the right. No undue retaliation was experienced, and the resultant disquietude of the enemy on the front enabled the 4/North Staffordshire to capture two prisoners.

On the 2nd the 106th Brigade was relieved by the 104th less the 19/Durham L.I., which remained at work in the forward area, and, on the 5th, the 105th Brigade with two battalions took over the line held by the 50th Brigade, and thus extended the 35th Division front as far north as the Broembeek, at a point 1,000 yards south-west of Turenne Crossing. Next day the 105th, together with the 4/North Staffordshire, relieved the battalions of the 104th Brigade.

The rain now ceased and the weather became fine and frosty. The country dried up considerably and the change was very welcome. Even a thaw brought comparatively little rain, and the temperature became mild.

Profiting by this, the enemy attempted a raid. At 5 a.m. on the 7th, a hostile party of from 15 to 20 men approached a post on the right flank of the 4/North Staffordshire. Rapid fire dispersed the attack, and the sergeant in charge led a small party in pursuit and captured four of their number (15th R.I.R., 2nd Guards Reserve Division). A further prisoner was taken on the following night. On the night 8th/9th the front line was taken over by the 174th and 175th Brigades of the 58th Division.

Divisional Headquarters now moved to Château Couthove near Proven, the 104th Brigade to Houtquerque, the 105th to School Camp near Poperinghe (after two days spent at Heerzele), the 106th to Road Camp between Poperinghe and Watou. The Pioneers remained at Boesinghe working in the Langemarck area, and on familiar places such as the Wijdendrift Road, Ney Wood, etc.

The relief was welcome. Although the weather had become dry, a fog generally hung over the country, and the atmosphere in that desolate region was depressing. Frequent reliefs were a necessity, but the infantry, in carrying them out, had to walk long distances on duckboard tracks and men entering the line had, generally, no better billet to look forward to than a damp and chilly shell hole. The ground became hard, and digging was toilsome. It was hoped, chiefly by those who did not know Flanders, that better conditions would prevail when the division next took over the line.

On the night 8th/9th also, the R.F.A. was relieved by the 57th Divisional Artillery. The 157th and 159th Brigades withdrew from the positions which they had held since October 18th [1] and moved to the neighbourhood of Handekot, from which place they marched to Arneke and Ledringhem respectively. The guns were left in their positions and taken over by relieving brigades. It was impossible to move them.

Since the middle of November the action of the artillery had consisted of a repetition of set bombardments and in answering calls for fire. No attack of any magnitude was attempted on our part, and the efforts on the part of the enemy were confined to spasmodic and unsuccessful attempts to regain the ground which he had lost in the recent operations. A forward gun of B/157 Battery on two occasions successfully engaged low-flying hostile aeroplanes which were harassing the front line, and D/157 Battery carried out a gas bombardment of a hostile battery situated in the centre of the forest.

Continuous shelling of the batteries and bombing of the wagon lines (necessitating a change of position) continued throughout the period, and the orders for the relief were greeted with much satisfaction. Brigadier-General Madocks received a very complimentary message from the G.O.C. R.A., XIX Corps, in which he thanked the 35th Divisional Artillery for the good work it had done whilst under his command. The casualties had been heavy ; less by shell fire than by gas, and exposure to weather for a prolonged period in unhealthy surroundings. Battery commanders had endeavoured to spare their men by keeping the gun detachments as small as was permitted by safety and the work required, and by sending others for a couple of days' rest at the wagon lines, but this system of relief, especially at times when the casualties were heavy, could only be carried out to a limited extent, and some, including the commanders, obtained no respite.

[1] On December 2nd the 157th had taken over three of the battery positions on the Broembeek in temporary relief of the 315th Brigade, R.F.A.

It is probable that the Flanders offensive entailed more strain on artillery drivers than any other period of the war. Driving up wagons by night to battery positions was a matter of normal routine, but pack transport was a more difficult operation. The physical exertion required of a small man to lead two large horses, loaded up with shells, stumbling over holes and mud, and often in the dark, was considerable. And the work was incessant. Pack transport does not facilitate a plenteous supply, and the number of rounds fired was very great. Ammunition supply in the Poelcapelle area was easier. The roads were more numerous and in better condition, and battery positions were generally situated closer to the main tracks.

Except that at intervals certain units were temporarily at work under the Royal Engineers, the battalions and batteries remained at rest and training until the beginning of January, 1918. The weather for the most part was fine and frosty, and the billets comfortable, so that the change from a vista of mud and wet shell holes was much appreciated.

During its service at Houthulst and Poelcapelle the following changes in personnel had occurred.

On October 27th, Lieut.-Colonel Vaughan gave up command of the 20/Lancashire Fusiliers and was transferred to the command of the 2/Manchester. His place was taken by Lieut.-Colonel Bicnill from the Middlesex. Major Heelis, of the same battalion, was appointed to the command of the depôt battalion.

On November 28th, Lieutenant W.O. Rushton, 18/Lancashire Fusiliers, was appointed Staff Captain, 104th Brigade, vice Captain H. N. Forbes, D.C.M., who became D.A.A.G. of the 46th Division.

Early in December, Captain M. M. Parry-Jones became G.S.O. 2 of the division, vice Captain H. J. P. Chichester Constable, D.S.O., who had been performing the duty for some weeks. Captain Chichester Constable was re-appointed in January and Captain Parry-Jones was transferred to the 3rd Division. Lieutenant G. W. Hodgkinson became G.S.O. 3 vice Captain H. J. P. Thomson. At this time, also, Lieut.-Colonel Greenwell returned from hospital and resumed command of the 19/Durham L.I.

Prior to the 17/West Yorkshire leaving the division, Lieut.-Colonel Hall had been evacuated sick, and Major Gill assumed temporary command.

CHAPTER XII

POELCAPELLE, 1918

THE year 1918 opened with a divisional assault at Arms, which was held on the 3rd and 4th. The weather was fine and frosty and the meeting was successful. Lieut.-General Sir C. Jacob, commanding II Corps, distributed the prizes to the successful competitors.

On the 7th the division once again began to take an active part in the war. On this day the 104th Brigade left Houtkerque and marched up to White Mill Camp, south of Elverdinghe, where it relieved the 175th Brigade in divisional reserve. Battalions were situated at White Mill and at camps between it and the canal bank.

Next day the brigade moved forward and relieved the 173rd Brigade, 58th (London) Division, in the line east of Poelcapelle. The relief was not pleasant. A heavy fall of snow disturbed the arrangements. In addition, the 20/Lancashire Fusiliers got caught in a barrage at Pheasant Farm, a ruin situated on the duckboard track known as Grouse Avenue, 1,500 yards west of Poelcapelle, and sustained 17 casualties. The relief was, however, completed without delay, and the troops were again on ground which had become familiar. Battalion headquarters were at Norfolk House, near Poelcapelle, and Souvenir House, east of Langemarck. The 106th Brigade moved up into the support area and the 105th to the White Mill Camp area. At the same time the Divisional Headquarters moved to the Canal Bank near Essex Farm, when General Franks assumed command of the line. The R.A. Headquarters also moved to the Canal Bank and took over command of the batteries in the line from the C.R.A., 58th Division. The batteries of the 35th D.A. completed the relief on the 13th, and the trench mortar batteries moved to Welsh Farm. Owing to the misty weather which prevailed, battery commanders had the greatest difficulty in registering and checking the calibrations of their guns. These had been taken over from out-going brigades, and paper

JANUARY 22, 1918

HISTORY OF THE 35TH DIVISION 181

records of shooting, however carefully compiled, were never deemed satisfactory by incoming commanders.

Meanwhile, the 19/Northumberland Fusiliers, which, since the middle of October, had been quartered in an uncomfortable and much-bombed camp near Boesinghe, were moved to Turco Camp, a collection of sand-bagged Nissen Huts near St. Jean. This camp, which had been especially well prepared, was much appreciated by the battalion. Work was begun on the tracks and lines of defence, and a congratulatory message from the Corps Commander testified to the excellence of the result.

The 35th Division was now the left division of the II Corps front. On its right was the 39th Division, and on its left the 18th Division, XIX Corps. In reserve was the 32nd Division, II Corps. The line taken over extended from the Lekkerboterbeek on the south to the line of the Broembeek and Ypres-Staden Railway on the north.[1]

There was a further fall of snow on the 14th. This was followed by two days and nights of heavy rain, after which snow again fell. Needless to say, the Steenbeek immediately rose in flood and washed away the bridges. B/159 Battery was once again flooded, and dead horses were washed down into the gun position.[2] The roads were submerged, and many of the duckboards of the tracks were displaced. During this deluge, on the 16th, the 105th Brigade was due to relieve the 104th, and the Royal Engineers had to exert all their energies to repair the damage in time. In this they were successful, and the relief was completed without hindrance.. The hostile artillery was at this period particularly quiet, and patrols of the 105th Brigade which went forward as much as 500 yards to investigate suspicious localities found no trace of the enemy.

On the 22nd the right of the 35th Division was extended in relief of the 39th Division. The 106th Brigade took over the line held by the 116th Brigade from the Lekkerboterbeek to a point 2,000 yards north-west of Passchendaele with headquarters at

[1] From the 13th General Franks temporarily commanded the II Corps and Brigadier-General Pollard commanded the division from that date until February 13th. Lieut.-Colonel Davson acted as C.R.A. from January 3rd to February 5th. Brigadier-General Madocks was in England. 157th Brigade Head-quarters was at Cane Post ; 159th at Adelphi House, near Iron Cross ; and batteries close to Langemarck. Lieut.-Colonel D. E. Forman commanded the brigade from January 14th.

[2] Major Hart was on leave when this happened and did not witness this second inundation of his battery.

Alberta House.[1] The right boundary of the division extended back from this spot to St. Julien. The division thus held the whole of the II Corps front with two brigades in the line. The 29th Division VIII Corps was on the right and the 32nd Division remained, as before, in reserve. The C.R.A., 35th Division, took over command of all the artillery covering the II Corps front.

On the 24th the 104th Brigade relieved the 105th in the front line. During this relief an unfortunate incident occurred when an incendiary shell entered the pill box known as Ferdan House, a company headquarters near Norfolk House, and killed the company commander of the 17/Lancashire Fusiliers, and Lieutenants Price and Hogan of the 15/Sherwood Foresters as well as two men. Two other officers and two other ranks were wounded, and the pill box set on fire. It was unlucky that one shell should enter through a small doorway and do so much damage, but similar incidents were not unknown throughout the war. Captured pill boxes, used as headquarters, were often unpleasant, in that the doorways naturally faced the enemy. Most of the headquarters near Houthulst were placed like this. So was Alberta House, and so was Taube Farm, in the front line, which had an enemy machine-gun laid on the entrance. For safety's sake a hole was cut in the back of this pill box, but as a rule the inmates accepted the risk. A good deal of risk was run at The Brewery in Poelcapelle.

In the early dawn of the 26th, under cover of mist, the enemy attempted a small raid against a post held by the 4/North Staffordshire. The raid was repulsed and two prisoners captured belonging to the 91st R.I.R., 2nd Guards Reserve Division.

Next day, the Kaiser's birthday, a similar raid took place against a post held by the 23/Manchester. This time, under cover of a thick fog, a party of about twenty of the enemy crept up and rushed the post from the rear. They succeeded in capturing a sergeant and 3 men. On leaving, the party was fired at by the adjacent post and one of the prisoners escaped; the others, however, were carried off. It would appear that enemy parties traversed some

[1] A group of pill boxes on the bank of the Steenbeek near St. Julien. The Headquarters, 23rd A.F.A. Brigade, also moved there, and, owing to the painful proximity of certain heavy howitzers, the Headquarters 159th Brigade, R.F.A., was moved from Adelphi House to Gournier Farm on the Ypres-Langemarck road in the same neighbourhood.

distance before making raids, as patrols had difficulty in locating hostile posts. An offensive patrol sent out from the 20/Lancashire Fusiliers on the night after this event in order to surprise a post on the Spriet road, advanced half a mile along the road without meeting any Germans.

On January 29th the 29th Division extended its line northwards, and the 4/Worcestershire relieved the 4/North Staffordshire. The 106th Brigade was now on a one-battalion front and carried out its own reliefs. The other two brigades relieved one another in the left sector. A relief took place on February 1st.

The night of the 1st/2nd was cold and a thick mist lay on the ground. From 1.30 a.m. to 2.15 a.m. the enemy lightly bombarded Helles House, a pill box in the front line which was occupied by a Lewis gun team of the 15/Cheshire. Suddenly from the mist appeared a party of 12 Germans. They rushed the post and knocked one of the sentries senseless. The other roused the team, but as soon as they appeared the enemy seized two of them as well as the gun and began to retire. They made an effort to take the other sentry, but after a very plucky fight with two of the enemy he succeeded in dragging them into a shell hole full of water and kicked himself free. The raiding party then made off. It was fired at by the next post and one man was killed (103rd R.I.R., 50th Division). A curious feature about this raid was that the Germans were all men of unusual physique and that they were armed only with revolvers. It was evidently a picked party.

A second raid was attempted on this night against Taube Farm, but was driven off by rifle and machine-gun fire.

At this time a change took place in the organization of the forces. Under instructions from the Army Council divisions were changed from a 13 battalion to a 10 battalion basis and this necessitated the breaking of many ties of mutual admiration and friendship which bound together units which had been fighting side by side for years. As far as the 35th Division was concerned, it meant the loss of the 20/Lancashire Fusiliers, the 16/Cheshire, the 14/Gloucester, the 23/Manchester, and the gain of the 12/Highland L.I.

Commencing on February 3rd the 16/Cheshire was withdrawn from the 105th Brigade and marched to Bridge Camp, whilst the

4/North Staffordshire was transferred to the 105th from the 106th. The 12/Highland L.I., from the 15th Division, arrived at Peselhoek near Vlamertinghe, and joined the 106th Brigade. Fifteen officers and 310 other ranks of the 16/Cheshire were sent to the sister battalion in the brigade, the remainder was transferred to the 1/6 Cheshire.

Three days later the 20/Lancashire Fusiliers and the 23/Manchester were disbanded. Nearly the whole of the officers and men of the former battalion were drafted to the other Lancashire battalions in the brigade. The personnel of the 23/Manchester were transferred to the 2nd, 11th, and 12th battalions of the same regiment.

Between February 8th and 16th the stores of these battalions had been disposed of, the details had joined the II Corps Reinforcement Camp at Merckeghem, and the battalions ceased to exist except that the details of the 23/Manchester, under Colonel Stevens, were formed into a new unit known as No. 12 Entrenching Battalion.

It remained for the 14/Gloucester to strike one last blow for the 35th Division before they were dispersed.

About 120 yards in front of the advanced posts and at a road junction close to the north bank of the Watervlietbeek stood three ruined buildings known as Gravel Farm. These buildings were strongly garrisoned by the enemy, and for a month past had been a source of annoyance to our patrols, as well as a centre of activity for hostile parties bent on examining the positions of our forward posts. It was therefore decided to raid and destroy this nest, and the task was entrusted to the 14/Gloucester. As the post was considered to be strongly fortified, and the garrison probably numerous, more artillery support was obtained than was usual in the case of a lesser raid. All known strong points in the neighbourhood were engaged by howitzers, and, whilst the field guns of the division barraged the line of advance and the approaches to the east, the 32nd Divisional Artillery opened fire on various points in the vicinity of Turenne Crossing. The raiding party, consisting of 38 men under 2nd Lieutenants Rundle, D.C.M., and Darley, started from Taube Farm and moved along the Watervlietbeek to a point about 200 yards south of the farm, where it waited until zero hour,

7 p.m. Owing to the men falling about in the darkness the movement was indicated to the enemy who thereupon opened machine-gun fire. Fortunately, before many casualties had been inflicted, the barrage fell and the raid advanced in two parties and, having successfully crossed the wire, reached the objective without further loss.

It was found that the buildings were not pill boxes proper, as had been suspected, but brick ruins reinforced with concrete and, in one case, with a cellar underneath. In the first of these 5 men were found; 1 man was made prisoner and the others, who resisted, were killed. In the second, 8 or 9 men took refuge in the cellar and refused to move. Bombs were thrown in and a Bangalore torpedo exploded. In the third, 3 other men were disposed of and about 20 more were killed or wounded outside. In addition about a dozen dead Germans were found, evidently killed by artillery fire. A machine-gun, half buried, was found and destroyed. The raiding party returned at the end of the time limit, half an hour, when the barrages ceased. Darkness and the bad going made it impossible to carry away the enemy wounded.

The Corps Commander wired his congratulations to the brigade commander and all concerned, and General Marindin in his report specially commended Major Wass and Captain Shufflebotham, M.C., for the careful way in which they had organized and prepared the raid.

The battalion was now relieved by the 15/Sherwood Foresters and, a week later, 12 officers and 250 men were transferred to the 13/Gloucester, and the remainder to the II Corps Reinforcement Camp. On the 6th representatives of *The Scotsman* and *The Glasgow Herald* visited the 18/Highland L.I. who were then in support at Wieltje.

Except for some artillery activity on the part of the enemy when Alberta House, the headquarters of the 106th Brigade, was heavily shelled for two days in succession, the next few days passed quietly, and on the 8th there began a reorganization of the line.

The II Corps front was in future to be held by three divisions instead of two, and on this account the 2nd Brigade, 1st Division, relieved the 106th Brigade and the 4/North Staffordshire from the Paddebeek to Besace Farm. The 17/Lancashire Fusiliers relieved the 15/Sherwood Foresters, and the 105th Brigade withdrew to the support line. The 104th Brigade now held the line between Besace Farm and the Broembeek, and on the next day the 19/Durham L.I. relieved the 5/6 Royal Scots of the 32nd Division which extended the line to Colombo House. At the same time the 157th Brigade, R.F.A., was relieved by the 25th Brigade, R.F.A., and moved northwards, in turn relieving the 65th, 123rd and " A " and " B "/161 Batteries in positions north-west of Langemarck. During this relief the enemy artillery, possibly erroneously, engaged the batteries of the 159th Brigade, R.F.A., which were stationary, and caused a certain amount of damage to guns and equipment. On the 11th General Madocks assumed command of the artillery covering the central section of the corps front.

In the early morning of the 11th a patrol of the 104th Brigade encountered, near Gravel Farm, a strong hostile party which was evidently intent upon a raid. Fire was opened and two or three of the enemy were killed. The hostile party then withdrew. One of the patrol was reported missing.

On the 15th at 8.30 p.m. the 18/Lancashire Fusiliers, which had relieved the 19/Durham L.I. on the 12th, raided the German positions at Turenne Crossing. The raiding party consisting of 2 officers (2nd Lieutenants Franks and Plenderleith) and 40 other ranks formed up astride the Aden House–Turenne Crossing road, and advanced under an intense barrage of artillery and machine-guns. The enemy's wire was thick and had to be cut by Bangalore torpedoes, which were fired by the 204th Company, R.E. Upon this, the hostile barrage descended on his own wire and posts. The crossing was stormed and, from a pill box situated between the road and railway, 11 prisoners were taken, including an officer and an officer aspirant. The garrison was known to have been stronger than this, but no trace of the remainder could be found. The casualties were slight. The prisoners belonged to the 114th I.R., 99th Division. Colonel Irvine specially commended the work of the Royal Engineers.

Next day the enemy retaliated with artillery fire on Varna Farm and the battery positions of the 157th Brigade, R.F.A. The 106th

February 28, 1918

Brigade then relieved the 104th, and the latter went into support. The 105th became reserve west of the canal.[1]

On the 22nd the 105th Brigade relieved the 106th in the line, and on the night 22nd/23rd the enemy attempted a raid against the right battalion, 15/Sherwood Foresters. The raiding party, estimated at 15 or 20 men, under a sharp barrage, advanced in the direction of Bower House, but was driven back by rifle fire.

The early morning of the 27th was marked by a very heavy hostile artillery fire on the divisional front lines. As an enemy raid appeared imminent, artillery support was asked for, but after half-an-hour the fire subsided without any attack having developed. In the evening, the 32nd Division carried out another successful raid on a large scale on Houthulst Forest in which the divisional artillery co-operated. In retaliation for this attack the front line was again shelled by the enemy.[2]

On the 28th the 105th Brigade carried out four simultaneous raids on enemy posts on its front. The two southernmost raids on Memling Farm and Gravel Farm were undertaken by the 15/Cheshire, and the others, against points to the east of Colombo House, by the 4/North Staffordshire. Each party was about forty strong. The raids were timed to start at 8 p.m.

The 25th Brigade, R.F.A., 1st Division, was attached to the 159th Brigade, R.F.A., for support of the raids of the 15/Cheshire, and the 161st Brigade, R.F.A., 32nd Division, was attached to the 157th Brigade, R.F.A., in support of the 4/North Staffordshire.

The raid on Memling Farm was commanded by 2nd Lieutenant G. D. Howells, and the party assembled without incident. An unfortunate accident marred the start as 2nd Lieutenant Howells, together with his servant and another man who were standing thirty or forty yards behind the point of assembly, were killed by one of the first shells of the barrage. This particular gun apparently fired short throughout the raid.

Notwithstanding this mishap to the commander, the party, under

[1] Following on the raid, the 32nd Division made a successful attack, in which the 35th D.A. co-operated, on enemy posts south of Houthulst Forest. Twenty-nine prisoners were captured and one machine-gun. Other machine-guns were destroyed.
[2] Information from prisoners captured by the 35th Division elicited the information that the result of this raid and bombardment necessitated hurried reliefs of certain enemy formations.

2nd Lieutenant Heape, advanced and reached the objective. Some bivouacs were found and destroyed, but there was no trace of any Germans. The party then returned having suffered no casualties except as stated.

The party raiding Gravel Farm was under command of 2nd Lieutenant G. K. Mowle, M.C., and from a line Taube House to the Watervlietbeek, advanced closely under what the raiding party described as an accurate barrage until it met a belt of wire some 300 yards from the farm. This was cut by a Bangalore torpedo, but soon afterwards a second belt was encountered and found to be intact. During the delay which ensued, parties of enemy were seen to be in rapid retreat. Fire was opened upon them and several casualties were caused. Having crossed the wire the party came upon a machine-gun post and killed the detachment, but the gun was buried, and in the time available the party was unable to dig it out. Enemy shelters were next encountered. The men in the first refused to surrender and were bombed. Six, including an officer, were killed, and two, both of whom were wounded, were captured. This shelter was set on fire, and the party went on to the next which was already on fire and empty. By this time Gravel Farm itself was by now burning fiercely and the enemy began to shell it. Lieutenant Mowle, considered that everything possible had been accomplished, ordered his men to withdraw to the forward posts, and, as a heavy barrage was by this time falling on the vicinity of Taube House, kept them there until the fire had subsided. The party, with the 2 prisoners, reached Taube House at 8.50 p.m., having had only 3 men wounded.

Colonel Cochran, in his covering report, especially mentioned the capacity for command exhibited by 2nd Lieutenant Mowle in this action.

The first of the raids of the 4/North Staffordshire was under command of 2nd Lieutenant W. H. Sharrat, and the party advanced along a road leading eastward from a point midway between 5 Chemins and Colombo House for a distance of 550 yards. The wretched condition of the ground in the line of advance made deployment impossible, and the party advanced in two columns in single file, one on each side of the road. It was not a desirable formation and the advancing columns were subjected to machine-gun fire from the left flank with which it was not possible to deal. Shortly afterwards a belt of wire across the road held up the advance. This was passed and later a group of elephant shelters strengthened with sandbags was encountered. These had been practically demolished by the artillery fire, and about twenty Germans were counted lying in the debris. A few more were bayonetted and one prisoner was taken. Machine-gun fire now opened from the right flank also, but the party advanced to the road junction which was the objective and then, according to orders, retired in a south-easterly direction to Angle Point. The casualties were 3 wounded.

The fourth raid of the night was under command of 2nd Lieutenant Zeederberg, and assembled at Colombo House. The party was to advance 500 yards along the forest road leading east and return by the same route. This party was subjected to machine-gun fire from five minutes before zero until the conclusion of the raid. Also, after the first hundred yards had been passed, it encountered a succession of obstacles consisting of felled trees and concertina wire, which were laid across the road about every 25 yards and hampered the advance to such an extent that many men were unable to reach the final objective before the time limit expired. Lieutenant Zeederberg, however, with some of the party, arrived at this point in spite of all difficulties. None of the enemy was encountered, but several were seen to retire in a northerly direction and were fired upon. The casualties were 1 killed and 2 wounded.

The prisoners captured at Gravel Farm belonged to the 22nd I.R., and the one captured by the 4/North Staffordshire, to the 156th I.R. Both of these regiments belonged to the 11th Reserve Division. Valuable information was obtained from the prisoners.

General Marindin in his report spoke highly of the accuracy of the barrages and the care bestowed upon them by the artillery brigade commanders, Colonel L. M. Wilson (157th) and Lieut.-Colonel D. E. Forman (159th), and also of the indefatigable work carried out in preparation of the raids by Captain C. J. Graham, acting Brigade Major, 105th Brigade.[1]

On March 1st the 105th Brigade was relieved by the 104th and moved into support. After a few days the battalions continued

[1] Captain Roupell, V.C., was on a course in England.

work on the Army Line, and the 106th Brigade carried out a practice scheme of manning it.

At 3 a.m. on the 5th, under cover of an intense bombardment, the 19/Durham L.I. raided some huts in the neighbourhood of what had been the objective of the 4/North Staffordshire on February 28th. The huts were reached, but the enemy had retired in face of the barrage, and no identifications were obtained. Two days previously, however, a sergeant of the 322 Pioneers had been captured at the advanced posts. In this raid 11 casualties were suffered through machine-gun fire.

Two days later, the 7th, the 17/Lancashire Fusiliers had a similar experience in a raid on Colibri Farm, close to Turenne Crossing. In this case the enemy were seen to be retiring, but no touch could be obtained. It seemed possible that after the experience of raids in February the enemy posts had orders to retire as soon as barrage fire opened and to reoccupy their positions later as circumstances permitted. The party of the 17/Lancashire Fusiliers, consisting of 3 officers and 50 men, reached its objective, but could accomplish little. Three men were wounded.

Next day the 106th Brigade took over the front line, and on the 9th it was relieved by battalions of the 1st and 32nd Divisions. The 35th Division then became G.H.Q. Reserve.

The 104th Brigade were in the neighbourhood of Elverdinghe, working on the Army Line; the 105th in camps round Eykhoek and Crombeke; the 106th at Dragon Camp near Vox Vrie, between Woesten and Poperinghe.

The artillery brigades were relieved on the 11th, 12th, and 13th; the 157th moved to its wagon lines near the canal, and the 159th to Crombeke. During the relief the wagon lines of the 157th Brigade, R.F.A., which were situated about a mile north of Ypres, were shelled. The casualties amounted to 12 men and 37 horses.

The Royal Engineers and the 19/Northumberland Fusiliers remained in the forward area.

At this time further reorganizations took place in the division. The 19/Northumberland Fusiliers were placed upon a three-company basis, and one company was disbanded. This battalion was still quartered at Turco Huts and was engaged in repairing duckboard tracks and assisting the battalions in support on work upon the

MARCH 13, 1918

corps defence lines. Colonel F. W. Daniell, D.S.O., left the battalion on the 24th to take up duties as Labour Commandant, X Corps, and his place was taken by Lieut.-Colonel W. P. S. Foord, D.S.O., late of the 14/Gloucester.

Another change was that the 104th, 105th, and 106th Machine-Gun Companies were reorganized to form the 35th M.G. Battalion of the Machine-Gun Corps under command of Colonel M. V. Blacker, M.C.

Lieut.-Colonel R. A. Irvine, C.M.G., D.S.O., gave up command of the 18/Lancashire Fusiliers on appointment as Director of Labour at G.H.Q., and his place was taken by Lieut.-Colonel L. M. Stevens, late of the 23/Manchester.[1]

[1] Lieut.-Colonel Irvine later commanded the 5th/6th Inniskillings in the 30th Division.

Plate VI

BRIGADIER-GENERAL W. R. N. MADOCKS, C.B., C.M.G., D.S.O.
Commanding Royal Artillery October 1917 to March 1919.

BRIGADIER-GENERAL A. J. TURNER, C.B., C.M.G., D.S.O.
Commanding 105th Infantry Brigade April 1918 to March 1919.

2nd LIEUTENANT H. F. PARSONS, V.C.
14th Battalion Gloucestershire Regiment.
Killed in action at The Knoll, 22nd August, 1917.

LIEUT-COLONEL W. H. ANDERSON, V.C.
12th Battalion Highland Light Infantry.
Killed in action at Maricourt, 25th March, 1918.

CHAPTER XIII

THE GERMAN OFFENSIVE, 1918

IT had been evident for some time that the enemy, profiting by political events in Russia, had been transferring large bodies of troops from the Eastern to the Western Front, and, although the magnitude of this movement was not within the knowledge of the troops, sufficient information was available to indicate a hostile offensive on a large scale in the near future.[1] That portion of the line which lay between Cambrai and the Somme was regarded as the area in which the battle would most likely take place.

It occasioned no surprise, therefore, when on March 21st, a message was received that the 35th Division was to be ready to move at a moment's notice, and when, a little later, it was rumoured that the enemy had attacked on a 50-mile front between the rivers Sensée and Oise. All work on the Army Line was stopped, and on the 23rd General Franks left for the south by motor-car. He was followed by the brigade commanders and by the C.R.A.[2] The troops entrained on the same day; the 104th Brigade, the 19/Northumberland Fusiliers, and 157th Brigade, R.F.A., at Peselhoek for Corbie; the 105th and 159th Brigade, R.F.A., at Rousbrugge for Mericourt l'Abbé; the 106th at Proven for Heilly.

The division now came under orders of the Fifth Army (General Sir H. Gough), the headquarters of which were at Villers Bretonneux, and the VII Corps (Lieut.-General Sir W. Congreve), the headquarters of which were at that time at Maricourt.[3] General

---

[1] The Bolsheviks assumed power on November 8th, 1917, and declared a "democratic peace."

[2] At this time General Sandilands was in England. The 104th Brigade was temporarily commanded by Lieut.-Colonel L. M. Stevens. Major B. C. H. Keenlyside commanded the 18/L.Fus.
General Madocks had been ordered to England on a Senior Officers' Course. Lieut.-Colonel Davson was acting C.R.A. Major J. H. K. Richardson was acting brigade major, and Lieutenant W. H. Riddell acting staff captain, R.A.

[3] It moved to Corbie at 11.30 p.m. on the 23rd.

Franks, having conferred with both these commanders, fixed his divisional headquarters at Mericourt-sur-Somme, and, at 2 a.m. on the 24th established an advanced headquarters at Maricourt. Arrangements were then made to relieve the tired troops of the 21st Division (Major-General D. G. M. Campbell) which had been offering a vigorous resistance to the enemy since his first onslaught upon them at Epéhy 70 hours previously. The line held by this division at this time was roughly between Cléry and Bouchavesnes.

Meanwhile the battalions had arrived at railhead, and the earlier arrivals marched to billeting places originally allotted to them, but as the plans had been changed it was necessary to divert them to conform to the new arrangements.

The first battalion to arrive was the 15/Cheshire, which reached Mericourt l'Abbé at 5 p.m. on the 23rd and marched (less one company left for detraining purposes) to Suzanne. It arrived there at 4 a.m. on the 24th and marched direct to Maricourt, arriving there at 6 a.m. on the 25th. General Marindin had meanwhile established his headquarters at Suzanne Château in the afternoon of the 23rd, and here information was received from details of units of the 21st Division that the enemy had captured Cléry and that a withdrawal had been ordered. General Marindin, therefore, gave instructions to collect all stragglers and organize them for defence. The 105th Trench Mortar Battery reached Suzanne at midnight 23rd/24th, and piqueted all roads leading to the village. " B " Company, 35th Battalion, Machine-Gun Corps, arrived shortly afterwards and sent an advanced guard to Eclusier, a hamlet on the Somme half a mile above Suzanne.

At 3.45 a.m. on the 24th General Franks reached Suzanne Château and ordered all troops to be diverted to Maricourt. At 5 a.m. the situation was explained to brigade commanders at a conference at Maricourt. The 105th Brigade was placed at the disposal of the G.O.C. 21st Division, and headquarters was occupied in a sunken road south-east of Hem Wood.

The enemy had by this time forced the exhausted troops of the 21st Division from the Cléry-Bouchavesnes Ridge and had gained possession of Bois Marrière and the high ground beyond it. The 15/Cheshire and 15/Sherwood Foresters, having had a short interval for breakfast, left Maricourt at 8 and 8.30 a.m., with a view to

HISTORY OF THE 35TH DIVISION

relieving the 21st Division and regaining possession of the ridge. These battalions moved to positions in a sunken road west of Hem Wood and in the valley north-west of Hindleg Wood respectively.

Meanwhile other battalions were reaching the battle front. The 17/Royal Scots, having detrained at Heilly at 7 p.m. on the 23rd, reached Bray at midnight and proceeded to piquet roads east of Cappy. On the return of General Pollard from the conference at Maricourt these orders were cancelled and the battalion marched to Maricourt, arriving there at 8 a.m. The battalion was then ordered to Bois de Hem in support of the two battalions of the 105th Brigade. The 12/Highland L.I. had reached Bray at 3 a.m. and Maricourt at 9 a.m. The battalion was subsequently placed under the orders of the G.O.C. 9th Division. The 17/ and 18/Lancashire Fusiliers had detrained at Corbie and marched to billeting areas at Vaux and Sailly Laurette. They were subsequently conveyed by motor bus to Bray and marched thence to Maricourt where they were placed in support.[1]

Owing to the congestion of the roads on account of transport columns moving back, of troops moving forward, and of civilian fugitives, the advance of the battalions was greatly impeded. As they came up they were moved into battle with no opportunity for rest after a railway journey of twelve hours and a long and trying march.

As soon as the 15/Cheshire and the 15/Sherwood Foresters had occupied the positions stated above, orders were given for these two battalions to counter attack and regain possession of the lost ground. The 15/Cheshire on the right deployed on a line three quarters of a mile west of Cléry, with its right on the Somme and its left at Howitzer Wood, and, in a spirited attack, recaptured the high ground north of the village. On the left the 15/Sherwood Foresters deployed north of Hem Wood, attacked in a north-easterly direction and continued this line as far as Maurepas.[2] A gap, however, existed between the two battalions, and no touch could be obtained with troops on the left.

These two battalions resisted several heavy attacks throughout the day and caused severe casualties to the enemy. The German

---

[1] Owing to entraining and detraining duties nearly every battalion was short of one company and was not complete in strength for twenty-four hours.

[2] This action was mentioned in Sir Douglas Haig's despatch of October 21st, 1918.

troops attacked in close formation, and it was reported that one Lewis gun team of the Sherwood Foresters, on one occasion, completely annihilated a hostile wave of 60 men. On the other hand, the losses in the front line became very heavy, and the supporting companies were called upon to reinforce the firing line. Towards 4.30 p.m. the enemy were outflanking the Sherwood Foresters from the north, and it appeared probable that the survivors of the front line would be overwhelmed by sheer weight of numbers. Fortunately, the remaining company of the battalion now arrived and was pushed in on the left. The enemy was then held on the ground originally gained. Great assistance was given at this point by two tanks, and the 15/Cheshire received valuable aid from a Canadian Motor M.G. Battery, and also from a portion of the 13/Sussex, 39th Division, which had been rallied by General Marindin and his staff and placed under command of Lieutenant Sutton, R.E. Signals. Lieutenant Sutton was killed whilst charging with his Signallers a party of the enemy which was impeding the advance on the right flank. The Signallers disposed of this party. Nevertheless, two companies of the 15/Cheshire were practically surrounded, and at this period the battalion had the misfortune to lose its Commanding Officer. Lieut.-Colonel Cochran; the Adjutant, Captain V. G. Barnett and Major H. F. A. Le Mesurier with about thirty men were so hemmed in by the enemy that all were killed or captured fighting to the last. Captain C. B. Kidd, M.C., and Lieutenant E. H. Hodson were also killed at this time. Many men succeeded in fighting their way through the enemy's ranks and rejoined their comrades. Major Harrison Johnston then assumed command.

At 5 p.m. orders were issued to withdraw to the line Curlu-Hardecourt.[1] This retirement was carried out in good order, covered by the 17/Royal Scots which had been in support south of Hem Wood.

Meanwhile on the north the 12/Highland L.I. had taken up a defensive position at Hardecourt, and, at 2 p.m., the battalion was ordered to capture Maurepas and the ridge north-east of it. Two

[1] Names of villages are mentioned in order to indicate definite points. In reality, such villages as Maurepas and Hardecourt were no longer in existence, and their positions could only be identified if one happened to step on brick rubble hidden amongst grass and weeds.

MARCH 25, 1918

companies led by Captains Johnstone and Graeme Taylor successfully accomplished this, but, on occupying the conquered ground, no troops could be found on either flank. Orders were then issued to evacuate this position and to withdraw to the Hardecourt Ridge. About 5 p.m. the remaining company joined the battalion. At 6 p.m. the position on the south was as follows. The 13/Sussex were upon the north bank of the Somme, the 17/Royal Scots carried the line to a point 100 yards north of the Maricourt-Cléry Road. It was prolonged for 1,500 yards due north by the 15/Cheshire, and from thence to Maurepas by the 15/Sherwood Foresters. General Marindin was in command of all troops on this portion of the front and had moved his headquarters to a quarry north of Curlu. General Franks had by now assumed command of the line held by the 9th, 21st, and 35th Divisions.

Whilst the 17/Royal Scots remained to cover the subsequent withdrawal, the remaining battalions continued the retirement to the line Curlu-Hardecourt, where it linked up with the 12/Highland L.I. A sharp attack by the enemy from a north-easterly direction was repulsed by rifle and machine-gun fire. As soon as the line was established and all wounded had been brought in, the 17/Royal Scots and 13/Sussex withdrew and took up a position on the right flank. By 8 p.m. all was in order and no further hostile attack developed on this day. Captain Stewart, R.A.M.C., attached 15/Cheshire, greatly distinguished himself during these successive withdrawals for the devotion he displayed in superintending the evacuation of all wounded. It is believed that none was left behind.

Meanwhile the 4/North Staffordshire, which had not detrained until 12 noon, had reached Maricourt, and at 8.50 p.m. sent forward two companies to reinforce the 15/Sherwood Foresters. The 18/Highland L.I. had reached Heilly at 12.45 p.m. and marched to Carnoy Valley, arriving there at 9 p.m. Subsequently a support position on the Maricourt-Briqueterie road was occupied, the outpost line in front running from Trones Wood to Favière Wood. The 19/Durham L.I. were in support 600 yards east of Maricourt, and the 19/Northumberland Fusiliers reached that place by march route at 8 p.m., and was placed at the disposal of the 106th Brigade which was temporarily attached to the 9th Division.

The line running through Favière Wood was held by composite battalions from the VII Corps Reinforcement Camp and were under the orders of Colonel Hunt.

Some of the artillery batteries of the 35th Division had reached the railheads late in the morning, but were not yet in the battle area. The D.A. Headquarters did not reach Heilly until 4 p.m. on the 24th. The acting C.R.A. and the acting brigade major had arrived by motor and reported to General Franks at Maricourt at 5 a.m. on the 24th. Positions for the incoming batteries in the neighbourhood of Hardecourt were then chosen. The field batteries which were to be transferred to the C.R.A., 35th Division, were in action south and south-east of Maurepas, but during the morning were withdrawn to positions south of Maricourt. The heavy artillery was in action south-west of Billon Wood. At 4 p.m. Colonel Davson took over command of the artillery covering the 35th Division (VII Corps) front from Brigadier-General Newcombe, C.R.A., 21st Division. Rear headquarters was established in Etingham Château at 6 p.m. The signallers and orderlies reached Maricourt during the night.[1]

During the night the remaining troops of the 21st Division were withdrawn from the fighting line and 60 Lewis gun teams and a tank brigade were attached to the 104th Brigade to supplement the defence of the Maricourt area.

The Corps Commander held a conference in a cellar in Maricourt at 9.30 p.m., which the G.O.C.'s 9th and 35th Divisions attended. The 35th Division Headquarters was then ordered to move back to Bray.

THE EVENTS OF THE 25TH MARCH

At 3 a.m. on the 25th, Major J. A. Cox, 2nd in command of the 12/Highland L.I., was informed that Colonel Anderson was missing and that a gap in the line existed between Trones Wood and Favière Wood. He went forward in charge of a party of 40 men, including 20 men of the 106th Trench Mortar Battery, and at 4 a.m. occupied

[1] The artillery, as taken over, comprised the remains of the 50th and 51st Brigades (9th Division), the 94th and 95th Brigades (21st Division), the 108th and 189th Army Brigades, also the 6th, 27th and 47th Heavy Artillery Brigades. There was no headquarter staff, and communications were in process of reorganization.

a position in the outpost line, south-east of Bernafay Wood. This party was vigorously attacked on two occasions but succeeded in holding the ground until some time later, when, all officers having become casualties, the remnant was forced back upon Briqueterie when they attached themselves to the 18/Highland L.I. Major Cox, however, had meanwhile discovered that Colonel Anderson was still commanding the battalion in Favière Wood.

At 7.45 a.m. the enemy opened a heavy barrage all along the line, and this was followed by a determined attack which advanced from the east in several waves. Immediately south of Trones Wood the outpost line was overwhelmed and forced back upon the 18/Highland L.I. The survivors were rallied by Major Gooderson and placed upon the left flank. The left company of this battalion, gallantly led by Captain Mower, delivered a counter attack and restored the situation after inflicting severe losses on the enemy. Further to the south, in front of the 12/Highland L.I., the enemy achieved some success and penetrated about 200 yards into Favière Wood. Colonel Anderson at once organized a counter attack and personally took command. This attack was a complete success. The situation was restored and 70 prisoners and 16 machine-guns were captured.

Between Maurepas and Curlu, the 15/Sherwood Foresters and the 15/Cheshire resisted all attacks made upon them at this time, and the counter barrage of the guns of the 21st D.A. and the 108th and 109th Army Brigades, R.F.A., which were now in position south-east of Maricourt, was particularly effective. The enemy barrage, however, caused considerable casualties to these two battalions as well as to the 17/Royal Scots in the sunken road in rear.

Meanwhile General Marindin had been summoned by the G.O.C. to Maricourt and had been placed in command of the right portion of the line. This, in addition to his own brigade, consisted of the 17/Royal Scots, the 104th Brigade, five battalions of what was known as Hunts Force, as well as artillery, tanks, machine-guns, and all details in Maricourt. The headquarters, as well as the artillery headquarters, occupied a semi-demolished building called "The Red Château" in Maricourt.

About 11 a.m. the pressure on the left flank increased, and reports were received from the 8th Hussars in Bernafay Wood that the enemy was in force in the northern portion of the wood and that large bodies could be seen moving west along the valley north of Montauban. Colonel Lawrenson therefore sent half of his reserve company to the assistance of the cavalry and to keep the left flank secure.

On receipt of this information General Pollard ordered the 19/Northumberland Fusiliers to Montauban to form a defensive flank, and the battalion, with two companies, eventually held the line in advance of the village from the Bazentin-le-Grand road for about 300 yards westward. The cavalry prolonged the line on the right in touch with the 18/Highland L.I. On the left of the 19/Northumberland Fusiliers was a portion of the Motor Machine-Gun Corps. The detached company of the 17/Royal Scots, which had lately arrived, moved up to prolong the line.

During the morning stragglers of various divisions returned on Maricourt. These were collected and organized for defence by the 105th Brigade Staff and were placed in positions north and north-east of the village. The 203rd Company, R.E., which was at work on some trenches, was of great assistance at this time and manned a portion of the line where it remained until the end of the day.

Meanwhile persistent and heavy attacks had continued against that portion of the line held by the 12/Highland L.I. By about 12 noon the enemy had penetrated on both flanks and more especially on the left where the details holding the outpost line had been forced back and exposed the left company. Colonel Anderson therefore ordered a withdrawal to the trenches north-east of Maricourt. This was successfully accomplished under cover of " A " Company which inflicted considerable loss upon the advancing enemy. The battalion now held the old trenches north-east of Maricourt in conjunction with the 203rd Company, R.E., except for the right company which had become detached and was in position south of Maricourt Wood. The hostile attacks were continued with determination, and the battalion was forced back through the Wood to the north of the village, when the enemy failed to make any further progress.

The result of this withdrawal was that the left flank of the 105th Brigade was exposed and that a considerable number of troops came back through Maricourt. General Marindin, Colonel Stevens, and their respective staffs, assisted by other officers present in the village, went out and collected these remnants and lined them up along the Maricourt-Cléry road. A counter attack was ther organized and these troops, assisted by two companies of the 4/North Staffordshire, and led by the above-mentioned officers, advanced and cleared the enemy from the wood. Some companies of the 17/ and 18/Lancashire Fusiliers also assisted. A noticeable feature of this engagement was the amount of shouting amongst the German troops. It was remarked afterwards that it appeared as if they had all gone mad.

Whilst the line was being restored in this sector the 18/Highland L.I. were being furiously assailed near Briqueterie. The first definite attack occurred at 2.30 p.m. and was beaten off. At 4.45 another assault was made by the enemy upon the front of the battalion and more especially at the point of its junction with the cavalry south of Bernafay Wood. The line was driven back, but the arrival of the 19/Durham L.I., which General Pollard had sent forward from Talus Boisé, changed the situation, and a counter attack not only restored the line but advanced it about 200 yards beyond that previously held.

Taking advantage of this movement, the 12/Highland L.I. advanced from the north end of Maricourt Wood, and, personally led by Colonel Anderson, drove back the enemy with loss over the crest towards Favière Wood. Unfortunately, Colonel Anderson, who throughout the day had displayed conspicuous gallantry, was killed in this attack, as also were the three company commanders. Major Cox, who succeeded to the command, was able to organize for defence only some 60 men. The fighting had split up the battalion, and it was night before it was united.[1]

[1] For his performance on the previous attacks, Colonel Anderson was awarded a posthumous V.C.

" For most conspicuous bravery, determination, and gallant leading of his command.

" The enemy attacked on the right of the battalion frontage, and succeeded in penetrating the wood held by our men. Owing to successive lines of the enemy following on closely there was the gravest danger that the flank of the whole position would be turned. Grasping the seriousness of the situation, Colonel Anderson made his way across the open in full view of the enemy now holding the wood on the right, and after much effort succeeded in gathering the remainder of the two right companies. He personally led the counter-attack and drove the enemy from the wood, capturing 12 machine-guns and 70 prisoners, and restoring the original line. (*Contd. on next page*)

The " break in " on Maricourt had allowed of enfilade fire being brought upon the right flank, and resulted in the front being withdrawn to the line Fargny Mill-Y Wood, which line was still held by the 15/Cheshire and the 15/Sherwood Foresters. The subsequent success of the counter attacks from Maricourt then permitted of its being continued along the old front trench line east of the village which was held by the 4/North Staffordshire. This battalion had advanced there with the counter attack.

The 17/Royal Scots were now holding the line from the Cléry Road along the eastern edge of Maricourt Wood. On their left were the VII Corps Reinforcement Details, which continued the line up the Briqueterie Road to link up with the 18/Highland L.I. The cavalry were still in position between this battalion and the 19/Northumberland Fusiliers who continued to hold their ground in spite of heavy losses.

It will be apparent from the above description that the left flanks of the 4/North Staffordshire, and also of the 15/Sherwood Foresters, whose left was in a salient south of Nameless Wood, were in a very exposed position. No troops were on the immediate left, and the supporting battalions and remainder of the line were 250 yards in rear. The flank was enfiladed by hostile machine-guns and was also exposed to bombing attacks.

Lieutenant Morgan, 15/Sherwood Foresters, here performed a meritorious action, when, with 3 men of his own battalion and 5 men of the North Staffordshire, he rushed a bombing party, bayonneted 8 of the enemy and then attacked a machine-gun team. The crew fled, taking the gun, and was pursued by Lieutenant Morgan and his men for three hundred yards.

At 7 p.m., the enemy having been reinforced, a further attack

---

" His conduct in leading the charge was quite fearless, and his most splendid example was the means of rallying and inspiring the men during a most critical hour.

" Later on the same day, in another position, the enemy had penetrated to within 300 yards of the village and were holding a timber yard in force. Colonel Anderson reorganized his men after they had been driven in, and brought them forward to a position of readiness for a counter attack. He led the attack in person and throughout showed the utmost disregard for his own safety. The counter-attack drove the enemy from his position, but resulted in this very gallant officer losing his life.

" He died fighting within the enemy's lines, setting a magnificent example to all who were privileged to serve under him."—*Lon. Gaz.*, 30667, *May 3rd*, 1918.

was made on the 18/Highland L.I., whose ammunition was at this time becoming exhausted, and for a time the situation was critical. The left of the battalion was driven back, but was reorganized and recovered the lost ground. On the left the village of Montauban had been subjected to heavy fire throughout the afternoon and evening, but no infantry attack was developed at this point. Captain Fawcus, 19/Northumberland Fusiliers, and some other officers were killed owing to these bombardments.

At this time, the general situation being quiet, it was arranged to relieve the outpost line by two battalions of the 104th Brigade. Accordingly, about 8.30 p.m., the 18/Lancashire Fusiliers relieved the 15/Sherwood Foresters, who retired to a position east of the Bray-Albert Road, and at 10 p.m. the 17/Lancashire Fusiliers relieved the 15/Cheshire, who retired to Suzanne. During the afternoon a composite brigade of the 21st Division, under Brigadier-General Headlam, was placed at the disposal of the G.O.C., 35th Division. This brigade arrived at Maricourt about 7 p.m.

During the morning of the 25th the artillery of the 35th Division had come into action, except "A"/157 and "D"/157 Batteries, which were delayed owing to a railway accident. Owing to the hostile advance it was impossible to occupy the sites which had been reconnoitred in the early morning. Instructions, therefore, were issued for the occupation of positions north and north-west of Maricourt. Battery commanders and staffs, however, during their reconnaissance, came under machine-gun fire, and, as there were grave doubts as to the batteries being able to maintain their positions, the C.R.A. ordered the guns to be placed between Maricourt and Billon Wood and south-east of the wood itself. Effective fire was able to be opened from midday onwards.

At 2 p.m. an alteration was made in the system of command. The heavy batteries had by now withdrawn to positions further in rear and General Newcombe assumed command of all artillery covering the 35th Division Front. The guns round Maricourt, designated the right group, were placed under the command of Colonel Davson with headquarters in Maricourt.[1]

[1] This group consisted of the 94th Brigade and details of the 95th (21st Division) situated 500 yards east of Billon Wood; 157th (less two batteries) and 159th Brigade (35th Division); 108th Army Brigade (east of Billon Wood), and 189th Army Brigade (1,000 yards north of Suzanne).

During the afternoon the VII Corps, and with it the 35th Division, was transferred from the Fifth to the Third Army (General Sir J. Byng) which, on this day, had assumed command of all troops north of the Somme.

At 9 p.m. the G.O.C. at Bray received a telegram from VII Corps which gave directions that the line was to be withdrawn to the Albert-Bray Road and that the retirement was to begin at once. This order was rendered necessary owing to events in the north where the enemy had managed to reach Courcelette and was threatening the line of the Ancre north of Albert.

This order reached the 105th Brigade about 10 p.m. and communicated to units concerned. As regards General Marindin's force the execution was complicated by the fact that it was composed of many different units and that, as regards some of them, a relief was actually in progress. In spite of difficulties a perfectly orderly withdrawal was carried out and all troops except the rear guard were clear of Maricourt area by 1.0 a.m. The rear guard, consisting of the 17/ and 18/ Lancashire Fusiliers and a portion of the 159th Brigade, R.F.A., remained in position until 2.45 a.m.

Although the order to withdraw was issued by the division at 9.10 p.m. for some reason it did not reach the 106th Brigade headquarters in Talus Boisé until after midnight, and the units did not receive their orders as early as others on their flanks.

The instructions were that the withdrawal should be *via* Carnoy, Mametz, Fricourt, and then by a road leading west of Happy Valley. The 12/ and 18/Highland L.I. were detailed as rear guard.

Before the orders reached the 18/Highland L.I. and the 19/Northumberland Fusiliers, the battalion of Hunts Force and the calvary had commenced to retire and both commanders threw back defensive flanks. At 1.45 a.m. this latter battalion was sharply attacked. This attack was directed against the right flank and the enemy did not perceive the isolation of the two companies of the battalion. The enemy's effort was repulsed with the loss of many killed and 1 prisoner—the second which had been captured during the day. The battalion then retired to Carnoy Valley. The 18/Highland L.I. remained in the line until 3 a.m., and passed Carnoy Valley at 5 a.m. All wounded were brought away.

During the night various dumps, R.F.C. Stores and aerodromes were set on fire by Army and Corps orders. This was no doubt a necessary precaution but the various fires must have conveyed information to the enemy that a withdrawal was contemplated.

THE EVENTS OF MARCH 26TH

The Retreat to The Ancre

At midnight 25th/26th the 35th Division Headquarters closed at Bray and opened at Sailly Laurette. It had been expected that the division would be called upon to hold the Bray Ridge but, about 2 a.m., orders were received from VII Corps and confirmed shortly afterwards in writing, that the corps was to fight on the line Albert-Bray without being so involved as to make retirement impossible. Retirement when made was to be to the north bank of the Ancre which was to be held again as a rearguard position, all bridges being destroyed after the crossing. Details were given as to the mode of retirement and the positions to be occupied when the troops crossed the Ancre.[1]

The withdrawal to the Bray-Albert road had been carried out without molestation from the enemy, and battalions which had been attached to other brigades now rejoined their own units, except the 19/Northumberland Fusiliers which remained attached to the 106th Brigade.

The front was now occupied as follows : on the right, round Bray, was General Headlam's Brigade of the 21st Division ; next to it, about half a mile north of Bray, was the 104th Brigade. This brigade held the front along the road past the western end of Happy Valley to the point formerly known as Forked Tree. The 105th Brigade extended from here in the direction of Méaulte, the 106th Brigade, which was later in getting into position, was in rear of the left flank with one battalion (the 18/Highland L.I.) linking up between the 105th Brigade and the 9th Division, which held the line from Méaulte to Albert. An outpost line was formed on the high ground north of Bray along the Fricourt road east of Happy Valley, and was then refused in a north-westerly direction. General Marindin's headquarters was fixed in Happy Valley.

For the purposes of the withdrawal General Franks had been placed in command of the combined troops of the 9th, 21st, and 35th

[1] *Vide* Appendix.

Divisions, and had undertaken to hold the position up to 10 a.m. General Pollard assumed command of the 35th Division and Colonel Lawrenson of the 106th Brigade.

The artillery in accordance with orders issued to the C.R.A. was now in positions as follows. The 157th and 159th Brigade in and around Bois de Tailles, south of the Bray-Corbie Road ; the 94th and 108th Brigades north-east of Sailley le Sec. The headquarters had, during the night, moved to Etinehem Château, and at 8.30 a.m. it moved to the cross roads on the Bray-Corbie road south-east of Morlancourt.

Owing to a change of position of the headquarters, 189th Brigade, notification of which, although sent, did not reach the C.R.A. until long after he had left Maricourt, the order for the withdrawal of this brigade was not delivered and subsequent messengers failed to find the new headquarters, so that, at 7 a.m., it was actually in front of the front line infantry.

The brigade commander, Lieut.-Colonel L. T. Raikes, D.S.O., on arrival at about 10.30 a.m., at a point west of Bray, received personal orders from the corps commander to retire north of the Ancre and take up a position to cover the crossing at Treux. Colonel Raikes reported this to the C.R.A. at 11 a.m., and the brigade then withdrew to a position south-west of Laviéville, less "D" Battery which had been attached to the 16th Division. Early in the morning this battery came into action at Bois de Tailles under command of the 157th Brigade, R.F.A., which was still short of two batteries.

The corps commander visited all units in the front line and impressed upon commanders that it was important to gain time for the removal of stores, but that units were not to become engaged so deeply as to prejudice their withdrawal.

Owing to the proposed withdrawal to the north bank of the Ancre, all transport, which previously had had orders to halt at Morlancourt, was ordered back over the river through Laviéville to Warloy. This subsequently proved a valuable precaution as the congestion of troops and guns in the few and narrow crossings was considerable.[1]

At 7 a.m. 35th Division Headquarters moved to Henencourt

---

[1] In view of this order rations had been dumped by divisional arrangements at intervals along the Bray-Albert Road. Some of the troops, especially those in the outpost line, could not obtain these, and suffered from hunger. Ammunition was also getting scarce.

Château, but General Franks spent most of the morning in Morlancourt where he explained the situation as indicated to him to representatives of the various commands.

Shortly before 11 a.m. hostile troops preceded by mounted scouts began to appear on the ridges east of the Bray-Albert Road. They advanced slowly, but soon began to make tentative essays against portions of the line. A strong effort made against the 9th Division and the left of the 105th Brigade was repulsed by rifle and machine-gun fire. The 15/Sherwood Foresters and the 15/Cheshire were heavily engaged for some hours and received valuable assistance from tanks operating on the left flank. By 1 p.m. the whole line was engaged, and strong forces covered by artillery fire attacked the right of the line. At 2 p.m. Major Hart rushed up a section of " B "/159 Battery to a point on the road 1.500 yards west of Bray, and, over open sights, engaged an enemy battery which had come into action in full view. A hundred rounds were fired and the battery was silenced. The section then withdrew.

The hostile pressure now became stronger and General Headlam, commanding the 21st Division composite force, in accordance with instructions that troops were not to be deeply involved, and that any retirement should be in echelon from the right, about 2 p.m. commenced the withdrawal of his brigade.[1] Colonel Stevens notified this movement of the 21st Division to General Marindin and stated that he was withdrawing his outpost line in order to conform. At 2.45 p.m. the main line of the 104th Brigade commenced to withdraw and at 3.15 p.m. the 105th Brigade in its turn commenced retirement. The artillery brigades in rear then limbered up. At the first intimation of the infantry retirement two batteries had been withdrawn from Bois de Tailles, and, about 3 p.m., came into action south of Morlancourt.

The position of the 106th Brigade was now as follows. A portion of the 18/Highland L.I. was still in the front line in touch with the 9th Division. One company was on the high ground east of Morlancourt, and, on its right, a portion of the 12/Highland L.I.[2] on

[1] By VII Corps order received at 1 p.m. Brigadier-General Headlam's force was to revert to the 21st Division when it took up a defensive position on the north bank of the Ancre.
[2] This battalion, as already stated, had been split up and was not yet reunited. The other portion conformed to the movements of the other troops and retired with them through Morlancourt.

the northern edge of Bois de Tailles. Two companies of the 19/ Northumberland Fusiliers were north of Morlancourt.[1] The 17/Royal Scots were withdrawing on Morlancourt preparing to act as rearguard for the division.

In addition, at 8 a.m., nucleus parties of the 21st Division and the Pioneers were formed into a force under Lieut.-Colonel McCulloch, and placed at the cross roads one mile south-east of Morlancourt. This force came under the orders of the G.O.C. 35th Division.

The enemy attacks were now being pressed forward, but the retirement was carried out in excellent order under cover of rearguards furnished by each brigade. The battalions suffered some loss from rifle and shell fire during this movement, but the enemy was held in check and many casualties inflicted on him. The 105th Brigade passed through the 106th about 4 p.m.

About 3 p.m. General Franks, then at Hennencourt Château, had a conversation over the telephone with the Corps Commander after which he left for Morlancourt, where about 4.15 p.m. he met Generals Pollard and Marindin. About 3.30 p.m. an order was issued by telephone from VII Corps which stated " Army orders that every effort must be made to check the enemy advance by disputing ground. It is to be distinctly understood that no retirement is to take place unless the tactical situation imperatively demands it."

This appeared to contradict VII Corps order 248 issued at 2.15 a.m., and General Franks consulted with the brigade commanders of the 105th and 106th as to the possibility of stopping the withdrawal and re-occupying the original Albert-Bray Line. The brigade commanders were of opinion that this could not now be carried out, and General Franks decided that to turn round and occupy the original line with jaded troops, with a shortage of ammunition, and with the enemy pressing hard, was out of the question. He therefore gave orders for the movement to continue.

At this time Morlancourt was congested with civilian carts, guns, tanks, and tired infantry. Fortunately, owing to the action of the rearguards, the troops were free from interference by the enemy, otherwise the crossing of the river by the passage allotted to the

---

[1] " Y " Company, which had not been deeply engaged at Maricourt, had retired with the 105th Brigade and was now ordered to rejoin the battalion.

HISTORY OF THE 35TH DIVISION

35th Division at Ville might have been a matter of some difficulty. The crossing immediately below, at Mericourt, had been assigned to the 21st Division and that above, at Dernancourt, to the 9th Division.

At 4.30 a.m. the 104th Brigade had crossed the Ancre and was taking up positions on the north bank covering Treux, Buire, and Ville. The 105th Brigade was passing through Morlancourt. The 106th was engaged with the enemy east of Morlancourt and McCulloch's Force was stationed to the south of it. Two batteries were in action in rear of McCulloch's Force. The 94th and 108th Brigades, R.F.A., were across the river, and 4 batteries of the 35th D.A. were between Morlancourt and Buire.

By 6.30 p.m. the 105th Brigade and the remainder of the artillery had crossed the river. The 12/Highland L.I. had retired fighting on Marett Wood, south of Treux, and, when all troops had crossed the Ancre, it retired to a sunken road 500 yards north of Buire where the detached portion was already in position. The 18/Highland L.I. retired by the north of Morlancourt and crossed the river about 7.30 p.m.

At 6.18 p.m. a telegram from VII Corps, timed 5.40 p.m., was received. This cancelled the retirement as laid down in order No. 248, and stated that the Bray-Albert Line was to be held at all costs, and that any retirement necessary was to be made on successive lines of defence with the right flank on the Somme and the left on the Ancre.

Notification of the issue of this order had previously been received by telephone, and General Franks, therefore, gave instructions for the high ground east of Morlancourt to be regained. At this time the units of the 105th Brigade were extended by the roadside between the Ancre and the railway in front of Buire, and were enjoying the first hot meal which they had had for several days. On receipt of the message, General Marindin ordered the 15/Sherwood Foresters to attack on the right *via* Buire, and the 4/North Staffordshire [1] on the left *via* Dernancourt. Two companies of the 15/Cheshire were ordered to support each attack, and, at the same time, a battery of the 94th Brigade, R.F.A., which had crossed the river during the afternoon, was ordered to Buire in support of the attack.

---

[1] Lieut.-Colonel Appleyard was a casualty from gas poisoning, and Captain Bache was commanding the battalion.

General Marindin then sent a message to the divisional commander describing the situation and stating that, although the order was being obeyed, he considered that the attack, made with men already tired, and ill supplied with ammunition, had small chance of success.

Shortly afterwards, by VII Corps order, the operation was cancelled, and officers were immediately despatched to stop the battalions. The 15/Sherwood Foresters were stopped as they were crossing the bridge at Ville-sur-Ancre, but there was some difficulty in getting in touch with the 4/North Staffordshire and finally the Brigade Intelligence Officer, Lieutenant Covington, and also Lieutenant Wills, the Signal Officer, went in search of them. The message did not reach the battalion and neither of the officers was seen again.[1]

Meanwhile the battalion had proceeded in.the direction of Morlancourt, and, as parties of men were discovered at work in close proximity, it was lined up facing the village whilst Captain Bache and Captain Graham, who was still acting as Brigade Major and had accompanied the battalion, went forward to reconnoitre. They were shot at both by the working party and later from the village, but naturally no trace could be found of the 15/Sherwood Foresters. The battalion was therefore disposed for defence with its left on the river whilst Captain Graham returned to obtain information. He then heard that the order to attack had been cancelled and sent a message to the battalion to this effect. The battalion withdrew at 1.30 a.m. on the 27th.

The 105th Brigade with the 15/Sherwood Foresters and 4/North Staffordshire was disposed along the railway line from the *Halte* at Buire to the cemetery in Dernancourt with outposts along the river bank and standing posts on the far side of the river amongst the woods and rushes. A strong point was established at a mill half a mile north-east of Ville-sur-Ancre. The 15/Cheshire [2] and Entrenching Battalion were in support. Bridge-heads were formed and the bridges prepared for demolition, but orders were given to hold the river line at all costs.

---

[1] Lieut. Covington was taken prisoner near Dernancourt, wounded in both knees. He escaped and swam the Ancre, and was rescued by some Australians.

[2] The party of the 15/Cheshire, which had been separated during the withdrawal, rejoined at this time. It suffered heavy casualties including Major Stewart, R.A.M.C.

On the right of the 105th Brigade was the 104th holding the river bank south-west of Buire with all three battalions in the line and headquarters in Buire. The 106th Brigade and the 19/Northumberland Fusiliers were in reserve at Laviéville. The G.O.C. Division visited the outpost line during the evening and returned to headquarters about 1 a.m.

Meanwhile, a staff officer from VII Corps had met General Marindin at Buire and had informed him that he had been placed in command of the division, and, as soon as the line was stabilized, conveyed him to Henencourt, which was reached at midnight. General Franks arrived an hour later.

This change of command was occasioned because it was considered that General Franks had misinterpreted the verbal instructions and orders issued in the morning of the 26th and that no retirement should have been made from the Bray-Albert Line. The question of responsibility was investigated at a later date, but the narration of the circumstances, except to state that the result helped to alleviate the commander's disappointment, does not fall within the scope of this history. The occurrence was a matter of regret to all ranks of the division.

The River Ancre, upon the banks of which the division was to be engaged for the next four days, rises a short distance above Miraumont and pursues a winding course between marshy meadows in a south-westerly direction for about twenty miles until it joins the Somme below Corbie.

The ground rises in down-like formation on either side, until, at distances varying from half a mile to a mile from the river bed, it attains a height of about 300 feet. Certain valleys penetrated into these downs, of which the most important to the 35th Division were two in number. One of these ran in a south-easterly direction for 200 yards from Ville to Morlancourt, and the other in a north-westerly direction from Buire to Laviéville.

Between Mericourt and Dernancourt the left bank was well wooded, and copses of elder interspersed with brushwood and rushes were scattered at intervals along both banks.

Along the river valley ran the railway line from Amiens to Douai. This railway crossed to the western side between Mericourt and Buire, and from there to Dernancourt was about 100 to 300 yards from the river bed. It was embanked for the most part, especially between Dernancourt and Albert where the embankment was about 30 feet high.

Below Albert the river was a considerable obstacle and this, with the railway embankment, made a welcome line of defence. The villages were not of great value for prolonged resistance. They were somewhat squalid, and built in a manner that brought back memories of the mud villages of the East. They, however, afforded cover, if not protection, and as they had only recently been evacuated, a certain number of comforts were obtained for the chilled and weary troops.

General Marindin assumed command of the divisional front on the morning of the 27th, and Lieut.-Colonel Crellin took temporary command of the 105th Brigade until the 31st inst., when Lieut.-Colonel Appleyard, having recovered, took his place.

At 10 a.m. on the 27th the enemy advanced in force from the Bray-Corbie Road, and, pivoting on Morlancourt, moved upon Dernancourt. This advance was broken up by artillery fire, but a retrograde movement of some troops of the division on the left for a time made the situation obscure. The VII Corps Entrenching Battalion was dispatched to line the ridge north-east of Buire and facing Dernancourt, and the 106th Brigade and 19/Northumberland Fusiliers were ordered up from Laviéville in support. These troops were under artillery fire as they moved forward, but the casualties were slight. The Northumberland Fusiliers waited on the reverse slope of a rise whilst the details of the 26th (South African) Brigade, which was now holding the railway embankment north of Dernancourt, organized a counter attack. Later, two companies of the Northumberland Fusiliers moved into close support and suffered somewhat heavily, but the situation then became normal.

One company of the 19/Durham L.I. was sent across the river to Treux and occupied the eastern outskirts.

The other troops along the river line were shelled during the day, and some casualties were caused. The advanced posts of the 35th Division on the far side of the Ancre were, however, able to inflict losses upon the enemy. Some of the battery positions were also searched for and subjected to fire, but without appreciable effect, except to "D"/159 Battery which, in order to obtain a longer range, had been moved close to Buire and was so heavily shelled that, after suffering some damage, it had to be withdrawn to its original position south of Bresle.

During the afternoon the 106th Brigade relieved the 105th in the line. The 17/Royal Scots relieved the 4/North Staffordshire, and the 12/Highland L.I., the 15/Sherwood Foresters and 15/Cheshire. The relieved battalions withdrew to sunken roads and quarries and remained in support.

The 19/Northumberland Fusiliers relieved the whole of the 26th Brigade, which, owing to losses in battle, scarcely exceeded the strength of one battalion, and during the night pushed patrols into Dernancourt. These came into contact with the enemy and some street fighting ensued.[1]

The night passed quietly, but rain fell heavily. In the darkness and confusion some parties in Dernancourt were either killed or captured.

THE ANCRE

March 28th to 31st, 1918.

At this time certain officers who had been in England when the division was ordered south made their way back by devious routes and various modes of conveyance. General Sandilands, having commandeered a canteen van, reached his brigade on the night of the 26th.

On the morning of the 28th General Madocks and Major Holland reached D.A. Headquarters at Henencourt, when General Madocks resumed command of the artillery. Captain Roupell, V.C., Brigade Major, 105th Brigade, also arrived, and for the next two days these were followed by other officers, N.C.O.'s, and men whose rank had not been adequate to obtain the more rapid modes of transit which had been employed by their seniors.

On the 28th the enemy made two separate attacks on the front held by the division.

[1] This brigade, which, in December, 1916, had relieved the 105th Brigade in " J " Sector at Arras, had been almost annihilated in a gallant defence at Marrières Wood near Cléry on March 24th. The 4th Australian Division relieved the remainder of the 9th, Division and the 3rd Australian Division came in on the right of the 35th.

The most northerly and most persistent of these took place from Dernancourt against the Northumberland Fusiliers who were lining the railway embankment for about 100 yards on each side of the archway where the road from Dernancourt passed underneath.

Soon after 5 a.m., under cover of a heavy barrage, a hostile attack in three waves descended the hillside from the Morlancourt–Méaulte road. Lewis gun fire was opened and after some checks and subsequent advances the assaulting lines were broken up and dispersed. Meanwhile, however, the enemy had succeeded in dribbling a fair number of troops into Dernancourt itself and, about 10 a.m., a force estimated as two battalions debouched from the village and formed a line in gardens and hedgerows about 200 yards from the embankment. At the same time a violent barrage was put down about 200 yards behind the railway. The position now became critical, not only on account of the losses occurring to the battalion and to the force of the enemy in front, but to the fact that ammunition was becoming very scarce.

Every effort was made by runners to renew the supply. Six thousand rounds were sent up by brigade headquarters, and this was eked out by bandoliers taken from killed and wounded men and from artillery gunners.

The bulk of the attack appeared to be developing against the left company, and a Lewis gun team under Corporal Dodds was sent to reinforce the threatened point. This N.C.O., who was subsequently killed, behaved in a most gallant manner and brought the gun into action well in advance of the embankment where it partially enfiladed the German line. The gun remained in action throughout the day. The detachment suffered severely from snipers in the houses in the village, but as men were killed they were replaced by volunteers from the firing line.

At 10.25 a.m. the barrage increased, and an attack appeared imminent. The casualties on the embankment were many, and Colonel Foord himself was wounded in the neck, but remained in command. The wounded were moved to the foot of the embankment, where they were attended to under fire by the Medical Officer (Captain Wilson). Colonel Foord now decided that the best defensive is the offensive, and gave orders for an attack with two companies. The risk was great, but the success was immediate and remarkable. About a hundred men rushed the enemy in his position and drove him into the village in such disorder that he left most of his machine-guns behind.

Artillery fire was then called for and the village subjected to a severe bombardment which practically blew it into the air and must have accounted for large numbers of the enemy.

Mention must be made of the services of Lance-Corporal Hogg, who, when a German sniper was taking toll of the men lying on the embankment, ran over it, slid down the face, and worked his way forward through the grass and bushes until he found a suitable spot. Here he waited until the sniper showed himself and then shot him dead. Later, in a similer manner, he killed the crew of a machine-gun. He regained the line in safety and took command of his platoon.[1]

The second series of attacks took place against the front of the 104th Brigade and was directed against the east edge of Marett Wood and the village of Treux.[2] These positions were held by the 18/Lancashire Fusiliers and the 19/Durham L.I. Three attacks took place. The first, at 6 a.m., was a small one and was stopped by Lewis gun fire. The others at 10 a.m. and 1 p.m. were delivered in some force. These attacks were all repulsed by a combination of artillery, machine-gun and rifle fire.

Meanwhile, two companies of the 18/Highland L.I., under Major Gooderson, had been sent to reinforce the 19/Northumberland Fusiliers. This battalion had been in support in the valley between Laviéville and Dernancourt, and in moving across the intervening ridge the companies were subjected to hostile artillery fire which caused many casualties. Having reached the embankment they at once became engaged with the enemy and assisted in stopping all further assaults.

The enemy then confined himself to shell fire. Heavy guns were turned upon Buire, and the 104th Brigade Headquarters which was in a chalk pit behind the village was bombarded for two hours and several casualties resulted. No attack developed.

At night the 105th Brigade relieved the 104th, the 15/Cheshire taking over the defence of Marett Wood. The remainder of the

---

[1] For this action Corporal Hogg was awarded the D.C.M.
[2] Marett Wood was on the hillside half-a-mile south of Treux and due east of Mericourt. It was about fifty acres in extent.

18/Highland L.I. moved up in support at Dernancourt and Colonel Lawrenson took over command of the sector from Colonel Foord who went to the dressing station. Captain Stabell commanded the 19/Northumberland Fusiliers.

In the evening the artillery made another attempt to push forward guns and " A " and " D " Batteries, 159th Brigade, succeeded in getting two sections each into positions in a hollow south of the Albert road. The 157th Brigade, R.F.A., changed position to the neighbourhood of Bresle.

The night was fairly quiet, but there was much rain.

The 29th was a comparatively quiet day on the divisional front but the 3rd Australian Division on the right was heavily attacked. This attack was repulsed with enormous loss to the hostile troops; who were allowed to approach within close range before fire was opened.

In the evening the 104th Brigade relieved the 106th in the left sector. The 17/Lancashire Fusiliers [1] took over the front at Dernancourt and the 19/Durham L.I. relieved the 17/Royal Scots between Dernancourt and Buire.

An unfortunate incident happened on this day owing to one of our own long range guns firing short and causing considerable loss to the 19/Northumberland Fusiliers about Dernancourt. One shell alone caused 29 casualties. On word being sent to headquarters the gun ceased firing.

A lesser accident of a similar nature befell the 104th Brigade next day, but this time one of the field batteries covering that portion of the line was at fault.

On the 30th the only incidents worthy of record were that the 3rd Australian Division was again attacked at noon with results as before, and that a patrol of the 4/North Staffordshire, under Lieutenants Dodman and Matthews, crossed the river and endeavoured to dislodge a party of the enemy known to be close to our lines in the neighbourhood of Ville. The hostile party proved to be stronger than was expected, and the patrol was compelled to withdraw without having accomplished its object.

At night the two Australian Divisions closed in and relieved the

---

[1] The battalion was at this time commanded by Major C. E. Jewell. Lieut.-Colonel Crook rejoined on the 29th.

battalions of the 35th Division. The 95th Brigade, R.F.A., and the 108th A.F.A. Brigade were transferred to the 4th Australian Division on the left, and the 35th Division Artillery came under command of the 3rd Australian Division.

On relief of the battalions, the 104th and 105th Brigades and the Pioneers, moved to La Houssoye, about five miles west of Buire, and the 106th Brigade to Heilly. Artillery Headquarters, which were at St. Laurent Farm, south of Bresle, now moved to Heilly also. The batteries remained in the line. The Royal Engineers marched back to Baisieux, the Train to Warloy, and the trench mortar batteries to Behaucourt. Divisional Headquarters moved to Pont Noyelles.

Before the 35th Division withdrew from the line the German advance on its front had been definitely stopped, and the troops of the division had just cause to congratulate themselves on being instrumental in determining this state of affairs. Every retirement which had been made had been ordered as part of a general plan and was not because the troops had been forced to relinquish positions.

Although since the night of the 26th, when the battalions took up their positions on the Ancre, the enemy had been able to make further advances both on the north and south, no ground was given up by the division. Indeed, on the contrary, some was gained, and there came a time, when, in spite of hostile attacks, the men in the firing line recognized that they held the upper hand.

For eight days they had had no rest and little food. They had been subjected to fighting of the most severe description with no prospect of relief, but neither fatigue nor losses in battle had diminished their fighting spirit.

The casualties in the week's fighting amounted approximately to 90 officers and 1,450 men.

CHAPTER XIV

Aveluy Wood

FOR the first three days of April, 1918, the infantry of the division were at rest, except that the 17/ and 18/Lancashire Fusiliers provided working parties for the Baisieux Line. On the 2nd the Corps Commander visited the division at La Houssoye and addressed the G.O.C., the brigade commanders and staffs, and the battalion commanders of the 104th and 105th Brigades, and thanked them for the work the division had done under very trying circumstances.

On April 4th rain fell all day. At 5 a.m. news was received that a German prisoner had stated that the enemy would attack south of the Somme at 5.30 a.m. This proved correct, except that the attack was launched an hour and a half later.

This attack involved the whole of the British troops south of the Somme and forced a withdrawal of the northern portion of the line to the west of Hamel.[1] Orders were received that the division was to be ready to move at half an hour's notice, and, at 3 p.m., the 104th Brigade was moved to Bonnay, under orders of the 3rd Australian Division, and the 105th Brigade to La Neuville. The 104th Brigade then held a defensive line on the Somme from Sailly-le-Sec to Corbie.

On the 5th the main German effort was made north of the Somme, when the attack extended from Dernancourt to Bucquoy, 12 miles further north.

The attack on Dernancourt alone in itself affected any troops of the 35th Division. At 7 a.m. an unusually heavy bombardment fell on Bresle and all the battery positions, and the batteries replied by firing a concentration on Morlancourt and the valley to the north of it, but, by 10 a.m., the enemy were reported to have crossed the railway at Dernancourt and, also, to be massing in Morlancourt. Thereafter the fighting in the former village became more violent,

[1] Two miles south of Sailly-le-Sec.

and the 52nd Australian Brigade sent urgent messages for increased fire. The artillery fire appeared to be effective and, in addition, C/159 Battery destroyed a large party of Germans east of Treux whilst D/159, which by now had been pushed up farther towards Buire, silenced a hostile battery which had advanced as far as Ville. Firing continued al! the afternoon, firstly on the woods round Dernancourt and afterwards to the north-west of it close to the quarry. At a later period this ground was made good and the fire was directed on the railway.

Bresle was shelled throughout the afternoon with H.E. and gas especially round the 159th Brigade Headquarters. Considerable casualties were caused, mainly to the personnel of the heavy artillery which occupied positions close to the village. The 157th Brigade Headquarters, east of St. Laurent Farm, was so heavily engaged that it became necessary to move it farther south. The enemy must have had great expectations of a break through at this point for not only were his batteries well advanced but, at 5.30 p.m., cavalry were reported in the woods around Ville and fire was turned upon them. At 6 p.m. the 106th Brigade, reinforced by machine-guns, was ordered up in support of the 4th Australian Division and moved to a line of trenches between Bresle and Baisieux. At 7 p.m. the situation became more quiet. The result of the day's fighting was that the 4th Australian Division had been driven from the railway at Dernancourt and held the high ground 1,000 yards farther back. The position at Buire and Ville remained as before.

It was after these two days' fighting that Marshal Foch, who, from March 26th, had been appointed Generalissimo of all the armies, sent his famous message, " The wave has spent itself upon the beach."

Orders were now received for the transfer of the 35th Division from the VII to the V Corps, Third Army, by bus to the Canaples Area. This was postponed except for the 106th Brigade, which concentrated at Franvillers in order to relieve the 142nd Brigade, 47th Division. The relief took place on the night 6th/7th, when the battalions made a ten-mile march in the rain and occupied the front line in Aveluy Wood. Meanwhile the remainder of the division had been temporarily attached to the Australian Corps, but a few hours later, the Headquarters, R.E., and 105th Brigade, were also

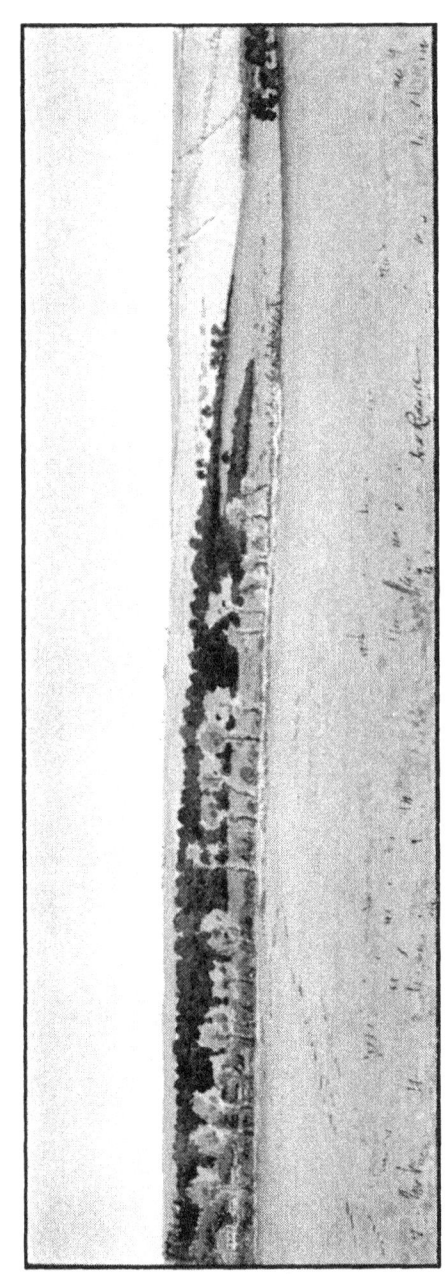

AVELUY WOOD   THE SOMME BATTLEFIELD BEYOND   MARTINSART CHATEAUX WOOD IN FOREGROUND.

transferred to the V Corps and marched to Puchevillers (Headquarters) Herisart and Toutencourt.[1]

The 104th Brigade remained holding the crossings of the Somme, until April 8th, when it was relieved and withdrew to billets and marched to Hedauville, a village just vacated by the 105th Brigade, which had taken over the right sector in Aveluy Wood with Headquarters at Senlis. The relief was carried out in intense darkness, and misfortune followed, as the medical officers of the 15/Cheshire and 4/North Staffordshire, Captains L. A. H. Bulkeley and A. L. Gardiner, were both killed on the 9th.

Aveluy Wood, which the 35th Division was to hold during the next two months, lies close to the right bank of the Ancre about two miles north of Albert. It had been reconnoitred by officers in July, 1916, at the beginning of the Somme battle, but in March, 1918, the situation did not inspire individuals with a desire to wander afield if it could be avoided. The wood was composed of well-grown trees which had not suffered to any great extent through shell fire. The undergrowth was very thick and visibility was difficult. A strip of marsh lay between the wood and the river. The enemy had gained a footing in the wood after his capture of Albert on the 26/27th of March, and, at the time the 35th Division took over the sector, the front line ran diagonally across it from the north-east corner to about 500 yards north of the south-west corner, or, roughly speaking, on the high ground which was about 130 feet above the river. South of the wood, in the river valley, lay the village of Aveluy, in German hands and visible from our lines. To the west, divided from the wood proper by a hollow, was the village of Martinsart, and 2,000 yards south-west of it, Bouzincourt. Both these places were subjected to a good deal of fire. The British front trench south of the wood lay along the high ground to the east of Bouzincourt, and from part of it a view could be obtained over the enemy's back areas including such points as the Albert-Bapaume road and Pozières Mill.[2]

---

[1] The V Corps (Lieut.-General Sir A. E. Fanshawe) held the line from Aveluy to Beaumont Hamel and consisted of the 12th, 17th, 38th, and 63rd Divisions. 106th Brigade Headquarters was in a sunken road three-quarters of a mile north-west of Martinsart.

[2] The right boundary of the 35th Division was on the Bouzincourt-Aveluy Road. The 12th Division was on the right. It was relieved by the 38th Division on April 11th.

On April 7th Major-General Marindin was confirmed in his appointment as divisional commander, and Brigadier-General Carton de Wiart, V.C., D.S.O., joined the division as G.O.C. 105th Brigade.

On the 11th the 104th Brigade relieved the 106th, and during its period in the line made some minor raids on hostile posts. On the same day the Australian Artillery relieved the 35th D.A. at Buire. The artillery had taken part in no further action of importance since the infantry moved north, but Bresle continued to receive considerable attention from the enemy's artillery, and the 159th Brigade Headquarters, after having had two billets destroyed was obliged to make use of a trench about 1,000 yards in rear.

At 4.30 a.m. on the 9th the village was enfiladed by a long-range gun from the north and a good many casualties were caused, various details which made use of the village as a billeting place being the greatest sufferers. Owing to the situation, it was necessary to keep the gun teams close to the batteries and those of the 159th Brigade were actually in the village, covered from hostile fire from the east by steep hillside which rose above it. Unfortunately, this enfilade fire did considerable damage to these teams, and for a time the shortage of horses caused some inconvenience.

The batteries then moved north. The 157th Brigade came into action between Senlis and Bouzincourt with headquarters in Senlis, and the 159th Brigade in a covering position north-east of Hedauville with headquarters in the village.[1] From this time the enemy began to shell Hedauville daily. It was fortunate that he did not do it two days earlier when the village was more crowded with troops. It eventually had to be discarded as a billeting place.

On the 11th three enemy aircraft fell in our lines. One of these was brought down by the 18/Lancashire Fusiliers by Lewis gun fire, for which act the battalion received the congratulations of the divisional commander. At this time hostile aeroplanes were very active on the front. A few days later a hostile machine came down intact in our lines and the pilot was captured.

On the 14th the 106th Brigade relieved the 105th in the right

---

[1] General Madocks took over command of the R.A. on the front of the 13th. The 77th Brigade, A.F.A. was attached and covered the left subsector. The 204th Company, R.E., were also in Senlis and suffered from shell fire. Practically the whole of the headquarters were either killed or wounded, and all correspondence was destroyed.

sector. Headquarters on the right brigade were moved from Senlis to the bank near Hedauville, and the reserve brigade headquarters from Hedauville Château also moved there. On the 17th the 105th Brigade relieved the 104th.

On the 16th our artillery knocked down the statue of the Virgin on Albert Cathedral, but the prophesy that its fall would herald the end of the war was not fulfilled with any suddenness.

At dawn on the 19th the 15/Cheshire made a slight advance along the left boundary of Aveluy Wood, and a forward post was established by a party under 2nd Lieutenant Gallagher, and next day a party of 25 under 2nd Lieutenant Tyson, under a Stokes bombardment, rushed an enemy post known as Lone Tree. Notwithstanding the fact that the party came under enfilade machine-gun fire, with the result that Lieutenant Tyson was wounded, 4 men killed, and 14 wounded, the post was reached and the garrison killed. Under the circumstances it could not be held, so, after all the wounded had been carried in, the party withdrew. The work of the stretcher-bearers was especially mentioned on this occasion and also one Private Crosby who went out on two occasions afterwards and brought in wounded men.

General Carton de Wiart was wounded at this time whilst walking along the road near Martinsart. It was the seventh time that he had been wounded in the war. Lieut.-Colonel L. M. Stevens was placed in temporary command of the 105th Brigade.

At the same time Captain J. N. O. Rycroft was appointed to the command of the 12/Highland L.I., and his place as brigade major, 106th Brigade, was taken by Captain C. N. Jervelund.

Preparations were now made for an attack on the hostile positions in Aveluy Wood and the valley to the south of it. This attack was to be made by the 35th and 38th Divisions. The main object was to capture the remaining high ground in the wood and also to deny to the enemy the commanding position west of Aveluy which overlooked our lines in advance of Bouzincourt. The left of the attack, about the centre of the wood, was to form a pivot and remain stationary, but farther south the distance of advance approached 500 yards. The artillery barrage was in the shape of a half-opened fan, and, as the batteries fired at an angle with the western " rib " of the fan, the calculation of lifts was somewhat complicated.

For the purposes of the attack the 104th Brigade relieved the 106th in the right sector, and, as the advance of this brigade was intimately connected with that of the 38th Division, the 104th Brigade was placed under its orders. The 38th Division took over the right half of the front of the 104th Brigade, the remainder was held by the 19/Durham L.I. as far as the south edge of Martinsart Wood. This battalion relieved the 18/Lancashire Fusiliers which became brigade support. Farther north, the front was held by the 15/Cheshire and 15/Sherwood Foresters. The 4/North Staffordshire was in reserve.

In order to increase the artillery support the 159th Brigade, R.F.A., evacuated the covering positions and came into action 2,000 yards farther east. With the 77th Brigade, R.F.A., it covered the northern sector, and the 157th Brigade covered the southern. The V Corps Heavy Artillery, and the 17th D.A. co-operated, whilst the Medium Trench Mortar Batteries were sited in and around Martinsart.

The attack commenced at 7.30 p.m., on the 22nd, at which hour the barrage descended.

The 19/Durham L.I., whilst waiting to attack, had suffered from a hostile barrage placed upon the support trenches and on Martinsart Wood, but this only lasted five minutes. When the battalion advanced over the open it was silhouetted against the setting sun and came under a devastating machine-gun fire. The right company (" W ") was fired on from both flanks; the commander, Captain Howes, was killed and 2nd Lieutenant Hall was wounded. This company was definitely held up after covering about 250 yards. The left company (" Y ") advanced without much difficulty for 400 yards when, owing to over-running the barrage, it was compelled to halt. Touch could not be obtained with troops on the right and left, and defensive flanks were thrown back.

Farther north, the 15/Cheshire with one company (" W ") in the front line, covered by a system of patrols under Lieutenant Harford, after advancing into the wood was held up by a strong point on the left which was part of the objective of the 15/Sherwood Foresters. On moving to render assistance in the capture of this strong point, Lieutenant Harford was severely wounded, and the advanced patrols suffered heavily. The company commander, Captain Milne, went forward to find out the cause of the delay and brought up fresh parties to assist, but heavy machine-gun fire was encountered and, except for a hostile post which was captured and consolidated, the troops had to be withdrawn to the original line. Captain Milne was killed. Lieutenant Harford was also killed as he was being brought in on a stretcher. Captain Warner ("Z" Company), advancing in support, was wounded and Sergeant Read, who took his place, shared the same fate.

This strong point which had stopped the advance of the 15/Sherwood Foresters was situated close to the edge of the wood and contained 3 machine-guns and a strong garrison. Apparently it had not suffered from the artillery bombardment. It held out until the end in spite of desperate and sustained efforts to take it.

The centre of the battalion was also delayed by two strong points, but after some sharp fighting these were both captured. An advance was then made to a hostile trench beyond. The left made progress until it was stopped by wire. By 9.30 p.m. the centre had advanced some 200 yards, but the flanks had made little headway.

At this time Lieut.-Colonel Greenwell, 19/Durham L.I., received information from 2nd Lieutenant Bell that the company was in touch with the 14/Royal Welch Fusiliers on the right, but that this battalion was also stopped [1] and that his left flank was in the air. Reinforcements were sent up to fill the gap which existed between the two companies and posts were dug and held. "W" Company, when relieved, had remaining only 1 officer, Lieutenant Chadwick, and 20 men out of the 140 which started.

The casualties in this attack amounted to 16 officers and 309 men killed, wounded, and missing. On the other hand it was reported that the enemy had suffered considerably, and 1 officer and 60 other ranks were captured.

Next day the 104th Brigade extended the flank to reoccupy that portion taken over by the 38th Division, and the 106th Brigade relieved the 105th in the left sector. On this day Brigadier-General A. J. Turner, C.M.G., D.SO. arrived to command the latter Brigade.

The next few days were quiet. The 159th Brigade, R.F.A., took over forward positions from the 157th Brigade, and the headquarters moved from Hedauville to Senlis. The 157th Brigade took

---

[1] This officer was killed shortly afterwards.

up the silent positions with headquarters in a cutting on the Warloy road. Hedauville was then handed over to the 17th Division. It was a nice village, but it received too many shells for comfort.

On the 27th the 17/Royal Scots had planned an attack on some hostile machine-gun posts on the edge of Aveluy Wood, and the place was bombarded by a 6-in. howitzer. At 8.30 p.m., the enemy, under a barrage, attacked the 12/Highland L.I. on the left. This attack was repulsed by artillery and rifle fire, but, owing to the continuous bombardment, the enterprise of the Royal Scots was postponed.

On the 26th Lieut.-Colonel Lawrenson, 18/Highland L.I., was seriously wounded in Aveluy Wood and died next day. The death of this officer, who had commanded the battalion almost since its formation, was deeply regretted by all ranks. Major Gooderson succeeded to the command of the battalion.

Another loss to the division, although also a matter of congratulation, was that Lieut.-Colonel Foord, who had just been granted a bar to his D.S.O., was appointed to command the 32nd Brigade. His place was temporarily filled by Major B. E. Sharp until the arrival of Lieut.-Colonel C. Hancock, D.S.O., on May 6th.

On the 27th, Captain Pulford, M.C., became D.T.M.O. vice Captain Fitzgerald who was appointed to the 4th Army Trench Mortar School. Captain Trench returned to duty as Staff Captain, R.A., and Lieutenant W. H. Riddell, who had been acting Staff Captain, returned to the Headquarters, 159th Brigade, R.F.A.

At this time, also, Lieut.-General Sir E. Fanshawe gave up command of the V Corps and his place was taken by Lieut.-General Shute.

During the first few days of May the infantry brigades were gradually relieved in the line by brigades of the 38th Division. The 104th Brigade and Royal Engineers marched back to Toutencourt, the 105th and Pioneers to Herissart, and the 106th to Rubempré. On the 4th the 12/Highland L.I. marched back to the neighbourhood of Hedauville, and two companies of the 19/Northumberland Fusiliers and the 204th and 205th Companies R.E. moved to Warloy. All these units commenced work on the Purple Line, which was in process of construction between Bouzincourt and Englebelmer. The artillery remained in the line. Artillery Headquarters moved to Contay, and General Madocks took command of all artillery covering the 38th Divisional front. Divisional Headquarters was at Toutencourt, but changed to Herissart on the 6th. On two days the Corps Commander visited the division and presented medal ribbons to those who had gained honours in the recent operations, and on the 8th the Commander-in-Chief visited divisional headquarters. A few days later the Army Commander visited the troops in training.

A composite battalion was now formed under Major McCulloch, 19/Durham L.I. This battalion, which was made up of one company from each battalion of the 104th Brigade, relieved the 12/Highland L.I. at the work on the Purple Line.

During the period that the infantry were in rest the line was comparatively quiet. The battery positions were shelled by the enemy almost daily, but only slight damage was done. The 157th Brigade relieved the 79th Brigade and were in action near Englebelmer. This area was subjected to continuous hostile fire. Both the batteries and the infantry supports suffered considerably. The "Lone Gun" which was situated just north of Bouzincourt and did valuable work by firing at night up the Aveluy-La-Boisselle road was vigorously searched for by the enemy, but without success. This gun evidently gave great annoyance to the German troops, for it was subjected to bombardments as long as the division remained in the sector. It was well dug in and never hit. The results of its shooting on the road were often visible in the morning from the trenches south of Martinsart Wood.

On the 10th the artillery supported an attack on the 114th Brigade on Aveluy Wood, which was only a partial success.[1] A week later the batteries assisted an effective raid against a post south of Aveluy Wood. This raid took place at 10.30 p.m., and from that hour until 2 a.m. all battery positions in the area were shelled with gas. As far as the 35th D.A. were concerned it had only a slight effect, although during the greater part of the time the men were working at the guns. Owing to the constant shelling of the wagon lines and the consequent casualties to horses, these were

[1] The first objectives were gained, but, whilst advancing on the second, one 18-pr. battery, shooting short, demoralized the attacking line. It is permissible to mention that this battery did not belong to the 35th D.A.

obliged to move from Forceville to Varennes and subsequently to Contay.[1]

The infantry battalions remained in rest until the 18th. The time was given up to training, sports, football, and musketry. Other forms of recreation included a visit from Mr. Leslie Henson's concert party. French troops attended some of these gatherings and were much interested, especially at the football and musketry. Hostile aeroplanes dropped some bombs in the vicinity of billets, and a long range gun occasionally fired at the villages as far back as eleven miles behind the line.

On the 11th the 17/Royal Scots and 15/Sherwood Foresters were moved to a camp north-east of Warloy for work on the lines, and on the 19th the 106th Brigade relieved the 113th Brigade in the centre sector at Aveluy.

Next day the 104th and 105th Brigades relieved the 114th and 115th respectively. This relief was interfered with by gas shelling. General Marindin assumed command of the line at 7.30 p.m. The headquarters was at Toutencourt.

On the 21st the two outer brigades closed in and relieved the 106th Brigade which moved to camps between Hedauville and Forceville and to dug-outs north-west of Senlis. Just prior to the relief the 18/Highland L.I. lost the whole crew of a machine-gun post owing to a direct hit by a shell. Seven men were killed; the gun itself was undamaged. Next day the infantry brigade headquarters in the bank south of Hedauville was heavily shelled during the morning.

The next few days were full of movement with raids and counter raids, but only a short reference can be made to them.

The enemy began by rushing a post of the 17/Lancashire Fusiliers and carrying off a Lewis gun and 2 men, but 1 man subsequently escaped. Later, a sniper was reported missing.

On the same day, the 23rd, the 15/Cheshire raided a hostile

---

[1] Varennes, like Senlis, was a village undermined with subterranean passages. These in Varennes were investigated by the R.E. as a possible shelter for reserve troops, but as the only entry was by means of a well shaft the idea was given up. Those in Senlis were used as brigade headquarters, both infantry and artillery, until May 6th, when the 159th Brigade moved close to the infantry headquarters in a bank near Hedauville. The Senlis passages were unhealthy—from a medical point of view.

trench facing Bouzincourt. It was found to be strongly held, and, after bombing the garrison, the patrol withdrew.

On the 24th, at 2.30 a.m., a party of the 4/North Staffordshire under 2nd Lieutenant Storr raided a post in the embankment south of Martinsart Wood. The wire round the post proved thick and the party, under machine-gun fire, withdrew to cover. It advanced again in search of another post but found no enemy and returned. During the early morning the 159th Brigade, R.F.A., dispersed some parties of the enemy which were believed to be part of a belated relief. At 11.15 p.m. the 15/Cheshire made another raid. This time it was on the post known as Lone Tree, on the Albert-Bouzincourt road, and a trench close to it, but found no enemy.

On the other hand, within a space of twelve hours, the Germans made five separate attempts upon posts of the 17/Lancashire Fusiliers but each time were repulsed.[1]

The 25th was devoted to artillery fire. Hostile shells appeared to be bursting all over the area. During the night brigade headquarters, batteries, and bivouacs were shelled by gas. On this night the 106th Brigade was due to relieve the 104th, and about 8 p.m., as the 18/Highland L.I. was paraded ready to move, a hostile aeroplane came down to within 300 feet and opened machine-gun fire. Five British planes then appeared and forced the intruder to the ground in the midst of the brigade headquarters. The machine, an Albatross, was undamaged ; the pilot was taken prisoner. He spoke English very well.

For the next two days this artillery activity continued, but was now mostly on the front lines. The Lone Gun, now manned by A/159 Battery, was shelled throughout the whole morning of the 26th, and all forward telephone lines of the brigade were cut. On two occasions S.O.S. signals were sent up, but no infantry attack developed although all indications seemed to point to one being in preparation.

The next two days saw a continuance of the shell fire. In addition to the front line the back areas were much harassed. At one time between 400 and 500 mustard gas shells were thrown into the area around Hedauville, and the 17/Lancashire Fusiliers were so pestered

---

[1] On this night the 63rd Division carried out a raid on a large scale between Aveluy and Hamel in which the 35th D.A. assisted. Two machine-guns and 24 prisoners were taken.

that they had to shift to other billeting ground. On the 28th, however, the battalion obtained some slight retribution when they shot down yet another enemy aeroplane with Lewis gun fire.

In the evening of the day the 12/Highland L.I. raided a sap head in Aveluy Wood. The party was unable to enter the post, but the garrison was destroyed by bombs.

ATTACK OF THE 1ST OF JUNE, 1918

On May 21st the G.O.C. received an intimation from V Corps that an attack would take place in the near future, and from that date preparations were made with regard to it.

The position selected for attack was the south-west portion of Aveluy Wood. The western boundary being from the point where the British front line entered the wood to the extreme south-west corner. The advance to be made was to the ride known as Ride 3, which at its junction with Ride D was not far distant from the British line to the north of it.[1] On the south, however, the distance from the starting-place on Heathcote's Bank to the final objective measured 520 yards.

Heavy and field artillery and machine-guns were to bombard the whole area on the night of May 30th/31st commencing at 12.55 a.m., on the 31st and continuing for 1 hour and 40 minutes. Gas projectors were to be fired into the ravine south-west of the wood, and a smoke barrage put down over the same area.

The area south of Martinsart Wood enclosed by Sauchiehall Trench, The Embankment, and the railway, which was known to be full of hostile machine-guns, was allotted to the 58th Divisional Artillery,[2] and the machine-guns of this division barraged patches east and south of this district. A smoke barrage to protect the right flank was also arranged for. The artillery of the division on the left also co-operated.

The actual assault was assigned to the 104th Brigade. General Sandilands had been injured whilst the brigade was in rest, and Lieut.-Colonel Stevens was in command.

---

[1] The rides in the wood running from west to east were lettered A, B, C, D, etc. A being on the southern edge. Those running from north to south were numbered 1, 2, 3, 4, etc. No. 1 being on the western edge. The rides crossed at right angles and enclosed spaces of from four to eight acres in extent.

[2] This division was now on the right.

The preliminary bombardment took place as arranged, except that, owing to the direction of the wind, the gas could not be liberated. The front trenches had been evacuated during the bombardment, and on reoccupation a German was discovered hiding in our lines. He belonged to the 24th Division, and thus gave information of a divisional relief.

Meanwhile the 104th Brigade had relieved the 106th in the left sector with the 19/Durham L.I. on the right, the 17/Lancashire Fusiliers on the left, and the 18/Lancashire Fusiliers in support. The 106th Brigade went into reserve. The 105th Brigade occupied the right sector, with the 15/Cheshire and 4/North Staffordshire in the line.

At 11.15 p.m. on May 31st, in order to allow of the heavy artillery shooting on the German front line, the front troops were withdrawn to selected positions. The bombardment opened at 11.25 p.m., and continued until 12.37 a.m. on June 1st. When it ceased the attacking troops took up their positions. The 17/Lancashire Fusiliers had two companies in the front and support trenches in the wood and two companies in Heathcote's Bank. The 18/Lancashire Fusiliers concentrated in the south end of Heathcote's Bank, and the 19/Durham L.I. were west of Martinsart.

Under cover of Heathcote's Bank were also assembled the 203rd Company, R.E., two platoons of the 19/Northumberland Fusiliers, and four Vicker's guns of the 35th M.G. Battalion. The Royal Engineers were to assist the infantry to consolidate in the Wood, and the Pioneers were to link up Heathcote's Bank with the southwest corner of the wood by a line of posts and eventually to join these to Sauchiehall Trench. The Vickers' guns were to accompany the attack.

At 3.25 a.m. the field artillery barrage of the 157th, 34th, and 159th Brigades, R.F.A., came down on the edge of the wood and a smoke-screen was thrown over the southern flank, but gas could not be used on this day either.

The first wave of the attack closely followed the barrage which advanced in a series of lifts from 50 to 100 yards at varying intervals. The valley between the two woods was crossed, and the west edge of Aveluy Wood successfully occupied. The Ravine opposite the south-west corner of the wood was assaulted by a platoon of the

18/Lancashire Fusiliers. This platoon suffered very heavily from machine-gun fire, and, in spite of gallant attempts, was unable to gain possession of the nullah. 2nd Lieutenant A. A. Armstrong, 19/Northumberland Fusiliers, who was following in rear with two platoons for the purpose of consolidation, advanced with one of them, and taking command of the remnants of the platoon of the 18/Lancashire Fusiliers, succeeded in capturing the ravine. Six of the enemy were captured and a few more were killed. Two machine-guns were also taken.[1]

All telephone lines were now cut and communication with battalion headquarters had to be done by runner or by power buzzer. Meanwhile, the right company of the 17/Lancashire Fusiliers had experienced very heavy fighting on the edge of the wood and had lost all its officers. By 5 a.m. this company was forced back to its original line. The companies on the left had also suffered severely from trench mortar fire, but this was dealt with by artillery and the troops were able to make headway.

The 18/Lancashire Fusiliers had pushed forward into the Wood and by 5.30 a.m. the right company was on the final objective and in touch with the centre company. Both companies began consolidating posts. This information was sent back by a prisoner who duly delivered it at battalion headquarters. It was later confirmed by a pigeon message. The Pioneers had kept in touch with the attacking infantry, and the remainder of the platoons under Lieutenant Hetherington had advanced and, under cover of a smoke-screen, commenced work on a chain of posts as had been ordered. Unfortunately, after half an hour, the smoke barrage was stopped and the party came under machine-gun fire from a point about 500 yards south-west of where the party was working, which necessitated picks and shovels being dispensed with and the work being completed with entrenching tools.

In the meantime the 17/Lancashire Fusiliers were having a hard struggle in the western fringe of the Wood and were making strenuous efforts along the edge in order to gain touch with the other battalion. One company of the 19/Durham L.I. was, therefore, ordered up in support, but contact was obtained without this company being called upon. Communications now became worse. The signallers

---

[1] For his actions during this day Lieutenant Armstrong was awarded the M.C.

were all casualties, the power buzzers broken by shell fire, and, owing to machine-gun fire from the right flank, runners were unable to reach the right company of the 18/Lancashire Fusiliers. Hostile artillery fire was also heavy to the west of the Wood and on Heathcote's Bank. General Marindin now sent instructions to employ the 19/Durham L.I. to improve the situation, but before this could be done the situation had changed.

About midday, the enemy brought up considerable reinforcements and counter attacked with great violence. In spite of determined resistance the troops in the Wood were gradually forced back, and a little later the 18/Lancashire Fusiliers and the 203rd Company, R.E., were obliged to withdraw across the open to Heathcote's Bank, taking with them the Pioneers, who had by now completed the chain of posts on which they were at work. Before retiring, all the wounded in the Wood, who could not be brought back were made as comfortable as possible, and the withdrawal was effected in good order in spite of the devastating effects of the hostile machine-guns to the south.

The remainder of the 19/Northumberland Fusiliers were almost annihilated in this withdrawal, but later the battalion sent out strong parties so that, by midnight, all the wounded had been brought in.[1]

The casualties were heavy and amounted to 6 officers killed or died of wounds, 13 wounded, and 1 wounded and missing. Of the other ranks 30 were killed, 215 wounded, and 74 missing, most of the latter being those wounded men who could not be brought in. In spite of losses the moral of the troops did not suffer in the slightest degree.

On the other hand the German losses were reported as being very severe both from the close fighting and especially from the artillery barrage, and this, seeing that the Wood was strongly held and both heavy and field guns had barraged it closely on two successive nights, was no doubt an accurate description. The prisoners actually brought in amounted to 2 officers and 75 men, and many others were accidentally killed after being conveyed to our lines. One batch of ten was destroyed by a German shell

[1] Congratulations on the behaviour of the Pioneers were received from the G.O.C.'s Army, Corps, Division, and Brigade.

when close to the dressing station. Six machine-guns were brought in, but several others, which had been collected at the edge of the wood ready for removal, had to be left there. A trench mortar was also captured.

At 9 p.m. the 12/Highland L.I. relieved the 17/Lancashire Fusiliers and the 17/Royal Scots relieved the other two battalions.

Except that artillery fire on both sides was above the normal the next few days passed without incident. Lieut.-Colonel Rycroft 12/Highland L.I., was slightly wounded and had to go to a rest camp. Major R. S. Dixon took command.

On the 5th the 104th Brigade relieved the 105th Brigade in the right sector. Lieut.-Colonel L. M. Stevens left the former brigade on appointment to command the 24th Brigade, 8th Division. General Sandilands returned to duty two days later.

Another attack on Aveluy Wood was now mooted, and the 105th Brigade was ordered to undertake it. With this attack in view, the 105th Brigade relieved the 104th Brigade in the right sector except for one battalion (the 18/L.F.) which remained in the line to hold the left battalion front. On the 10th at 2.32 a.m., under an artillery bombardment, 1,062 concentrated gas drums were projected on to the enemy's positions opposite the left sub-sector. The bombardment was carried out by the divisional artillery, corps heavy artillery, and 6-in. trench mortars, and was preparatory to the infant y attack. It was continued on the following morning, and wire was cut round the hostile posts east of Bouzincourt. The 105th Brigade sent out fighting patrols along the whole line, but found the hostile wire very strong, and the enemy, naturally, very much on the alert.

On the left the Germans carried out their first successful raid against the 12/Highland L.I. and carried off 2 men from one of their posts.

Next day, under Third Army Orders, the projected operation was cancelled owing to the inability of the 18th Division to co-operate on the right as had been planned. The 104th Brigade then relieved the 105th Brigade in the right sector.

At the same time the 315th A.F.A. Brigade began to relieve the 34th A.F.A. Brigade.

At this time Lieut.-Colonel Johnston, 15/Cheshire, and Major

Dixon, commanding 12/Highland L.I., both became ill and were evacuated to hospital. Their places were filled by Lieut.-Colonel Hodson and Captain Houston. Colonel Rycroft returned to the 12/Highland L.I. on the 13th.

Lieut.-Colonel D. E. Forman left the divisional artillery to take command of the 33rd Brigade, R.F.A., and his place in command of the 35th D.A.C. was taken by Major A. T. Gruncell.

On the 14th some minor alterations were made in the location of battalions owing to V Corps order that the forward area should be thinned out and the troops distributed in depth, and, on the 15th, the relief of the 35th Division by the 12th Division commenced. On this day the 62nd and 63rd Brigades, R.F.A., relieved the 157th and 159th Brigades. The latter then marched to Raincheval. On the 16th the 105th and 106th Brigades [1] were relieved by the 35th and 37th and marched to Puchevillers and Warloy respectively. The 15/Cheshire marched to Acheux for work under the C.R.E., V Corps.[2] The D.A.C. marched to Raincheval. The Trench Mortar Batteries moved there on the following day.

On the 17th the 104th Brigade was relieved by the 36th Brigade and battalions marched to Warloy, headquarters to Beauquesres. The battalions were moved also to Beauquesnes on the 18th. The machine-gun relief was then completed. The 19/Northumberland Fusiliers marched to Raincheval, except one company, which went to Acheux for work on the Purple Line.

At the conclusion of the relief divisional headquarters moved to Val Vion and Beauquesnes, and the division became G.H.Q. Reserve and Left Support Division of V Corps.

From now until June 29th the troops were resting and training. A composite battalion of the 104th Brigade, under Captain Bell, 19/Durham L.I., relieved the 15/Cheshire at Acheux, and the 205th Field Company, R.E., relieved the 204th. An epidemic of influenza broke out about this time and caused a considerable amount of sickness. It was not confined to the 35th Division, but was noticeable in the whole army in France.

During this period of rest Major C. E. Jewels, D.S.O., M.C., was transferred from the 17/Lancashire Fusiliers to command the 18th

---

[1] Prior to the relief the 19/Durham L.I. made a small raid on some hostile posts.
[2] This battalion rejoined on the 22nd.

Battalion. Colonel L. M. Wilson left the 157th Brigade, R.F.A. on appointment as Deputy Director of Artillery at the War Office· Major J. Webster commanded the brigade until the arrival of Lieut.-Colonel J. de B. Cowan from the 6th D.A. on July 6th. Major P. H. Richardson rejoined and reassumed command of B/157 Battery.

On the 27th Major H. R. McCulloch was appointed to the of the 19/Durham L.I. vice Lieut.-Colonel W. B. Greenwell who became Assistant Instructor at the Senior Officers' School, Aldershot.

At the end of the month orders were received that the division would move north, and rumours spread around that a further German offensive was to be expected in that quarter.

On the day before departure Beauquesnes was bombed by hostile aeroplanes. One or two men were wounded and fires broke out, but were subdued after an hour's work.

After leaving this area the 35th Division was not again called upon to fight in woodlands, and there is no record of any member having expressed regret at the circumstance.

Forest fighting is not the easiest form of warfare, and the memory of Houthulst and Aveluy—not to mention the smaller woodlands —must conjure up recollections to the infantry of bitter struggles under difficulties both seen and unseen. Thick undergrowth impeded both movement and vision, and the sombre atmosphere of the forest does not assist in stimulating the cheerfulness of troops in the forward lines. The fact that, under such conditions, two costly attacks did not impair the buoyancy of spirit of the troops engaged, is a tribute to the fighting qualities of the division. Evidence goes to prove that the German troops, who, of course, had equal difficulties to contend with, disliked our operations in Aveluy Wood, and would have been better pleased if they had not been undertaken.

As regards the artillery, woodland fighting is anathema. Registration is impossible, and observation of fire defies the efforts of the most persistent of battery commanders. Shrapnel catch the tops of the trees, burst before they are intended, and a barrage becomes irregular. This was the case in woods that were, or were becoming, skeletons : and Aveluy was not a skeleton.

CHAPTER XV

LOCRE

ON June 30th the division entrained at Doullens and Candas for the XIX Corps Area (Lieut.-General Sir H. E. Watts). The 104th Brigade detrained at St. Omer and marched to Tattinghem; the 105th at Wizernes and billeted in the neighbourhood; the 106th at Arques and marched to Ebblinghem. The artillery detrained at all three places and concentrated at Wormhout and Ouderzeele. The 19/Northumberland Fusiliers were at Hallines. Divisional Headquarters spent the day at Wizernes.

The division was once again in the area which had been occupied on the first arrival in France two-and-a-half years before, but next day all units moved forward by omnibus and march route to the area between Winnizeele and Abeele and were accommodated partly in billets and partly in camp. The 104th Brigade relieved three battalions of the French 71st Division in reserve.

On July 3rd the positions were as follows:—The 104th Brigade was moving up to relieve the French 217th Regiment in the Locre sector, and advanced parties of the 17/Lancashire Fusiliers, the Machine-Gun Battalion and the Trench Mortar Batteries went into the line with the French. The 105th Brigade was partly at Arques and partly at Abeele. The 106th was at Winnizeele. The Pioneers were at Godewaersvelde. The artillery was in the act of taking up reserve positions 2,000 yards south-west of Poperinghe, relieving the French 7th divisional artillery.

On the 4th the 104th Brigade began the relief of the 217th French Regiment; the 105th relieved the 104th in the Abeele area; the 106th moved to Godewaersvelde, the 18/Highland L.I. relieving a battalion of the 221 French Regiment in the line of the Locre sector. The artillery put two guns per battery into the line in the neighbourhood of Westoutre.

During the next two days the relief was completed.

July 6, 1918

The G.O.C. took over command of the Locre sector at 8 a.m. on the 6th, with headquarters at Le Mort Homme (La Montagne) in a quarry one mile north-east of Mont des Cats. Rear headquarters was at Terdeghem. The division was under the tactical command of the French XVI Corps, but was administered by the British XIX Corps.[1] The 41st Division was on the left, and the 41st French Division, which was in process of relief by the 36th British Division, was on the right. The 104th Brigade was on the left at the Scherpenberg, the 105th, which had relieved the 358th French Regiment on the previous night, was in the centre on Mont Rouge, and the 106th on the right on Mont Vidaigne and Mont Noir.

The country in which the 35th Division was destined to fight for the next month is chiefly noteworthy in that it contained many of those isolated hills which rise at intervals above the Flanders Plain, the best known of which lie in a straight line from west to east, namely, Cassel, Mont des Cats, and Kemmel. Cassel, with its town, for long the headquarters of the Second Army, and its numerous windmills was to become familiar to the troops of the division. Mont des Cats, crowned by the buildings of the Trappist Monastery, was a notable feature in the landscape, and the once beautiful and verdure-clad Kemmel was, when the 35th Division arrived in the area, a stark memorial of the desolation of warfare.

Between Mont des Cats and Kemmel is a range running from north-east to south-west including Scherpenberg, isolated to the north, and Mont Rouge, Mont Vidaigne, and Mont Noir. These latter joined together to form one chain about two miles in length, and rising about 300 feet above the level of the plain. Since 1914 this region had been a reserve billeting area, but the events of the 9th and 10th of April had brought it once more into the battle zone. The heavy onslaughts of fresh German troops against British divisions, many of which had already been deeply engaged farther south, had compelled the Commander-in-Chief to ask for assistance from the French. On the 16th these reinforcements began to arrive and eventually came into line from the Kemmel-Messines road to the Flanche Becque, north of Bailleul. On April 25th a violent bombardment followed by an overwhelming attack had forced our allies

[1] The British X Corps, Lieut.-General R. B. Stephens, took over the line on the 8th instant. The 35th Division was transferred to it. The other divisions were the 30th and 31st.

from Kemmel Hill and back across the intervening low ground to the east of the Scherpenberg-Mont Noir line. Here, in spite of further enemy efforts, the hostile advance was stopped and some successful counter attacks improved the position and re-took the village of Locre, part of which had been lost.[1] This German success on the south seriously threatened the communications in the Salient and made necessary a withdrawal of the line east of Ypres. Any further success in this area might have made necessary the evacuation of Ypres itself. As it was, the advantage gained by the enemy necessitated the Ypres-Poperinghe road being camouflaged as far as Vlamertinghe.

Such was the situation when the 35th Division took over the line, and instructions were issued to the effect that no further withdrawal was to be thought of, and that any movement made was to be in advance.

The enemy commenced operations at once. At 4.15 a.m. on the 7th a party of about 30 attempted a raid on a post of the 17/Lancashire Fusiliers near Locre Hospice. A sharp hand-to-hand fight ensued, and the enemy was driven off with casualties, leaving identifications. From 3.30 p.m. to 6 p.m. a destructive shoot was carried out against C/159 Battery, which was situated close under the hills, and considerable damage was done to the equipment and to the position. On the 8th Scherpenberg was shelled throughout the day.

Heavy thunderstorms possibly stopped any hostile infantry movements, but the headquarters of the division was bombarded and 5 casualties caused by a direct hit on the General Staff Office. Mont Rouge was shelled by howitzers (5·9 in.), and the left portion of the front line also received attention.

The communications forward of the line of heights were in full view of the enemy, and in most cases reliefs, supply parties, etc., could only move at night.

The next few days were very wet but fairly quiet. An enemy raid on the left battalion front was repulsed, and a patrol encounter in front of the centre brigade caused a few casualties.

On the night 14th/15th the 18/Lancashire Fusiliers under a

---

[1] Locre is about 1,000 yards south-east of the summit of Mont Rouge and 150 feet below it.

July 18, 1918

Stokes mortar and artillery barrage carried out a raid on the enemy position 1,200 yards east of Locre and north of the Kemmel road. The advance was checked owing to the trench mortar barrage falling short, and on account of this the party on the right had to withdraw. A few minutes later it appeared probable that enemy bombs were also falling in front of the hostile wire in addition to our own. In spite of this, efforts were made to reach the trench which was the point of attack. On the right 2nd Lieutenant Hill got through the wire, whilst it was being cut by a bangalore torpedo, and his section followed him. This party came under machine-gun and rifle fire, and Lieutenant Hill was wounded in the arm and knocked over by a bomb. Undaunted by this he led his men forward, bombed the trench, and silenced the machine-gun.

2nd Lieutenant Silliton, on the left, also entered the trench with two sections and searched a big dug-out, but found it empty. The delay caused by the short shooting of the mortars made further progress impossible, and the party withdrew.

Later on, a patrol under Captain Rigby, M.C., went out to search for killed and wounded. This patrol penetrated the wire for the second time by the gap made by the torpedo on the right. Corporal Gripps, 203rd Company R.E., had fired this. He also afterwards brought in a wounded man on his back from the hostile trench.

It was considered that the reason the raid did not achieve greater success was due to the delay and confusion caused by the short shooting of the Stokes. A considerable increase in hostile artillery activity on the next day was apparently the result of it.[1]

As intelligence indicated a hostile attack on the army front on the 18th, intense harassing fire was carried out on the night 17th/18th between 10 p.m. and 3.15 a.m., and again at noon on the 18th. No attack developed, and except that Locre was heavily shelled, the day was abnormally quiet.[2] On the 20th the 12/Highland L.I. occupied several hostile posts, which the enemy made no attempt to retake. Booby traps were found in some of them, but were destroyed without mishap. The 105th Brigade advanced the posts held by it in order to conform. A patrol of the 4/North Stafford-

---

[1] Whilst this raid was in progress the XIX Corps on the left carried out a successful attack east of Dickebush Lake.

[2] It was on this day that the great French counter attack took place on a 27-mile front between Soissons and Château-Thierry.

shire advanced on a machine-gun post but found it unexpectedly empty, and two nights later, in reply to an abortive German raid, a patrol attempted to force its way through the wire of an enemy strong point, but was held up with bombs and rifle fire. A hand-to-hand fight ensued, and one German was killed. The patrol leader and two others were afterwards found to be missing. Hostile fire now increased again, and on the 25th the battery positions were subjected to a severe bombardment. Both A/159 and B/159 Batteries lost guns.

The project was now formed that an attack should be made on the high ground known as the Dranoutre Ridge. This operation, which was to be on a somewhat large scale, was entrusted to the 106th Brigade, and accordingly, in order to allow of the necessary preparations, on the night 25th/26th, the 17/Royal Scots and the 12/Highland L.I. were relieved in the line by two battalions of the 90th Brigade, 30th Division (15th and 16th London battalions). On the following night the 18/Highland L.I. were relieved, and the command of the right sector passed to the G.O.C. 90th Brigade. Simultaneously, the 77th Brigade, A.F.A., came under orders of the C.R.A., 35th Division.[1] At the same date General Marindin, by desire of the Corps Commander, moved his headquarters to the rear position at Terdeghem. The C.R.A. and C.R.E. remained at Le Mort Homme.

On the night of the 27th, at 11.30 p.m., a very successful operation was carried out by the 19/Durham L.I. against the enemy trenches opposite the Hospice at Locre. The force consisted of 28 other ranks of " X " Company under Captains Smith and Ryall and 32 of " Z " Company under 2nd Lieutenants Dyer and Jordan. Captain H. Heaton, M.C., supervised the enterprise.

The party got into position in front of its lines before zero, and bangalore torpedoes were placed in the enemy wire. Then, under an accurate artillery and Stokes mortar barrage, the party advanced and entered the enemy work, at two points. It was soon evident that either a relief was in progress or that the enemy was forming up for an attack, for the trenches were full of men, many of whom lined up on the parapet. Fierce hand-to-hand fighting followed the entry of the Durhams in which at least 20 of the enemy were killed.

---

[1] It was relieved by the 149th Brigade, R.F.A., on the 31st.

On the left, Captain Ryall with some men rushed a machine-gun post and, although himself seriously wounded, eventually captured it and killed the crew. Subsequently, with the assistance of his servant, he brought the gun back to our lines.

The enemy troops fought bravely and showed little or no inclination to surrender. It was, therefore, necessary to exercise extreme measures in dealing with them. Four prisoners were sent back to headquarters, but, owing to recalcitration on their part, only 2 could be delivered alive. In addition to those overcome in the actual fighting, about 50 dead were counted in the trench, who presumably had been killed by the barrage. None of the Durhams was killed. In addition to Captain Ryall, Captain Smith and Lieutenants Dyer and Jordan were slightly wounded, as well as about 20 men.[1] The battalion was then relieved by the 17/Lancashire Fusiliers.

On the 29th the Army and Corps Commanders inspected the 106th Brigade, which was then training for attack in the Sylvester Cappel Area, and on this day the 27th Battalion of the 2nd Canadian Division was attached to the 35th Division for instruction in the line. On the 31st this battalion relieved the 19/Durham L.I. in reserve in the left sector, and the Durhams moved back to camp near Terdeghem.

Mont Rouge had now been heavily shelled for three days in succession and, in addition to this, the enemy appeared to be adopting our methods of dropping sudden crashes of fire on sensitive spots. Some damage was done, notably to the advanced wagon line of the 159th Brigade, R.F.A., but, generally, the casualties were not in proportion to the expenditure of ammunition. *Per contra*, it was stated by prisoners that our harassing fire by night was causing the enemy great inconvenience.

On August 1st the 17/Lancashire Fusiliers celebrated Minden Day by raiding the German trenches a thousand yards east of Locre. Two platoons started under Lieutenants Stott and Worthington. No artillery or Stokes barrage was employed. Lieutenant Stott's party entered the trench and captured a prisoner. The rest of the garrison were either killed or fled. When returning with the

---

[1] For this action Captain Ryall and Lieutenant Jordan were awarded the M.C. Lieutenant Jordan was again wounded on October 14th.

prisoner the party was attacked from the rear, and in the confusion the prisoner escaped. Lieutenant Worthington's party came under heavy machine-gun fire and was unable to accomplish its mission. Next day the battalion was relieved in the line by the 27th Canadian Battalion.

On the same night, the 15/Cheshire were being relieved by the 4/North Staffordshire, but one platoon of " Y " Company stayed in the line and raided an enemy post south of Locre on the Locre-Dranoutre road. This post was found to be empty, but after further reconnaissance another was located on the right flank and was rushed. The commander, 2nd Lieutenant Hutson, killed the sentry, and the post was bombed. The platoon then withdrew under machine-gun fire. The battalion afterwards retired to bivouacs at Boeshepe.

The 106th Brigade now moved forward preparatory to the attack on Dranoutre. The 105th Brigade Headquarters shifted to Mont Vidaigne to make room for the 106th. The weather became very wet, and owing to the fact that a strip of marshy ground had to be crossed in the proposed attack, it was decided to postpone it until a more favourable date. Accordingly, the 106th Brigade moved back into reserve.

The line was now reorganized into a two-battalion front with the 105th Brigade on the right and the 104th on the left. The 90th Brigade rejoined the 30th Division. The artillery was apportioned to correspond. The 159th Brigade, R.F.A., and the 38th Brigade, A.F.A., under Major Hart, forming the right group, and the 157th Brigade, R.F.A., under Lieut.-Colonel Cowan, the left.

On the 4th the 104th Brigade Headquarters, which was situated in an embankment on a by-road about 1,200 yards west Scherpenberg, was bombarded from 1 p.m. to 7.45 p.m., the last hour of which was intense. Some casualties were caused. At 11 p.m. a party of 50 of the 18/Lancashire Fusiliers under 2nd Lieutenants Rutherford and Allen, supported by a Stokes mortar and artillery barrage, raided the enemy trenches south-east of Locre. The wire was cut and the trench entered, but the enemy had retired. The casualties amounted to 1 killed, 3 wounded, and 3 missing (including 1 sapper).

The day of the 5th was very wet, and the night was worse. The

106th Brigade had moved into the line again preparatory to the proposed attack. The prospects, however, were so unfavourable that, after consultation with the Corps Commander, it was finally decided to abandon the enterprise. This decision was much regretted, as the attack had been carefully prepared, and, with fine weather, success was thought to be assured. What added to the disappointment was that the enemy was stated to be showing signs of retreat, and all ranks felt a strong desire to be closer on his heels than was the case in 1917. The rumours as regards this particular sector proved premature as two patrols of the 19/Durham L.I. reconnoitred the forward area on the night of the 7th, and, although certain posts were found to be unoccupied, the enemy was in strength farther in rear and showed no inclination to move.

On this day the Divisional Headquarters, which for the last few days had been at Le Mort Homme, moved back to Terdeghem, and the relief of the 35th Division by the 30th Division commenced. It was completed on the 9th, and battalions marched back to the rear areas. The artillery followed two days later. The 104th Brigade was between Cassel and Terdeghem; the 105th at Ecke and St. Sylvestre Cappel; 106th at Ecke and Steinworde. The Pioneers, who had been at work on trenches in the neighbourhood of Locre, were also relieved and marched from Boeshepe to St. Marie Cappel. The artillery brigades, after leaving one section per battery in reserve positions south of Abeele, marched to camps between Cassel and Terdeghem.

On Sunday, August 11th, His Majesty the King, who was on a visit to the front and who, on the 6th, had visited the troops in training and spoken to divisional commanders, attended a Parade Service at Terdeghem at which General Marindin and representatives of brigades and units were present.

Whilst the infantry battalions continued training and musketry in the rear areas, a portion of the artillery, the 35th Machine-Gun Battalion, and the Pioneers again moved forward on attachment to the 30th Division. The batteries, on the 16th, took up supporting positions, and on the 21st, under the 36th Division, assisted in the barrage covering the attack which the 35th Division had been obliged to forego and which resulted in the capture of the Dranoutre Ridge by the 30th Division. A hundred prisoners were taken.[1] Most of the batteries then withdrew to reserve positions.

At this time it became evident that the enemy intended to relinquish the Lys Salient, the maintenance of which was proving costly in men. On August 18th British troops had advanced opposite Merville and, next day, the town itself was captured. Although there were as yet no strong indications of a retreat on the north of the Salient, this, with other losses of ground, such as at Dranoutre, hastened his impending departure.

On the 29th the 105th Brigade and two companies of the Machine-Gun Battalion moved up in support on the St. Jan Cappel sector and relieved the 108th Brigade, 36th Division. Fires during the night made it clear that the enemy was actually withdrawing in the direction of Bailleul, and, on the 30th, the town was found to be unoccupied. The proposed relief of the 36th Division was immediately cancelled, and the 105th Brigade returned to its rest area. The other brigades stood fast.

On the 31st orders were received that the 35th Division was to be transferred to the II Corps (Lieut.-General Sir Claud Jacob). It moved next day.

During the period included in this chapter the following changes had taken place :—

Lieutenant P. S. Abraham, Intelligence Officer, R.A., was transferred as Intelligence Officer to R.A., IV Corps. On July 15th Major Chichester Constable, G.S.O. 2, was appointed G.S.O. 2 to the I.G. of Training, G.H.Q. His place was taken by Major Sir G. P. D. Pauncefort-Duncombe, Bart., D.S.O. On the 24th Captain Hodgkinson, G.S.O. 3, became Brigade Major, 105th Brigade, vice Captain Coe, who went to the 14th Division, and Lieutenant Harrison, who was A.D.C., became G.S.O. 3. On August 10th Lieutenant Maitland-Mackgill-Crichton, Black Watch, became A.D.C. to the G.O.C.[2]

---

[1] It was on this day that the battle of Bapaume commenced. Albert was recaptured on the 22nd and Bray on the 24th.
[2] In addition to above the Headquarter Staff at this time consisted of Lieut.-Colonel Thorpe, G.S.O.I., Lieut.-Colonel Farmar, A.Q.M.G. ; Major Viccars, D.A.Q.M.G. ; Major Bury, D.A.G. ; Colonel Huddleston, A.D.M.S. ; Major Stower, D.A.D.O.S. ; Major Johnston, O.C.A.S.C., and Major Wood, Camp Commandant.

On August 13th Lieut.-Colonel Crook went to England on six months' duty, and Major G. Mackereth, M.C., temporarily commanded the 17/Lancashire Fusiliers. On the 14th Major R. T. Holland, M.C., R.A., was appointed G.S.O. 2 of the 9th Division, and Major A. J. R. Kennedy, D.S.O., succeeded him as Brigade Major, R.A.

CHAPTER XVI

YPRES

ACCORDING to the orders received on August 31st, the 35th Division was to relieve the 30th American Division on the right section of the II Corps front, on the front Voormezeele-Zillebeke, by September 5th. The 14th Division was on the left, and the 34th Division, XIX Corps, on the right. The artillery was to go at once into action covering the 14th Division.

* On September 1st the 159th Brigade, R.F.A., relieved the 152nd Brigade, 34th Division, in positions between Ypres and Brielen, with headquarters at Machine-gun Farm. On the next day the 157th Brigade, R.F.A., occupied positions in the same neighbourhood vacated by the 160th Brigade, R.F.A. The D.A.C. and wagon lines were at Handekot and Hamhoek. The C.R.A. then took command of the artillery covering the 14th Division, with headquarters at Château Couthove.

On September 2nd, also, the Divisional Headquarters and the 104th Brigade moved to Heerzeele, the 105th Brigade to Tunnelling Camp, 3 miles north-west of Poperinghe, and the 106th Brigade to St. Jan de Biezen.

On the 3rd the 106th Brigade relieved the 119th U.S.A. Regiment in the right sub-sector of the Canal sector, and two companies of the Machine-Gun Battalion relieved the American Machine-Gunners in the left sub-sector.

Next day the 105th Brigade commenced the relief of the 120th U.S.A. Regiment in the left sub-sector. Headquarters were in huts 1,000 yards south of Vlamertinghe. The machine-gun relief was completed and the command of the line passed to General Marindin at 6 p.m. on this day. Headquarters were at Vogeltji Convent near Château Lovie in the Proven Area. The 66th D.A. covered the front. The 104th Brigade was in reserve between Poperinghe and Vlamertinghe. Both the 105th and 106th Brigades were interfered with by gas shelling during the relief, and a certain number of casualties was caused in the 4/North Staffordshire and the 12/Highland L.I.

The line now held was familiar to many of those in the division who had served in the Ypres Salient in the earlier stages of the war, but noticeable changes had occurred. Ypres itself had settled more nearly to the earth and many once familiar landmarks had disappeared. The Pilckem Ridge was once more in German hands, and tracks to the north of the town, which had been used in safety a year before were now, once again, under hostile observation. On the other hand the enemy had evacuated Kemmel on August 31st, and observation from that quarter was denied him.

The line as taken over extended from Moated Grange, south of Voormezeele, on the south, to the canal at the crossing of the Ypres-Lille road about 1,000 yards to the north-east. It crossed the canal here and continued in an almost straight line in the direction of the road and railway crossing, south-west of Zillebeke Lake, and later was extended to the lake itself (September 13th).

Numerous tracks, mostly corrugated with wood, spread out in all directions behind the lines and, as far as supplies and reliefs were concerned, the troops were able to regard the prospect of rain with equanimity. And rain came very shortly afterwards.

As soon as the battalions had taken over, they commenced patrolling towards the front. On the 4th a daylight patrol of the 12/Highland L.I., under Lieutenants Young and Bethune, advanced 1,000 yards. A fight with the enemy ensued, in which a Lewis gun was destroyed. On the 5th the 159th Brigade, R.F.A., commenced to withdraw from action north of Ypres, and, by the 7th, had taken up positions south-west of the town covering the 35th Division, with observation posts on the ramparts of Ypres, one at the Lille Gate and another at the south-east bastion.

On this day a strong patrol of the 15/Cheshire, under Lieutenant Shaw, went out in the mist at 10.30 a.m. Two hostile posts were found to be unoccupied, but, on proceeding farther, a third was met with and rushed. Six prisoners were captured, two of them being wounded. The patrol withdrew without casualties. These prisoners stated that a British offensive on this front was considered an unlikely contingency, and that our propaganda leaflets were read with interest if not with enjoyment. They further stated that an officer had told them that the 35th British Division was against them, and that they had been warned that it was "a fighting division." [1]

A few quiet days passed and then the 104th Brigade relieved the 105th in the left sector. A patrol encounter of the 17/Lancashire Fusiliers on the following day (9th) had unfortunate results, and, in the end, 3 men were reported missing. On the two following days further encounters took place. In the first of these the party came under heavy machine-gun fire from Spoil Bank, a bank on the canal one mile east of Voormezeele, and the Commander, 2nd Lieutenant Edwards, was wounded. Three patrols were out on the 11th, and one of these, under Lieutenant Cooke, reached Blauwe Poort Farm, half a mile south of Zillebeke Lake, and bombed the garrison. No prisoners, however, were taken in these encounters. Patrols of the 106th Brigades were unable to get within close touch of the enemy, although they penetrated to White Horse Cellars, close to St. Eloi.

Meanwhile the 157th Brigade, R.F.A., had relieved the 64th Brigade, R.F.A., and was now covering the right sector of the divisional front. The activities of this brigade had, for the last week, been confined to harassing fire and to supporting a minor operation on the part of the Belgians. On the 10th the number of rounds allotted for harassing fire was reduced. For the purpose of deceiving the enemy as to the number of guns on the front shooting was carried out by "active sections," and most of the guns remained silent.

Next day the 105th Brigade relieved the 106th, and the latter became divisional reserve. At the same time the active section of D/159 Battery was moved into Ypres.

From the 13th onwards there was a noticeable increase in the amount of hostile fire. On this day the 19/Durham L.I., which had relieved the 17/Lancashire Fusiliers, captured a corporal and 4 men of the 40th Saxon Division—a new identification. This hostile patrol approached one of our posts at dawn. Lance-Corporal Cranney, who was in charge of the post in question, gave orders

[1] The above information is taken from an official summary of interrogation. It must appear remarkable how soon the knowledge of the change of front reached the German Staff.

that fire should be withheld, and then, when the enemy was within 30 yards, he rushed out with 5 men and captured the whole. Meanwhile, patrols of the 105th Brigade had located the line of hostile posts as being 1,000 yards distant from our line. At 10 p.m. the 35th D.A. bombarded Hill 60 with 1,000 rounds of gas shells.

At 10 a.m. on the 15th the front held by the 35th Division was transferred from the II to the XIX Corps.

On this day the infantry of the division, under a light artillery barrage, advanced the whole line of front to a depth varying from 600 to 1,000 yards.

Zero hour was 10.28 p.m. On the right the 4/North Staffordshire advanced with the right flank moving almost due south, and a little to the east of Moated Grange. Practically no opposition was met with in this direction, and posts were established in the old French Trench leading to Spoil Bank. On the immediate left, two hostile posts were captured by the 15/Sherwood Foresters, and a platoon then went forward to clear the dug-outs and tunnels in Spoil Bank. Seven of the enemy were found here, of whom 5 were killed and 2 taken prisoners. To the north of the Sherwood Foresters was the 18/Lancashire Fusiliers. The covering party of the left platoon came upon an untouched belt of wire, south of Blauwe Poort Farm, but gaps were cut in this without delay. Two enemy posts were rushed before the machine-guns could be brought into action, and a third, from which the defenders merely fired a few rifle shots, was taken immediately afterwards. The garrison of the farm of La Chapelle offered some resistance, but it was surrounded, and a corporal, 14 men, and a machine-gun captured. 2nd Lieutenant Rewcastle, who was on the right, endeavoured to exploit his success, but, although his patrol advanced some 600 yards, no further trace of the enemy was found. The booty was 27 prisoners, 1 heavy machine-gun, and 1 light machine-gun.

The right of the 19/Durham L.I., under 2nd Lieutenant Reid, advancing on Blauwe Poort Farm, encountered a certain amount of opposition from small posts which patrols had previously found unoccupied. In the fighting which ensued Lieutenant Reid was hit and is believed to have been killed (search parties failed to find him), and the attack lost direction. The advance was continued and a post established a little north of the farm.

HISTORY OF THE 35TH DIVISION

The centre platoon, under Lieutenant Shepley, met with considerable resistance. The enemy was in strength and at one time succeeded in forcing back the advancing troops, but they returned to the attack and finally gained and held all objectives. Many of the enemy were killed and a number of prisoners taken. On the left centre, Lieutenant Dales succeeded in capturing Manor Farm with but little opposition, and, on the left (2nd Lieutenant Leach), the objectives were gained without difficulty. The enemy at this point ran away. The battalion captured 25 prisoners and 2 machine-guns. One German was found next morning hiding from the left platoon. In view of future operations this advance was of some importance. It gave more room for deployment of the left and centre brigades in the impending attack, and enabled machine-guns to be brought within effective range for barrage purposes. The casualties were slight, whilst those of the enemy were heavy. Congratulations on the success were received from the higher commanders.

In all, 49 prisoners and 4 machine-guns were captured. The prisoners belonged to the 40th Saxon Division, and their moral was not good : neither was their condition.

On the two following days more prisoners were captured. The 15/Sherwood Foresters took 4 from a post near Spoil Bank, and under Lieutenant Mann, a party of the 15/Cheshire took 1 N.C.O. from the outskirts of St. Eloi. A German sergeant was killed at the same time. Next day another patrol got caught in a barrage, and Lieutenant Stott was killed.

On the 16th the 106th Brigade relieved the 104th in the line, and, on the 19th, the 105th Brigade was relieved by the 42nd Brigade, 14th Division. The battalions marched to School Camp. Both the brigade headquarters of the 104th and 105th were at St. Dunstan's, behind Belgian Château. The 159th Brigade R.F.A. Headquarters was close beside them at Assam Farm, and the 157th Brigade, R.F.A., south of Vlamertinghe. The batteries of the 157th Brigade were now covering the 42nd Brigade under the 14th Division. The Divisional headquarters and D.A. now moved to Waratah Camp.

The 106th Brigade was now holding the whole of the divisional front, but, except for artillery activity on the part of the enemy, no operation of importance took place. Major A. G. Scougal, of the 17/Royal Scots, was killed on the 16th, and his place as second-in-command was taken by Major Murray, 18/Highland L.I.

On the 22nd a day which had originally been fixed for the beginning of the advance, the troops began to take up forward positions. The 17/Lancashire Fusiliers moved to the front line, and relieved two companies of the 17/Royal Scots. The headquarters were in Swan Château. The 18/Lancashire Fusiliers was in support and the 19/Durham L.I. in reserve.

The 4/North Staffordshire and the 15/Sherwood Foresters relieved the 18/Highland L.I. Headquarters was at Bedford House. Next day these two battalions were relieved by the 15/Cheshire.

These somewhat complicated reliefs had been arranged firstly, in order to conceal the projected attack, and secondly to give some respite to the troops who were to make the actual assault. Between now and September 27th all units took up their battle positions. The front was arranged as follows :—

The sector held by the 35th Division was known as Trois Rois from the village of that name, situated on the Lille road, about half a mile south of Ypres. On the extreme right, 500 yards north of the canal at Spoil Bank and behind La Chapelle, was the 4/North Staffordshire with one company in the front line. On its left was the 15/Sherwood Foresters with two companies aligned along the line of "Middlesex Road." The 15/Cheshire was in brigade reserve about Bedford House.[1]

The 104th Brigade was in the centre of the line, with the 18/Lancashire Fusiliers on the right and the 19/Durham L.I. on the left. Each had two companies in the front line. The 17/Lancashire Fusiliers was in reserve. The head-quarters of both brigades were at Woodcote House.

On the left was the 106th Brigade with one company of the 17/Royal Scots in the front line between the railway and Zillebeke Lake, with the 12/Highland L.I., the actual attacking battalion, immediately behind. The 18/Highland L.I. were in support, and the 17/Royal Scots in reserve north of Belgian Château. Brigade

---

[1] Middlesex Road was a plank road made in the previous year. It ran northeast from Voormezeele to a point south of Manor Farm where it connected with other roads running east and south-east. It was in fairly good condition.

headquarters was in a dug-out in the railway embankment east of Trois Rois.

The artillery covering the front was divided into three groups. Right Group: Lieut.-Colonel Lyons, D.S.O.; 187th Brigade, R.F.A., and B/159 Battery. Centre Group: Lieut.-Colonel Cowan; 157th Brigade, R.F.A., and A/159 Battery. Left Group: Lieut.-Colonel Davson; remainder of 159th Brigade and 173rd Brigade, R.F.A. All batteries were gradually moved up to forward positions in readiness to support the forthcoming attack.

Two companies of the 101st Machine-Gun Battalion were also attached to the 35th Division.

In addition a certain number of heavy guns had been brought up by degrees and were now in position covering the front of attack.

During these days certain alterations occurred in the personnel. Lieut.-Colonel J. Jones, M.C., of the Durham L.I., joined the 17/Lancashire Fusiliers, and Major Meskereth resumed the rank of second in command. Major Stewart, D.S.O., M.C., R.A.M.C., who had been wounded in March, rejoined the 15/Cheshire, and Lieut.-Colonel Farmar, A.Q.M.G., left the division and was succeeded by Lieut.-Colonel Jones, King's Liverpool Regiment.

Plate IV

MAJOR-GENERAL A. H. MARINDIN, C.B., D.S.O.
Commanding 105th Infantry Brigade May 1916 to March 1918.
Commanding Division March 1918 to March 1919.

SEPTEMBER 28, 1918

CHAPTER XVII

THE FINAL ADVANCE

Events of September 28th to October 2nd

THE first objective to be gained on the 28th extended from the canal, south-east of Battle Wood, through Klein Zillebeke, and thence along the ridge to a point south-east of Sanctuary Wood. In order to allow the left brigade to come up, the right and centre brigades were to make a pause on a line from The Bluff to a point just north-east of Zwartelen, after which the troops were to continue to the first objective. On reaching this, the right brigade was to stand fast and allow the 41st Division to pass through it.

The barrage opened at 5.25 a.m. It was reported as accurate and effective, although, in order not to give away the forward positions of the batteries, no registration had been attempted. The assaulting infantry had occupied their assembly positions between 2 and 3 a.m., and, at 5.30 a.m., the whole line advanced. The barrage advanced in lifts of 100 yards in three minutes, and the infantry kept close up to it.[1] Rain had begun to fall at zero hour, and this, with the pitted nature of the ground, made the advance difficult, but, in spite of this handicap, the time was well kept.

On the right the 105th Brigade advanced steadily for an hour, and reached the line of pause—an advance of 1,500 yards—where the assaulting companies were reorganized. After a halt of 40 minutes the advance was resumed. Little opposition was met with and a large number of prisoners was captured. By 8.30 a.m. the line from Buffs Bank, round the east of Battle Wood to the railway embankment was in possession of the troops. About 650 prisoners were captured, including a battalion commander and his staff, 2 field guns, 7 trench mortars, and 22 machine-guns.

---

[1] Double pauses were made at 500, 1,000, and 1,500 yards. The barrage consisted of shrapnel and H.E., in equal proportion. Shrapnel 10 per cent. on graze. One round in eight of smoke.

In the centre the 104th Brigade advanced without incident. The line running east of Hill 60 and the Caterpillar was reached with but slight opposition, and by 8.30 a.m. the battalions were on the line Klein Zillebeke–Canada Tunnels. Patrols of the 18/Lancashire Fusiliers were then pushed out to Jehovah Trench, and this, after a certain amount of opposition from hostile machine-guns, was captured by 11 a.m. From this position a platoon under 2nd Lieutenant Arnold advanced and, after a sharp struggle with the detachments, captured 3 field guns which were in action close to the road, about 1,000 yards east of Klein Zillebeke.

Meanwhile, the 17/Lancashire Fusiliers, which had been following up the attack, had passed through the 18/Lancashire Fusiliers and the 19/Durham L.I. and were preparing for the advance on Zanvoorde. This battalion was subjected to heavy machine-gun fire from the valley of the Bassevillebeke, which lay across its front, and from the high ground farther to the east on which Zanvoorde stands. Owing to this, the commander decided to outflank the ridge from the north and, about 4 p.m., reported that Zanvoorde was taken. As appeared later, this was not accurate. The western spurs of the ridge had been captured, but the site of the village itself, which lay on a spur running out in a south-easterly direction, had not been occupied. The enemy attempted to counter attack from Tenbrielen on to this spur, but was repulsed, and, under the impression that the final objective had been reached, the battalion consolidated the position.

On the left the 106th Brigade, with the 12/Highland L.I. leading, advanced with little opposition except in Zillebeke village, where the enemy attempted to make a stand. These parties were summarily dealt with, and the advance continued. Hedge Street Tunnels were reached at 6.45 a.m., and Tor Top Tunnels and Canada Tunnels were captured by 7.30 a.m. A line was then consolidate about 500 yards beyond them. At this time the enemy made some attempt to interfere, but was dispersed by Lewis gun fire.[1]

The 18/Highland L.I., which had been advancing in support, now arrived preparatory to passing through and advancing on the second objective, Alaska Houses, midway between Zanvoorde and

---

[1] Hedge Street Tunnels and Tor Top Tunnels are on Observatory Ridge immediately south of Sanctuary Wood, and about 1¼ miles east of Zillebeke. Canada Tunnels lie one mile to the south-west. These were all deeply dug German works.

Gheluvelt. This battalion in its advance suffered some loss from hostile howitzer fire, 4 of its officers being wounded. When close to the fist objective it was engaged by a low-flying hostile aeroplane, which was brought down by Lewis gun and rifle fire. The battalion advanced from the first objective at 9.50 a.m., and came under heavy machine-gun fire from Shrewsbury Forest, which caused a certain number of casualties. Regardless of this, the troops pushed forward, but touch appeared to be lost with the 104th Brigade, and also with the division on the left. In reality, the troops of the 104th Brigade were aware of the position of the 18/Highland L.I. at this time, but actual touch was not established with the 29th Division until after midday, when patrols of 17/Royal Scots filled the gap.

When approaching Alaska Houses the left company of the 18/Highland L.I. was fired on at point blank range by field guns, and many casualties were inflicted. A party which was sent to try to capture these guns reported that they had apparently withdrawn, but as at about this time, 3 guns were captured by the 12/Highland L.I., it is probable that they were the same pieces. Alaska Houses were captured at 12.30 p.m. The position was then consolidated and patrols pushed forward to Ugly Wood. The 17/Royal Scots were then disposed on the right of the 18/Highland L.I.

The 12/ and 18/Highland L.I. between them captured 5 officers and 220 men, 4 77-mm. guns, 1 5.9-in. howitzer, and about 20 machine-guns.

As soon as the first objective was reached the 157th and 159th Brigades, R.F.A., moved forward to the vicinity of Verbrandenmolen and Zillebeke, which places were reached about midday. The various batteries now reverted to brigade control, and the attached brigades rejoined their own divisions. The batteries in the advance suffered some casualties from shell fire and mines. One gun of D /157 Battery was destroyed by a shell, and one section of C/159 Battery was temporarily put out of action through the horses treading on tin canisters filled with explosive which were buried in the roadways east of Zillebeke. Several other traps of a similar nature were picked up before damage was done. All artillery units found the roads and tracks in very bad condition, and progress was slower than had been hoped. C/159 (Major Goss) and the section of D/159 Batteries, which were hastening forward to support the second advance of the 106th Brigade, were unable to do so except by bursts of fire on Gheluvelt and the Gheluvelt–Zanvoorde road so that the 17/Royal Scots and the 18/Highland L.I. made good their objective at Alaska Houses with practically no artillery support.

Towards evening these guns were in action about Hedge Street Tunnels.

In the afternoon, on the right, B/157 Battery and one section of D/157 went forward from Verbrandenmolen as advanced guard. B/157 (Major P. H. Richardson) was fired on whilst in column of route by a machine-gun. This was located, and one gun rapidly brought into action destroyed it at the eighth round. Later, as these batteries were coming into action, forty rounds were showered upon them by a hostile 105 mm. battery. These howitzers were marked and engaged over open sights with the result that the detachments were scattered and the guns ceased fire. They were subsequently captured by the infantry of the 41st Division. In the evening B/157 and D/157 batteries withdrew to Corner House, 500 yards east of Hill 60. During the day the divisional artillery fired 37,500 rounds.

Immediately after the advance the Royal Engineers and Pioneers commenced to work on the roads and tracks which were practically obliterated. The transport was moved up to the neighbourhood of Zillebeke Lake, and until such time as the roads were made passable rations and ammunition was sent up by pack animals.

In the evening the G.O.C. visited the brigadiers at Tor Top Tunnels and Woodcote House. Gathering darkness had made impossible any further advance on this day, but the results gained surpassed anything that had previously been carried out by the division. In addition to an advance of 6,000 yards[1] over ground, a considerable portion of which had not been in the allied possession since 1914, historic places such as Hill 60, Caterpillar, Sanctuary Wood, and Shrewsbury Forest had finally been wrested from German hands.

---

[1] Direct measurement. The walking distance from the original line to Zanvoorde is about four miles.

HISTORY OF THE 35TH DIVISION 261

Upwards of 800 prisoners had been captured in addition to field guns, machine-guns and trench mortars. The casualties for the day amounted to 573.

During the night orders for the next day's fighting were issued. The 105th Brigade was to move up *via* Zanvoorde and capture the line Tenbrielen–Blagnaert Farm. If all went well the advance was to continue to Wervicq. The 106th Brigade was to be in support, and the 104th was to remain on the final objective, and was detailed for the defence of the line as far south as the canal.

The 105th Brigade was therefore relieved by the 104th (18/L.F.) and the battalions concentrated at Klein Zillebeke. At 8 a.m. the 15/Cheshire, forming the advanced guard, began to move on Tenbrielen *via* Zanvoorde. The other two battalions formed the main body. Owing to the mist and the fact that the track from Klein Zillebeke to Zanvoorde was almost obliterated, the leading battalion lost direction and advanced along the road to Hollebeke Château. When the mistake was discovered, General Turner was of opinion that it was too late to go back and decided to advance on Zanvoorde from the west.

On reaching the western slopes of the Zanvoorde ridge the battalions in turn deployed in attack formation. On the arrival of the 15/Cheshire at the outskirts of what had once been the village, heavy machine-gun fire was opened on the battalion. One officer (Lieutenant Tyson) and several men were killed, and many more were wounded. This was unexpected, as the village was assumed to be in our hands.[1] An attempt to envelop these machine-guns failed, and further casualties were incurred. An artillery barrage was now called for which was supplied by A/157 Battery (Major Wallers) at Corner House, and C/157 Battery (Major Webster) firing from a position 500 yards south-east of Klein Zillebeke. This barrage crept through the village from the western to the eastern edge, and, under it, three companies of the 15/Cheshire again attacked. But the machine-guns were too well protected to be silenced by field guns, and no success was achieved. It was now 12.30 p.m., and General Turner sent word to Colonel Johnston that no further attack was to be made, and at the same time issued orders

[1] This village was reduced to a heap of rubble. The Germans had put up a notice board to mark its site.

for enveloping attacks to be made by the 15/Sherwood Foresters and the 4/North Staffordshire.

Meanwhile B/159 Battery and two sections of D/159 (Major J. H. K. Richardson) had overcome the difficulties of the side tracks and had advanced from their positions east of Zillebeke to the neighbourhood of Hollebeke Château,[1] from which place they were able to bring effective fire on Zandvoorde in support of the attack. After a sharp fight the whole of the Zandvoorde ridge was cleared of the enemy, and the two battalions followed up their success. The 15/Sherwood Foresters advanced on Tenbrielen, the 4/North Staffordshire towards Blegnaert's Farm, whilst the 17/Royal Scots prolonged the left.

The enemy, by means of well-posted machine-guns, strongly contested this advance, but, in spite of the difficulty of keeping direction, the troops overcame all opposition, and about 7.30 p.m. the new front was made good.

On receipt of information at 1 p.m. that the advance had been held up at Zanvoorde, General Marindin, who was then at Woodcote House, called up General Pollard on the telephone and gave him instructions that, if the advance of the 105th Brigade was delayed, the 106th must push through to Tenbrielen, and that he, General Pollard, was to take command of all advarced troops.

As the 105th Brigade now seemed to have gained the upper hand, General Pollard limited his orders to moving the 17/Royal Scots up on the left of the 4/North Staffordshire. This battalion, therefore, advanced with its right on the Zanvoorde–Tenbrielen road. Progress was slow owing to heavy shelling and machine-gun fire, but the advance of one company of the 12/Highland L.I. upon hostile positions beyond the Gaverbeek relieved the situation. An attempted counter attack on the part of the enemy was overcome by the two leading companies, under Captains Craig and Matley, and the advance was not delayed. By nightfall the battalion had reached to within 500 yards of Blegnaert Farm, and patrols were pushed forward to it.

The 18/Highland L.I. and the 12/Highland L.I. (less C Company, which had pushed forward as stated) had, meanwhile,

---

[1] The other section of D/159 was, with C/159, at this time one mile south-west of Gheluvelt.

September 29, 1918

moved forward in close support of the 17/Royal Scots, and in the evening dug in in a position in rear of them. The former battalion, in its assembly position north-west of Zanvoorde, had suffered considerably from gas shelling. It became necessary for all ranks to wear gas masks, which further increased the difficulty of crossing the country. At one period of the day a considerable number of gas shells were fired upon the area of advance, but later, the battery which fired them either ran short of this class of ammunition or retired.

The situation at nightfall was that the 15/Sherwood Foresters were north of Tenbrielen, the 17/Royal Scots on the line Tenbrielen–Blegnaerts Farm, and the 18/Highland L.I. in close support. The 4/North Staffordshire was fortifying the line Zanvoorde–Tenbrielen, and the 12/Highland L.I., in rear of the other battalions of the 106th Brigade. B/159 Battery was in close support of the infantry, and other batteries moving up as fast as the state of the roads permitted.

So far as this particular portion of the front was concerned the 35th Divison had now reached the utmost limit of the British advance on the 19th of October, 1914, and henceforward it was to fight on virgin soil. The western slopes of the ridge over which the division had passed were a maze of disused trenches and neglected wire. Although many of these trenches bore evidence of not having been regularly occupied for some time, they were deep, still in good repair, and constituted a serious obstacle to the passage of troops. The artillery, indeed, were confined to two roads, one on each flank of the divisional line of advance. These trenches opened one's eyes to the extent of cover for reserves which the enemy possessed during the years of struggle for the Ypres Salient. From now onwards trenches were left behind and open warfare prevailed.

General Pollard now issued orders that the advance should be continued at 6.15 a.m., next morning, and asked that artillery support should be given for the bombardment of Wervicq. Accordingly the divisional artillery was placed under his control, and support was also obtained from heavy howitzers. A bombardment of Wervicq was ordered from 5.50 to 6.50 a.m., but the result was probably not very effective. It had rained heavily all night, and although the gun teams hooked in before dawn, and the batteries moved off in the dark, the state of the roads was such that they had the greatest difficulty in getting forward. Only one section of B/159 Battery succeeded in arriving within effective range before zero hour. It came into action at the cross roads a quarter of a mile east of Houthem. The remainder of the battery and D/159 joined it shortly afterwards. The 157th Brigade, R.F.A., in order to open fire at the prescribed time, dropped into action to the east of Kortewilde. More advanced positions were occupied later in the morning.

A/159 Battery (Major Youl) fired from its overnight position, and then advanced to a position between Kortwilde and Tenbrielen. C/159 which, on the 28th had been far advanced on the left flank in support of the 106th Brigade, had been obliged to make a wide detour to the north in order to cross the ridge. On the afternoon of the 29th it was north of Zanvoorde, and owing to the intersected country it was not till midday on the 30th that it came within effective range of Wervicq at a spot 1,000 yards west of Tenbrielen.

The infantry advanced at 6.15 a.m. The 12/Highland L.I. were on the right; the 18/Highland L.I. on the left. The 15/Cheshire and 17/Royal Scots were in support.

Rain fell and a strong wind was blowing, but the opposition from the enemy was slight, and the advance progressed successfully until within 1,000 yards of the railway north of Wervicq. Here the forward movement was checked by machine-gun fire from the front and both flanks. The right flank of the 12/Highland L.I. was now close to a group of houses known as Krommen Peerlaar Cabaret, and more cottages lay to the south-west of them. The leading company of the 15/Cheshire was accordingly called up from support and moved out on the right flank to clear away the machine-guns. Shortly afterwards two companies of the 12/Highland L.I. succeeded in penetrating into the outskirts of Wervicq but were compelled to withdraw owing to machine-gun fire which enfiladed the right flank. Another company of 15/Cheshire then came up and the supporting company of the 12/Highland L.I. was ordered to advance to the south-east.

The 18/Highland L.I. was suffering severely from machine-guns on the left flank, especially from a farm on the Wervicq–Gheluvelt road, but the left supporting company pushed out to the left and succeeded in reducing them to silence. The right of the battalion still continued to advance, but the left was definitely held up, and two companies of the 17/Royal Scots were brought up as reinforcements. These companies made good the ground, and reached a point within 400 yards of the suburbs, north of the railway. In the course of their manœuvres to patrol the left, these companies had crossed a thick belt of wire, and shortly afterwards heavy fire was opened upon them from the left flank. This flank was exposed as no touch could be obtained with the troops of the 29th Division. The fire was located as coming from a group of pill boxes. One of these was rushed and the garrison captured, but it was found impossible to clear the other machine-guns from their position. By this time the strength of the companies was greatly reduced. All the officers were casualties, as was also a large proportion of the N.C.O.'s. The enemy now made a counter attack upon the flank of the support companies, and it became necessary to withdraw. All the leading troops were successfully brought back except the remnants of two platoons which were so far advanced that they were unable to extricate themselves. The right of the 18/Highland L.I. had meanwhile forced its way as far forward as the railway embankment, but the troops could not maintain this position, and eventually established themselves upon a ridge about 500 yards to the north of it.

General Pollard, accompanied by General Turner from advanced headquarters on the Zanvoorde–Tenbrielen road, had gone forward to investigate the situation. He decided that further progress could not be made without systematic artillery preparation, and returned to headquarters to arrange it.

Meanwhile, at 11 a.m., the 29th Division was reported to be east of Gheluwe, and the 104th Brigade was ordered up towards Menin to connect with General Pollard's force at Reeke.[1] The brigade left Klein Zillebeke at 12.30 p.m. Shortly afterwards the G.O.C. received a message from General Pollard and also from the G.O.C. 3, who was acting as liaison officer, giving details of the infantry dispositions and stating that the divisional artillery was moving on Wervicq.

---

[1] Owing to numerical weakness General Pollard was unable to extend his left to Reeke. This village was 1200 yards north-east of Wervicq.

A message was sent to General Pollard to say that heavy artillery would be employed, and that it was hoped the advance of the 104th Brigade would lessen the pressure.

The 104th Brigade, however, had in the meantime met with strong resistance in the neighbourhood of America Cabaret, and no direct touch was obtained with the 29th Division which had had to relinquish its hold of Gheluwe. At nightfall the 104th Brigade established a line beyond America Cabaret facing east and south-east, with the 18/Lancashire Fusiliers on the left and the 19/Durham L.I. on the right. Orders were then issued that the infantry should stand on the ground gained.

During the night definite touch was obtained with the troops of the 29th Division.

The 104th Brigade continued its advance at dawn on October 1st, but little progress was made as the machine-gun fire was heavy all along the front. It now became apparent that the brigade was confronted by the well-known Gheluwe Switch, a strong line of trenches and pill boxes which had been constructed some twelve months previously, and which was designed in order to cover Menin. General Sandilands reported that it would not be captured except by a pre-arranged attack. The 105th and 106th Brigades were still maintaining their positions, but their numbers did not permit of their taking part in any serious action.[1]

At this time the 41st Division marched across the rear of the 35th, being under orders to capture the Terhand Line and the 104th Brigade were allotted the task of attacking the high ground north of Wervicq and west of Reeke. The 157th Brigade, R.F.A., was placed at the disposal of General Sandilands, and the batteries moved to positions south-west of Blegnaert Farm. At the same time the 30th Division closed up, and, in the evening, relieved General Pollard's force and the 159th Brigade, R.F.A. The infantry marched to Kruiseeke and the artillery to Zillebeke Lake.

During the night October 1st/2nd General Sandilands received orders to capture the high ground west of Reeke in conjunction with the 41st Division, which was to attack on the immediate left. The attack was carried out by the 17/Lancashire Fusiliers, and

---

[1] The 105th and 106th Brigades were at this moment only 900 and 500 strong, respectively. The trench strengths on September 28th had been 2,280 and 2,050.

commenced at 6 a.m., after a preliminary bombardment by the 157th Brigade, R.F.A., The troops met with strong opposition and made very little progress. The attack of the 41st Division was also held up, and a second attempt in the afternoon failed to make any impression on the enemy. In the evening the 104th Brigade was relieved by the 103rd Brigade, 34th Division, and withdrew to Kruiseeke. The 157th Brigade, R.F.A., marched to Brisbane Camp, near Belgian Battery Corner, south-west of Ypres.

The front line, as handed over by the infantry, was three miles in advance of that from which they had started on the morning of September 30th. They had carried out their orders and captured the high ground overlooking Wervicq, but owing to opposition and heavy losses had not been able to extend the front as far to the east as had been intended.

The difficulties of making headway during the latter part of the advance may be attributed to the open country over which they were operating, and to the lack of power in the artillery support. The bombardment of Wervicq had been ordered for 5.50 a.m., and this was complied with; but, as it happened, the nests of machine-guns which delayed the advance were first encountered about 1,200 yards north of the town. Between dawn and the time when the forward lines came to grips with the enemy, battery commanders were unable to arrange any reliable system of communication, and the result was that pill boxes and isolated houses had to be assaulted without effective covering fire. Could this have been given, the infantry might have been able to hold on to the positions so hardly won in the outskirts of the town, and the losses during the day would possibly have been less than they were.

This temporary interruption of the advance, however, was of little account when compared with all that the division had accomplished in the first four days' fighting. The total advance had been about eight miles over very difficult country, and in most inclement weather. During this time 1,100 prisoners had been captured as well as 42 guns and unnumbered machine-guns, trench mortars, and other articles of equipment.

As the line advanced the evacuation of the wounded became a serious problem. The line for stretcher-bearers being through Zanvoorde to Klein Zellebeke—a road which was knee-deep in mud—Zwarteleen and thence along Middlesex Road. On October 1st motor ambulances were brought by the Lille Road to Hollebeke and then to Tenbrielen. In this way the carrying distance was greatly shortened.

The same difficulties were experienced by ration parties moving in the opposite direction. It is greatly to the credit of all concerned that the troops were at no time short of food.

At the end of the operations the fighting spirit of the all ranks remained as high as ever. This was fully proved very shortly afterwards.

Events from October 3rd to 16th

On October 3rd the 104th Brigade marched back to the area to the south of Zillebeke Lake, with headquarters in the railway embankment.[1] The 105th and 106th Brigades moved to billets south-west of Ypres. The headquarters of the 105th was south of Vlamertinghe, and of the 106th at St. Dunstan's. One complete day's rest was enjoyed at these places.

The Corps Commander, having been assured that, in spite of losses, the division was quite equal to further operations, instructions were issued as to the next attack.

With this in view, on the night of the 5th/6th, the 104th Brigade and 105th Brigade, less the 4/North Staffordshire and two companies of the 15/Cheshire, marched up the Menin Road and took over the line held by the 107th Brigade, 36th Division, which then sideslipped to the north. This line consisted of a series of detached posts just east of the Gheluwe-Wijfwegen-Dadizeele road. The left flank was on the road to Moorseele and the right flank on the Gheluwe road due west of Artoishoek. The headquarters were in pill boxes just south of Terhand. On the 6th two batteries of each brigade, under command of the O.C. 159th Brigade, went into action south of Terhand. One gun per battery was entailed to supply harassing fire by day and night.

On the 7th many hostile shells were fired on the positions held by the division, and Lieut.-Colonel W. G. W. Crellin, D.S.O., commanding 15/Sherwood Foresters, was severely wounded by one

[1] The 18/L.F. marched through Ypres with the band playing. It was probably the first British military band to play in Ypres.

OCTOBER 13, 1918

of these. This gallant and able officer unfortunately died next day in the casualty clearing station.

Owing to the postponement of the projected attack the 104th and 105th Brigades were relieved in the line by the 106th. The 104th Brigade withdrew to Gheluvelt, and the 105th to their former billets south of Vlamertinghe. They remained in these positions until October 11th, when they again occupied the front line. The 106th Brigade withdrew to Gheluvelt.[1]

Meanwhile, the Pioneers, amongst other works, had been preparing a divisional headquarters at Jackdaw Tunnels, near Sanctuary Wood, and re-making the roads leading to it. The headquarters moved there on the 12th.

The 13th was very wet. It was the day when the troops were due to take up their assembly positions preparatory to the next attack. The objective of the attack was a line from a point on the Terhand-Courtrai road, 1,600 yards south of Gulleghem, on the left to a slight rise 2,000 yards south of Moorseele, on a bye-road between that place and Wevelghem. This line lay at an oblique angle, with the direct line of advance. The distance from it varied from 8,000 yards on the left to 6,200 yards on the right. It was a form of advance which previous experience had shown to be difficult but, as the whole army was making a slanting movement, it was unavoidable. The objective, when gained, would bring the division within reach of the crossings of the Lys. The dispositions of the troops were as follows :—

The 105th Brigade was on the right. The 15/Cheshire was in front with two companies in the line, and the 15/Sherwood Foresters (Lieut.-Colonel H. Morton, D.S.O., M.C.) in support at 500 yards distance. The 104th Brigade was on the left. The 17/Lancashire Fusiliers on the left on a four platoon front, carrying out the attack up to the second pause of the barrage, *i.e.*, at 3,000 yards. The 19/Durham L.I. was in rear of the left and the 18/Lancashire Fusiliers on the right. The 106th Brigade was in reserve in rear of Terhand. The divisional artillery, less one battery of 18-prs. and one section of 4·5-in. howitzers per brigade, was on the line Terhand–Molenhock. The 119th A.F.A. Brigade was also in action, and was to carry on the barrage beyond the 3,000 yards. As the barrage

[1] Captain L. H. Bradney, Welsh Guards, joined as brigade major at this time.

started the two detached batteries and the howitzers were to move forward with the infantry to carry on the barrage beyond the line reached by the 119th A.F.A. Brigade. The remainder of the artillery was to advance as soon as the limit of range was reached. In this way the barrage would be continuous. The lifts were 100 yards in two minutes with a pause of 15 minutes in addition at every 1,500 yards. A series of thermite shells were to be fired on the left flank in order to give direction to the infantry. Heavy artillery were detailed for counter battery work, and to fire on certain farms beyond the range of the field guns.

Between 4.30 a.m. and 5 a.m. the enemy put down a defensive barrage on the assembly positions which caused some casualties to the troops, but did not interfere with the preparations for attack.

The advance commenced at 5.35 a.m. There was a thick, white mist on the ground, and, in addition, a number of gas shells were fired by the enemy. The mist certainly helped to cover the assembly, but afterwards increased the difficulty of keeping direction. The gas shells were more annoying than destructive. One burst in the ventilator of the 104th Brigade Headquarters at Peteuvin Wood, between Terhand and Wijfwegen.

During the first period of the attack the 15/Cheshire met with considerable opposition, but this was overcome without delaying the advance. The objective was reached by both the leading battalions at about 7.15 a.m. Thereupon the 15/Sherwood Foresters passed through the 15/Cheshire and the 18/Lancashire Fusiliers, and the 19/Durham L.I. passed through the 17/Lancashire Fusiliers. This battalion had encountered numerous machine-gun and infantry posts and in overcoming them the conduct of Captain Atkinson and 2nd Lieuts. Aspden, Stephenson, and Drummond was especially noticeable. 2nd Lieut. Aspden was killed. He was awarded a posthumous M.C. Unfortunately this battalion lost its commanding officer, Lieut.-Colonel Jones. He had gone forward to keep his men from getting too close under the barrage and was mortally wounded in doing so. He died next day.

Owing to the fog the Sherwood Foresters to some extent lost direction, and bore too much to the right. This was partly due to the advance of the 41st Division being behind time, and the troops naturally turned towards the fire directed on to their right flank.

They came upon the final objective at Cabin's Copse, 500 yards north of Wijnberg. The advance here was strongly opposed, and some field guns fired over open sights at the advancing infantry. Two of these guns were captured, after the teams had been shot, but the remainder made their escape under cover of machine-gun fire. The 18/Lancashire Fusiliers continued to the final objective without much difficulty, but the 19/Durham L.I., on the left, had to stop some 500 yards short of it, as the 36th Division was held up in front of Gulleghem. Some sharp fighting took place here, in which Lieutenant Chadwick and Sergeant Robertson distinguished themselves. As a further attack on this place was decided upon for the next morning the infantry of the 104th Brigade stood fast.

Meanwhile, the 4/North Staffordshire had been pushed up on the left of the Sherwood Foresters, had linked up with the 104th Brigade, and established a line actually in advance of that which had been ordered. In the afternoon the 41st Division, on the right, occupied the front allotted to it, and the 15/Cheshire closed in to the left.

Meanwhile, the artillery had carried out the programme arranged for it. At the commencement of the barrage B/157 and B/159 Batteries, with two sections of howitzers, advanced down the Moorselle road. Unfortunately this road was the only direct line of advance in the neighbourhood, and was common to both the 35th and 36th Divisions. It was kept under fire by the enemy and, in the advance, B/157 Battery came under a burst of fire and suffered several casualties amongst the horses, which caused a slight delay. B/159 avoided the same fate by wheeling off the road and advancing for a short distance across country, the condition of which, fortunately, made such a movement possible. These batteries came into action about 1,000 yards east of Kazelberg (one section of B/159 at the cross roads north of Herthoek) and carried on the barrage. The howitzers arrived shortly afterwards.

As soon as the original barrage was finished the remainder of the batteries limbered up and between 8.15 and 10 a.m. were in action south-east of Moorselle. Some of these batteries were delayed by casualties to the horses and by the congestion of traffic on the road. C/159 took the risk of using side tracks across country, and in this manner saved considerable time. The dense fog and the smoke which hung over the battlefield made it very difficult for the battery commanders to find out the exact positions of the infantry, and, in addition, the officer in liaison between the 105th Brigade and the 159th Brigade, R.F.A., and his two signallers, were all wounded as the battalions changed over, and for a time the brigade headquarters was denied all information.

On the other hand the fog made it possible for the batteries to keep in much closer touch than would have been the case on a clear day. As an instance of this it may be mentioned that the O.C. and advanced patrols of C/159 Battery entered Silver Farm with the infantry front line. Machine-gun fire from Gulleghem, Kloefhoek, and Kappelhoek were all dealt with, and A/ and D/157 (Major Phillipps) successfully broke up an enemy concentration north of Gulleghem. This was considered to be the preparation of a counter stroke. The final positions of all batteries were between Moorselle and Wijnberg.

The attack was renewed at 9 a.m. on the 15th of October. The objective was the high ground at Schoon-Water and Kappelhoek.

The 18/Lancashire Fusiliers and the 19/Durham L.I. advanced on the left, and, as the 36th Division was now in possession of Gulleghem, no difficulty was experienced in occupying the line of the Gulleghem-Wevelghem road, and the spurs to the east of it. On the right the 4/North Staffordshire supported by the 15/Sherwood Foresters captured the high ground south-east of Kappelhoek. Considerable opposition was met with from machine-guns posted in houses in the outskirts of Welveghem, but this was ignored, and a line established from Kloefhoek to Kappelhoek. Patrols then advanced, in conjunction with the 104th Brigade and the 41st Division, and established posts in advance of this line. After dark a patrol of the 15/Sherwood Foresters reached Welveghem Church, and one of the 4/North Staffordshire passed through Welveghem and advanced as far as the river Lys at Lauwe. It rained all night.

Since dawn on the previous day the troops had advanced nearly five miles. Upwards of 500 prisoners and 43 guns were captured, 12 150-mm., 19 105-mm. howitzers, and 12 77-mm. guns. A large number of trench mortars, machine-guns and equipment also fell into our hands. The enemy appeared to have been taken by surprise, and to have been to some extent demoralized by the rapidity of the advance.[1]

The Passage of the Lys

Orders were now issued that the country was to be cleared as far as the banks of the Lys, and the 106th Brigade was detailed for the attack. A conference took place at the 104th Brigade Headquarters at Elba Corner at 11.30 p.m., when the details were arranged. The conference ended at 12.15 a.m. on the 16th, and the attack began at 5.30 a.m. The artillery supplied a creeping barrage.

The 106th Brigade passed through the other two brigades and deployed, with the 18/Highland L.I. on the right and the 12/Highland L.I. on the left, on the low ground east of the Schoon-Water Spur.[2]

At the commencement there was little resistance by the enemy, and, in spite of the heavy going, the advance progressed favourably. After crossing the Welveghem-Bisseghem road, however, severe opposition was met with. Then both artillery and trench mortar fire was opened on the troops from the far bank, and machine-guns from the tile works west of Marcke and from the other houses beyond the river became somewhat destructive.

The ground on the banks of the river was flat and open, and, as it was impossible to get in touch with the enemy on the far side, a line was taken up which encircled Bisseghem on the left, and continuing within 500 yards of the river up to a point on the left bank between Welveghem and Marcke. Brigade headquarters were established in the German aerodrome south-west of Bisseghem.

The 35th Division had become acquainted with the Lys when they first went into the line in the spring of 1916. This river rises amongst the low hills of Artois and flows to Aire where it is canalized.

[1] On the 14th, when the advance party of A/159 Battery rode into a hostile gun position at a farm between Moorseele and Herthoek, they found twenty or thirty dead or dying Germans in a loft above a barn. These had evidently been put out of action by the heavy artillery counter battery fire, before they could reach their guns. Others were lying beside the guns. The battery had not fired a round and yet it bore evidence of being in a high state of discipline.

[2] Kloefhoek and Kappelhoek lie between Welveghem and Gulleghem. Schoon-Water is 1000 yards due south of the latter place.

T

After that it passes St. Venant, Merville, Armentières, Menin, and Courtrai, and finally joins the Scheldt at Ghent. In its middle and lower courses it is impassable by infantry, and, as the bridges had been destroyed, it was necessary that they should be restored before the troops could come to grips with the enemy.

During the day of the 17th the troops occupied their positions. The 106th Brigade along the river, the 104th in support south-west of Moorseele, and the 105th in reserve. Most of the batteries were in action east of the Gulleghem–Welveghem road. At 7.5 p.m. an order was received at divisional headquarters, which was now at Terhand, that the Lys was to be bridged at once, and that patrols were to cross the river and cover the operations.

The 204th Field Company had already moved forward with pontoon equipment for this purpose. Three places were chosen: (a) opposite the railway Halte at Marcke, where a side road ran down to the river; (b) on the Bisseghem–Marcke road, and (c) opposite the north-east corner of Bisseghem. The enemy was holding the south bank in some force.

At 10 p.m. an artillery barrage from all three brigades was put down and, under this, the bridging parties advanced. The southernmost bridge (a) opposite Marcke could not be made owing to the magnitude of the task and the strong hostile opposition. On the Bisseghem-Marcke road (b) bridge was constructed by connecting up two half-sunk barges by a foot-bridge. The sappers were working in gas masks, and the night was dark. The C.R.E. specially mentioned the energy and resolution of Lieutenant Stranack in completing this work. At the third point the bridge was partially constructed, but work had to be suspended owing to heavy machine-gun fire and gas shelling.

Parties of the 18/Highland L.I. crossed over and established posts on the farther bank, and, shortly after midnight, a party of the 17/Royal Scots, under Lieutenant Inman,[1] also passed the bridge and raided the enemy posts north of Marcke. It returned at dawn having accounted for several of the enemy and bringing back 3 prisoners.[2]

The troops engaged were quite prepared to exploit these successes,

[1] The Commander, Lieutenant Harvey, was wounded at the start.
[2] On this day the Belgians entered Ostend and Bruges, and the British Douai and Lille.

but, owing to the general situation, instructions had been received that the river was not to be forced in face of strong opposition. Also, the reported presence of many civilians in Marcke made an effective artillery barrage for covering an advance a matter of some difficulty.

On the morning of the 18th divisional headquarters moved forward to Herthoek. General Marindin had gone forward to the 106th Brigade headquarters, where he received a message that the 35th Division were to capture Marcke as soon as possible, and that the X Corps, on the right, were to make good the line of the Courtrai–Aelbeke road.[1]

The 106th Brigade was detailed for the attack, and in the evening the 17/Royal Scots crossed the river by a single plank bridge at a bend of the river, west of the tile works. The battalions formed up, facing east on a two-company front. One company of the 18/Highland L.I. was in reserve, and acted as a " mopping-up " party. The attack commenced at 10 p.m. under a creeping barrage, and, by 11.30 p.m., all the railway crossings and the eastern exits of Marcke had been captured. Twenty-four prisoners and 4 machine-guns were taken. The enemy showed little disposition to resist the attack.

During the afternoon the 104th Brigade had concentrated between Moorseele and Bisseghem, and, at 11 p.m., the 17/Lancashire Fusiliers (now under command of Major G. Mackereth, M.C.) and the 19/Durham L.I. passed across the river by the above-mentioned foot-bridge and took up positions behind the 106th Brigade.

During the night all three companies of the Royal Engineers were hard at work on the bridges over the Lys. They were fit for traffic by 3 a.m. Seven bridges in all were made, and two more substantial ones were completed next day. A couple of chance shells fell amongst the 205th Company, and caused casualties to 25 men and 11 horses.

At 5.30 a.m. on October 19th the 104th Brigade attacked on a three-battalion front. The 17/Lancashire Fusiliers on the right, the 18/Lancashire Fusiliers in the centre, and the 19/Durham L.I. on the left. A creeping barrage of all three artillery brigades

[1] The 24th Division was now on the right. It had received the 41st Division on the 15th. This division had crossed over to the left, relieved the 36th, and was now in the outskirts of Courtrai.

covered the advance. A thick mist covered the ground, but there was little opposition, and, in a short time, the troops were on the line of the Aelbeke–Courtrai road. The line was then advanced to the road from Walle to Rolleghem, which was reached by 7 a.m. This was nearly the final objective, but patrols pushed out towards t'Hooghe.[1] Some opposition was met with here, but, eventually, the Courtrai–Coyghem road was occupied and patrols of the 19/Durham L.I. were sent on into Courtrai. They were the first British troops to enter the town and received an ovation from the inhabitants.

The 105th Brigade had been in support north-east of Lauwe and, at 8.30 a.m., took up a position at Pottelberg, south of Courtrai. A patrol of the 15/Sherwood Foresters then entered the town.[2]

At 11 a.m. the three field artillery brigades began to cross the bridges and took up positions east and south of Marcke. The 10th Brigade, R.G.A. (2 batteries of 6-in. howitzers) and the 150th and 159th Batteries, R.G.A., 60-prs., advanced to the neighbourhood of Bisseghem.

The operations had been eminently successful, and cordial congratulations were received from the Corps Commander. The troops were received with acclamation by the inhabitants of Marcke, over 1,000 of whom had been released from German bondage. Coffee was freely offered to the men. It was all they had to offer.

[1] A small village 1½ miles south-east. of Courtrai on the Coyghem road.
[2] The Mayor and some members of the Corporation of Nottingham visited the battalion on this day. During their return across the Lys they experienced a good deal of gas shelling.

CHAPTER XVIII

THE BATTLE OF SWEVEGHEM

ABOUT midday on the 19th orders were received from XIX Corps that the eventual objective of the Corps was that portion of the line of the Scheldt between the canal junction at Bossuyt to the eastern exits of Avelghem; that the advance was to be resumed on the morrow by the 35th Division; that it should establish a starting line Rolleghem–Knock—east of t'Hooge, and, as the left moved forward, prolong the line to the canal at a point two miles east of Courtrai.

The objective given was from the cross roads at Le Chat Cabaret, east of Belleghem, to the canal at Pont Levis No. 2, north of Knokke. The right portion of this ran along a ridge to the village of Kreupel; the left was on low ground up to the canal. Afterwards, a further objective was given which entailed an advance to some high ground some 2,000 yards in advance which afterwards became known as the Hoogstraatje Ridge. The village of that name stood on the centre of the ridge about a mile south of Knokke.

The fulfilment of these orders entailed a wide movement on the part of the troops forming the left flank before they got on the line of their objective, and complicated the provision of artillery support. The total advance contemplated, after the troops had taken up their positions, amounted, on an average, to 6,000 yards. The 34th Division, X Corps, was to attack on the right, and the 29th Division, II Corps, on the left. One brigade of the 41st Division was placed at the disposal of the G.O.C. 35th Division as divisional reserve.

The 104th Brigade formed the right of the division, and the 105th the left. The 106th Brigade was in support. Both the attacking brigades had all three battalions in the line. No set barrage of artillery was attempted. The troops were ordered to advance as in open warfare. The 159th Brigade, R.F.A., was attached to the 105th Brigade, and the 157th to the 106th. The 119th A.F.A.

Brigade supported the attack of the 104th Brigade, each battalion having a section attached to it. The morning was very wet, but the weather improved later.

At 7 a.m. on the 20th the right brigade advanced. The 17/Lancashire Fusiliers on the right made good progress, and by 9 a.m. had gained the high ground south-east of Belleghem. By midday the line had advanced on to the final objective. The 18/Lancashire Fusiliers met with more opposition, and did not reach the final objective until the evening. On the left of the brigade the 19/Durham L.I. encountered stiff resistance from the start, and were held up at the approach to the first ridge. The ridge was shelled by the artillery, and it was then assaulted and captured. The battalion had now to cross some low ground, and at the second ridge the same performance was repeated, but by 6.30 p.m. the troops were in possession of the objective and of 7 prisoners.

The 105th Brigade moved off at 4.45 a.m., and the attack commenced at 6.15 a.m. The battalions, in order from right to left, were the 15/Cheshire, 15/Sherwood Foresters, and 4/North Staffordshire. The two battalions on the right reached their assembly positions without incident, but the 4/North Staffordshire, whilst deploying, was fired on by machine-guns in farms on the front and left flank. Considerable opposition was experienced at the hamlet of Blokken, where 2 150-mm. howitzers fired at the troops over open sights.

About 7 a.m. the 15/Cheshire captured the village of Berkstraat. A thousand yards beyond the village, and about 100 feet below it, flowed a muddy stream called the Keibeek, which meandered across the front and passed under the canal. It was little more than a wide ditch for field draining, but it was an impediment, and the approach was covered by machine-guns from houses immediately in rear, and from others on the high ground 1,000 yards farther on. This brought the attack to a halt. One battery was advancing with the infantry, but the others of the 159th Brigade were still covering the advance from positions east and south-east of Marcke, and, at the time, it was difficult to bring fire to bear on the various points of resistance. The forward movement was, therefore, temporarily checked. The 15/Sherwood Foresters had also been subjected to machine-gun fire, and the progress was slow. The open nature of the country exposed the troops, but advantage was taken of the deep ditches, and by crawling up these many machine-gun rests and farms were outflanked and captured. Eventually, at the outskirts of Sweveghem the advance came to a standstill.

The batteries had now reached the limits of range and advanced in a north-easterly direction. The roads were few and bad. They were also congested with infantry transport so that time was lost in taking up new positions. By 9 a.m., however, all batteries were well forward and intense fire was brought to bear on Sweveghem. For a time the situation in Sweveghem was so obscure that the battery commander concerned, who was with the battalion commander, did not dare to open fire. When, however, the Sherwood Foresters, who had previously fought their way, step by step, as far as the church, were heavily counter attacked, and forced back to the western edge, an intense barrage was put down on the village. This proved effective and, under it the infantry renewed the attack and succeeded in capturing the village and emerging on the eastern side.

A battery of the 157th Brigade had, meanwhile, been called upon to reinforce the fire on the first objective—the Kreupel Ridge—and the hostile fire was to some extent reduced. By 3 p.m. the 15/Cheshire had driven the enemy from the line of the Keibeek and by the evening had gained the summit of the ridge. Here vigorous resistance was encountered from a strongly-held farm called Kapelle Milaine.

In the meantime the 4/North Staffordshire had reached the canal, had captured 2 howitzers, and were making progress towards their objective. The 19/Durham L.I. were also making progress.

On receiving the various reports at about 2 p.m. General Marindin, who was then visiting brigade headquarters, had decided that he would not use the reserve brigade, but would leave the 104th and 105th Brigades to complete the capture of the Kreupel Ridge, and send the 106th Brigade to the south to make a flank attack on the Hoogstraatje Ridge, which, if successful, would not only gain possession of the final objective, but would force the enemy to retire from the positions which he held to the west of it. This attack was planned for 5.15 p.m., and a barrage of all artillery was arranged to start near the south-western end, clear of the 104th Brigade positions, and move in a north-easterly direction up to the canal.

In accordance with this order the 157th Brigade, R.F.A., moved its guns to positions east of Marionetteberg. During the afternoon the battery commanders of this brigade had been reconnoitring new positions. A party consisting of Majors Waller and P. H. Richardson, Captains Phillipps and C. F. Morgan, and Lieutenants Holbrook and Carlyon had reached a road embankment 1,700 yards south-east of t'Hooghe when heavy machine-gun fire was opened upon them from the east. The position of these guns was located and the party proceeded under cover of the embankment to the front line, where it was found that this was apparently one of the machine-gun nests which was obstructing the infantry at this point. The officers mentioned, being satisfied that they knew the position of the gun, or guns, borrowed 2 Lewis guns and some rifles from the infantry and took them to a farm on a flank. Fire was opened from this point on to the farm-house determined, and about forty of the enemy were driven from the buildings. Captain Morgan and Lieutenants Holbrook and Carlyon hurried forward to the farm and found it vacated. Having cut through a thick belt of wire, the party reached another farm from which fire was opened on the retreating enemy. Another post, which the enemy were endeavouring to establish on the right, was also engaged. Some of the enemy were killed : the others ran away. The officers then finished their reconnaissance and rejoined their batteries. The accident of their having been able to locate this point of defence was of material assistance.

When the 106th Brigade received orders to make a flank attack the two Highland L.I. battalions were west of t'Hooghe. The 17/Royal Scots were farther in advance ready to support the 105th Brigade. The Highland L.I., each accompanied by a section of the machine-gun Battalion, accordingly marched down the Courtrai–Coyghem road to Eigendaele Bosch, a distance of three miles. The 17/Royal Scots moved eastwards and waited in an assembly position north-west of Kreupel. It now began to rain again, and this, with other causes, delayed the march of the 12/Highland L.I., so that by the time the battalion had passed through the Lancashire Fusiliers it was seven o'clock, and the artillery barrage was finished.

Three companies of the 12/Highland L.I. and two and a half sections of C Company Machine-Gun Battalion in advanced guard formation, moved forward along the road from Eigender Bosch to Hoogstraatje, whilst B Company moved along a parallel road, 800 yards to the north. Z Company, 18/Highland L.I., followed the main part of the battalion to establish posts as the attack progressed ; the remainder of the battalion was disposed, ready to pass through the 12/Highland L.I. as opportunity offered.

At first the attack proceeded well, but at 9 p.m. the leading company (D) of the 12/Highland L.I., was held up by heavy machine-gun fire from Molen le Claere. The remainder of the battalion left the road and took up defensive positions to the south, whilst D Company attempted to clear the buildings. At the same time B Company, on the other road, was checked at a farm at an embanked road junction called Laatste Oortje by fire coming from another embanked road to the east. Laatste Oortje Farm was occupied and put in a state of defence by Y Company, 18/Highland L.I., the civilian inhabitants stating that the enemy had just left, and now held a post farther east.

At 11.20 p.m. D Company, 12/Highland L.I., were still in difficulties. Strong wire had been encountered, and fire appeared to be coming from various points. Artillery fire was called for, and the company extended to its left, gaining touch with B Company.

General Pollard now sent orders to the 17/Royal Scots to advance and join hands with the 12/Highland L.I., and complete the capture of the ridge. The battalion, therefore, with a section of the Machine-gun Battalion, passed through the 15/Cheshire, and advanced along the road from t'Hooghe to Laatste Oortje. The advance was without incident until after the vanguard had crossed the Kreupel ridge, and reached the low ground beyond it and then a Very light shot up and fire was opened from several directions. A patrol under 2nd Lieutenant Inman advanced under covering fire from the Machine-Gun Section and subdued the enemy in front. Having thus cleared the way for 600 yards, the main body again advanced, and deployed astride the road. From this point the battalion then pushed straight on to the objective and occupied a line from Molen le Claere, which had just been cleared by the

October 21, 1918

12/Highland L.I. to Hoogstraatje. This was about 4.50 a.m. on the 21st. At the same time the 15/Cheshire captured Kapelle Milaene. An officer's patrol of the Royal Scots was now sent towards the canal, and after a sharp struggle with hostile machine-guns, cleared the whole flank. Other patrols turned back to the left rear and captured some enemy posts still existing there. A few prisoners were taken. It was evident that the enemy had prepared to defend the canal from a frontal attack from the east as the posts were found dug and wired for defence from that direction. This no doubt accounted for the fact that the hostile resistance on the left half of the divisional front had been more accentuated than on the right. The 4/North Staffordshire did not reach Pont Levis No. 2 until 10 p.m.

Between 7 a.m. and 9 a.m. on the 21st the troops of the 41st Division passed through those of the 35th Division and occupied the line. The latter then withdrew to billets in and around Courtrai, except the 17/Royal Scots and the 4/North Staffordshire, which remained in the battle area until next day.

The 35th Division had now been fighting for six days and had concluded with a strenuous battle extending for 23 hours. The cultivated portions of the country were composed of very sticky mud, and the negotiation of it would have been a high trial, even to men who had not to fight a battle in addition. When relieved the troops were soaked to the skin, cold, and very exhausted. But the exhaustion was physical, not mental, and in no way impaired their efficiency.

The total prisoners taken in the six days' fighting amounted to 650. The casualties for the 20th/21st were 49 killed, 200 wounded, 27 missing.

The 35th Division remained in and around Courtrai until the 26th. The 105th Brigade being in the barracks and monastery of Pottelberg. On the 24th divisional headquarters moved to a château on the road between Courtrai and Sweveghem and the 106th Brigade marched to Sweveghem to assist the 41st Division if called upon. This division was due to attack on the 25th up to the River Scheldt, and the 35th was due to relieve it on completion of the attack.

Meanwhile, there were rejoicings in Courtrai. The populace were pleased and excited. Those who had troops billeted upon them did everything possible to make them comfortable, and official receptions were held to greet the higher commanders.

On the 25th the bands of the division played in the Grande Place, and on the 28th the Corps Commander made his official entry into Courtrai. On this occasion the pipers of the 106th Brigade played in the Place. The kilts as well as the pipes excited a great deal of interest and curiosity amongst the inhabitants.

At this time Lieut.-Colonel McCulloch, 19/Durham L.I., returned to England for a tour of duty. His place was taken by Major B. C. H. Keenlyside, 18/Lancashire Fusiliers.

THE FIGHT ON THE SCHELDT

On the night 26th/27th the 35th Division relieved the 41st Division on the Corps front. Since taking over on the morning of the 21st the 41st Division had advanced the line about 5,500 yards. It had also side-slipped to the left, and the 29th Division had been withdrawn. Concurrently with this relief, the 30th Division relieved the 34th on the right, and the 31st relieved the 9th on the left.

The line as taken over extended from Autryve on the Scheldt, to Avelghem, and thence along the main road to near Waffelstraat. From that place it bent back to the north-west and ended up a mile to the south of Okkerwijk. The 106th Brigade occupied the portion between Autryve and Avelghem, and the 104th the remainder. The 105th was in support east of Sweveghem. Divisional headquarters was at Sweveghem.

At 5 a.m. on the 27th the 17/Lancashire Fusiliers on the right, and the 18/Lancashire Fusiliers on the left, pushed forward strong patrols in a north-easterly direction. Severe opposition was met with from the high ground about Tieghem. Artillery fire from across the Scheldt also opened on the troops. The line was advanced about 200 yards and held until midday, but it then had to be withdrawn. A certain number of casualties had been suffered, but 3 prisoners were brought in. Next day the enemy kept up continuous artillery fire on the positions. In the evening the 19/Durham L.I., from Krote, relieved the 17/Lancashire Fusiliers.

Orders were now received for an attack along the left bank of the Scheldt. Two objections were given. The first was the line Waermaerde to 500 yards south of Tieghem ; the second from Kerkhove to Haelendries. The attack was to be supported by a barrage moving at the rate of 100 yards in 3 minutes, and XIX Corps arranged a smoke screen by heavy artillery to cover the attacking troops from the hostile positions on their right flank beyond the Scheldt, and also to neutralize the batteries and machine-guns in that direction. Many guns were allotted for this purpose. The 104th Brigade was detailed for the attack, and the 106th Brigade to form a defensive flank along the river as the attack moved forward.

On the 29th divisional headquarters was bombed, and on the 30th Sweveghem was shelled, and a large number of casualties was caused amongst horses. Also the headquarters of the 19/Durham L.I., at Bosch, which had been chosen as battalion headquarters for the brigade, was completely destroyed by 150-mm. howitzers. This bombardment lasted for two hours. The headquarters moved to Driesch. A new brigade headquarters was chosen 2,000 yards west of Avelghem.

Meanwhile the batteries moved into positions selected to support the attack. The operation was difficult as the terrain was in full view of Mont de l'Enclus on the far side of the Scheldt. The movement, however, was successfully carried out. The 157th Brigade advanced from positions north-west of Moen to the neighbourhood of Driesh and Bosch. The 159th Brigade advanced two batteries to Ooteghem ; the others were already in action south of this place. The 119th Brigade, A.F.A., also moved forward. The 10th Brigade, R.G.A., 6-in. howitzers prepared to fire on certain farms and cross roads. Some of these guns advanced as far as Avelghem, within 1,500 yards of the hostile machine-guns.

During the night of the 30th/31st, which was very dark, the battalions of the 104th Brigade took positions with the right on the Scheldt, east of Avelghem. The 19/Durham L.I. on the right ; 17/Lancashire Fusiliers, centre ; 18/Lancashire Fusiliers, left. They advanced with two companies in the front line and two in support, ready to continue the advance after the first objective had been gained. The 15/Cheshire was in reserve.

The attack was launched at 5.25 a.m. A certain amount of

opposition was experienced from machine-gun posts, but these were all overrun, and by 6.40 a.m. the line of the first objectives had been captured. This included the villages of Kapelwijk, Hofdries, Waffelstraat, Vierschaat, Hulstraat, Molenhoek, Waffelstraat (another one), Meerschstraat, Oostende, Rugge, Trappelstraat, and Waermaerde. The last three were consolidated as a flank defence by the 19/Durham L.I. and B Company, 35th Machine-Gun Battalion. Shortly afterwards the 17/Royal Scots extended their line to Rugge, and took over the defence. The detonators of charges placed by the enemy in the bridges at Rugge were removed in time by an N.C.O. of the 184th Tunneling Company, R.E.

In conjunction with the division on the left a pause of two hours was made on the first objective. Meanwhile the 157th Brigade, R.F.A., kept up a covering fire whilst the two other brigades advanced to positions to the west of Tieghem. A certain number of shells had been fired at the batteries whilst in action and during the advance, but few casualties resulted, and, at 8.10 a.m., the 119th and 159th Brigades were in occupation of their forward positions. From these a smoke barrage was fired in order to conceal the further advance from the right bank of the river. The 157th Brigade continued the covering barrage.

The advance was resumed at 8.45 a.m. The opposition was more severe, but was insufficient to hinder the troops. On this occasion, apparently for the first time, tracer bullets were used by the enemy. The result was unfortunate for him as the position of his machine-guns was thereby disclosed. The final objective was captured at 9.55 a.m., and with it the villages of Kruisstraat, Vossenhoek, Tenhove, Haelendries, Varent, and Kerkhove. The enemy appeared to be retreating on Audenarde.

At 12.10 orders were received by the G.O.C. that the success was to be exploited, and that the village of Eeuwhoek, which lay about 1,000 yards farther on, was to be seized if possible. This was successfully carried out, and by 2.30 p.m. patrols of the 17/Lancashire Fusiliers had reached Eeuwhoek and Meesche, which were on the Scheldt south of Elseghem, and established posts in both places. The 18/Lancashire Fusiliers on the left were obliged to limit their advance, owing to the fact that the 31st Division was contained in front of Merkegemhoek. On the right the 19/Durham

November 1, 1918

L.I. had also pushed forward and held the bank of the river. Major Keenlyside had been wounded but he continued in command until the end of the day.

Although the morning had been clear the weather afterwards became dull, and the amount of smoke shell and high explosive fired by heavy guns made good observation by the enemy almost impossible. As an example of the bewilderment produced it may be mentioned that a German aviator entirely lost his bearings and descended intact amongst the 159th Brigade gun positions.

As will be seen from the number of villages captured this tract of country was very densely populated, and, in spite of all efforts to clear them from the war zone, large numbers of the inhabitants were still in the farms and villages. They, unfortunately, suffered from the warfare passing by them, particularly from the hostile gas shells which were fired indiscriminately over the countryside. The attitude of these unfortunates to the German prisoners was pathetic evidence of the treatment which they had experienced.

The attack was a complete success, and many messages of congratulation were received by the 104th Brigade from the higher commands. As a result of driving in this wedge on the flank, the French, next day, were able to make a long advance in the direction of Audenarde. On November 1st the Army Commander visited the division and offered his congratulations in person.

The prisoners amounted to 6 officers and 270 other ranks. In addition there were captured 3 guns, 80 machine-guns, some trench mortars, 2 motor ambulances (complete with German wounded), wireless sets, listening sets, messenger dogs, and a variety of other articles. Numerous machine-guns and trench mortars were discovered damaged by gun fire, and not brought in.

The casualties amounted to 428 of all ranks. The 18/Lancashire Fusiliers were the chief sufferers. Considering their exposed position on the river bank the 19/Durham L.I. were somewhat fortunate. This was probably due to the efficient smoke screen formed by the heavy artillery.

The German losses were heavy. In addition to those killed by the infantry, large numbers of dead were found who had evidently been killed by gun fire.

The infantry were very complimentary about the artillery barrage. One battalion described it as the best it had seen. If this were so—as far as the 157th and 159th Brigades were concerned —it was a fitting conclusion to three and a half years of close co-operation. For it was the last set barrage that the 35th Divisional Artillery fired in the War.

CHAPTER XIX

THE CROSSING OF THE SCHELDT : THE ARMISTICE

ON the night of November 1st/2nd the 104th and 105th Brigades were relieved by the 41st Division. The 106th Brigade had been relieved on the previous night.

During the day a very valuable and daring reconnaissance was carried out by Sir E. Pauncefort Duncombe, who penetrated up to Kwaadestraat and Elseghem and brought back information from the inhabitants that the enemy was in full retreat, but was still holding these places with machine-guns.

On the next day this officer was posted as brigade major to the 165th Brigade, and his place as G.S.O. 2 was taken by Major A. E. Sanderson, D.S.O. At this time, also, Lieut.-Colonel W. Rigby, D.S.O., Royal Irish Rifles, assumed command of the 19/Durham L.I. A few days later Lieut.-Colonel Sherbrooke, R.A., joined as G.S.O. 1, vice Lieut.-Colonel Thorpe who was appointed to the Tank Corps.

On relief the brigades retired to rest billets. The 104th to Staceghem, the 105th to Marcke, and the 106th to Cheval Rouge.

At night Sweveghem was bombed by aeroplanes. A good deal of damage was done. All the houses round " Q " office were wrecked, and some injury caused to the office. One bomb dropped in the mess of Y Company, 19/Northumberland Fusiliers. Lieutenants Davies and Hall were killed, and three other officers wounded. Casualties were also inflicted on the Machine-Gun Battalion.

The Royal Engineers and Pioneers now made preparations for passing the infantry across the Scheldt in the next advance. Bridging materials were obtained, also canvas boats, and practices took place in ferrying the 104th and 105th Brigades across the Lys. With a little practice the Pioneers became efficient in the art of ferrying, but not before some exciting and amusing incidents had taken place.

On November 4th the division was ordered to take over that portion of the line of the Scheldt which lay between a point east of Rugge (across the northern arm of the river) to Tenhove. The 18/Highland L.I. and the 15/Sherwood Foresters [1] occupied this line under command of the 106th Brigade.[2] Attempts were made to cross the river, but owing to lack of means, were unsuccessful. The 157th Brigade, R.F.A., also moved forward and came into action north of Bosch. One company of the 19/Northumberland Fusiliers marched to Ingoyghem and established a dump, in preparation of work in connection with the bridging of the Scheldt. On the 7th the 159th Brigade, R.F.A., moved up and occupied silent positions between Tieghem and the river. The 104th Brigade was moved nearer to the point of operations. The proposed attack was arranged for the 11th, but during the night 8th/9th news was received that the enemy was retiring from the river, and that patrols of both the 41st Division and the French had crossed. Orders were at once despatched to the 105th Brigade that the troops were to cross by any means at their disposal. The 104th Brigade was ordered up to Tieghem.

At 5.30 a.m. on the 9th the 18/Highland L.I., by making use of a canvas boat and other material which was lying about, managed to pass one company across the Scheldt. This company advanced as far as the railway line beyond Berchem. The rest of the battalion followed as rapidly as possible and established a line along the railway.

At 7 a.m. the 15/Sherwood Foresters commenced to cross by ferry, and also by the bridge of Tenhove which was put in order by the Royal Engineers. A floating foot-bridge was subsequently erected by the Royal Engineers, and the troops which followed were able to make use of this.

At midday the 15/Sherwood Foresters and the 18/Highland L.I., with the 15/Cheshire in support, advanced from the Berchem Railway and reached a line stretching from the north of Kleinhoogveld to 800 yards east of Kraai, 4,000 yards farther on, and beyond the objective which had been planned for the attack of the

---

[1] Lieut.-Colonel Morton went to hospital on the 6th. Major Johnson commanded in his absence.
[2] The 105th Brigade assumed command on the 7th inst. General Pollard was ill with influenza. Lieut.-Colonel Rycroft commanded the 106th Brigade.

11th. Outposts were then pushed forward to the Renaix-Nukerke road.

Meanwhile the 104th Brigade, which was in billets around Staceghem, had, in the early morning, received orders to march at once. The brigade started at 9.30 a.m., crossed the Scheldt at 5.30 p.m., and after a march of fourteen miles, billeted at Berchem. B/159 Battery crossed by a bridge on the left erected by the 41st Division, and took up a position near Berchem. By strenuous work the Engineers and Pioneers made the bridges and approaches available for wheeled traffic. This work was completed by midnight.

The 104th Brigade was now ordered to pass through the 105th and continue the pursuit. The troops started at 7 a.m. on the 10th with the 18/Lancashire Fusiliers and B/159 Battery as advanced guard. The Renaix–Nukerke road was crossed at 9 a.m., and the advance was continued without opposition. Brigade headquarters reached Louise-Marie at midday, and received an enthusiastic reception from the inhabitants. Bread, cigars, apples, etc., were handed out to the troops, and Belgian flags made their appearance. A similar procedure took place in all the villages which were entered. The people appeared to be beside themselves with joy. At Lousie Marie the nuns in the convent insisted on General Sandilands visiting the Mother Superior, who was very ill. She had feared that she might die before she had seen a British soldier.

The troops passed on and by 5 p.m. had occupied the line Boekanter–Boschstraat, which was the objective given in Corps Orders. The 18/Lancashire Fusiliers entended their outpost line in front of the objective, having accomplished an advanced guard march of 13,500 yards. Except for a few mounted patrols, little opposition was encountered. One prisoner was taken.

Meanwhile, in rear, the other brigades were also on the move. The 105th Headquarters was at Quaremont with battalions at Zandstraat and Pensemont. The 106th at Kalverstraat, with battalions at Mont l'Eclus and Sulsique. R.A. headquarters was near Knokt. All batteries were now across the river. The 159th Brigade was affiliated to the 104th Brigade and marched to Audenhove. The 157th Brigade was north-west of Renaix.

Divisional headquarters moved to a château east of Mont l'Eclus.

Although opposition was practically non-existent the troops had difficulties to contend with, inseparable from a forced march in an unknown country. The personnel of the artillery and transport, especially, had heavy work in clearing roads and filling up mine craters to allow of the passage of wheeled traffic. All ranks, however, were consumed with excitement, and thought of nothing but moving forward.

In the evening the rumour spread abroad that an armistice had been signed. At 8.30 a.m. on the 11th a wire was received at divisional headquarters that hostilities would cease at 11 a.m., and that every effort was to be made to reach the line of the Dendre by that time. Orders were sent to the 104th Brigade, which had previously received instructions to reach the line Everbecq-Kalenberge, and the troops marched at 9 a.m. The 17/Lancashire Fusiliers were now leading.

At 9.30 a.m. General Marindin left his headquarters in his car with his A.D.C., Lieutenant Crichton. Having passed by columns of artillery on the march, he reached the 104th Brigade headquarters near Boschstraat, and pushed on towards Grammont. Excited crowds were met here who threw flowers and climbed on the steps of the car in order to shake hands. A French patrol then reported a hostile machine-gun on the far side of the river Dendre. The general and A.D.C. left the car and walked down to the bridge which they reached before 11 o'clock. Shortly afterwards some cyclists of the leading battalion arrived and established posts at the bridges in Grammont. X Company of the battalion followed with B/159 Battery which came into action covering the bridges. The 17/Lancashire Fusiliers occupied Grammont. The 19/Durham L.I. halted at Everbecq and the 18/Lancashire Fusiliers at Paricke. The 159th Brigade, R.F.A., came into action east of that place.

A few German prisoners were captured in Grammont, and about 200 British prisoners, who had been released, streamed back across the river.

The 105th Brigade was now in the neighbourhood of Audenhove, and the 106th Brigade at Boschstraat and Tenberg. The troops did not advance beyond these positions because the war had come to an end.

CONCLUSION

On November 12th, much to the disappointment of everybody, news came that the 35th Division would not advance into Germany. As the division was in advance of the general line it had been hoped that the progress might continue still farther, or, failing that, that the troops might be left in occupation of their present positions which were novel, pleasantly situated, and free from the marks of war. But it was not to be, and, on the 13th, the units commenced their backward movement over ground which had become familiar in more exciting circumstances.

The order given was that the division should march back to billets in the St. Omer area, and the various phases of the return journey, which appeared to be an anti-climax, may be but briefly related. The Scheldt was passed at Berchem, the Lys at Harlebeke. Whilst at Harlebeke the Army Commander visited the division and spoke to all the brigade commanders and the C.R.A. Thence the troops marched to Menin and along the long Menin Road to Ypres.

On November 28th, whilst passing through Ypres, the Royal Scots were inspected by their colonel-in-chief. Princess Mary had been visiting the stations of the various women's corps in Flanders, and, whilst in Ypres, noticed some cyclists of the Royal Scots. She stopped them, enquired about their battalion and, on hearing it was on the march from Menin, she expressed a wish to see it march past her.

Rain fell heavily but Her Royal Highness waited nearly two hours until the battalion entered the city. The effect on the battalion was electrical. The weary march in pitiless rain through that expanse of desolation traversed by the Menin Road was forgotten, and the Royal Scots marched back through Ypres in the spirit of elation which had filled them when they advanced from it on the same day two months before.

At the conclusion of the march the various units were collected as follows :—Divisional Headquarters at Eperlecques : R.A. Brigades at Serques, Moulle, and Tilques ; D.A.C. and Trench Mortar Batteries at Nieurleb and St. Momelin ; 104th Brigade at Merckeghem, Volkerinckhove, and Bollezeele ; 105th Brigade at

HISTORY OF THE 35TH DIVISION

Bayenghem and Monnecove ; 106th to Millain ; 19/Northumberland Fusiliers at Hellebroucq ; Royal Engineers at Nordausques. The time was employed in recreation, concerts by the much appreciated "Sparklets," and other troupes instituted by units—and education. Under this last heading many hours were spent by the rank and file in studying intricate problems of philosophy and mathematics, and so fitting themselves for the civil life which lay ahead of them. The scheme of education would probably have become a success if its tenour had not been broken by demobilization. This began with the miners on December 11th, and as there was a large number of miners in the division, gaps were left in education classes, football teams, and other associations, and many of those who were left began to grow restless.

Towards the end of January trouble broke out in Calais, and the infantry was ordered there to preserve order. This unpleasant piece of work lasted for about five days, at the end of which the 106th Brigade returned to Millain. The other brigades remained in the neighbourhood of Calais for another month.

Before it was disbanded the 35th Division was destined to achieve one more success in Flanders, but of a more peaceful nature than those which were past. Since Christmas a football competition had been in progress, and, after several well-contested matches, the 159th Brigade, R.F.A., was chosen to represent the 35th Division in the Army Competition at Brussels. Four hard games were witnessed there, and in the end the division bore the cup in triumph back to the St. Omer area.

During the early part of March the G.O.C. presented colours to various battalions, and on the 16th, after having bade farewell to all the units whom he had commanded, General Marindin handed over command of the division to take command of the 3rd Highland Brigade on the Rhine.

After this the disintegration became rapid. General Pollard left to command the embarkation brigade at Dunkerque, and General Sandilands commanded the remnants of the division. General Madocks and several of the staff officers departed to take up other appointments.

Finally, on April 9th, the artillery embarked at Dunkerque and proceeded to Ripon for demobilization. The infantry followed some ten days later, and by the end of the month the 35th Division ceased to exist except in the memories of those who had had the honour of serving in it.

APPENDIX I.

Honours.

V.C.

Lt.-Col. H. W. Anderson, 12/H.L.I.
2nd Lt. H. F. Parsons, 14/Glos.

C.B.

Maj.-Gen. G. MacK. Franks.
Brig.-Gen. W. R. N. Madocks.
Maj.-Gen. A. H. Marindin.
Maj.-Gen. R. J. Pinney.

Maj.-Gen. J. H. W. Pollard.
Brig.-Gen. J. W. Sandilands.
Brig.-Gen. A. J. Turner.

C.M.G.

Lt.-Col. H. M. Davson.
Brig.-Gen. H. O'Donnell.

Brig.-Gen. J. W. Sandilands.

D.S.O.

2nd Lt. R. S. Bauld, 18/L.F.
Major A. N. Braithwaite, 17/W.Y.
Lt.-Col. R. C. Browne-Clayton, 16/Ches.
Lt.-Col. H. P. G. Cochran, 15/Ches.
Major W. L. Crawford, 20/L.F.
Lt.-Col. W. A. W. Crellin, 15/S.F.
Lt.-Col. H. M. Davson, R.F.A.
Lt.-Col. F. W. Daniell, 19/N.F.
Major J. K. Ewart, R.A.S.C.
Lt.-Col. W. P. S. Foord, 14/Glos, 19/N.F. Bar.
Major J. H. Gill, 17/W.Y.
Major V. E. Gooderson, 18/H.L.I.
Lt.-Col. W. P. Greenwell, 19/D.L.I.
Lt.-Col. D. M. B. Hall, 4/N.S.
Major R. D. Harisson, 159/R.F.A.
Major G. A. Hart, 159/R.F.A.
Lt.-Col. R. A. Irvine, 18/L.F.
Lt.-Col. C. E. Jewels, 18/L.F., 20/L.F. Bar.

Lt.-Col. Harrison Johnston, 15/Ches.
Major J. W. Lloyd-Davies, R.E.
Brig.-Gen. A. H. Marindin, 105th Bde.
Lt.-Col. A. W. Mills, 17/L.F.
Major T. H. Minshall, R.E.
Major A. W. Muir, 19/N.F.
Lt.-Col. W. A. Murray, 18/H.L.I., 17/R.S.
Lt.-Col. C. R. Newman, D.H.Q.
Brig.-Gen. J. H. W. Pollard, 106th Bde.
Lt.-Col. H. W. Rushton, R.E.
Capt. H. D. Ryalls, 16/Ches.
Capt. B. A. Russell, 14/Glos.
Lt.-Col. L. M. Stevens, 23/Man., 18/L.F.
Capt. F. N. Stewart, R.A.M.C.
Major A. E. V. Trestrail, 16/Ches.
Lt.-Col. E. Vaughan, 20/L.F.
Major J. E. Viccars, D.H.Q.
Capt. J. H. Worsley, 4/N.S.

M.C.

2nd Lt. R. R. Aitken, 12/H.L.I.
Lt. T. W. Allen, 15/Ches.
2nd Lt. C. W. Almack, Q./R.H.A.
2nd Lt. H. A. Armstrong, 19/N.F.
Capt. H. Armstrong, 19/N.F.
2nd Lt. M. Arnold, 18/L.F.
2nd Lt. F. Aspden, 17/L.F.
Capt. C. S. Atkinson, 17/L.F. Bar.
Lt. W. Baker, 14/Glos.
Capt. S. A. Ball, R.A.M.C.

2nd Lt. W. G. Barnes, 4/N.S.
Lt. H. E. Bethune, 12/H.L.I.
Capt. W. H. Bird, 4/N.S.
Lt. H. Bowditch, D.A.C.
Capt. A. N. Braithwaite, 17/W.Y.
Capt. S. Brown, R.A.M.C.
Capt. D. Burnett, 16/Ches.
Lt. J. Callan, 12/H.L.I. Bar.
Capt. A. Campbell-Balfour, 18/H.L.I.
Capt. A. J. Chesney, D.H.Q.

HISTORY OF THE 35TH DIVISION

Capt. R. A. S. Coke, 20/L.F.
Capt. C. H. Cooke, 19/N.F.
2nd Lt. G. S. Cormack, 18/L.F.
2nd Lt. J. E. Coutts, 18/L.F.
Capt. E. Curran, 157/R.F.A.
Major H. S. Dawson, N.F.
Lt. W. J. Dean, 19/N.F.
Capt. W. A. Dimouline, Signals.
2nd Lt. W. Dobinson, 18/L.F.
Lt. A. F. Draper, R.A.M.C.
Capt. G. A. Duncan, 18/L.F.
Capt. W. Duns, 15/S.F.
Capt. C. E. Dyer, 4/N.S.
2nd Lt. W. Dyson, 157/R.F.A.
Lt. C. W. Farrish, 157/R.F.A.
Capt. J. Fawcett, 19/N.F.
Capt. W. Fawcus, 19/N.F.
2nd Lt. E. W. R. FitzGerald, 157/R.F.A.
2nd Lt. — Franks, 18/L.F.
2nd Lt. H. G. S. Franks, 159/R.F.A.
2nd Lt. J. A. Fraser, 105/M.G.C. (9/R. Scots Fus.).
2nd Lt. A. E. V. Gallon, 18/L.F.
Lt. — Gardiner, 18/L.F.
Capt. — Gelagher, 16/Ches.
Capt. M. A. Gibb, 4/N.S.
Capt. M. Mends Gibson, 157/R.F.A.
Capt. G. de C. Glover, 105th Bde.
Major V. W. Goss, 159/R.F.A.
2nd Lt. D. R. Grant, 19/N.F.
2nd Lt. S. Greener, 18/L.F.
Lt. W. A. Hanrick, 159/R.F.A.
Capt. R. P. Harrison, D.H.-Q.
Major G. A. Hart, 159/R.F.A.
Lt. F. Harwood, 157/R.F.A.
2nd Lt. R. M. Harwood, 157/R.F.A.
Lt. R. S. Heath, 17/L.F.
Lt. R. T. Helsby, R.A.M.C.
Capt. S. H. Hempson, 20/L.F.
Capt. H. Henstock, 4/N.S.
Capt. C. H. Hewson, 159/R.F.A.
Lt. W. E. Hicks, 19/N.F.
Capt. G. W. Hodgkinson, 105th Bde.
Capt. W. Hodson, 15/Ches.
Capt. D. F. Holman, 4/N.S.
Lt. C. Huntley, 17/L.F. (North Fus.).
2nd Lt. R. Irvine, 20/L.F.
2nd Lt. R. Jackson, 157/R.F.A.
2nd Lt. H. Jarvis, 17/R.S.
Major A. S. Johnson, 15/S.F.
R.M.S. R. T. Jones, 15/Ches.
Lt. and Qmr. T. Keay, 17/L.F.
Major J. Keith, 157/R.F.A.
Capt. W. T. Kelly, 106th T.M.B.
Capt. Kennedy, 18/H.L.I.
C.S.M. P. Kerr, 17/R.S.
Capt. C. B. Kidd, 15/Ches.

Capt. Kinred, 14/Glos.
Major H. F. A. Le Mesurier, 106th T.M.B.
Lt. H. Lewis, 18/L.F.
Lt. O. Lloyd, 4/N.S.
Lt. A. D. Loch, 17/R.S.
Lt. H. F. S. Lowery, 17/R.S.
Major W. T. Luck, 157/R.F.A.
Capt. R. C. Lyons, 157/R.F.A.
Major J. W. Lloyd-Davies, R.E.
Capt. D. J. McAfee, R.A.M.C.
Lt. R. MacGregor, 157/R.F.A. Bar.
Lt. A. S. McIver, 18/H.L.I.
2nd Lt. R. L. Maitland-Heriot, 157/R.F.A.
Lt. R. F. M. McKevitt, 17/L.F.
2nd Lt. P. Merrick, 18/H.L.I.
Lt. G. M. Miller, 15/S.F.
Lt. R. A. Moir, Signals.
Lt. C. F. Morgan, 157/R.F.A.
Capt. A. W. Muir, 19/N.F.
Capt. A. W. Murray, 18/H.L.I.
Lt. T. W. Murray, 159/R.F.A.
Capt. R. E. Newland, R.A.M.C. (Aust.).
Major G. A. Pinney, 159/R.F.A.
Capt. G. Phillips, 157/R.F.A.
2nd Lt. — Plenderleith, 18/L.F.
Capt. A. A. Pocock, 19/N.F.
C.S.M. C. H. Price, 19/N.F.
Lt. E. O. Prothero, 19/N.F.
Capt. C. W. Pulford, Y/35 T.M.B.
2nd Lt. F. A. Raynes, 17/R.S.
2nd Lt. H. Redfern, 18/L.F.
Capt. W. Rennison, 17/L.F.
2nd Lt. J. J. Rewcastle, 18/L.F. Bar.
Lt. A. Richardson, 157/R.F.A.
Capt. J. H. K. Richardson, 159/R.F.A.
Capt. P. H. Richardson, 157/R.F.A.
Capt. E. Rigby, 18/L.F.
Capt. F. A. D. Roberts, 18/L.F.
2nd Lt. J. C. Robertson, 18/H.L.I.
Capt. R. C. R. Robinson, 17/L.V.
Capt. H. A. Rowell, R.A.M.C.
Lt. M. H. Rose, 23/Manchester.
Major L. H. Ross, 106th Bde.
Lt. T. A. Roxburgh, 159/R.F.A.
Capt. W. O. Rushton, 104th Bde.
Capt. A. G. Scougal, 17/R.S.
Lt. C. W. Sewell, 15/S.F.
Rev. J. J. Sheridan, C.F.
Capt. E. J. S. Shufflebotham, 14/Glos.
2nd Lt. J. Sillitor, 18/L.F.
Rev. G. Smissen, C.F.
Capt. A. Stabell, 19/N.F.
2nd Lt. H. W. Stanton, 12/H.L.I.
Capt. F. D. Stephenson, 159/R.F.A.
2nd Lt. E. C. Stephenson, 17/L.F. (East York.).
Capt. F. N. Stewart, R.A.M.C.

HISTORY OF THE 35TH DIVISION

Major L. A. W. Stower, D.H.-Q.
2nd Lt. J. M. Summers, 18/H.L.I.
2nd Lt. J. D. Taggart, X/35 T.M.B.
2nd Lt. C. F. Tissingham, 15/Ches. Bar.
Capt. R. W. Train, 106th Bde.
Capt. S. J. le P. Trench, R.F.A.
Lt. D. M. Weatherstone, 17/R.S.
Major J. Webster, 157/R.F.A.
Capt. C. E. Wilson, R.A.M.C.

2nd Lt. A. E. Winn, Y/35 T.M.B.
2nd Lt. M. R. Wood, 18/L.F.
Lt. H. Woodward, 4/N.S.
Lt. H. M. Woodyer, 15/Ches.
Capt. J. N. Wootton, 105/T.M.B.
Capt. Rev. J. K. Worley, C.F.
2nd Lt. R. A. Wylie, 17/R.S.
2nd Lt. F. St. G. Yorke, 18/H.L.I.
Capt. W. Young, 17/W.Y.

D.C.M.

Cpl. — Bloor, 18/L.F.
Pte. J. H. Britwell, 17/L.F.
Pte. S. Wall, 17/L.F.
Pte. — Burns, 15/Ches.
Cpl. — Workman, 18/H.L.I.
Gr. — Monk, 158/R.F.A.
Sgt. C. W. Empson, 158/R.F.A.
Sgt. J. McKean, 159/R.F.A.
Gr. S. McEwen, 163/R.F.A.
Sgt. S. Harvey, 15/Ches.
Sgt. — Williams, 15/Ches.
Cpl. W. McGovern, 20/L.F.
B.S.M. W. G. Taylor, 159/R.F.A.
C.S.M. — Smith, 18/H.L.I.
C.S.M. — McGuillan, 18/H.L.I.
Cpl. W. Pincher, 17/R.S.
L.-Cpl. — Lees, 15/Ches.
Pte. J. Dobson, 19/N.F.
Sgt. T. A. Brown, V/35 T.M.B.
Pte. W. A. Johnson, 16/Ches.
C.S.M. R. Mayer, 10/L.F.
L.-Cpl. — Grundy, 20/L.F.

L.-Cpl. — Utterly, 18/L.F.
Pte. — Bertwick, 17/L.F.
C.S.M. R. Maskill, 18/L.F.
Sgt. W. J. Dean, 19/N.F.
Adjt. M. Levy, R.F.A., Interpreter.
Pte. W. Sholisar, 17/L.F.
B.S.M. A. H. Cook, 157/R.F.A.
Sgt. W. Berry, 157/R.F.A.
Cpl. T. Coombs, X/35 T.M.B.
Pte. J. Watt, 17/R.S.
L.-Cpl. J. Hallar, 12/H.L.I.
C.S.M. R. Crawford, 12/H.L.I.
Sgt. A. White, 17/R.S.
Sgt. H. C. Patterson, 159/R.F.A.
Pte. H. Holt, 4/N.S.
Pte. A. Sibbering, 4/N.S.
Pte. J. H. Bratton, 4/N.S.
C.S.M. — Kenton, 15/Ches.
Sgt. — Bush, 15/Ches.
Sgt. — Fay, 15/Ches.
Pte. A. Walmsley, 17/L.F.
Sgt. G. H. King, Signals.

M.M.

Sgt. A. Hare, 23/Man.
Cpl. J. O'Connor, 23/Man.
Pte. A. Lee, 23/Man.
Pte. W. Townley, 23/Man.
Pte. J. H. Carmont, 23/Man.
Pte. G. Wright, 17/L.F.
Pte. B. Taylor, 17/L.F.
Sgt. — Williams, 15/Ches.
L.-Cpl. — Sands, 15/Ches.
Pte. — Emmens, 15/Ches.
L.-Cpl. — Smith, 15/Ches.
L.-Cpl. — Turner, 14/Glos.
Pte. J. H. Fowler, 14/Glos.
Cpl. — Roskett, M.G.C.
Pte. — Vero, 17/W.Y.
Pte. — Marshall, 17/W.Y.
L.-Cpl. A. O'Donnell, 18/H.L.I.
Pte. — Rolleston, 18/H.L.I.
Gr. A. McKibbon, 159/R.F.A.
Gr. H. Macdonald, 159/R.F.A.
Sgt. W. Riley, 159/R.F.A.

Gr. — Lord, 159/R.F.A.
Gr. — Morgan, 159/R.F.A.
Gr. — Flannagan, 159/R.F.A.
Gr. — Rencastle, 159/R.F.A.
Cpl. — Bulley, 159/R.F.A.
Driver — Farnworth, 159/R.F.A.
Pte. — Rice, 20/L.F.
Cpl. R. J. Townson, 157/R.F.A.
Gr. A. J. Martin, 157/R.F.A.
Dr. Antonio Cusmano, 157/R.F.A.
Cpl. J. Smith, 159/R.F.A.
Br. J. Yuill, 159/R.F.A.
Gr. A. McKay, 159/R.F.A.
Sgt. — Homerf, 18/L.F.
L.-Cpl. — Algie, 18/L.F.
Pte. — Lemaitre, 18/L.F.
a/C.S.M. — Ryle, 17/W.Y.
Pte. — Walsh, 17/W.Y.
Pte. — Whitelaw, 17/W.Y.
Pte. — Bridgemont, 17/W.Y.
Cpl. G. Bull, 157/R.F.A.

HISTORY OF THE 35TH DIVISION

L.-Cpl. G. Stringer, 17/L.F.
L.-Cpl. A. Wilkinson, 17/L.F.
a/B.S.M. J. J. Stewart, 157/R.F.A.
L.-Cpl. — Legg, 18/H.L.I.
Cpl. — Brown, 18/H.L.I.
Sgt. J. Coutts, R.F.A.
Sgt. J. Watt, R.F.A.
Gr. G. Cowie, R.F.A.
Cpl. — Rose, 16/Ches.
Pte. A. Mizon, 18/L.F.
Cpl. R. Stamon, 20/L.F.
Cpl. W. Grundy, 20/L.F.
Pte. E. Price, 20/L.F.
Pte. T. Gorier, 20/L.F.
Pte. — McPhail, 17/R.S.
Pte. — Prior, 17/R.S.
Cpl. — Williams, 17/R.S.
Br. P. Ecclesff, Z/35 T.M.B.
Gr. W. Higginbotham, Y/35 T.M.B.
L.-Sgt. J. Craig, 20/L.F.
Sgt. C. Betterby, 20/L.F.
Pte. J. Gerance, 20/L.F.
Pte. J. MacGuire, 20/L.F.
Pte. J. Pearce, 14/Glos.
Pte. A Bidwell, 14/Glos.
Pte. W. G. Harding, 14/Glos.
Pte. A. Bunce, 14/Glos.
Sgt. — Johnston, 15/Ches.
Sgt. — Waring, 15/Ches.
Pte. — Kemp, 15/Ches.
Pte. — Pugh, 15/Ches.
a/Sgt. W. Haynes, 17/R.S.
a/Sgt. W. B. Donaldson, 17/R.S.
L.-Cpl. T. Ley, 17/R.S.
Cpl. T. Neally, 17/R.S.
Pte. F. Blackburn, 19/N.F.
Sgt. J. B. Robson, 19/N.F.
Sgt. G. Masterton, 159/R.F.A.
Br. A. Kemp, 159/R.F.A.
Cpl. C. Coomber, Y/35 T.M.B.
Cpl. W. A. King, R.E. Bar.
Br. A. McKibbin, 159/R.F.A. Bar.
Gr. H. Chalmers, 157/R.F.A.
Sgt. T. Hackett, 18/L.F.
Cpl. R. Woodend, 18/L.F.
L.-Sgt. R. Dawson, 18/L.F.
L.-Sgt. F. Roberts, 18/L.F.
Pte. H. Bray, 18/L.F.
Cpl. J. Curran, 20/L.F.
Pte. A. Guest, 20/L.F.
Sgt. C. Brocklebank, 20/L.F.
Sgt. H. C. Bolton, 20/L.F.
Cpl. — Ames, 16/Ches.
Cpl. — Moat, 16/Ches.
Pte. — Hudson, 16/Ches.
Pte. — Band, 16/Ches.
Pte. — Titterton, 16/Ches.
Pte. — Marshall, 16/Ches.
Pte. — Walker, 16/Ches.
Cpl. — Long, 14/Glos.
Pte. — Budgett, 14/Glos.
Pte. — Blake, 14/Glos.
Pte. — Cowl, 14/Glos.
Pte. — Darch, 14/Glos.
L.-Cpl. — Fitton, 18/L.F.
Cpl. — Waldron, 18/L.F.
Sgt. — Steadman, 18/L.F.
Pte. — Morris, 18/L.F.
Sgt. — Beetham, 18/L.F.
Sgt. W. Ramsay, 17/R.S.
L.-Cpl. A. Leigh, 17/R.S.
Pte. A. Forrest, 17/R.S.
Pte. W. Still, 17/R.S.
Pte. W. Davie, 17/R.S.
Sgt. G. H. Beaming, D.A.C.
Br. G. Burgess, 159/R.F.A.
Dr. J. Richardson, 159/R.F.A.
Gr. J. Hughes, 157/R.F.A.
Sgt. J. Thomson, 157/R.F.A.
Sgt. A. L. Christie, 159/R.F.A.
Gr. G. Hewett, 157/R.F.A.
Sgt. T. Gray, 157/R.F.A.
SS. J. Peters, 157/R.F.A.
Br. W. Marshall, 159/R.F.A.
Br. W. Dickson, 159/R.F.A.
Gr. D. McLean, 159/R.F.A.
Br. F. H. Hollis, D.A.C.
Sgt. — Brooking, 159/R.F.A.
Cpl. W. Appleby, 157/R.F.A.
Br. M. Maclean, 157/R.F.A.
Sgt. W. Killen, 157/R.F.A.
Cpl. J. McBryde, 159/R.F.A.
Sgt. T. Moore, 4/N.S.
Dr. F. Goodier, 157/R.F.A.
Cpl. — Hewitt, 157/R.F.A. Bar.
Gr. — Carr, 159/R.F.A.
Dr. J. H. Henderson, D.A.C.
Sgt. — Dixon, 19/D.L.I.
Pte. — Pearson, 19/D.L.I.
Pte. — Taylor, 17/L.F.
Cpl. — Eastham, 18/L.F.
Pte. — Patton, 18/L.F.
Pte. — Twist, 18/L.F.
Pte. S. Smith, 18/L.F.
Pte. — Boardman, 18/L.F.
Pte. — Boynton, 18/L.F.
Pte. — Ashby, 18/L.F.
Pte. — Gukenbiehe, 18/N.F.
Sgt. W. S. Scorer, 19/N.F.
Pte. R. Hopper, 19/N.F.
Sgt. J. W. Coxon, 19/N.F.
Sgt. W. Gaskett, 157/R.F.A.
Sgt. A. Smart, 157/R.F.A.
Sgt. E. Price, 157/R.F.A.

Gr. T. N. Smith, 157/R.F.A.
Dr. D. Park, 157/R.F.A.
Gr. L. Stenhouse, X/35 T.M.B.
Gr. — Schofield, Y/35 T.M.B.
Gr. — Harrington, Y/35 T.M.B.
Cpl. G. Maughan, 19/N.F.
Pte. R. McKibbon, 19/N.F.
Pte. I. Riches, 19/N.F.
Gr. C. J. Nicholas, 159/R.F.A.
Gr. S. Fuller, 159/R.F.A.
Pte. B. Rees, 17/L.F.   Bar.
Pte. T. Diggle, 17/L.F.   Bar.
Pte. T. Lord, 17/L.F.
Pte. F. Jones, 17/L.F.
Pte. A. Carr, 17/L.F.
Pte. B. Heyworth, 17/L.F.
Pte. A. Burgess, 17/L.F.
Sgt. M'Colm, 159/R.F.A.
Gr. — McShane, 159/R.F.A.
Sgt. J. Coutts, 157/R.F.A.
Sgt. N. Gaskett, 157/R.F.A.
Cpl. F. E. Lynn, Y/35 T.M.B.
Dr. J. Holt, D.A.C.
Cpl. A. Webster, R.E.
L.-Cpl. R. Clark, R.E.
L.-Cpl. P. Perrin, R.E.
Sap. E. G. Cockin, R.E.
Pr. J. Pritchard, R.E.
Pte. A. Ross, 17/R.S.
Pte. J. Fleming, 17/R.S.
Sgt. J. Lord, 17/L.F.   Bar.
Pte. J. Nicholls, 17/L.F.
L.-Sgt. R. Harthill, 17/L.F.
Sgt. E. Seddon, 17/L.F.
Pte. P. Rivett, 17/L.F.
Pte. P. Almond, 17/L.F.
L.-Sgt. J. Rigby, 17/L.F.
Cpl. A. Fielding, 17/L.F.
Pte. C. P. Heath, 17/L.F.
Pte. J. H. Meakin, 17/L.F.
Pte. E. Holland, 17/L.F.
Pte. W. Carradus, 17/L.F.
a/Sgt. C. Holmes, 17/L.F.
Cpl. W. Reveley, 19/N.F.
Cpl. L. McHughtry, 19/N.F.
Pte. J. B. Thompson, 19/N.F.
Cpl. S. Field, 19/N.F.
Sap. A. E. Marshall, R.E.
Sap. R. B. Gale, R.E.
Sap. E. Swain, R.E.
Sap. A. T. Childs, R.E.
Sap. T. Palmer, R.E.
Sgt. D. G. O'Hea, 12/H.L.I.   Bar.
L.-Cpl. C. Nicholas, 12/H.L.I.
L.-Cpl. D. Rate, 12/H.L.I.
Cpl. W. Brown, 12/H.L.I.
Pte. G. W. Graham, 17/R.S.

Pte. M. McNamee, 17/R.S.
Pte. W. Milne, 17/R.S.
Pte. W. H. Clark, 17/R.S.
Cpl. H. C. Clarke, 17/R.S.
Cpl. C. Pritchard, 17/R.S.
L.-Cpl. A. Nicol, 17/R.S.
Gr. W. C. Jackson, 159/R.F.A.
Gr. G. F. Waters, D.A.C.
Sgt. J. W. Woodcock, 4/N.S.   Bar.
Pte. J. Russell, 4/N.S.
Pte. J. Smith, 4/N.S.
Pte. L. Hall, 4/N.S.
L.-Cpl. J. Barrett, 4/N.S.
Sgt. C. A. Kemp, R.E.
Sap C. T. Wilson, R.E.
Cpl. T. Yorke, 19/N.F.
Pte. A. T. Wilson, 4/N.S.
Pte. W. Walton, 4/N.S.
Sgt. E. Guilder, 4/N.S.
L.-Cpl. I. Derbyshire, 4/N.S.
L.-Cpl. H. G. Paragreen, 4/N.S.
L.-Cpl. W. C. Lawton, 4/N.S.
Pte. — Aspinall, 15/Ches.
Pte. — Potter, 15/Ches.
Pte. — Jones, 15/Ches.
R.S.M. — Lyon, 15/Ches.
L.-Cpl. — Newlots, 15/Ches.
L.-Cpl. — Pratt, 15/Ches.
Sgt. — O'Connor, 15/Ches.
Pte. — Reynolds, 15/Ches.
Pte. — Smith, 15/Ches.
Pte. — Madeley, 15/Ches.
Pte. — Smith, 15/Ches.
Pte. — Llewellyn, 15/Ches.
Pte. — Scholes, 15/Ches.
Pte. — Hoddinott, 15/Ches.
Sgt. — Baird, 15/Ches.
Cpl. — Nightingall, 15/Ches.
Cpl. — Johnson, 15/Ches.
Pte. — Hardman, 15/Ches.
Pte. — Brown, 15/Ches.
Sgt. — Elliott, 15/Ches.
Pte. J. R. Angus, 19/N.E.
L.-Cpl. E. Todd, 19/N.F.
Pte. S. Clark, 19/N.F.
C.Q.M.S. A. E. Haram, 19/N.F.
Sgt. G. Rooke, 17/L.F.
Sgt. E. Tetlow, 17/L.F.   Bar.
C.S.M. C. W. Chamberlain, 17/L.F.
Sgt. R. H. Garnett, 17/L.F.
Sgt. C. Parsons, 17/L.F.
Sgt. F. S. Rowland, 17/L.F.
Cpl. T. Pemberton, 17/L.F.
L.-Cpl. J. Francis, 17/L.F.
L.-Cpl. S. Kendall, 17/L.F.
Pte. W. Thomas, 17/L.F.
Pte. E. Spear, 17/L.F.

HISTORY OF THE 35TH DIVISION

Pte. C. B. Hodgkiss, 17/L.F.
Pte. C. Lane, 17/L.F.
Pte. P. Broughton, 17/L.F.
Pte. J. Holden, 17/L.F.
Pte. J. M. Gregson, 17/L.F.
Pte. J. E. Mincher, 17/L.F.
Pte. C. P. Gray, 17/L.F.
Pte. H. Knowles, 17/L.F.
Pte. G. Wilkes, 17/L.F.
Pte. R. T. Kershaw, 17/L.F.
Pte. A. Mole, 17/L.F.
Pte. J. Pendell, 17/L.F.
Pte. I. Winstanley, 17/L.F.
Pte. W. Williams, 17/L.F.
Pte. W. Connor, 17/L.F.
Pte. R. Horwarth, 17/L.F.
Sgt. D. Barnett, 18/L.F.
Sgt. J. Hackett, 18/L.F.
Cpl. J. M. Mullin, 18/L.F.
C.S.M. G. Chapman, 18/L.F.
Cpl. — Knight, 18/L.F.
Cpl. J. Donacher, 18/L.F.
Cpl. — Button, 18/L.F.
Cpl. J. O'Brien, 18/L.F.
Cpl. W. Lill, 18/L.F..
L.-Sgt. J. Brown, 18/L.F.
Pte. H. Prince, 18/L.F.
Pte. W. Riddicks, 18/L.F.
Pte. W. Robson, 18/L.F.

Pte. A. Pickup, 18/L.F.
Pte. J. Hilbraid, 18/L.F.
Pte. T. Woodhead, 18/L.F.
Pte. R. J. Monks, 18/L.F.
Pte. H. Kelly, 18/L.F.
Pte. A. A. Roberts, 18/L.F.
Cpl. W. Tomlinson, 157/R.F.A.
Cpl. A. Davidson, 159/R.F.A.
Cpl. E. G. Webb, D.A.C.
L.-Br. J. Rough, R.A.
Br. H. Gough, 157/R.F.A.
L.-Sgt. J. W. Wardle, 19/N.F.
Sgt. L. Smith, 19/N.F.
Pte. J. A. Harrison, 19/N.F.
Pte T. Forster, 19/N.F.
Pte. J. Simpson, 19/N.F.
Pte. W. Timlin, 19/N.F.
Pte. W. E. Stainburn, 19/N.F.
Pte. W. Summerside, 19/N.F.
Sgt. T. Marwick, 19/N.F.
Sgt. I. Jackson, 19/N.F.
Cpl. S. R. Lonsdale, 19/N.F.
Sgt. T. Leach, 19/N.F.
Cpl. J. E. Jobson, 19/N.F.
Pte. E. Emmerson, 19/N.F.
Sgt. A. Rayner, R.F.A.
Cpl. J. E. Rust, R.F.A.
SS.. J. Ross, R.F.A.
Cpl. G. Ball, 157/R.F.A.

M.S.M.

B.Q.M.S. — Gerrard, 159/R.F.A.
Sgt. W. Smith, 19/N.F.
Sgt. J. Hulme, 19/N.F.
Sgt. F. W. Erle, 159/R.F.A.
L.-Br. — Whalley, 159/R.F.A.
Gr. J. H. Smith, 157/R.F.A.
Sgt. J. Duckworth, D.A.C.
Sgt. J. Brandon, 4/N.S.
L.-Sgt. W. Heathcote, 4/N.S.
Sgt. C. J. Fuller, R.E.

Sgt. J. H. Martin, R.E.
Sgt. H. W. Noyle, R.E.
Pte. S. Roberts, 19/N.F.
L.-Cpl. F. Gibson, 19/N.F.
Sgt. F. E. Pagett, 19/N.F.
Sgt. T. W. Harrison, 19/N.F.
C.S.M. J. Whitton, 19/N.F.
Cpl. T. J. Brownbridge, 19/N.F.
Cpl. S. McMorran, 17/R.S.
R.Q.M.S. J. Richardson, 19/N.F.

Foreign Decorations.

Legion of Honour.

Maj.-Gen. A. H. Marindin.
Maj.-Gen. R. J. Pinney.

Order of the Crown.

Maj.-Gen. G. MacK. Franks.
Maj.-Gen. A. H. Marindin.
Brig.-Gen. J. H. W. Pollard.

Croix de Guerre.

Maj.-Gen. R. J. Pinney.
Maj.-Gen. A. H. Marindin.
Maj.-Gen. G. M. Franks.
Brig.-Gen. W. R. N. Madocks.
Brig.-Gen. J. H. W. Pollard.
Brig.-Gen. A. J. Turner.
Brig.-Gen. J. W. Sandilands.
Lt.-Col. H. W. Thorp, D.H.Q.
Major R. T. Holland, R.A.
Sgt. — Francis, 18/L.F.

Capt. F. K. Simmons, 104th Bde.
Major P. H. Richardson, R.F.A.
B.S.M. C. Butler, 157/R.F.A.
Driver J. Sheriffe, 157/R.F.A.
Lt. W. S. Wrinch, 20/L.F.
Lt. R. T. Helsby, R.A.M.C.
Pte. — Ham, 20/L.F.
C.S.M. P. Coulter, 16 Ches.
Sgt. — Battle, 17/L.F.

Croix de Guerre (Belgian).

Maj.-Gen. G. M. Franks.
Maj.-Gen. A. H. Marindin.
Brig.-Gen. J. H. W. Pollard.
Capt. F. Gordon, 17/R.S.
Sgt. T. McGinney, 17/R.S.
Capt. — Cruickshank, 157/R.F.A.

B.S.M. F. Beer, 159/R.F.A.
Dr. J. Mullin, 159/R.F.A.
Cpl. W. Wicken, 157/R.F.A.
Sgt. — Birmingham, 17/L.F.
Sgt. — Moat, 17/L.F.

Medaille Militaire.

Cpl. H. Hodgkiss, X/35 T.M.B.
M. Rufin (Intr.), 159/R.F.A.

Note.—The honours of the 15/Sherwood Foresters are not given in the War Diaries. Some of the other lists are incomplete as names of recipients are omitted.

x

APPENDIX II.
CASUALTY LISTS.
R.F.A. UNITS.

Date	157/Brigade Officers			157/Brigade O.R.			159/Brigade Officers			159/Brigade O.R.			T.M. Batteries Officers			T.M. Batteries O.R.			Royal Engineers Officers			Royal Engineers O.R.		
	K	W	M	K	W	M	K	W	M	K	W	M	K	W	M	K	W	M	K	W	M	K	W	M
1916																								
February																								
March						1																		
April	1			1	32		1	1		1	4								1	2			1	1
May	1	4		12	14		1	1			3	1								1		3	5	
June		1		6				4		7	24											8	56	
July					2		1			1	3								1	3		4	23	
August					3									1									1	
September		1						1			2						2						1	
October																								
November																							5	
December																								
Total	2	6		18	53	1	3	6		9	39	1		1			7		1	7		18	93	
1917																								
January	1										2												1	
February																								
March	1			2			1	3		10													1	
April				2	8					2	8			2		1	1					2	2	
May		1			3					1	2					2							5	
June				1	7		1	2			2												3	
July	2	2		1	8						2												9	
August	1			1	3		1	1			2									2			2	
September					6		2			5														
October	7				15			1		8	4					1	1		3	1		1	23	1
November		3		11	38		2	3		1	29					3	3					2	29	
December				2	10						24								3	1		2	2	
Total	3	15		20	100		5	11		12	88			4		7	21		6	4		8	77	1

HISTORY OF THE 35TH DIVISION

Date 1918	157/Brigade Officers K. W. M.	157/Brigade O.R. K. W. M.	159/Brigade Officers K. W. M.	159/Brigade O.R. K. W. M.	T.M. Batteries Officers K. W. M.	T.M. Batteries O.R. K. W. M.	Royal Engineers Officers K. W. M.	Royal Engineers O.R. K. W. M.
January	1	3						1 11
February	2	3	1	1 5		1 2		2
March	1	22	2	10 2		2		4 16
April	1	8	2	10 14			2	7 79
May		16	1	2 18				1 2
June		7		3		8		8 14 3
July	1	8	1	1 14	1	1		3 9
August	1	2 4	2	2 5				1
September	1	4 27	3	25 1		4		4 11
October		3 37		34			2	10 24
November		1 3					1	
Total	2 8	16 133 3	1 10	16 130 1	1	2 17	1 4	38 169 4
Grand Total	7 29	54 286 4	9 27	37 257 1	6	9 45	8 15	64 339 5

	158/Brigade Officers K. W. M.	158/Brigade O.R. K. W. M.	163/Brigade Officers K. W. M.	163/Brigade O.R. K. W. M.
1916	4 6	3 20	1	2 47

D.A.C.

	Officers K. W. M.	O.R. K. W. M.
1916	1	1 2
1917		6 23
1918		5 9
Total	1	12 34

APPENDIX II—Continued.

Date	17/Royal Scots Officers K	W	M	O.R. K	W	M	19/North. Fus. Officers K	W	M	O.R. K	W	M	17/West Yorks. Officers K	W	M	O.R. K	W	M	17/Lancs. Fus. Officers K	W	M	O.R. K	W	M
1916																								
February	—	—	—	7	4	—	—	—	—	—	1	—	—	—	—	—	—	—	1	2	—	1	6	—
March	—	1	—	6	6	—	—	—	—	2	—	1	—	—	—	2	3	—	—	3	—	6	15	—
April	—	—	—	9	14	—	—	—	—	3	4	—	—	1	—	3	9	—	—	—	—	1	6	—
May	—	—	—	3	12	—	—	1	—	2	6	—	1	2	—	6	22	—	—	—	—	5	9	—
June	—	4	—	21	2	—	1	1	—	5	6	—	1	1	—	6	5	—	—	—	—	3	9	—
July	2	1	—	—	69	4	1	—	—	19	23	—	1	12	—	43	255	—	1	9	2	36	206	9
August	—	—	—	—	5	—	1	—	—	9	12	—	—	2	—	13	61	—	—	5	—	11	105	31
September	—	—	—	2	8	—	—	—	—	—	9	—	—	—	—	—	20	—	—	1	—	1	14	—
October	—	2	—	7	24	—	—	—	—	1	—	—	—	—	—	4	2	—	—	2	—	12	15	25
November	—	—	—	7	19	—	—	—	—	5	—	—	—	—	—	—	8	—	—	—	—	—	3	—
December	—	—	—	—	—	—	—	—	—	—	2	—	—	—	—	—	—	—	—	—	—	—	—	—
Total	2	8	—	62	163	4	3	2	—	46	64	—	3	18	—	79	387	—	4	23	2	76	388	65
1917																								
January	—	—	—	2	1	—	—	—	—	—	—	—	—	—	—	—	—	—	—	—	—	—	1	—
February	—	—	—	—	6	—	—	—	—	1	—	—	—	1	—	—	—	—	—	3	—	4	6	—
March	—	—	—	—	—	—	—	—	—	—	—	—	—	—	—	—	—	—	—	1	—	3	3	—
April	—	—	—	—	—	—	—	—	—	—	—	—	—	—	—	—	—	—	—	1	—	13	37	2
May	—	—	—	7	12	—	—	—	—	1	3	—	—	—	—	1	8	—	—	—	—	1	—	—
June	—	—	—	3	10	—	—	—	—	10	2	—	—	—	—	6	2	—	—	3	—	4	9	—
July	—	—	—	12	74	—	—	—	—	4	8	—	—	6	—	7	3	—	—	1	—	7	43	—
August	1	—	—	2	11	—	—	—	—	3	2	—	—	1	—	7	8	—	—	3	—	—	54	—
September	—	—	—	13	62	2	—	—	—	5	4	—	2	—	5	7	56	53	—	1	—	—	4	—
October	—	3	—	15	38	—	—	—	—	3	—	—	—	6	—	7	17	—	4	9	—	32	150	5
November	—	—	—	—	—	—	—	1	—	1	3	—	—	—	—	—	48	45	—	—	—	3	5	—
December	1	—	—	—	—	1	—	—	—	—	8	—	—	—	—	—	—	10	—	—	—	3	3	—
Total	2	4	—	54	214	3	—	1	—	28	33	—	2	13	5	29	142	108	4	22	2	67	324	7

308

APPENDIX II—*Continued.*

Date	17/Royal Scots Officers K. W. M.	17/Royal Scots O.R. K. W. M.	19/North. Fus. Officers K. W. M.	19/North. Fus. O.R. K. W. M.	17/West Yorks. Officers K. W. M.	17/West Yorks. O.R. K. W. M.	17/Lancs. Fus. Officers K. W. M.	17/Lancs. Fus. O.R. K. W. M.
1918								
January		1 5		3	DISBANDED			1 9
February		4 9		2			1	1 9
March	3 2	30 155 40	2 2	22 17 2			1 8 1	6 86 37
April	1	9 28	1	13 47			3 1	7 29 1
May		.8 23	1					
June	1	2 29	1 1	6 3			8	7 37, 2
July	1	7 18		6 1			2 7	7 93 13
August		13		2 6			1 1	15 24
September	3 9	59 245 38		2 5			4	4 6
October	1	8 54		1 9				24 96 10
November			2 3	2 4			5 9	29 217 32
Total	8 14 1	128 579 78	7 6	48 104 3	5 31 5	108 529 108	9 40 2	101 606 96
Grand Total	12 26 1	244 956 85	10 9	122 201 3			17 85 4	244 1318 168

310 HISTORY OF THE 35TH DIVISION

Date	18/Lancs. Fus. Officers K. W. M.	18/Lancs. Fus. O.R. K. W. M.	20/Lancs. Fus. Officers K. W. M.	20/Lancs. Fus. O.R. K. W. M.	15/Cheshire Officers K. W. M.	15/Cheshire O.R. K. W. M.	16/Cheshire Officers K. W. M.	16/Cheshire O.R. K. W. M.
1916								
February		1 6		4 12		3 10		7 29
March	2 3	6 15	1 1	2 3		4 22		4 24
April		1 6		6 6		6 13		2 8
May	3	5 9		2 2			1	1
June		3 9						
July	1	36 206 9	2 10	39 119 13	2 1	37 195 8	1	38 235 7
August	9 5 1 2	11 105 31	2 2 1	10 62 6	1 6 1 1 1	7 20 2	1 9	4 39
September				1 10		4 32		4 35
October				3 22 2		4 34		4 29
November	2	12 14	1 1	1 17	1 1	8 30 5	1 2	5 14 1
December		15 25		2				2
Total	4 32 2	76 388 65	5 14 2	68 253 21	4 12	73 357 15	1 13	70 415 8
1917								
January								
February	1	1		2				
March	3	21 2		8 1 7 6	1	2 8 2		6 18 19
April	1	34 61 16	1 3	20 64 6	1	7 19 4	5	6 33 4
May	1	1 3		1 4 3	1	1 13 1	4	14 3
June	1	6 4		3		1 6	1 1	5
July	3	6 13	1	9		1 7	1 1	5
August	1	3 52		2 20			1	21
September	1	11 1	5 1	1 27 178 7 12	2	48 151	1 9	3
October	3 11	36 151 76	1	27 178 8	2	21 144 4 1	8	41 173 114
November		2 17		3 8		9 94		5 14
December		3		1		2		8 1
Total	4 16 2	88 288 93	2 10 1	63 309 19	2 7	89 444 14	4 24 1	66 294 141

HISTORY OF THE 35TH DIVISION

Date	18/Lancs. Fus. Officers K. W. M.			18/Lancs. Fus. O.R. K. W. M.			20/Lancs. Fus. Officers K. W. M.			20/Lancs. Fus. O.R. K. W. M.			15/Cheshire Officers K. W. M.			15/Cheshire O.R. K. W. M.			16/Cheshire Officers K. W. M.			16/Cheshire O.R. K. W. M.		
1918																								
January		1			12			2			36													
February	3	4	2	28	13		DISBANDED							1		4	3		DISBANDED			5	3	
March	3	4	2	28	130	84							3	8	7	32	176	209						
April		4		1	35								3	8		14	118	7						
May				3	42									2		4	76	1						
June	4	5	1	30	137	5							1	1		8	31	3						
July		3		20	64									2			10							
August													1	3		14	118	2						
September		9	1	30	154	16							2	7		37	158	19						
October		13		48	221	49							1				5							
November					3																			
Total	7	39	4	162	811	154		2			36		11	32	7	120	706	246		5			5	3
Grand Total	18	87	8	326	1487	312	7	26	3	131	598	40	17	51	7	282	1507	275	5	37	1	141	712	149

APPENDIX II—*Continued.*

Date	14/Gloster Officers			14/Gloster O.R.			15/Sher. Forest Officers			15/Sher. Forest O.R.			23/Manchester Officers			23/Manchester O.R.			4/N. Stafford Officers			4/N. Stafford O.R.		
	K.	W.	M.	K.	W.	M.	K.	W.	M.	K.	W.	M.	K.	W.	M.	K.	W.	M.	K.	W.	M.	K.	W.	M.
1916																								
February	—	1	—	3	—	—	1	—	—	4	3	—	1	—	—	2	7	—						
March	—	—	—	5	12	—	1	—	—	12	10	—	—	3	—	1	14	—						
April	—	—	—	3	14	—	—	3	2	1	29	26	—	2	—	8	12	—						
May	2	4	—	9	25	8	—	9	—	—	4	—	1	1	—	1	24	24						
June	2	6	—	6	126	10	8	—	—	64	249	36	4	7	—	42	213	24						
July	—	3	—	28	87	9	—	1	—	3	24	—	1	4	—	20	62	—						
August	—	—	—	6	3	—	—	—	—	—	—	—	—	2	—	3	9	—						
September	—	—	—	6	16	—	1	1	—	6	44	8	—	—	—	6	65	—						
October	1	—	—	1	13	—	2	2	1	10	29	8	—	—	—	2	8	—						
November																—	2	—						
December																								
Total	6	14	—	68	296	27	13	15	3	100	392	78	7	19	—	85	424	25						
1917																								
January	1	—	—	7	—	—	—	—	—	—	10	—	—	—	—	3	4	—						
February	—	—	—	1	—	—	—	—	—	—	—	1	—	1	—	—	10	—						
March	—	1	—	—	17	—	—	—	—	—	—	—	—	—	—	2	14	—						
April	2	2	—	2	4	—	2	—	—	18	6	—	—	1	—	1	20	—						
May	1	2	—	1	6	—	2	—	—	1	41	15	—	—	—	7	4	—						
June	2	—	—	6	20	—	—	1	—	1	4	—	—	—	—	3	1	—						
July	2	—	—	6	20	—	—	—	—	—	3	—	—	—	—	—	44	3						
August	—	1	—	8	32	—	—	—	—	25	53	5	—	—	—	19	146	62						
September	—	—	—	2	7	—	3	—	—	24	198	30	5	5	—	1	3	—						
October	1	8	—	74	177	33	1	—	—	—	16	—	9	5	—	—	6	—						
November				2	10	—	2	3	1	—	1	—	1	—	—									
December				—	4	—																		
Total	5	18	1	108	298	33	2	9	1	70	332	51	11	13	1	37	252	65						

HISTORY OF THE 35TH DIVISION

Date	14/Glo'ster Officers K. W. M.	14/Glo'ster O.R. K. W. M.	15/Sher. Forest. Officers K. W. M.	15/Sher. Forest. O.R. K. W. M.	23/Manchester Officers K. W. M.	23/Manchester O.R. K. W. M.	4/N. Stafford Officers K. W. M.	4/N. Stafford O.R. K. W. M.
1918								
January			4 1	2 15	1	4		
February	DISBANDED	2	1	2 12	DISBANDED			5 29 1
March			1 3 7	24 154 246			2 5 1	20 125 61
April			1 5 1	27 120 21			1 2	14 76
May				5 29			4	4 92
June			1	21 43 5			1	1 9
July				4				7 34
August			3	28 89 8				6
September				36 168 43			1 8	29 194 32
October			3 14 1				1 9	23 177 18
November				10			1	
Total		2	10 27 10	145 644 323	1	4	6 30 1	103 742 112
Grand Total	11 32 1	176 596 60	25 51 14	315 1368 452	18 33 1	122 680 90	6 30 1	103 742 112

APPENDIX II—*Continued.*

	19/D.L.I.						12/H.L.I.						18/H.L.I.						Staff					
	Officers			O.R.			Officers			O.R.			Officers			O.R.			M.G.C. Officers			Signals O.R.		
Date 1916	K.	W.	M.	K.	W.	M.	K.	W.	M.	K.	W.	M.	K.	W.	M.	K.	W.	M.	K.	W.	M.	K.	W.	M.
February																								
March		1																		2			1	
April				4	19								1	2		11	16					2	5	
May				7	21									1		3	11					2	12	
June				3	4									1		1	13							
July	1	8		33	220								4	13		40	202	3				15	47	
August	1	3		25	85									1		2	24					1	32	
September																5	17							
October		3		6	18								1	1		9	8							
November																	23							
December																								
Total	3	14		78	367								2	22	1	72	317	3						
1917																								
January																								
February																								
March																								
April																	3							
May	2	1		5	53									1			4							
June														1		2	9	2						
July					26									2		4	8							
August					26								1	12		42	29	4					2	
September		16		20	100												260	1		2		16	54	3
October				21	124												4					1	2	
November														3			7							
December																								
Total	2	17		46	329								2	18		48	317	7						

HISTORY OF THE 35TH DIVISION

Date	19/D.L.I. Officers K. W. M.	19/D.L.I. O.R. K. W. M.	12/H.L.I. Officers K. W. M.	12/H.L.I. O.R. K. W. M.	18/H.L.I. Officers K. W. M.	18/H.L.I. O.R. K. W. M.	Staff M.G.C. Officers K. W. M.	Staff Signals O.R. K. W. M.
1918								
January								
February								
March	3 6 1	36 103 20	7 8 1	1 3	6	1 7	1	1
April			1	33 187 110	1 1	54 172	1 1 1	5
May	2	3 21	8	16 75	2 1	1 6		1
June	1	6 57		1 126	1 6	9 15		
July	3	20	1	11 59		10 94		
August				1 22		1 2		
September	2	21 132 12	4 8	30 159 5	1 9	26 147 12	2 3	12 51
October	1 8	31 18 29	2	4 41 7	1 2	18 46		12 106
November								
Total	4 22 1	97 520 61	11 28 1	97 672 122	6 25	120 489 12	*	*
Grand Total	9 52 1	221 1216 61	11 28 1	97 672 122	10 65 1	240 1123 22	*	*

* Complete records not available.

APPENDIX III.

Original Order of Battle.

Commander	Major-General R. J. Pinney.
A.D.C.	Lieut. J. A. Pinney.
Camp Commandant	2nd Lieut. W. R. G. Pearson.
G.S.O. 1.	Lieut.-Colonel R. N. Greathead.
G.S.O. 2.	Major W. M. Stewart.
G.S.O. 3.	Major R. A. Steel.
A.A. and Q.M.G.	Lieut.-Colonel A. W. Hasted, C.M.G.
D.A.A. and Q.M.G.	Major N. E. B. Bellairs.
D.A.Q.M.G.	Major G. H. Gill.
A.D.M.S.	Colonel H. O. Trevor.
D.A.D.M.S.	Major P. Davidson, D.S.O.
A.D.V.S.	Captain W. H. Taylor.
D.A.D.O.S.	Lieut. T. H. Cullen.
A.P.M.	Captain C. N. B. Hamilton.

104th *Infantry Brigade.*

Commander	Brig.-General G. M. Mackenzie.
Brigade-Major	Captain B. L. Montgomery, D.S.O.
Staff-Captain	Captain the Hon. J. M. Balfour.
17/Lancs. Fus.	Lieut.-Colonel W. J. McWhinnie.
18/Lancs. Fus.	Lieut.-Colonel R. A. Irvine, C.M.G.
20/Lancs. Fus.	Lieut.-Colonel C. R. G. Mayne, D.S.O.
23/Manchester	Lieut.-Colonel R. P. Smith.

105th *Infantry Brigade.*

Commander	Brig.-General J. G. Hunter, C.B.
Brigade-Major	Major G. N. Dyer.
Staff-Captain	Captain R. O. Hall.
15/Cheshire	Lieut.-Colonel F. H. M. Newell.
16/Cheshire	Lieut.-Colonel R. Browne-Clayton.
14/Gloucestershire	Lieut.-Colonel G. C. Roberts.
15/Sherwood F.	Lieut.-Colonel H. A. Hill.

106th *Infantry Brigade.*

Commander	Brig.-General H. O'Donnell.

Brigade-Major ..	.. Captain C. T. Tomes.
Staff-Captain ..	.. Captain G. B. J. Monfries.
17/Royal Scots ..	.. Lieut.-Colonel R. D. Cheales.
17/West Yorkshire	.. Lieut.-Colonel H. A. Moore.
19/Durham L.I. ..	.. Lieut.-Colonel L. S. Stoney.
18/Highland L.I.	.. Lieut.-Colonel R. R. Lawrenson.

Pioneers Battalion.

19/Northumberland Fus.   Lieut.-Colonel F. W. Daniell.

Divisional Artillery.

Commander ..	.. Brig.-General W. C. Staveley, C.B.
Brigade-Major ..	.. Major P. G. Robinson.
Staff-Captain ..	.. Captain R. M. Rendle.
157th Brigade R.F.A.	.. Lieut.-Colonel G. Milne.
158th Brigade R.F.A.	.. Lieut.-Colonel T. P. Ritzema.
159th Brigade R.F.A.	.. Lieut.-Colonel W. Lamont.
163rd Brigade R.F.A.	.. Lieut.-Colonel Guy Simonds.
35/D.A.C. ..	.. Lieut.-Colonel E. W. Chance.

Divisional Engineers.

C.R.E.	.. Lieut.-Colonel H. W. Rushton.
Adjutant	.. Lieut. B. C. Dening.
203rd Field Co. ..	.. Captain K. N. Pye.
204th Field Co. ..	.. Major T. H. Minshall.
205th Field Co. ..	.. Major J. A. Murdock.

35th Divisional Signals.

O.C.	.. Major R. L. Pearson.
Cable Section E. ..	.. Lieut. E. M. Sutton.
Cable Section T. ..	.. 2nd Lieut. M. Tomson.
104th Bde. Sec. ..	.. Lieut. J. B. McLaren.
105th Bde. Sec. ..	.. Lieut. H. R. Otty.
106th Bde. Sec. ..	.. 2nd Lieut. H. V. Tennant.

35th Divisional Train.

O.C.	.. Major F. E. Johnson.
O.C. H.Q. Co. ..	.. Major T. P. Ellis.
O.C. No. 2 Co. ..	.. Lieut. B. W. F. Farrell.
O.C. No. 3 Co. ..	.. Lieut. L. D. B. Monier-Williams.
O.C. No. 4 Co. ..	.. Lieut. J. F. Stewart.

APPENDIX IV.

ORDER OF BATTLE, *November*, 1916.

List of Units, 35th Division, showing Commanding Officers.

Commander : Major-General A. J. S. LANDON, C.B.

Unit.	C.O.
104th Inf. Bde. ..	.. G.O.C. Brig.-General J. W. Sandilands, C.M.G., D.S.O.
17/Lancs. Fus. ..	.. Lieut.-Colonel A. M. Mills.
18/Lancs. Fus. ..	.. Lieut.-Colonel R. A. Irvine, C.M.G.
20/Lancs. Fus. ..	.. Lieut.-Colonel E. Vaughan.
23/Manchester Regt.	.. Lieut.-Colonel L. M. Stevens.
104/Machine Gun Co.	.. Major O. M. Parker.
105th Inf. Bde. ..	.. G.O.C. Brig.-General A. H. Marindin.
15/Cheshire Regt.	.. Lieut.-Colonel H. P. G. Cochran.
16/Cheshire Regt.	.. Major R. Worthington.
14/Glostershire Regt.	.. Lieut.-Colonel W. P. S. Foord.
15/Notts and Derby Regt.	Lieut.-Colonel R. N. S. Gordon.
105/Machine Gun Co.	.. Major A. D. Gordon.
106th Inf. Bde. ..	.. G.O.C. Brig.-General H. O'Donnell.
17/Royal Scots ..	.. Major E. T. Weston.
17/West Yorks Regt.	.. Lieut.-Colonel F. St. J. Atkinson.
19/Durham L.I. ..	.. Lieut.-Colonel B. C. Dent.
18/Highland L.I. ..	.. Lieut.-Colonel R. R. Laurenson.
106/Machine Gun Co.	.. Captain C. W. Merison.
Div. Artillery ..	.. G.O.C. Brig.-General W. C. Staveley, C.B.
157th Bde. R.F.A.	.. Lieut.-Colonel D. B. Stewart, D.S.O.
158th Bde. R.F.A.	.. Lieut.-Colonel P. H. Fawcett.
159th Bde. R.F.A.	.. Lieut.-Colonel H. M. Davson.

Div. Amm. Col.	Lieut.-Colonel A. H. Berly.
Div. R.E.	C.R.E. Lieut.-Colonel H. W. Rushton.
203rd Field Co.	Captain K. W. Pye.
204th Field Co.	Major T. H. Minshall.
205th Field Co.	Captain W. F. Mewton.
Div. Sig. Co. ..` ..	Captain G. R. Smallwood.
35th Div. Train	Lieut.-Colonel F. E. Johnson.
S.S.O.	Major J. K. Ewart.
Div. Supply Col.	Capt. E. D. M. Humphries.
A.D.M.S.	Colonel H. O. Trevor.
D.A.D.M.S.	Captain T. G. Fleming.
105th Field Ambce. ..	Lieut.-Colonel G. H. Richard.
106th Field Ambce. ..	Lieut.-Colonel J. Fairbairn.
107th Field Ambce. ..	Lieut.-Colonel R. Hemphill.
75th San. Sect.	Captain J. Teare. (T)
19/Northld. Fus. (Pnrs.) ..	Lieut.-Colonel F. W. Daniell.
A.D.V.S.	Major W. H. Taylor.
Mobile Vet. Section ..	Captain W. B. de Vine.

APPENDIX V.

ORDER OF BATTLE, *October*, 1918.

Headquarters

Commander	.. Major-General A. H. Marindin, D.S.O., p.s.c.
A.D.C. ..	.. Captain D. E. C. Wood.
A.D.C. ..	.. Lieut. J. D. Maitland-Mackgill-Crighton.
G.S.O. 1. ..	.. Lieut.-Colonel H. W. B. Thorp, D.S.O., p.s.c.
G.S.O. 2. (act.)	.. Major Sir E. P. D. Pauncefort-Duncombe, Bart., D.S.O.
G.S.O. 3 ..	.. Captain R. P. Harrison.
Intell. Officer	.. Lieut. A. I. Chesney.
A.A. and Q.M.G. ..	Lieut.-Colonel L. M. Jones, D.S.O.
D.A.A.G. ..	.. Major R. F. Bury.
D.A.Q.M.G.	.. Major J. E. Viccars, D.S.O.
A.D.M.S. ..	.. Colonel W. E. Hudleston, C.M.G., D.S.O.
D.A.D.M.S.	.. Major H. A. Rowell, M.C.
D.A.D.V.S.	.. Major W. H. Taylor.
D.A.D.O.S.	.. Major L. A. W. Stower, M.C.
D.A.P.M. ..	.. Captain W. B. Litherland, M.C.
Claims Officer	.. Captain G. E. D. Warmington.
Gas Officer	.. Captain J. Hume.
Sen. Chaplain D.C.G.	Rev. J. Thom, M.C.
Sen. Chaplain P.C.D.	Rev. J. F. Dolan.

Divisional Artillery

Commander	.. Brig.-General W. R. N. Madocks, C.M.G., D.S.O., p.s.c.
Brig.-Major	.. Major A. J. R. Kennedy, D.S.O.
Staff Capt.	.. Captain S. J. le P. Trench, M.C.
157th Bde. R.F.A.	Lieut.-Colonel J. de B. Cowan.
Batt. Commanders	Major Waller, Major P. H. Richardson, M.C., Major J. Webster, M.C., Major G. Phillips, M.C.
159th Bde. R.F.A.	Lieut.-Colonel H. M. Davson, D.S.O.

HISTORY OF THE 35TH DIVISION

Batt. Commanders   Major Youl, Major G. A. Hart, D.S.O., Major V. W. Goss, M.C., Major J. H. K. Richardson, M.C.
D.A.C. ..   Major A. C. Gruncell.
D.T.M. Officer   Captain C. W. Pulford, M.C.
X/35 T.M.B.   Lieut. J. G. Whitehead.
Y/35 T.M.B.   Captain S. Baraclough.

Royal Engineers
Commander   Lieut.-Colonel J. W. Skipwith.
Adjutant ..   Captain G. W. Bost, M.C.
203rd Field Co.   Major M. L. Cobb, M.C.
204th Field Co.   Major W. G. Baker.
205th Field Co.   Major E. A. T. Dillon.

Divisional Signaling Company
Commanding   Major W. I. Bell, M.C.
2nd in Command..   Captain W. A. Dimoline, M.C.

104th Infantry Brigade
Commander   Brig.-General J. W. Sandilands, C.M.G., D.S.O., p.s.c.
Bde. Major   Captain F. K. Simmons, M.V.O.
Act. Bde. Major ..   Captain G. W. Miller, M.C.
Staff Capt.   Captain W. O. Rushton, M.C.
Intell. Officer   2nd Lieut. C. S. Cuthbertson.

17/Lanc. Fus.
O. Commanding ..   Lieut.-Colonel J. Jones, M.C.
2nd in Command..   Major G. Mackereth, M.C.

18/Lanc. Fus. ..
O. Commanding ..   Lieut.-Colonel C. E. Jewels, D.S.O., M.C.
2nd in Command..   Major B. C. H. Keenlyside.

19/Durham L.I.
O. Commanding ..   Lieut.-Colonel W. R. McCulloch.
2nd in Command..   Captain J. W. Waller.

HISTORY OF THE 35TH DIVISION

104 T.M.B.
O. Commanding .. Captain W. L. Caldwell.

105th Infantry Brigade
Commander .. Brig. Gen. A. J. Turner, C.M.G, D.S.O., p.s.c.
Bde. Major .. Captain G. W. Hodgkinson.
Staff Capt. .. Captain W. H. Robson.
Intell. Off. .. Lieut. L. B. Eyre.

15/Cheshire
O. Commanding .. Lieut.-Colonel H. Johnston. D.S.O.
2nd in Command.. Major A. E. Y. Trestrail.

15/Sherwood Foresters
O. Commanding .. Major H. Morton, D.S.O., M.C.
2nd in Command.. Major A. S. Johnson, M.C.

4/North Staff.
O. Commanding .. Lieut.-Colonel D. M. B. Hall.
2nd in Command.. Major H. Meredith.

105th T.M.B.
O. Commanding .. Captain J. N. Wootton, M.C.

106th Infantry Brigade
Commander .. Brig.-General J. H. W. Pollard, C.B., C.M.G., p.s.c.
Bde. Major .. Captain J. H. Bradney.
Staff Capt. .. Captain R. W. Train.
Intell. Officer .. Lieut. G. R. McColl.

17/Royal Scots
O. Commanding .. Lieut.-Colonel W. A. Murray, M.C.
2nd in Command.. Major J. Gordon.

12/Highland L.I.
O. Commanding .. Lieut.-Colonel J. N. O. Rycroft, D.S.O., M.C.
2nd in Command.. Major R. S. Dixon, D.S.O., M.C.

18/Highland L.I.
O. Commanding .. Lieut.-Colonel V. E. Gooderson, D.S.O.
2nd-in-Command.. Captain R. Dagger.

106/*T.M.F.*
O. Commanding .. Captain W. D. Ronald.

Divisional Troops
19/*Northumberland Fus.*
O. Commanding .. Lieut.-Colonel C. Hancock, D.S.O.
2nd in Command.. Major B. E. Sharp.

35*th Btn. M.G.C.*
O. Commanding .. Lieut.-Colonel N. V. Blacker, M.C.
2nd in Command.. Major W. H. C. Ramsden.

Div. Emp. Co.
O. Commanding .. Captain H. J. Craig.

Comdr. Div. Train Lieut.-Colonel F. E. Johnson, D.S.O.
S.S.O. .. .. Major J. K. Ewart, D.S.O.
Adjutant .. .. Captain R. Chignell.

105*th Field Ambce.* Lieut.-Colonel C. Scaife.

106*th Field Ambce.* Lieut.-Colonel E. Phillips, M.C.

107*th Field Ambce.* Lieut.-Colonel R. Hemphill, D.S.O.

45*th Mobile Vet. Section*
O. Commanding .. Captain R. H. Stalker.

APPENDIX VI.

Corps Routine Orders.

By Lieut.-General Sir R. C. B. Haking, K.C.B.

Headquarters, 9th June, 1916.

The Corps Commander has much pleasure in publishing the following letter received this morning:

To First Army

"The Commander-in-Chief is of the opinion that the behaviour of the troops of the 35th Division on the occasion of the action of 30th May was most creditable."

(Sd.) L. E. Kiggell, *Lieut.-General,*
Chief of General Staff.

To XI Corps.

"The G.O.C. First Army has great pleasure in forwarding the above letter for your information."

(Sd.) S. H. Wilson, *Lieut.-Col., G.S.,*
First Army.

The Corps Commander wishes to emphasise the fact that the successful repulse of the enemy's attack was due to two main causes:—

(1) The gallant manner in which the troops of the 105th Brigade withstood the intense preliminary bombardment.

(2) The delivery of an immediate counterstroke across the open by the troops of the 104th and 105th Infantry Brigades to restore the line and drive the enemy back.

(Sd.) H. C. Holman, *Brig.-Gen.,*
D.A. and Q.M.G. XI Corps.

APPENDIX VII.

Brigade Routine Orders.

By Brigadier-General A. H. Marindin, commanding 105th (Infantry) Brigade. 24.10.17

Complimentary.

1. The following message from Lieut.-General Lord Cavan, Commanding XIV Army Corps, addressed to 35th Division, begins : " I heartily thank and congratulate you and whole Division on splendid fighting qualities shown to-day. Best German troops were driven back, at heavy cost I know, but result is that your Division secured left flank of Army. Army Commander is thoroughly satisfied."

2. The following letter has been received by the Brig.-General from the Commander of the French Regiment (3 Battalions), which attacked on our left :—

My General,

I hear from Lieut. Covington of the success of your fine Brigade. In the name of the 201st Regt. and on my own part I wish to tell you how great an honour we feel it to fight alongside your valiant troops.

The memory of our intimate liaison with the 105th Brigade will remain warm in our hearts.

Believe my General in my most respectful devotion

(Sd.) Mongin.

The Brigadier has sent the following reply :—

My dear Colonel,

I wish to express my most warm thanks for your kind letter. It was a very great honour for me and my Brigade to fight alongside the First Division of the glorious French Army.

My Brigade and myself offer you our most sincere congratulations on the success which you and your famous Regiment have achieved to-day, and we are very proud that we have been allowed to fight in close liaison with the 201st Regiment.

Believe my dear Colonel,
etc.
(Sgd.) A. H. Marindin.
(Sgd.) D. C. Hamilton,
Brigade-Major,
105th Infantry Brigade.

APPENDIX VIII.

4/NORTH STAFFORD REGIMENT.

Previous History.

The 4/N. Staff. left Canterbury for Southampton on October 6th, 1917, landing at Havre on October 8th. They left Havre on the 10th and went by train to Bapaume, marching to camp at Fremicourt. Here they were attached to the 57th Division. On October 13th the four companies were attached to four battalions of the 167th, 168th and 169th Brigades, 57th Division, for training in trench warfare, and on October 16th suffered their first casualties: 1 O.R. killed and 1 wounded.

On the 18th the Battalion reassembled at Fremicourt. On the 22nd they were again attached to units of the 57th Division by companies for training in the line, remaining in the line until the 28th.

On November 1st they went into the line as a battalion opposite Pronville.

November 4th : Casualties.—2nd Lieut. F. W. C. Sienis missing (on patrol), 1 O.R. killed, 2 wounded
November 5th :   1 O.R. killed, 3 wounded.

On November 6th the Battalion returned to Fremicourt.

They left Fremicourt by bus on November 9th, billeted that night at Arras, and the next night at Bruay, and the next at Thiennes, arriving November 14th at Stienvoorde, and the next day marched *via* Poperinghe and Vlamertinghe to camp near Château des Trois-Tours, where they joined the 106th Brigade.

17/WEST YORK.

Subsequent History.

On November 14th the Battalion was inspected by the G.O.C. 106th Brigade, who then took leave of the Battalion. On November 15th the G.O.C. 35th Division inspected and took leave of the Battalion.

HISTORY OF THE 35TH DIVISION   333

On November 16th the Battalion finally left the 35th Division and came under the orders of the C.E. XIX Corps for work on the railways and road in the forward area ; moving that night to Elrerdinghe, where they relieved the 16/Cheshire at Wellington Camp.

From November 17th-30th they were so employed, having on the 17th 5 O.R. wounded, and on the 30th 2 O.R. wounded.

On December 1st the Battalion marched to Thienshoek ; thence the next day to Merville ; the following day to L'Eclème *via* Robecq, and on the 4th to Barlen ; on the 5th to Acq.

On the 6th the Battalion was inspected by the G.O.C. 31st Division and 70 men were transferred to " Tanks."

On December 7th : The majority of the remainder of the Battalion went to the 15th Battalion, West York ; 14 men only going to the 16/West York, and some of the transport personnel to the 18/West York.

APPENDIX IX.

VII Corps Order No. 248. March 26th, 1918.

Issued to Signals 2.15 a.m.

VII Corps will fight to-day on the line Albert-Bray in order to delay the enemy as long as possible without being so involved as to make retirement impossible. Retirement when made will be to the north of the Ancre, which is to be held again as a rearguard position, all bridges being destroyed after the crossing. They will be prepared for demolition under orders of the C.E. VII Corps.

Retirement will be from the right. 21st Division *via* Méricourt L'Abbé, 35th Division *via* Ville, 9th Division *via* Dernancourt and Albert, the left of the 9th Division pivoting on Albert. Transport to move as early as possible, 21st and 35th Divisions on Baizieux 9th Division on Lavieville. Artillery will take up positions on the North Bank of the Ancre to cover the crossing. Heavy artillery will come into position north of the main Albert-Amiens road on the line Lavieville-Bresle-Baizieux.

On reaching the new position the right flank of the 21st Division will rest on Ribemont and will be covered by two thousand details under Lieut.-Colonel Hadow, Black Watch, who will previously have taken up a position on the line Heilly-Ribemont. These details will come under the command of G.O.C. 21st Division, when the latter reaches the new line. Left of 21st Division will rest on Buire, right of 35th Division on Buire left on Dernancourt, right of 9th Division on Dernancourt left on Albert, where touch must be maintained with V Corps.

In the event of the Albert-Bray line being broken, divisions will make their way fighting to the locations given on the North Bank of the Ancre.

    Div. H.Qs., 9th Div., Millencourt.
     21st and 35th Divs., Bresle.
    Corps H.Q., Montigny.

Acknowledge by wire.   *Signed by* :—
          A. Hore-Ruthuen,
          B.G.G.S., VII Corps.

INDEX

A

Aberdeen, Lord Provost of, 3
Abraham, Lieut. P. S., 246
Aden House, 166
Ainsworth, Capt. R. W., 20
Aitken, Lieut. R. R., App. I.
Alaska Houses, 259
Allan, Sir H. H., 37
Allen, Lieut. T. W., 244 ; App. I.
Allenby, Lord, 64
Almachi, Lieut., 140
Almond, Pte., App. I.
Ancre, The, 205 et seq.
Anderson, Lieut.-Col. H. W., 198, App. I.
Angus, Pte., App. I.
Armstrong, Capt. H., App. I.
Armstrong, Lieut. H. A., 232 ; App. I.
Arnold, Lieut. M., 258 ; App. I.
Appleby, Col. W., App. I.
Appleyard, Lieut.-Col. W., 173, 209, 212
Arras, 56 et seq.
Aspden, Lieut. F., 270 ; App. I.
Aspinal, Pte., App. I.
Atkinson, Lieut.-Col. F. St. J., App I.
Atkinson, Capt. C. S., 270 ; App. I.
Aveluy Wood, 219 et seq.
Aylward, Lieut. R. N., 23

B

Bacon, Capt., 140
Baker, Lieut. W., App. I.
Baker, Major W. G., App. V.
Balderson, Pte., 125
Balfour, Capt. J. M., App. III.
Ball, Capt. S. A., Appl. I.
Bannatyne, Major, 18
Baraclough, Capt., App. V.
Barber, Lieut., 151
Barclay, Lieut. H. B., 132
Barnes, Lieut. W. G., App. I.
Barnett, Capt. V. G., 196
Barrie, Capt., 141
Batteries, R.F.A. :
  A/157 : 62, 107, 177, 261, 272
  B/157 : 107, 115, 123, 128, 177, 260, 271

Batteries, R.F.A. (continued) :
  C/157 : 75, 106, 123, 125, 129, 261
  D/157 : 42, 84, 107, 260, 272
  D/158 : 62
  A/159 : 42, 91, 96, 99, 112, 120, 129, 153, 216, 229, 242, 255, 264, 273
  B/159 : 18, 58, 83, 92, 96, 112, 130, 153, 181, 207, 242, 255, 262, 263, 271, 292, 293
  C/159 : 15, 25, 95, 96, 112, 130, 153, 220, 240, 259, 264, 271
  D/159 : 42, 96, 123, 172, 212, 216, 220, 251, 259, 262, 264
Battle, Sgt., App. I.
Battle Wood, 257
Bauld, Lieut. R. S., App. I.
Baxter, Lieut., 89
Bedford, Lieut.-Col. W. G., 9, 16, 19
Beer, B.-S.-M., App. I.
Bell, Major W. I., App. V.
Bell, Capt. (D.L.I.), 225, 235
Bell-Smythe, Brig.-Gen., 127
Bellairs, Major N. E. B., App. III.
Bernafay Wood, 36, 199, 201
Berly, Lieut.-Col. A. H., App. IV
Berry, Lieut. G. W., 146
Bertwick, Pte., App. I.
Bethell, Lieut.-Col., 168
Bethune, Lieut. H. E., 250 ; App. I.
Bicknill, Lieut.-Col., 178
Bigland, Mr. Alfred, 1
Billon Wood, 198-203
Bird, Capt. W. H., App. I.
Bird Cage, The, 126 et seq., 152
Birmingham, Sgt., App. I.
Blackwell, Lieut. C. W., 124
Blacker, Lieut.-Col., M.V., 191, App. V.
Blagnaert Farm, 261
Blair, Lieut. J., 39
Blauwe Poort Farm, 252
Blenkinsop, Lieut., 110
Bloor, Cpl., 24 ; App. I.
Bluff, The, 257
Board, Sgt., 125 ; App. I.
Bois Marrière, 194
Boot, Lieut., 79
Bost, Capt. G. W., App. V.

HISTORY OF THE 35TH DIVISION

Bouzincourt, 221.
Bowditch, Lieut. H., App. I.
Bradney, Capt. L. H., 269
Braithwaite, Major A. N., App. I.
Bray, 207
Bresle, 219
Brigades, R.F.A. :
  157th : 3, 9, 13, 14, 16, 25, 41, 52, 58, 83, 93, 95, 97, 102, 106, 113, 120, 125, 136, 157, 172, 177, 186, 190, 193, 206, 216, 220, 222, 224, 231, 244, 251, 253, 255, 259, 264, 266, 267, 278, 280, 285, 291 ; App. II.
  158th : 3, 9, 14, 25, 41, 52, 58, 84 ; App. II.
  159th : 3, 14, 25, 41, 52, 58, 83, 84, 88, 92, 95, 112, 120, 123, 157, 170, 172, 177, 182, 186, 190, 193, 204, 206, 220, 224, 228, 231, 243, 244, 249, 253, 255, 259, 266, 276, 278, 285, 291, 293 ; App. II.
  163rd (Howitzers) : 4, 9, 14, 25, 43, 52 ; App. II.
Brigades, Infantry :
  104th : 2, 8, 9, 12, 14, 17, 27, 36, 40, 45, 46, 49, 56, 60, 64, 74, 80, 84, 87, 91, 101, 105, 118, 124, 129, 135, 142, 144, 153, 157, 161, 166, 169, 172, 175, 180, 182, 186, 187, 189, 193, 198, 199, 203, 205, 207, 209, 211, 215, 219, 222, 224, 226, 230, 234, 235, 238, 244, 246, 249, 251, 253, 258, 261, 266, 268, 269, 274, 275, 278, 280, 284, 285, 287, 290, 292, 293 ; App. II.
  105th : 2, 8, 9, 12, 14, 16, 25, 27, 30, 31, 38, 40, 45, 50, 53, 56, 60, 64, 78, 80, 84, 87, 93, 101, 105, 108, 114, 118, 122, 128, 134, 151, 154, 157, 163, 166, 168, 169, 171, 175, 182, 186, 187, 189, 193, 194, 200, 204, 205, 207, 215, 219, 220, 223, 226, 234, 235, 238, 241, 244, 246, 249, 251, 253, 257, 261, 262, 266, 268, 269, 276, 278, 280, 283, 284, 290, 293 ; App. II.
  106th : 2, 8, 9, 12. 16, 17, 19, 27, 30, 36, 38, 41, 45, 50, 53, 56, 60, 66, 80, 84, 87, 101, 105, 108, 118, 122, 127, 134, 151, 154, 157, 159, 168, 169, 171, 173, 176, 180, 185, 190, 193, 197, 204, 205, 209, 211, 212, 213, 216, 222, 224, 226, 229, 235, 238, 242, 243, 253, 258, 261, 262, 266, 268, 273, 275, 278, 280, 283, 284, 285, 290, 293 ; App. II.

Britwell, Pte., App. I.
Brown, Sgt. T. A., App. I.
Brown, Capt. S., App. I.
Brown, Lieut., 23
Browne-Clayton, Col., 47, 81 ; App. III.
Bryan, Capt., 141
Bryce, Capt., 79
Bucquoy, 219
Buffs Bank, 257
Buire, 212, 215, 220
Bulkeley, Capt., L. A. H., 221
Burke, Capt. A. M., 97
Burkett, Lieut., 131
Burnett, Capt. D., 128 ; App. I.
Burns, Pte., App. I.
Bury, Major, 246
Butler, Lieut. F. J., 131
Butler, B.-S.-M., App. I.
Butt, Capt., 22
Burt, Lieut., 96
Byng, Lord, 204

C

Cabin's Copse, 271
Caldwell, Capt. W. L., App. V.
Callan, Lieut. J., App. I.
Campbell, Major-Gen. D. G. M., 194
Campbell-Balfour, Capt. A., App. I.
Canada Tunnels, 258
Canal Wood, 134
Carlyon, Lieut., 281
Carver, Sgt., 111
Chadwick, Lieut., 225, 271
Chaffey, Lieut. C. R., 91
Chance, Lieut.-Col. E. W., App. III.
Cheales, Lieut.-Col., 16, 132
Cheans, Lieut.-Col. R. D., App. III.
Cheshire Regt. :
  15th Battn., 2, 20, 34, 46, 50, 60, 71, 74, 87, 90, 93, 105, 123, 128, 135, 139, 166, 168, 175, 183, 187, 194, 196, 199, 202, 207, 210, 213, 215, 221, 223, 228, 235, 244, 250, 254, 261, 264, 269, 271, 229, 280, 282, 285, 291 ; App. II.
  16th Battn., 2, 13, 17, 31, 34, 46, 49, 50, 90, 93, 106, 108, 111, 122, 135, 137, 160, 172, 183 ; App. II.
Chesney, Capt. A. J., App. 1 & IV.
Chignell, Capt. R., App. V.
Christie, Capt., 13
Clayton, Col. Browne, 47, 81 ; App. III.
Clery-Bouchavesnes, 194
Climo, Major V. C., 24
Cobb, Major M. L., App. V.

INDEX 339

Cochran, Lieut.-Col. H. P. G., 34, 114, 196 ; App. I & IV.
Coe, Capt., 246
Coke, Capt. R. A. S., App. I.
Colombo House, 163 et seq.
Cook, Capt. C. H., App. I.
Cook, Sgt., 33
Cooke, Lieut. (Lancs. Fus.), 251
Congreve, Lieut.-Gen. Sir W. N., 28, 193
Constable, Major C., 178, 246
Cormack, Lieut. G. S., App. I.
Corps : II, 173, 246 ; III, 122, 125 ; IV, 87, 93, 95 ; V, 220, 230 ; VI, 52, 60 ; VII, 193, 204, 205 ; VIII, 27 ; IX, 241 ; X, 45, 239, 275 ; XI, 8 ; XIII, 28, 30, 38, 52 ; XIV, 46, 157, 160 ; XV, 116, 120 ; XIX, 169, 173, 238, 252, 278, 285
Corrington, Lieut., 210
Coulter, C.-S.-M., App. I.
Courtrai, 275
Cowan, Capt., 14
Cowan, Lieut.-Col. J. de B., 236, 244, 255 ; App. V.
Cowl, Pte., App. I.
Coutts, Lieut. J. E., App. I.
Coyle, Cpl., 174
Cox, Major J. A., 198, 201
Craig, Capt., 262
Cranney, L./Cpl., 251; App. I.
Crawford, Capt. A. B., 18
Crawford, Major W. L., App. I.
Crellin, Lieut.-Col. A. W., 212, 268 ; App. I.
Cressey, Capt., 143
Crook, Lieut.-Col., 37, 81, 162, 216, 247
Crosby, Pte., 223
Cruickshank, Capt., App. I.
Cullen, Major, 17
Curlu, 196, 199
Curran, Capt. E., App. I.
Cuthbertson, Lieut. C. S., App. V.

D

Daggar, Capt. R., App. V.
Dales, Lieut., 253
Daniell, Lieut.-Col. F. W., 4, 18, 191 ; App. I, III & IV.
Darch, Pte., App. I.
Darley, Major C. B., 94
Davidson, Major P., App. III.
Davies, Lieut. R. C., 22
Davis, Brig.-Gen. Price, 10

Davson, Lieut.-Col. H. M, 25, 30., 58, 84, 136, 168, 171, 181, 193, 198, 203, 255 ; App. I, IV & V.
Dawson, Major-Gen., 24
Dawson, Major H. S., App. I.
de Wiart, Brig.-Gen. C., 222, 223
Dean, Lieut. W. J., App. I.
Dent, Lieut.-Col. B. C., 84, 94, 163 ; App. IV.
Dernancourt, 210, 214, 219
Dibb, Cpl., 111
Dillon, Major E. A. T., App. V.
Dimouline, Capt. W. A., App. I & V.
Divisions : 1st, 173, 190 ; 2nd, 38, 43rd ; 3rd, 38, 40 ; 5th, 25 ; 9th, 197, 205, 207, 209, 213, 284 ; 12th, 74, 235 ; 14th, 249 ; 17th, 173, 226 ; 18th, 181 ; 19th, 8, 9, 14 ; 21st, 194, 197, 203, 205, 207, 209 ; 24th, 47, 275 ; 29th, 27, 182, 183, 259, 265, 266, 278, 284 ; 30th, 40, 239, 242, 245, 266, 284 ; 31st, 239, 284, 286 ; 32nd, 98, 102, 113, 181, 187, 190 ; 34th, 144, 159, 161, 168, 278, 294 ; 36th, 245, 246, 268, 271, 275 ; 38th, 8, 9, 21, 221, 223, 225, 226 ; 39th, 181 ; 40th, 125 ; 41st, 239, 260, 266, 271, 275, 283, 290, 291 ; 42nd, 220 ; 50th, 168, 169 ; 58th, 176 ; 59th, 107, 109, 120 ; 61st, 97, 101, 113 ; 63rd, 229. Australian, 3rd, 216, 219 ; 4th, 216, 217, 220. American, 30th, 249
Dixon, Major R. S., 234, 235 ; App. V.
Dobbie, Sir J., 2
Dodman, Lieut., 214
Doidge, Capt. R. C., 10
Dranoutre Ridge, 242, 246
Draper, Lieut. A. F., 164 ; App. I.
Drummond, Lieut., 270
Du Cane, Lieut.-Gen. Sir J., 116
Duckworth, Lieut., 13
Duncan, Capt. G. A., App. I.
Dunlop, Sir T., 3
Dunn, Lieut., 69
Duns, Capt. C. E., App. I.
Durandeau, Lieut., 10
Durham, Earl of, 2
Durham Light Infantry : 19th Batt., 2, 8, 36, 38, 50, 66, 76, 90, 102, 110, 129, 137, 145, 148, 168, 171, 174, 176, 186, 190, 197, 212, 216, 224, 231, 233, 242, 254, 258, 266, 269, 271, 275, 279, 280, 284, 285, 287, 293 ; App. II.
Dyer, Capt. C. E., 242 ; App. I.
Dyer, Major G. N., App. III.

Dyson, Lieut. W., App. I.

E
East, Lieut. K. D., 19
Edinburgh. Lord Provost of, 2
Edwards, Lieut. (Lancs. Fus.), 257
Ellis, Major T. P., App. III.
Empson, Sgt. C. W., App. I.
Epéhey, 118, 126
Erle, Sgt., App. I.
Evans, Brig.-Gen. W., 171, 172
Ewart, Major J. K., App. I, IV & V.
Eyre, Lieut. L. B., App. V.

F
Fairbairn, Lieut.-Col. J., App. IV.
Fanshawe, Lieut.-Gen. Sir A. E., 221, 226
Fargny Mill, 202
Farman, Lieut.-Col. H., 155, 246, 255
Farmer, Lieut. J. B., 115
Farrar, Lieut., 13
Farrell, Lieut. B. W. F., App. III.
Farrish, Lieut. C. W., 154 ; App. I.
Fauquissart, 12
Favière Wood, 197, 199
Fawcett, Capt. J., App. I.
Fawcett, Lieut.-Col. P. H., 16, 58, 81 ; App. IV.
Fawcus, Capt. W., App. I.
Fitzgerald, Lieut. E. W. R., 74, 80 ; App. I.
Fleming, Capt. T. G., App. IV.
Foord, Lieut.-Col. W. P. S., 163, 191, 214, 216, 226 ; App. I & IV.
Forbes, Capt. H. N., 178
Forester, Lieut., 78
Forman, Lieut.-Col. D. E., 181, 189, 235
Forster, Capt. G. R., 146
Forster, Lieut. P. R., 149
Foulkes, Major, 38
Francis, Sgt., App. I.
Franks, Lieut. (Lancs. Fus.), 186 ; App. I.
Franks, Lieut. (R.A.), App. I.
Franks, Major-Gen. G. Mac K., 127, 173, 180, 193, 197, 198, 205, 208 ; App. I.
Frost, Lieut., 20
Furnival, Major, 25

G
Gallagher, Lieut., 223
Gallon, Lieut. A. E. V., App. I.
Gardiner, Lieut., 24 ; App. I.
Gardiner, Capt. A. L., 221
Gauche Wood, 125
Gelagher, Capt., App. I.
Gerance, Pte., App. I.
Gerrard, Sgt., App. I.
Gheulwe Switch, 266
Gibb, Capt. M. A., App. I.
Gibbon, Capt., 130
Gibbons, Lieut., 108
Gibson, Capt. M. M., App. I.
Gill, Major S. H., 178 ; App. I & III.
Gillemont Farm, 126, 134, 141
Glasgow, Lord Provost of, 3
Glass, Lieut. W. B. K., 143
Glover, Capt. G. de C., 25, 47, 82 ; App. I.
Gloucestershire Regt. : 14th Battn., 2, 21, 22, 33, 46, 48, 50, 87, 89, 93, 105, 114, 122, 125, 135, 137, 140, 154, 163, 166, 183, 184 ; App. II.
Golightly, Lieut. G. F., 111
Gonnelieu, 118
Gooderson, Lieut.-Col. V. E., 171, 199, 215, 226,; App. I & IV.
Gordon, Major A. D., App. IV
Gordon, Major J., App. V.
Gordon, Col. R. N. S., 34, 114 ; App. IV.
Goss, Major V. W., 25, 94; App. I & V.
Gough, Gen. Sir H., 193
Grace, Lieut. T., 140
Graeme-Taylor, Capt., 197
Graham, Capt. C. J., 189, 210
Grant, Lieut. D. R., App. I.
Gravel Farm, 188
Gray, Lieut., 110
Greathead, Lieut.-Col. R.N., App. III.
Greener, Lieut. S., App. I.
Greenwell, Lieut.-Col. W. P., 94, 111, 171, 178, 225, 236 ; App. I.
Gricourt, 101
Gripps, Cpl., 241
Gruncell, Major A. T., 235 ; App. V.
Grundy, L./Cpl., App. I.
Guillemont, 47
Gukenbiehe, Pte., App. I.

H
Haddon, Lieut., 111
Hadow, Capt. E. G., 121
Haldane, Lieut.-Gen. Sir A., 60, 64
Hall, Capt. R. O., 25 ; App. III.
Hall, Lieut.-Col. P. S., 132, 178
Hall, Lieut.-Col. D. M. B.,App. I & V.
Hallendries, 288
Ham, Pte., App. I.
Hamilton, Capt. C. N. B., 25 ; App. III.

INDEX

Hamilton, Lieut. J. R., 143
Hancock, Lieut.-Col. C., 226 ; App. V.
Hanrick, Lieut. W. A., 80 ; App. I.
Hardecourt, 196
Harford, Lieut. 224
Hare, Sgt., 18, App. I.
Hare, Lieut.-Col., 155
Harris, Lieut., 166
Harisson, Major R. P., 43. 62, 95, 152 ; App. I & V.
Harvey, Capt. M. M., 20, 164
Harvey, Sgt., App. I.
Hart, Major G. A., 181, 207 ; App. I & V.
Harwood, Capt., 3
Harwood, Lieut. R. M., App. I.
Harwood, Lieut. F., App. I.
Hasler, Lieut., 123
Hasted, Lieut.-Col. A. W., App. III.
Headlam, Brig.-Gen., 203, 207
Heape, Capt. R. S., 109, 162
Heaton, Capt. H., 242
Heath, Lieut. R. S., App. I.
Heathcote, Lieut.-Col. R. E. M., 132, 152
Heelis, Major, 162, 178
Helmsley, Lieut. R. T., App. I.
Hempson, Capt. S. H., App. I.
Hemphill, Lieut.-Col. R., App. IV & V.
Hemstock ; Capt. H., 79 ; App. I.
Hetherington, Lieut., 232
Hewson, Capt. C. H., App. I.
Hicks, Lieut. W. E., App. I.
Highland Light Infantry :
12th Battn., 183, 196, 197, 199, 200, 204, 207, 209, 213, 226, 229, 230, 234, 241, 242, 250, 258, 262, 264, 273, 282 ; App. II
18th Battn., 3, 13, 36, 38, 50, 66, 80, 81, 102, 128, 135, 141, 145, 154, 168, 173, 197, 199, 200, 203, 204, 205, 207, 209, 215, 238, 242, 254, 258, 262, 264, 273, 274, 275, 282, 291 ; App. II
Hill, Lieut. (Lancs. Fus.), 241
Hill, Lieut.-Col. H. A., App. III.
Hill " 60," 252
Hindenberg Line, 95, 121
Hodgkiss, Major, App. I.
Hodgkinson, Capt. G. W., 178, 246, App. I & V.
Hodson, Capt. H., 115
Hodson, Capt. W., App. I.
Hodson, Lieut.-Col., 235
Hogg, Major C. M. T., 24
Hogg, L./Cpl., 225

Holbrook, Lieut., 281
Holland, Major, 25, 213 ; App. I.
Holman, Capt. D. F., App. I.
Honnecourt Wood, 119, 135
Houston, Capt., 235
Houthulst, 157
Howells, Lieut. G. D., 187
Howes, Capt., 224
Huddlestone, Col. W. E., 246 ; App. V
Huffan, Major S., 132, 171
Hulson, Capt., 9
Hunt, Col., 198
Hunt, Pte., 77
Hunter, Brig.-Gen. J. G., 2, 17 ; App. III.
Hunter-Weston, Lieut.-Gen. Sir A. G., 27
Huntley, Lieut. C., App. I.
Hume, Capt. J., App. V.
Humphries, Capt. E. D. M., App. IV.

I

Inman, Lieut., 274, 282
Irvine, Lieut.-Col. R. A., 186, 191 ; App. I, III & IV.
Irvine, Lieut. R., 113 ; App. I.

J

Jackson, Capt. 145
Jackson, Lieut. R., App. I.
Jacob, Lieut.-Gen. Sir C., 180, 246
Jarvis, Lieut. H., App. I.
Jehovah Trench, 258
Jenkins, Lieut. H. F. O., 92
Jervelund, Capt. C. N., 223
Jewell, Lieut.-Col. C. E., 216, 235 ; App. I & V.
Johnson, Lieut., 78
Johnson, Pte. W. A., App. I.
Johnson, Major A. S., App. I & V.
Johnson, Lieut.-Col. F. E., App. III, IV & V
Johnston, Lieut. (Cheshires), 140
Johnston, Lieut.-Col. H., 2, 8, 17, 234, 261 ; App. I & V.
Johnstone, Capt. (H.L.I.), 197
Jones, Lieut., 61
Jones, Lieut.-Col. J., 255, 270 ; App. V.
Jones, Lieut.-Col. (King's Liverpools), 255
Jones, R.-S.-M. R. T., App. I.
Jordan, Lieut., 242
Judge, Lieut., 69

K

Kappelhoek, 272
Keay, Lieut., App. I.
Keenlyside, Major B. C. H., 284, 287 ; App. V.
Keith, Major J., 25, 107 ; App. I.
Kelly, Capt. W. T,. App. I.
Kemp, Bmdr., App. I.
Kennedy, Major A. J. R., 247 ; App. V.
Kennedy, Capt., 113 ; App. I.
Kerr, C.-S.-M. P. App. I.
Kidd, Capt. C. B., App. I.
King George, H.M., 245
King, Col., App. I.
Kinred, Capt., 21
Kitchener, Lord, 1, 3, 9
Klein Zillebeke, 258
Knoll, The, 134, 137 et seq.
Kreupel Ridge, 280

L

La Chapelle, 252
Laatste Oortje, 282
Lamont, Lieut.-Col. W., 4, 9 ; App. III.
Lancashire Fusiliers :
  17th Battn., 2, 8, 9, 14, 21, 37, 46, 51, 66, 102, 104, 107, 109, 118, 121, 130, 143, 153, 160, 163, 166, 186, 190, 200, 203, 204, 216, 219, 228, 231, 234, 238, 240, 243, 251, 254, 258, 266, 269, 295, 279, 284, 285, 286, 293 ; App. II.
  18th Battn., 2, 9, 19, 21, 23, 37, 40, 46, 87, 93, 104, 107, 118, 121, 130, 153, 165, 175, 186, 200, 204, 219, 222, 224, 231, 234, 240, 244, 252, 254, 258, 266, 269, 271, 279, 284, 285, 286, 292, 293 ; App. II.
  20th Battn., 2, 13, 37, 40, 51, 87, 93, 104, 105, 108, 113, 128, 131, 143, 162, 163, 168, 180, 183 ; App. II.
Lancashire Hussars, 19
Landon, Major-Gen. A. J. S., 64, 127
Langtree, Lieut., 42
Lascelles, Capt. R. G., 94
Laurenson, Lieut.-Col. R. R., 200, 206, 226 ; App. III & IV.
Lawrenson, Lieut. R. F., 94
Layman, Lieut., 9
Le Mesurier, Major H. F. A., 61, 196 ; App. I.
Lee, Pte., 18
Lees, Cpl., App. I.
Leigh, Cpl., App. I.
Les Trois Sauvages, 110
Lewis, Lieut. H., App. I.
Ley, Pte., App. I.
Lihons, 87
Litherland, Capt. W. B., App. V.
Little Priel Farm, 130, 139
Lloyd, Lieut. O., App. I.
Lloyd-Davies, Major J. W., App. I.
Loch, Lieut. A. D., App. I.
Locre, 238 et seq.
Long, Cpl., App. I.
Lone Tree, 229
Lowery, Lieut. H. F. S., App. I.
Luck, Major W. T., App. I.
Lumsden, Major, 13
Lyons, Capt. R. C., App. I.
Lyons, Lieut.-Col., 255
Lys, Passage of, 273 et seq.

M

MacGregor, Lieut. R., App. I.
Mackenzie, Brig.-Gen. G. M., 2, 16 ; App. III.
Mackenzie, Lieut. G., 143
Mackereth, Major, 247, 255, 275 ; App. V.
Macwhinnie, Lieut.-Col. W. J., 16 ; App. III.
McAfee, Capt. D. J., App. I.
McColl, Lieut. G. R., App. V.
McCulloch, Lieut.-Col. W. R., 208, 209, 236, 284 ; App. V.
McEwen, Gunner S., App. I.
McGinney, Sgt., App. I.
McGovern, Cpl. W., App. I.
McGuillan, C.-S.-M., App. I.
McIver, Lieut. A. S., App. I.
McKean, Sgt., App. I.
McKevitt, Lieut. R. F. M., App. I.
McKnight, Lieut., 73
McLaren, Lieut. A., 33
McVaxen, Lieut. J. B., App. III.
Machine Gun Coy. : 104th, 18, 191 ; 105th, 191 ; 106th, 191
Machine Gun Battn. : 35th, 191, 194, 231, 238, 245, 246, 282, 286 ; App. II.
Madocks, Brig.-Gen. W. R. N., 171, 172, 177, 213, 222, 227, 295 ; App. I & V.
Magnan, Gen., 36
Maitland, Major R., 81, 83
Maitland-Heriot, Lieut. R. L., App. I
Maitland-Mackgill-Crichton, Lieut., 246 ; App. V.
Mann, Lieut., 253

INDEX

Manchester Regt. ; 23rd Battn., 2, 9, 17, 35, 37, 40, 46, 49, 66, 87, 102, 105, 109, 124, 130, 135, 143, 160, 166, 175, 182, 183 ; App. II.
Mansfield, Mr. Alfred, 1
Maricourt, 200, 203
Marett Wood, 209, 215
Martinsart, 221, 224, 230
Martin, Sgt. J. H., App. I.
Mary, H.R.H. Princess, 294
Marindin, Major-Gen. A. H., 18, 34, 112, 124, 137, 144, 164, 185, 189, 194, 199, 200, 204, 205, 207, 208, 209, 211, 222, 228, 233, 242, 245, 262, 275, 280, 293 ; 295, App. I, IV & V.
Maskill, C.-S.-M., App. I.
Mason, Lieut., 131
Matley, Capt., 262
Matthews, Lieut. (N. Staffs.), 216
Maurepas, 196, 199
Maxwell, Lieut.-Col. E. L., 20
Mayne, Lieut.-Col. C. R. P., 25 ; App. III.
Mayer, C.-S.-M., App. I.
Meldrum, Lieut., 22
Menendez, Lieut., 23
Meredith, Major H., App. V.
Merison, Capt. C. W., App. IV
Merrick, Lieut. P., App. I.
Merville, 246
Metcalfe, Major C. H. F., 94, 132
Miller, Capt. G. W., 140 ; App. V.
Millington, Capt., 163, 165
Mills, Lieut.-Col. A. W., 17, 37, 74, 81 ; App. I & IV.
Milne, Capt., 48, 224
Milne, Lieut.-Col. G., 3, 8 ; App. III.
Milward, Capt., 25
Minshall, Major T. H., App. I & III.
Mitchell, Lieut., 48
Moat, Sgt., App. I.
Moated Grange, 252
Moir, Lieut. R., App. I.
Monfries, Capt. G. B. J., App. III.
Monies-Williams, Lieut., App. III.
Monk, Gunner, App. I.
Montauban, 36, 38, 200, 203
Montgomery, Capt. B. C., 94 ; App. III .
Moore, Lieut.-Col. H. A., App. III.
Morgan, L./Cpl., 139 ; App. I.
Morgan, Capt. C. F., 202, 281
Morlancourt, 208, 212, 219
Morland, Gen. Sir T., 45
Morton, Lieut.-Col. H., 269, 291 ; App. V.

Mowle, Lieut. G. K., 107, 188
Mullen, Dr. J., App. I.
Murdoch, Major J. A., 4 ; App. III.
Murray, Lieut.-Col. W. A., 141 ; App. I & V.
Murray, Capt. A. W., App. I.
Murray, Lieut. T. W., App. I.
Muir, Major A. W., 41 ; App. I.

N
Nameless Wood, 202
Napier, Sgt., 77
Neuve Chapelle, 12
Newcombe, Brig.-Gen., 198, 203
Newell, Lieut.-Col. F. H. M., 114 ; App. III
Newland, Capt. R. E., App. I.
Newman, Lieut.-Col. C. R., 155 ; App. I.
Nicholson, Capt. K. J., 94
Nicol, Pte., App. I.
Noakes, Capt., 110
North Staffordshire Regt., 4th Battn., 173, 176, 182, 183, 184, 186, 187, 197, 201, 202, 209, 213, 216, 221, 224, 229, 241, 244, 250, 252, 254, 262, 271, 272, 279, 280, 283 ; App. II.
Northumberland Fusiliers, 19th Battn., 4, 24, 27, 45, 51, 128, 172, 181, 190, 193, 197, 200, 202, 205, 208, 211, 212, 235, 238
Nutall, Lieut., 13

O
O'Connor, Cpl., 18 ; App. I.
O'Donnell, Brig.-Gen. H., 3, 39, 114 ; App. III & IV.
O'Donnell, L./Cpl. A., App. I.
O'Hea, Sgt., App. I.
Oakhanger Wood, 50
Oliver, Lieut. G. B., 24
Oliver, Capt. W. J., 110
Ossus Wood, 134, 142
Otter, Lieut. H. R., App. III.

P
Panama House, 104 et seq.
Parker, Major O. M., App. IV.
Parry, Lieut., 175
Parry-Jones, Capt. M. M., 178
Parsons, Major, 25
Parsons, Lieut. H. F., 141 ; App. I.
Passchendaele, 158
Pauncefort-Duncombe, Major Sir G. P. D., 246, 290 ; App. V.
Pearson, Major N. L., 4 ; App. III.

Pearson, Lieut. W. R. G., 78 ; App. I.
Perkins, Brig.-Gen. A. E. J., 136
Phillips, Major G., 281 ; App. I & V.
Pilckem Ridge, 159
Pincher, Cpl. W., App. I.
Pinney, Major G. A., 42 ; App. I & III.
Pinney, Major-Gen. R. J., 4, 21, 34, 36, 38, 51, 64 ; App. I & III.
Playfer, Capt., 107
Plenderleith, Lieut., 186 ; App. I.
Plumer, Lord, 174
Pocock, Capt. A. A., App. I.
Poelcappelle, 171 et seq., 180
Pollard, Brig.-Gen. J. H. W., 114, 160, 181, 200, 206, 208, 262, 263, 265, 282, 291, 295 ; App. I & V.
Potter, Major, 72, 83
Powell, Lieut., 74
Price, C.-S.-M., App. I.
Prothero, Lieut. E. O., App. I.
Pugh, Pte., App. I.
Pulford, Capt. C. W., 94, 226 ; App. I & V.
Pulteney, Lieut.-Gen. Sir W. F., 122
Pye, Capt. K. N., 4 ; App. III.

R

Raikes, Lieut.-Col. L. T., 206
Rainbird, Sgt., 22 ; App. I.
Ramsden, Major W. H. C., App. V.
Ranken, Lieut.-Col. T., 118
Rawlinson, Lord, 174
Raynes, Lieut. F. A., App. I.
Read, Sgt., 225 ; App. I.
Redfern, Lieut. H., App. I.
Reid, Lieut. (D.L.I.), 252
Rendel, Capt. R. M., 22 ; App. III.
Rennison, Capt. W., App. I.
Renwick, Mr. G., 4
Rewcastle, Lieut. J. J., App. I.
Rhodes, Sgt., 76
Riccard, Lieut.-Col. C. B. J., 94
Richard, Lieut., 172
Richardson, Major J. H. K., 193 ; App. I & V.
Richardson, Major P. H., 236, 260, 262, 281 ; App. I, V.
Riddell, Capt. W. H., Intro. xi, 193, 226
Rigby, Capt. (Lancs. Fus.), 241 ; App. I.
Rigby, Lieut.-Col. W., 290
Riley, Capt., 43
Ritzema, Col. T. B., 3, 16 ; App. III.
Roberts, Capt. F. A. D., App. I.
Roberts, Sgt., App. I.
Roberts, Col., 22 ; App. III.
Robertson, Sgt., 271
Robertson, Lieut. J. C., App. I.
Robinson, Capt. R. C. R., App. I.
Robinson, Major P. G., 25 ; App. III.
Robson, Capt. W. H., App. V.
Ronald, Capt. W. D., App. V.
Ronnsoy, 151
Rose, Lieut. M. H., 219 ; App. I.
Rose, Lieut. A. D., 92
Rosieres,
Rosebery, Earl, 2
Ross, Major L. H., App. I.
Rowell, Capt. H. A., App. I & V.
Roupell, Capt. G. R. P., 82, 213
Royal Engineers :
  203rd Field Coy., 4, 27, 172, 181, 200, 231, 260, 275, 290, 292 ; App. II.
  204th Field Coy., 4, 16, 27, 69, 181, 186, 226, 235, 260, 274, 275, 290, 292 ; App. II.
  205th Field Coy., 4, 27, 226, 235, 260, 275, 290, 292 ; App. II.
  35th Divl. Signal Coy., 4
Royal Scots : 17th Battn., 2, 9, 12, 36, 38, 50, 73, 91, 102, 105, 114, 129, 135, 152, 160, 169, 174, 196, 197, 199, 200, 213, 216, 226, 228, 242, 254, 259, 260, 262, 264, 275, 282, 286 ; App. II.
Roxburgh, Lieut. T. A., App. I.
Rundle, Lieut., 184
Ruscastle, Lieut., 252
Rushton, Capt. W. O., 178 ; App. I & V.
Rushton, Lieut.-Col. H. W., 4, 25, 155 ; App. I, III & IV.
Russell, Capt. B. A., 164 ; App. I.
Rutherford, Lieut., 244
Ryall, Capt. (D.L.I.), 242
Ryalls, Capt. B. A., 31, 48,; App. I.
Rycroft, Lieut.-Col. H. N. O., 223, 234, 235, 291 ; App. V.

S

Saint, Lieut.-Col. E. T., 81, 94
St. Jan Cappel, 246
Sanctuary Wood, 257
Sandilands, Brig.-Gen. J. W., 16, 74, 124, 162, 166, 193, 213, 230, 234, 266, 292, 295 ; App. I, IV & V.
Sanderson, Major A. E., 290
Sands, L./Cpl., App. I.
Sauchiell Trench, 230
Savy Wood, 97
Scaife, Lieut.-Col., App. V.

INDEX 345

Scheldt, The, 284 et seq.
Scheldt, The, crossing of, 290 et seq.
Scherpenberg, 240
Schofield, Gunner, App. I.
Schofield, Lieut. R. B., 33
Schorn-Water, 272
Scougal, Major A. G., 38, 254 ; App. I.
Seely, General, 114
Sharp, Major B. E., 226 ; App. V.
Sharrat, Lieut. W. H., App. I.
Shaw-Stewart, Lieut.-Col. D. H., 136
Shaw, Lieut. (Cheshires), 250
Shepley, Lieut., 253
Sherbrooke, Lieut., 290
Sheridan, Rev. J. J., App. I.
Sherwood Foresters : 15th Battn., 2, 13, 20, 31, 34, 37, 41, 46, 50, 68, 70, 79, 87, 93, 111, 114, 128, 135, 139, 163, 166, 173, 175, 186, 194, 197, 199, 202, 207, 209, 213, 224, 228, 253, 254, 262, 263, 269, 271, 272, 276, 279, 291 ; App. II.
Sholiser, Pte. W., App. I.
Shooter, Sgt.-Major, 16 ; App. I.
Short, Lieut., 175
Shufflebotham, Capt. E. J. S., 185 ; App. I.
Shultz, Capt. G. E., 140
Shute, Lieut.-Gen., 226
Sibbering, Pte. A., App. I.
Sillitor, Lieut. J., 241 ; App. I.
Simmons, Capt. F. K., 132 ; App. I & V.
Simonds, Lieut.-Col. G., App. III.
Skipwith, Lieut.-Col. J. W., 155 ; App. V.
Slinger, Lieut. G. N., 80
Smallwood, Capt. G. R., App. IV.
Smart, Sgt., App. I.
Smissen, Rev. G., App. I.
Smith, Gunner, App. I.
Smith, Lieut.-Col. R. P., App. III.
Smith, C.-S.-M., App. I.
Smith, Lieut. (D.L.I.), 66
Smith, Lieut. K., 78
Smith, Lieut. R., 174
Somerville Wood, 108, 109
Somme, The, 27
Spoil Bank, 252
Stabell, Capt., 216 ; App. I.
Stalker, Capt., App. II.
Stansfield, Lieut., 24
Staff, Sgt., 110
Stanton, Lieut. H. W., App. I.
Staveley, Brig.-Gen. W. C., 4, 19, 25, 81, 95, 97, 160, 168, 171 ; App. IV.
Steel, Major R. A., App. III.

Stenhouse, Gunner, App. I.
Stephenson, Capt. F. D., App. I.
Stephenson, Lieut. E. C., App. I.
Stephens, Lieut.-Gen. R. B., 160, 239
Stevens, Lieut.-Col. L. M., 191, 193, 200, 207, 223, 230, 234; App. I & IV.
Stevens, Capt. F. C., 43
Stevenson, Cpl. (D.L.I.), 77
Stewart, Lieut.-Col. D. B., 17, 19, 24, 30, 43, 58, 84, 127 ; App. IV
Stewart, Capt. F. N. (R.A.M.C.), 197; App. I.
Stewart, Major W. M., App. III.
Stoney, Lieut.-Col. L. S., 38 ; App. III.
Stott, Lieut., 243
Stower, Major L. A. W., App. I.
Stranack, Lieut., 274
Stringer, Sgt., 109 ; App. I.
Strong, Lieut. Vesey, 24
Storr, Lieut., 229
Struth, Lieut., 152
Styles, Lieut. A. C., 33
Summers, Lieut. J. M., App. I.
Sutton, Lieut. E. M., 196 ; App. III.
Swain, Pte., App. I.
Swallow, Lieut., 69
Sweveghem, 278 et seq.
Swoter, Major L. A., App. V.
Symons, Lieut.-Col , 17, 19, 43

T

Taggart, Sir J., 3
Taggart, Lieut. J. D., App. I.
Taylor, Pte., App. I.
Taylor, B.-S.-M., 96 ; App. I.
Taylor, Major W. H., App. IV & V.
Teare, Capt. J., App. IV.
Temperley, Major R., 4
Tenbrillen, 261
Tennant, Lieut. H. V., App. III.
Terhand Line, 266, 269
Thirlwell, Major H. W., 17
Thom, Rev. J., App. V.
Thomlinson, Lieut.-Col. W., 3
Thomson, Capt. H. J. P., 178
Thomson, Sgt., J., App. I.
Thorp, Lieut.-Col. H. W. B., 155, 246, 290 ; App. V.
Tissingham, Lieut. C. F., 140 ; App. I.
Tomes, Capt. C. T., App. III.
Tomson, Lieut. M., App. III.
Toop, Capt., 22
Topham, Lieut., 125
Torrence, Lieut., 162
Townley, Pte., 18
Train, Capt. R. W., App. I & V.

Trench, Capt. S. J. le P., 22, 95, 226 ; App. I & V.
Trench Mortar Batteries :
V/35 : 59, 94 ; App. II.
X/35 : 14, 59, 238 ; App. II.
Y/35 : 14, 59, 238 ; App. II.
Z/35 : 15, 59, 138, 238 ; App. II.
106th : 198
Trestrail, Major A. E. V., App. I & V.
Treux, 215, 220
Trevor, Col. H. O., App. III & IV
Trois Rois, 254.
Trones Wood, 40, 197
Tudor, Brig.-Gen., 83
Turner, Brig.-Gen., 261, 265 ; App. V.
Twin Copses, 106
Tyler, Brig.-Gen. J. A., 99
Tyson, Lieut., 223, 261

U
Upson, Sgt., 23 ; App. I.
Utterly, L./Cpl., App. I.

V
Vaughan, Lieut.-Col. E., 64, 162, 178, App. I & IV.
Vernon, Lieut.-Col., 22
Viccars, Major J. E., 246 ; App. I & V.
Vickery, Lieut.-Col., 171
Ville-sur-Ancre, 210
Vine, Capt. W. B. de, App. IV.

W
Waermaerde, 285
Wales, H.R.H. Prince of, 160
Wall, Pte. S., App. I.
Waller, Lieut., 94
Waller, Major, 116, 261, 281 ; App. V.
Wallis, Lieut. A., 153
Warburton, Lieut., 69
Waring, Sgt., App. I.
Warmington, Capt. G. E. D., App. V.
Warner, Capt., 225
Wass, Major, 185
Waterlot Farm, 31
Watson, Sgt. (W. Yorks), 121
Watts, Lieut.-Gen. Sir H. E., 238
Weatherstone, Lieut., App. I.
Webster, Major J., 236, 261 : App. I & V.
Wervicq, 263 *et seq.*
Welbourne, Lieut., 78
West Ham, Mayor of, 4

West Yorkshire Regt. : 17th Battn., 2, 9, 36, 38, 50, 66, 71, 91, 92, 105, 109, 120, 122, 137, 148, 152 ; App. II.
Weston, Major E. T., App. IV
White, Capt. (R.A.), 96
White, Lieut. (W. Yorks), 92
Whitehead, Lieut. J. G., App. V.
Wilcocks, Sgt.-Major, 69
Wilkinson, Sgt. (Cheshires), 146
Williams, Capt. G. S. de M., 19
Williams, Sgt. (Cheshires), App. I.
Williamson, Sgt., 109
Willis, Major G. S. C., 67
Willis, Lieut. (R. Scots), 73.
Wills, Lieut., 210
Wilson, Brig.-Gen. F. A., 160, 171, 189
Wilson, Col. L. M., 132, 136, 236
Wilson, Capt. C. E., App. I.
Winn, Lieut. A. E., App. I.
Winstanley, Pte., 139
Wolfe, Lieut., 125
Wolstenholme, Capt., 20, 80
Wood, Lieut. (Cheshires), 123
Wood, Capt. M. R., 162 ; App. I.
Wood, Capt. D. E. C., App. V.
Woodyer, Lieut. H. M., App. I.
Woolconbe, Lieut.-Gen. Sir C. L., 93
Woodrow, Lieut., 115
Wootton, Capt. J. N., App. I & II.
Workman, Cpl., App. I.
Worley, Rev. J. K., App. I.
Worsley, Capt. J. H., App. I.
Worthington, Lieut., 243
Worthington, Major R., 115 ; App. IV.
Wrinch, Lieut. W. S., App. I.
Wylie, Lieut. R. A., App. I.

Y
Ypres, Third Battle of, 158
Ypres, 1918, 249
Yorke, Lieut. F. St. G., 13 ; App. I.
Yorke, Cpl. T., App. I.
Youl, Major, 264 ; App. V.
Young, Lieut. (H.L.I.), 250
Young, Capt. W., App. I.

Z
Zanvoorde, 258, 261
Zillebeke, 258

www.ingramcontent.com/pod-product-compliance
Lightning Source LLC
Chambersburg PA
CBHW021829220426
43663CB00005B/179